ᴅᴜᴍʙᴀʀᴛᴏɴ ᴏᴀᴋꜱ
ᴍᴇᴅɪᴇᴠᴀʟ ʟɪʙʀᴀʀʏ

Jan M. Ziolkowski, General Editor

APOCALYPSE

PSEUDO-METHODIUS

AN ALEXANDRIAN WORLD

CHRONICLE

DOML 14

Apocalypse
PSEUDO-METHODIUS

An Alexandrian
World Chronicle

Edited and Translated by

BENJAMIN GARSTAD

DUMBARTON OAKS
MEDIEVAL LIBRARY

HARVARD UNIVERSITY PRESS
CAMBRIDGE, MASSACHUSETTS
LONDON, ENGLAND
2012

Reprinted with corrections 2014

Library of Congress Cataloging-in-Publication Data
Pseudo-Methodius.
    [Apokalypsis. English, Greek, & Latin]
    Apocalypse of Pseudo-Methodius. An Alexandrian world chronicle /
edited and translated by Benjamin Garstad.
    p. cm. — (Dumbarton Oaks medieval library ; DOML 14)
    English and Latin.
    Includes bibliographical references (p.) and indexes.
    ISBN 978-0-674-05307-6 (alk. paper)
    1. Apocalyptic literature. 2. History, Ancient — Chronology. I. Garstad,
Benjamin. II. Excerpta Latina barbari. English & Latin. III. Title.
    BS646.P8413 2012
    270.2 — dc23   2011036263

Contents

Introduction

The original *Apocalypse,* or *Revelations,* wrongly attributed to
Saint Methodius of Olympus (a Christian bishop and author
martyred ca. 311), was composed in Syriac by an unknown
author in response to the first Arab invasions and the establishment of the caliphate. Internal evidence has recently allowed scholars to fix the date of composition very close to
692.[1] According to the Syriac text, the dominion of the Ishmaelites — the term referring to the descendants of Ishmael
(the elder son of Abraham), which Pseudo-Methodius consistently uses for the Arabs[2] — will last for ten "weeks of
years," or seventy years (the Greek and Latin versions have
seven "weeks"). If this period is taken to begin with the date
of the Hejira in 622, the last "week of years" would be the
span of time from 685 to 692. It has been proposed that
the *Apocalypse* was written at some time during these seven
years, and probably toward their end, because these seven
years saw the introduction of tax reforms by the caliphate
that substantially increased the tax burden on Christians,
and as a consequence increased the incentive for Christians
to avoid the poll tax by committing apostasy and converting
to Islam. Pseudo-Methodius sees this as the "falling away"

vii

from the Church foreseen by the apostle Paul and clearly considers it to be the most detrimental result of the Ishmaelite invasion. Reinink refines this date by linking the focus in the *Apocalypse* on Jerusalem to the building of the Dome of the Rock on the Temple Mount by the caliph 'Abd al-Malik in 691. This construction was supposed to supplant the Christian presence in the Holy City by appropriating a shrine for Islam and to indicate the stability and permanence of Muslim rule. Considering the prominence in Pseudo-Methodius's composition of the themes of the immanent demise of Arab rule and the redemption of Jerusalem by the Roman emperor, he may well have written in response to the building of the Dome of the Rock and the message it was intended to convey. At any rate, the *Apocalypse* could not have been written later than 694, when its influence is first to be seen in other Syriac works.[3]

Not much can be said about the identity of the author. Even his theological affiliation is difficult to discern. The preface to the Syriac *Apocalypse* says that Methodius received his vision on "the mountain of Senegar," Mount Singara (or Sinjar) northwest of Mosul, and the real author of the *Apocalypse* probably came from this same place.[4] Singara was a stronghold of the Monophysite community in Mesopotamia. This, along with the prominent place accorded to Ethiopia, the most powerful Monophysite kingdom of his day, in the author's eschatology suggests that he was himself a Monophysite. But his belief in the supremacy of the Roman Empire and his fervent expectation of deliverance from the Ishmaelites and restoration of the Church through the activity of the Roman emperor indicate that he belonged to the Melchite Church, which adhered to the Chalcedonian

creed. Perhaps Pseudo-Methodius did not intend to reveal his own denomination. Reinink has proposed that the author of the *Apocalypse* saw Arab rule and the inducements to apostasy as the real threat to the Church, rose above sectarian wrangling, addressed himself to all Christians, and offered the ruler of the Christian Roman Empire as the hope of all the faithful, of whatever party, in Arab-occupied lands.[5] The *Apocalypse* was never taken to be a document belonging to any particular faction within Christianity.

The *Apocalypse* was translated from Syriac into Greek and from Greek into Latin, all fairly rapidly. We can say practically nothing about the circumstances of the Greek translation, but as it must fall between the Syriac composition and the Latin translation we can at least date it in broad terms. The earliest manuscript of the Latin text seems to have been written sometime before 727,[6] and we have no reason to believe that this manuscript was produced simultaneously with the translation itself. Certain linguistic details of the translation indicate that it was made into the Vulgar Latin of Merovingian Gaul.[7] One Peter, a monk, claims responsibility for the Latin translation, but while he makes his moral ardor clear, he does not convey anything about his life. So within the space of some thirty-five years the *Apocalypse* was written in Syriac beyond one end of the Mediterranean, translated into Greek at some intermediate time and place, and then rendered from Greek into Latin beyond the far shores of the sea, all while the geopolitical turmoil which provoked its composition and transmission continued to rage unabated.

The influence of the *Apocalypse* of Pseudo-Methodius throughout the Christian world was immense. In the East,

it retained its currency in its original Syriac milieu, inspiring further eschatological works, and gained further readers in Armenia and the Arab-speaking world. The Byzantine apocalyptic tradition was irrevocably transformed by Pseudo-Methodius, and practically all subsequent Greek apocalypses found their themes and motifs in this work. At least two Old Slavonic translations were made from the Greek *Apocalypse,* one before the eleventh century (perhaps at the end of the ninth century) and another in the thirteenth or fourteenth century, and extracts from the *Apocalypse* found their way into the Russian *Primary Chronicle* and other historical works.[8]

In the West, the Latin *Apocalypse* is represented by a manuscript tradition that rivals the classics and the Church fathers in its extent.[9] The popularity of Pseudo-Methodius is also evident in the multitude of vernacular translations. For instance, numerous Middle English versions were produced in prose and verse.[10] The earliest printed edition dates from 1470, and several more followed. This work that helped to make sense of the first Arab onslaughts took on fresh resonance over the centuries as new and strange enemies arose in the East, seemingly appearing out of nowhere. The Mongols were identified with the Unclean Nations led by Gog and Magog,[11] and broadsheets with excerpts from the *Apocalypse* were printed in Vienna during the Turkish siege of 1683.[12] But Pseudo-Methodius not only enabled medieval Europe to recognize exotic and distressing invaders, but also shaped the eschatological expectations of Christendom. Joachim of Fiore, the great apocalyptic voice of the Middle Ages, may have neglected Pseudo-Methodius, but his

followers read and adapted the *Apocalypse* with great enthusiasm.[13]

If the influence of Pseudo-Methodius was vast, the sources that he drew on in composing his *Apocalypse* were encompassed within a much smaller orbit. The principal source is the Bible, and Pseudo-Methodius draws on it for everything from evocative imagery to the structure of his expectations about the end of days. But the biblical passages he selects to emphasize may not be the ones a modern reader might expect to find in a work of eschatology. The Revelation of Saint John, for instance, is not mentioned at all; it was inconsistent with the very positive view of the Roman Empire espoused in the *Apocalypse,* and was in fact ignored by much of the Byzantine apocalyptic tradition. Nor does he depend to any great extent on the Book of Ezekiel, where Gog and Magog are most fully described. Rather, Pseudo-Methodius takes the outline of his vision of the end of the world from the brief eschatology in 2 Thessalonians 2:1–12. In reading this passage, great stress is placed on the Roman Empire as "he who now letteth" (v. 7), preventing the rise of the Antichrist. An obscure verse at Psalm 68:31, "Ethiopia shall soon stretch out her hands unto God," recurs several times to make the Roman Empire the final world kingdom and to explain the final surrender of the dominion of the world by the last Roman emperor. And an elaborate allegorical interpretation of Jacob's blessing of Dan (Genesis 49:17–18) sets out the circumstances of the reign of the Antichrist and the last days. The Greek and Latin translators were well aware of the biblical allusions and quotations woven into the *Apocalypse* and turned to the

standard biblical texts in their own languages, rather than translating passages afresh.

The prophetic vision of Pseudo-Methodius takes in the entire extent of history from Adam to the Second Coming, and for the first part of the *Apocalypse,* which refers to the past, he depends on a few Syriac sources. Much of the historical portion of the *Apocalypse* is based on the *Cave of Treasures,* attributed to the fourth-century Ephraem the Syrian but probably composed in the sixth century. It offers an account of the patriarchs and kings in Christ's genealogy from the Creation to the Crucifixion. It provided Pseudo-Methodius with a chronology and various characters and incidents, such as Jonetos, the fourth son of Noah, and his dealings with Nimrod, that would have been novel and unfamiliar to the Greek and Latin (as well as Syriac) traditions of Christian history writing based on Eusebius. Alexander the Great's encounter with Gog and Magog in the *Apocalypse* is based on material in Syriac versions of the legends about Alexander, the *Alexander Legend* and *Alexander Poem,* but Pseudo-Methodius himself was the source for this incident in later recensions of the Greek *Alexander Romance.*[14] The account of Alexander's mother, Chouseth, however, and her second marriage after his death, which knits together the kingdoms of Rome, Greece, and Ethiopia, seems to be an invention of Pseudo-Methodius.

The *Apocalypse* is also indebted to the typology that is so important in the Syriac interpretation of scripture and history.[15] The chiliastic chronology of Pseudo-Methodius's history, to begin with, is based on typology. The course of time runs through seven chiliads, or millennia, which correspond to the seven days of creation, for "one day is with the Lord

as a thousand years" (Psalm 90:4, 2 Peter 3:8). Certain individuals and nations who have a part in the past are also considered types of others who will appear in the future. The first invasion of the Ishmaelites, or Midianites, has specific parallels with the second invasion of the Ishmaelites, the Arabs. Gideon, who defeats the Ishmaelites, and Alexander, who with the help of God preserves the world from the Unclean Nations, are types of the last Roman emperor.

Perhaps few works are as evocative of the anxiety of the Middle Ages as the *Apocalypse* of Pseudo-Methodius. It is a real anxiety, occasioned by the pressure of immense and shocking geopolitical forces, and it is focused on the very real calamities of subjection and servitude, poverty and exile. It is an existential anxiety inasmuch as the text itself demonstrates that individual identity was bound up with the stability of society and government. As an expression of and response to this anxiety the *Apocalypse* is equally characteristic. Neither a series of jeremiads nor introspective soul-searching, it is a sweeping narrative and a meditation on the course of human history. Yet as vividly as the miseries are seen and as bleak as the prospects seem, the message of the *Apocalypse* is profoundly positive. The invasion of the Ishmaelites may disturb but cannot demolish the dominion of the Roman Empire, the kingdom of the Christians, and even when all lawful power and authority are removed from the earth and the Antichrist reigns, the order of the world will be redeemed by Christ's triumphal return.

The *Apocalypse* of Pseudo-Methodius contains frequent and substantial excerpts from the Bible, and although the translations presented in this volume were made into common early Byzantine Greek and early medieval Vulgar Latin,

these biblical passages affect the tone and diction of the work. I have tried to convey this in the translation. Where the medieval translator quotes verbatim from the Septuagint, the Greek New Testament, or the Vulgate, I have given the equivalent passage from the Authorized Version (noting any variations from the lectionary reading in *italics*), so as to give the reader the same impression of familiar, authoritative, yet somewhat archaic scripture. Outside the biblical quotations I have retained in recognizably "biblical" terms the words and phrases borrowed from the Bible. I have made no effort to render the *Apocalypse* into modern colloquial English, because the Greek and Latin translators aimed for an elevated and arcane register appropriate to prophecy, and their first readers would have recognized this.

The Greek and Latin texts in this volume are based on those scrupulously edited by Aerts and Kortekaas, and it is no exaggeration to say that this project would have been impossible without their work. I acknowledge myself a dwarf perched precariously on the shoulders of giants.

OUTLINE OF THE APOCALYPSE OF PSEUDO-METHODIUS

1–2 the family of Adam, the spread of fornication, the Flood

3–5.1 the descendants of Noah, establishment of kingdoms, wars between them, invasion of Sampsisano

5.2–9 first invasion of the *oikoumene* by the sons of Ishmael, defeated by Gideon, a prophecy of their second invasion and its defeat by Rome

CHRONOLOGY OF THE APOCALYPSE OF PSEUDO-METHODIUS

790 Babylon established and ruled by Nimrod (3.6)

— Pontipos made king of the sons of Ham (3.6)

799 (third year of Nimrod) city of Jonetos built for Jonetos (3.6)

— Ham and Japheth at war (3.7)

4th millennium

37 [seventy-fourth year of Reu] Ham and Japheth at war, Egyptians defeated by kingdom of Nimrod (4.1)

— Eresdes, descendant of Nimrod, conquers Ham and the lands of the west (4.2)

982 Chosdro, sons of Eresdes, defeats the sons of Ham (4.3–4)

5th millennium

5 Sampsisano of the tribe of Jonetos invades from the East (5.1)

— sons of Ishmael pushed out from the desert of Yathrib, lay waste the inhabited world for 60 years, defeated by Gideon (5.2–8)

— kings in Babylon, Medes and Persians (6–7)

— conquests of Alexander, imprisonment of the Unclean Nations (8)

— Byzas marries Chouseth (9.1–4)

— Romulus Armelaus marries Byzantia, their sons reign in Rome, Byzantium, and Alexandria (9.4–6)

[a prophecy of future events follows from this point]

7th millennium

— Persia destroyed, the sons of Ishmael invade, Romans defeated at Gabaoth (10.6–11.3)

— king of the Romans defeats the Ishmaelites (13.11–13)

— invasion of the Unclean Nations defeated (13.19–21)

— king of the Romans dwells in Jerusalem (13.21)

— the son of perdition appears (13.21, 14.2)

— the cross assumed into heaven, the king of the Romans dies, authority abolished (14.2–6)

— the son of perdition revealed, many deceived by his signs and wonders, he occupies the Temple in Jerusalem (14.6–10)

— Enoch and Elijah refute the son of perdition (14.11–12)

— the Son of Man comes in glory (14.13)

AN ALEXANDRIAN WORLD CHRONICLE

The *Excerpta Latina Barbari* has never received the attention to which its interest entitles it. The text, or at least its Greek original, furnishes an important link in the Christian chronicle tradition, marking a transition from the sparse and tabular *Canons* of Eusebius of Caesarea to the fuller narratives of the popular world chronicles by John Malalas and his followers. The arrival of the original in Gaul and its translation into Latin provide a telling example of the acquisition and adaptation of a Greek literary work to meet the demands of

the culture of the Merovingian Franks. The details of the *Excerpta,* moreover, are sufficiently varied that they offer not only evidence of the texts of authors from Manetho to Julius Africanus, but also the first attestation of the names of the Three Wise Men of the Nativity story. The *Excerpta* also contains one of the earliest versions of the legendary history of Alexander to circulate in the Latin West, as well as a euhemeristic narrative of the gods as early mortal kings whose possible influences still remain to be investigated. The text is also a valuable testament to the Vulgar Latin of eighth-century Gaul. Nevertheless, the *Excerpta* is not easy of approach, by turns daunting and despicable, and has suffered generations of unwarranted and unfortunate neglect.

The text of the sole surviving manuscript (Paris, Bibliothèque Nationale, MS Lat. 4884) received the name *Excerpta Latina Barbari* from the sixteenth-century French humanist Joseph Justus Scaliger, after he had exerted his erudition and ingenuity to restore what he considered a testimony to the *Chronicle* of Eusebius to his standards of sense and legibility.[16] Scaliger recognized the work as the Latin translation of a Greek Christian world chronicle. "The Latin extracts of the barbarian" summed up Scaliger's judgment of the capacity of the translator in both Greek and Latin. Barbarous Latin notwithstanding—and it is not really that bad by the standards of the day in which it was translated—the manuscript Scaliger knew, the one preserved in the Bibliothèque Nationale, is our sole witness to the translation, and to the chronicle itself, since the Greek original is now lost.

The *Excerpta* is not the result of a single act of writing. Although the stratigraphy of its composition is obscure and confused, we can tease out a provenance for the extant

version from various hints, bold and faint, within the text itself. In the early fifth century a Greek chronicle was prepared in Alexandria that included a chronology with brief, mostly biblical elaborations and a series of king lists that constituted the raw material of the chronology. A little more than a century later this chronicle was augmented and adapted, perhaps in Constantinople, and sent as a diplomatic gift to the Frankish king, Theudebert I. Some two centuries after its arrival in Gaul the chronicle was translated into Latin, apparently to aid the efforts of missionaries working on the Saxon frontier of the Frankish kingdom.

The Alexandrian origin of the basic text of the chronicle is evident from a number of details. First of all, it depends in one instance on the Alexandrian text of the Bible. Quoting Genesis 6:2, the *Excerpta* speaks of "the angels of God seeing the daughters of men" (1.1.2), and while both the Septuagint and the Vulgate have "the sons of God" in this verse, the Alexandrian text, like the *Excerpta,* speaks of "the angels of God." The *Excerpta* regularly refers to Alexander the Great as *conditor,* or "the Founder," a title he probably would not have borne outside Alexandria. After Alexander the chronography traces the passage of years according to the reigns of the Ptolemaic kings of Egypt and ends on a somewhat wistful note with the cessation of kingship in Egypt (1.9.3). Beginning with the death of John the Baptist (2.9.2), certain events, particularly those commemorated by the Church or significant points in the civic and ecclesiastical history of Alexandria, are dated according to the Egyptian as well as the Roman calendar. Finally, the end of the Roman consul list is interspersed with notes on the succession of Alexandrian patriarchs and prefects.

This original Alexandrian composition consisted of a chronology and a collection of king lists that provided the raw data of the chronology. This two-part structure imitated the *Chronicle* of Eusebius. Like the *Excerpta,* the *Chronicle* comprised a chronography laying out in the form of king lists and references to earlier historians the evidence for Eusebius's synthesis and a table of canons which allowed the time lines of various kingdoms to be seen running in parallel columns. The *Excerpta*'s chronology covered the time from Adam to Cleopatra VII and at regular intervals calculated the period from Adam to the ruler or event in question. For the most part the chronology was a bare succession of the lives of patriarchs or the reigns of kings, but at certain points it was elaborated with biblical quotations, with notes on significant events, and particularly with a lengthy description, ultimately based on the *Book of Jubilees,* of the dispersion of the nations which followed the confusion of tongues at the Tower of Babel.[17] With this inclusion the chronicle tradition (other examples of the Table of Nations are to be found in similar works) attempted, in tracing all the peoples of the inhabited earth back to the three sons of Noah, to be as geographically comprehensive as its time lines were chronologically comprehensive. The chronology in the *Excerpta* follows the sequence of biblical patriarchs and kings up to the final capture of Jerusalem by Nebuchadnezzar (1.7.6), then the kings of Babylon, the Medes, and the Persians up to the conquests of Alexander, and from him the Ptolemies up to the rise of Rome. But this is not the only chronological structure imposed on the material. There are also intimations of the millenarian chronology devised by Julius Africanus, according to which the millennia of the world's existence

reflected the seven days of Creation, with Christ born at the precise midpoint of the sixth millennium. The *Excerpta* does mark such epochal points as the dispersion of the nations at—approximately—the middle of the "cosmic week" (1.1.3) and Christ's Incarnation 5,500 years from Adam (2.8.4), in accord with Africanus's scheme, and hints at the fulfillment of Daniel's prophecies by "weeks" (1.8.2, 2.6.5), but apart from these few instances it is hard to see how Africanus's system has determined the structure of the *Excerpta*.[18] The king lists in the second part of the *Excerpta* cover the various peoples mentioned in the chronology and all of the kingdoms included in Eusebius's *Canons* (except the Israelites, whose king lists are fully presented in the first part). The king lists end with a lengthy list of Roman consuls that can be seen as a continuation of the chronology. Originally notices on events seem to have run alongside the consul list, but later these came to be embedded in the list itself. It is otherwise difficult to explain why events that should occur in the same year or succeeding years are separated by several consular years. Toward the end of the chronicle there is evidence of a partisan ecclesiastical tendency. The chronicler praises the Nicene Creed (2.10.2), notes the exile of Athanasius (2.10.4), refers to Arius and his followers as heretics (2.10.2, 2.11.1), and follows the Orthodox succession of Alexandrian patriarchs, revealing his own Nicene sympathies at a time when feelings on the matter, especially in Egypt, might still have been quite raw. The chronicle concludes with the consulate of Valentinian and Eutropius in 387, but the last event mentioned is the end of the episcopate of Theophilus in 412 (2.11.3). Since the author chose no signifi-

cant date to close his work, the chronicle was probably prepared shortly after the latest date mentioned.

The chronicle as it was constituted at this stage seems to
belong to a family of Alexandrian Christian world chronicles. Other examples of this family survive only fragmen-
tarily, in the form of scraps of parchment and papyrus. A
parchment sheet written at the end of the fourth or beginning of the fifth century is preserved in the Staatliche Mu-
seen, Berlin (P. Berlin 13296), and covers the period from
251 to 338, showing a remarkable consistency with the content of the *Excerpta*.[19] The other set of fragments, commonly
called the *Alexandrian World Chronicle,* was collected by the
Russian Egyptologist W. Goleniščev and is more extensive,
including material up to 392.[20] This manuscript has been
dated to the early fifth century, but the most authoritative
dating, on the basis of the script, sets the writing in the period 675–700,[21] though the fifth century may very well remain a viable date for the composition of the text that provided the archetype for this manuscript. Once again, the
remains of the *Alexandrian World Chronicle* often parallel material found in the *Excerpta*.[22] But while the *Excerpta* preserves the entire text in translation, the fragments of the
other chronicles reveal what must have been an important
aspect of the original: its illustrations. In each case the
Greek text of the fragments is interspersed with crude but
abundant illuminations depicting people, events, cities, and
other features of the ordered world. Apart from an initial
letter on the first page, the Latin text of the *Excerpta* is not
illuminated, but gaps left in the text, many of them prepared
with captions in smaller letters, make it apparent that the

manuscript was intended to be illustrated, no doubt on the pattern of the Greek original (see the Notes to the Texts). It is even possible in some cases, with a little imagination, to insert the surviving illustrations from the Greek fragments —for instance, the translation of the relics of Saints Andrew and Luke, the principal illustration on the Berlin parchment, and the figure of Theophilus of Alexandria and his triumph over the Serapeum from the Goleniščev Papyrus— into the empty spaces left in our Latin manuscript. On the whole the *Excerpta* manuscript gives us an idea of how extensive the program of illustrations was in its original conception and the subjects that attracted the illuminator's attention, if not the style in which he worked.

The *Excerpta* is also part of broader Byzantine chronicle tradition, which may not have a common source but shares an extensive stock not only of information, but also of passages with their specific wording. The examples of this tradition which are both best preserved and most extensive as well as most relevant to the *Excerpta* may be the *Chronicon Paschale* and the *Chronography* of George the Syncellus. The anonymous *Chronicon Paschale*, or *Easter Chronicle*, covers the period from Adam to Heraclius and was most likely written in Constantinople shortly after its end point of 630.[23] It preserves the fullest Greek version of the Table of Nations and so can help us reconstruct an abstruse and difficult portion of the text that the *Excerpta* translator attempted to render into Latin. The aid of the *Chronicon Paschale* at this juncture can be supplemented with the so-called *Liber Generationis*, a Latin text derived from Greek sources, perhaps Hippolytus chief among them,[24] which is found in two versions appended respectively to the *Chronicle of 334* and the *Chronicle*

of Fredegar (ca. 658).[25] The compiler of the *Liber Generationis* not only takes us back closer to the original Christian tradition of the Table of Nations, but he also seems to have understood his material somewhat better than the *Excerpta* translator. George the Syncellus wrote his *Chronography* in 808–810 and covered the period from Creation to the reign of Diocletian.[26] His version of the Table of Nations is not as full as that of the *Chronicon Paschale,* but he does offer passages parallel to the content of the *Excerpta* which are not found in other Greek chronicles. The precise relations between the chronicles noted here and the *Excerpta* present a complex and probably intractable problem, but suffice it to say that at certain points there are obvious parallels between the texts, and it is possible to discern in these other chronicles the exact Greek words the *Excerpta* is trying to render into Latin and make some sense of the errors in the translation and the transmission of our Latin text.

The description of the chronicle's primary composition and its parallels, however, does not account for all of the contents of the *Excerpta,* let alone for its arrival in Gaul and translation into Latin. We must turn to a number of anomalous features of the *Excerpta*. First, the list of Roman consuls which concludes the *Excerpta* ends in 387 and covers events up to 412, but the list of Roman emperors which precedes it (2.7.1–3) continues up to the reign of Anastasius (491–518). Then there is the list of Latin kings from Aeneas to Romulus, an altogether muddled document, which appears twice in the *Excerpta* (1.6.4, 2.4.1) and both times includes a "Francus Silvius" among the number of proto-Roman kings. Finally, while most of the chronicle consists of brief and hurried notices on rulers and their reigns, computations, and a

few remarkable people and events, there are two instances of protracted narrative apart from paraphrases of the Bible. One treats the pagan gods as ancient human kings and the other deals with Alexander the Great.

The extended list of Roman emperors points to the early sixth century and "Francus" to the ultimate destination of the *Excerpta* in Frankish Gaul; taken together, these features suggest an explanation for the lengthy narrative passages. Theudebert I (534–548), the king of the Austrasian Franks, was courted as an ally by Justinian, receiving embassies and letters from 536,[27] until in 539 he marched into Italy at the head of an army which attacked both Ostrogoths and Byzantines.[28] Theudebert's expedition put paid to the diplomatic efforts of the Byzantine emperor, but we should not be surprised if while they lasted they included the gift of a book, particularly a richly illustrated book like the original of the *Excerpta*. This would explain the adaptations and additions made to the original. Extending the list of Roman emperors to Anastasius would bring the chronicle as a whole more or less up to date. John Lydus, a civil servant and professor of rhetoric at Constantinople, notes that sixth-century Byzantine scholars posited an eponymous founder of the Frankish race,[29] and the inclusion of Francus Silvius among the early Latin kings would unite the Franks and the Romans by bonds of blood and common ancestry. This kinship could have been the basis of a claim to Frankish military aid on the part of the Byzantine "Romans" as they endeavored to recapture their original capital. It may also have been intended to allow the Byzantines to save face as they anticipated the formal cession of Roman territory to Frankish control that took place in 540.[30] The *Excerpta*'s account

of Alexander the Great makes him not only the liberator of the nations of the West, including the Romans, from all of the despotic peoples of the East who hold them in bondage, but also a worshipper of the True God in Jerusalem (1.8.4–6).[31] This seems to be a veiled call upon Theudebert to the pious pursuit of military glory in emulation of Alexander, freeing Rome and the believers in the True God from their Oriental oppressors. The Byzantines were aware of the eastern origins of the Ostrogoths ("East-Goths"), and one of the epistles of Justinian supposedly appealed to the shared Catholic faith of the Romans and the Franks against the Arian heresy of the Goths.[32] Including the grounds for a comparison of Alexander and Theudebert may also have aimed to flatter the pretensions of the Frankish king, who, alone among all barbarian kings, was known in Byzantium to have minted gold coins in his own name and to have entertained designs on the imperial city itself.[33] The narrative explaining the gods as mortal kings (1.6.1–3) may have been just as purposeful. If the conversion of the Franks to Christianity was considered precarious or superficial at Byzantium before Theudebert's invasion of Italy, all doubt must have evaporated when it was reported that the Franks had sacrificed Gothic women and children to celebrate their victory.[34] A derogatory description of the gods would, it might have been hoped, bolster the Christian convictions of the Frankish king, at least, and trickle down to his subjects.

At some time between 536 and 539, then, the Alexandrian world chronicle was manipulated with the intention of presenting the finished product to Theudebert as a gift that might induce him to pursue the ends of the Byzantine regime. We may assume that the preparation of such an

official document took place at Constantinople, but the references to Alexander as "the Founder" in material we assume to have been added at this stage suggest that the alterations, like the original composition, were undertaken in Alexandria. At any rate, the changes were made in the Byzantine East. All of the added material has affinities with certain passages in the *Chronicle* of John Malalas. Inasmuch as the confusions of the *Excerpta*'s Latin king list can be explained at all, they must be elucidated by reference to Malalas's early Italian history.[35] Not that Malalas is a source for the *Excerpta;* rather his work is further evidence for the circulation of the material that went into the Greek *Excerpta* at this second stage of its composition. Malalas cites a source for his account of Alexander, which is remarkably similar to the one in the *Excerpta,* the lost historian Bouttios.[36] Thus the *Excerpta* and Malalas are both independent witnesses to this fragment of the text of Bouttios on Alexander. It does not seem unlikely that Bouttios is also the common source for the account of "Picus, who is also Zeus" and his dynasty in the *Excerpta* and the parallel "Picus-Zeus narrative" in Malalas.[37]

It may seem odd that an Alexandrian chronicle should be selected to serve the purposes of a diplomatic mission that must have been organized in Constantinople, but the scenario we have attempted to reconstruct is not unlikely. Although Egypt became increasingly isolated in the course of the fifth century, there was still regular communication between Alexandria and Constantinople on the part of the upper echelons of the imperial bureaucracy and clergy, the very parties who might be expected to orchestrate the means of persuasion in elite circles.[38] Justinian's marked bias

in favor of the Chalcedonian party need not have excluded the use of a chronicle from Monophysite Alexandria. Not only had Monophysitism been favored during the lengthy reign of Anastasius, and recruits to the imperial chancery from this time were unlikely to have disappeared with the accession of Justin, but there was also a Monophysite party at the court of Justinian under the patronage of the empress Theodora. Moreover, the chronicle's religious orientation is not, after all, Monophysite but Athanasian, that is, anti-Arian. Furthermore, what was a firm bias in favor of the sympathies of Egypt when the chronicle was first written must have seemed neutral or at least agreeable to all parties in the controversies of the sixth century. Indeed, the explicitly Athanasian stance of the chronicle may have been one of the features that suggested it for the purpose we have proposed. As an emphatically Nicene document, it execrates the very Arian creed espoused by the Ostrogoths and recalls the grounds upon which Justinian summoned the aid of Theudebert.

While there is a plausible explanation for the arrival of the *Excerpta*'s Greek original in Gaul, the genesis of its Latin needs to be addressed. At the outset, three negative suggestions might be made in this regard. First, the ascription of the chronicle to "George, bishop of Amiens, or Victor, bishop of Tours" in a marginal gloss added by a later hand is little more than a guess as to the possible identity of the translator. Second, the chronicle was not translated for the purposes of presentation. Enough readers of Greek could be found in Gaul to make the contents of the *Excerpta* plain to Theudebert or any of his courtiers.[39] The embassy, no doubt conversant in Greek, that made the presentation may

have wished to retain some control over the Frankish reading of the text, control which would diminish as the text became more widely accessible. The teaching of Latin in Constantinople, moreover, may have waned in the course of the sixth century, but throughout the reign of Justinian the Latin of the imperial chancery remained far above the standard demonstrated by the *Excerpta* translator. Third, the translation was made for largely different reasons than the initial presentation. It is not so much that the translator was unsympathetic to claims of kinship between Franks and Romans or calls to pious war-making as that he was insufficiently learned to detect the allusive and cryptic manner of their presentation. Francus Silvius would not have been included among the Latin kings by someone so unaware of the Troy legend as to be unable to distinguish between *Ilios* (Troy) and *helios* (sun).[40]

The manuscript itself points to the occasion of the translation. The single text of the *Excerpta* was written somewhere in northern France, most probably Corbie, in the eighth century.[41] The one illumination executed in the manuscript, the initial *P,* has affinities with the illustrations of the Corbie Psalter.[42] Corbie was not only famous for its library and scriptorium, but at its foundation in the seventh century it was also an outpost on the frontier of Christendom and one of the centers of the missionary effort that would push that frontier back in the succeeding years. Evangelism and learning, indeed, went hand in hand in this period. But more than circumstantial evidence suggests that the translation of the *Excerpta* was a product of these twinned efforts at saving souls and cultivating the mind.

In the *Excerpta*'s account of the gods, the magical prac-

tices by which Faunus-Hermes, the son of Picus-Zeus, deceived the Egyptians are enumerated and include the "neighing of horses" along with the "speech of birds" and "the divination of the dead and other evils" (1.6.2). This odd mention of horse augury has a corollary in an eighth-century list of folk practices and more obviously pagan rites, the *Indiculus superstitionum et paganiarum* (Little Index of Superstitions and Pagan Practices), which refers (item 13) to "auguries of birds or horses or cattle" *(De auguriis vel avium vel equorum vel bovium)*. Unlike many of the other items on this list, horse augury does not appear to be a commonplace borrowed from an authoritative literary source and so probably represents a custom actually observed by the compiler of the list. The *Indiculus* is appended to the capitulary of the Council of Liftinis or Estienne (742/3) along with a baptismal formula in an Old Saxon dialect for renouncing the Devil and confessing the Trinity, and all of these documents are generally agreed to be associated with the work of Saint Boniface to convert the Saxons and Thuringians.[43] The mention in the *Excerpta* of a hippomancy (prophecy from horses), which the *Indiculus* suggests was prevalent among the pagan peoples beyond the Rhine, taken together with the text's provenance, indicates that the *Excerpta* may have been translated as an aid to the eighth-century missionary effort among the Germans. An instance of horse augury was not necessarily interpolated into the text by the translator—the practice, after all, had good classical warrant[44]—but its occurrence might have commended a new use for the text.

Numerous indications point to a correspondence between the substance of a world chronicle and the material

of missionary preaching in northwestern Europe. Martin of Braga's influential *De correctione rusticorum* (The Amendment of Peasant Ways) began with the Creation and fall of Satan and traced the course of history to the Last Judgment.[45] Pirmin of Reichenau, who worked in the Alemannic mission field in the early eighth century, included an account of salvation history in his *De singulis libris canonicis scarapsus* (excerpts from the Individual Canonical Books), a handbook for proselytizing. Daniel of Winchester advised Saint Boniface to begin his dialogues with the heathen by discussing the origins of the world from their perspective and from that of the Christians.[46] Louis the Pious is supposed to have instructed Ebo of Reims to trace the history of the world from Creation to Christ for the benefit of the Danes he set out to convert.[47] But the Christian account of world history could, by and large, be derived from the Bible. The real benefit of the *Excerpta* lay in its euhemeristic account of the heathen gods as disreputable men whose actual existence could be situated in the bygone ages of history.

Accounts of the gods that emphasized the elements prominent in the *Excerpta*'s version of the Picus-Zeus narrative were familiar in the argument against paganism as it was known to the Franks. Caesarius of Arles had spoken of the gods as depraved men who lived in a specific historical time in a sermon against using the names of pagan gods for the days of the week.[48] Martin of Braga fit the gods into the Christian scheme of world history, explaining that demons had adopted the names of particularly wicked men and women.[49] Martin's work exerted a palpable influence on the missionaries at work north and east of Francia, including

Eligius of Noyon and Pirmin of Reichenau, although they have left no record of having employed the account of the gods in the *De correctione rusticorum* (The Amendment of Peasant Ways). Ælfric and Wulfstan, however, clearly composed their euhemeristic accounts of the gods with an eye to Martin of Braga.[50] According to Gregory of Tours, the Frankish queen Clothilda insisted, in arguing against the paganism of her husband, Clovis, that the gods he worshipped were in fact men and censured the flight of Saturn, the libidinous ways of Jupiter, and the sorcery of Mars and Mercury.[51] Two things are especially remarkable about Gregory's presentation of the euhemerism he attributes to Clothilda. It is sufficient to denounce the gods of a pagan Frank under the names of the Greco-Roman pantheon, more or less as they appear in the *Excerpta,* and the discreditable points of myth to which Clothilda is made to draw Clovis's attention are echoed in the *Excerpta:* the departure of Cronus before his son Picus-Zeus, not once, but twice; the seductions of Picus-Zeus; and the magical jugglery of Faunus-Hermes. Daniel of Winchester's advice on missionary preaching to Boniface also included the injunction to stress the genealogies of the pagan gods and to deduce from this their humanity and the fact that, like them, the world itself must have a beginning.[52] All told, the *Excerpta*'s world history and its account of the gods would seem to have fit rather comfortably into the missionary preaching of the Franks.

A history which made the pagan gods out to be kings of the distant past might have some obvious potential in the repertoire of missionary preaching on a theoretical level, but in order to effectively persuade potential converts

among the heathen, a euhemeristic narrative must bear some resemblance to the traditional myth of the pagans it addresses. The *Excerpta* seems to have exhibited such similarities to the myth of the Germanic peoples beyond the Rhine. The baptismal formula that accompanies the *Indiculus* includes the "words of the Devil" that the candidate is to renounce, namely "Thunaer ende Uuoden ende Saxnote" (Thunaer and Woden and Saxnote), and indicates that in addition to their distinctive national god, Saxnote, the Saxons worshipped such recognizable figures from the Germanic pantheon as Donar or Thor and Woden or Odin. While practically nothing is known about Saxon myth, it may nevertheless have shared some features with the better-attested, if later and far removed, Old Norse mythological material. The Picus-Zeus narrative exhibits noteworthy affinities with our pagan and Christian sources on the Norse gods. The gods, especially the chief ones, are consistently presented as wanderers who seduce women and engage in impressive feats of sorcery.[53] The Picus-Zeus narrative, an account of the gods as the first kings of the Roman realm, moreover, might have been particularly effective in the Saxon mission field if Hauck's interpretation of certain gold bracteate medallions as depictions of the chief god of the Saxons in the guise of the Roman emperor is correct.[54] Both the Saxons and the missionaries addressing them would be discussing their gods in terms of the rulers of the Roman Empire or its predecessor in the west, the primal kingdom of Italy.

The *Excerpta* has certain affinities with the *Apocalypse* of Pseudo-Methodius that justify the presentation of the two texts in the same volume. Both texts were originally com-

posed in the East. Indeed, both were first written outside the orbit of the metropolitan culture of Constantinople, and both were co-opted by that same culture for purposes of its own. And both were ultimately translated into Latin in Merovingian Gaul in the eighth century. These texts offer evidence of the persistence of a pan-Mediterranean culture in a period when scholars have been inclined to see fragmentation and isolation. They embodied a late antique outlook that sought to embrace all time and space within the compass of the authoritative texts of the Christian tradition. Yet this vision of the world was not exclusive; it was broad and muscular enough to find a place not only for a great hero of the classical world like Alexander, but also for the pagan gods themselves. Perhaps this perspective resonated with readers at a time when the world did seem to be breaking apart. For all their similarities, however, the *Excerpta* and the *Apocalypse* differ in one significant way. While there are no signs, apart from some ninth- or tenth-century marginalia, that the *Excerpta* was read until the Renaissance or exerted any influence, the readership of the *Apocalypse* in several languages was immense and its grim and pervasive impact so profound that it might be said to have been sublimated into the thought of the Middle Ages and the societies to which they gave birth.

I would like to thank Michelle Bezenar of the MacEwan University Library, who saw to it that a very small library was sufficient to the needs of a rather rarefied undertaking; Richard Stoneman, Willem Aerts, Kevin van Bladel, and

Danuta Shanzer, who all offered their encouragement and advice; the MacEwan Research Council, which provided some financial support for this project; and the readers for the Dumbarton Oaks Medieval Library, Michael Winterbottom and Michael Herren. Finally, I owe a great debt of gratitude to my wife for her patience, understanding, and cooperation.

Roxannae,
sine qua non

NOTES

1 S. Brock, "Syriac Views of Emergent Islam," in *Studies on the First Century of Islamic Society,* ed. G. Juynboll (Carbondale: Southern Illinois University Press, 1982), 18–19; G. Reinink, "Pseudo-Methodius: A Concept of History in Response to the Rise of Islam," in *The Byzantine and Early Islamic Near East,* I: *Problems in the Literary Source Material,* ed. A. Cameron and L. Conrad (Princeton: Darwin, 1992), 178–86.

2 On the origins and implications of this terminology for the Arabs, see F. Millar, "Hagar, Ishmael, Josephus and the Origins of Islam," *Journal of Jewish Studies* 44 (1993): 23–45; idem, "The Theodosian Empire (408–450) and the Arabs: Saracens or Ishmaelites?" in *Cultural Borrowings and Ethnic Appropriations in Antiquity,* ed. E. Gruen (Stuttgart: Franz Steiner, 2005), 297–314.

3 G. Reinink, "Der edessenische 'Pseudo-Methodius,'" *Byzantinische Zeitschrift* 83 (1990): 33–34.

4 Reinink, "Pseudo-Methodius: A Concept of History," 160 and n. 53.

5 Ibid., 167–68.

6 The Codex Bernensis, Burgerbibliothek 611. See M. Verhelst, "Pseudo-Methodius, Revelationes: Textgeschichte und kritische Edition. Ein Leuven-Groninger Forschungsprojekt," in *The Use and Abuse of Eschatology in the Middle Ages,* ed. W. Verbeke et al. (Leuven: Leuven University Press, 1988), 114 (#4).

7 Aerts and Kortekaas, *Die Apokalypse des Pseudo Methodius* (569/97), 28–29.

8 S. Cross, "The Earliest Allusion in Slavic Literature to the Revelations

of Pseudo-Methodius," *Speculum* 4 (1929): 329–39; Thomson, "The Slavonic Translations of Pseudo-Methodius," 143–55.

9 A. Perry, *Dialogus inter Militem et Clericum, Richard FitzRalph's Sermon: "Defensio Curatorum," and Methodius: the Bygynnyng of the World and the Ende of Worldes, by John Trevisa,* Early English Texts Society no. 167 (London: Humphrey Milford, 1925), xxxvii–xliii, lists the numerous manuscripts of the Latin Pseudo-Methodius in England alone. See also M. Twomey, "The *Revelationes* of Pseudo-Methodius and Scriptural Study at Salisbury in the Eleventh Century," in *Sources of Wisdom: Old English and Early Medieval Latin Studies in Honour of Thomas D. Hill,* ed. C. Wright, F. Biggs, and T. Hall (Toronto: University of Toronto Press, 2007), 370–86.

10 C. D'Evelyn, "The Middle-English Metrical Version of the Revelations of Methodius: With a Study of the Influence of Methodius in Middle-English Writings," *Publications of the Modern Language Association of America* 33 (1918): 135–203.

11 P. Jackson, "Medieval Christendom's Encounter with the Alien," *Historical Research* 74 (2001): 347–69.

12 Aerts and Kortekaas, *Die Apokalypse des Pseudo Methodius* (569/97), 35.

13 P. Alexander, "The Diffusion of Byzantine Apocalypses in the Medieval West and the Beginnings of Joachimism," in *Prophecy and Millenarianism: Essays in Honour of Marjorie Reeves,* ed. A. Williams (Burnt Hill: Longman, 1980), 53–106.

14 E. A. Wallis Budge, trans., *The History of Alexander the Great, Being the Syriac Version of Pseudo-Callisthenes* (Cambridge: Cambridge University Press, 1889); R. Stoneman, *Alexander the Great: A Life in Legend* (New Haven: Yale University Press, 2008), 170–85.

15 Reinink, "Pseudo-Methodius: A Concept of History," 153, 164–67.

16 J. Scaliger, *Thesaurus temporum* (Leiden: Thomas Basson, 1606), vol. 2, 44, *titulus.* See C. Frick, "Joseph Justus Scaliger und die Excerpta Latina Barbari," *Rheinisches Museum für Philologie* 43 (1888): 123–27; A. Grafton, *Joseph Scaliger: A Study in the History of Classical Scholarship* (Oxford: Clarendon, 1993), vol. 2, 560–69.

17 See J. Piilonen, *Hippolytus Romanus, Epiphanius Cypriensis and Anastasius Sinaita: A Study of the* ΔΙΑΜΕΡΙΣΜΟΣ ΤΗΣ ΓΗΣ (Helsinki: Suomalainen Tiedeakatemia, 1974); J. Scott, *Geography in Early Judaism and Christianity: The Book of Jubilees* (Cambridge: Cambridge University Press, 2002), esp. 135–58.

18 *Iulius Africanus, Chronographiae: The Extant Fragments,* ed. M. Wallraff et al. (Berlin: Walter de Gruyter, 2007), xxxvi–xxxviii. The editors of this latest collection of fragments would actually attribute a number of the king lists in the second half of the *Excerpta* to Africanus, at least at second hand.

19 H. Lietzmann, "Ein Blatt aus einer antiken Weltchronik," in *Quantulacumque: Studies Presented to Kirsopp Lake,* ed. R. Casey et al. (London: Christophers, 1937), 339–48.

20 A. Bauer and J. Strzygowski, *Eine Alexandrinische Weltchronik. Text und Miniaturen eines griechischen Papyrus der Sammlung W. Goleniščev, Denkschriften der kaiserlichen Akademie der Wissenschaften in Wien, philosophisch-historische Klasse* 51 (Vienna: Carl Gerold's Sohn, 1905).

21 Bauer and Strzygowski, *Eine Alexandrinische Weltchronik,* 83; O. Kurz, "The Date of the Alexandrian World Chronicle," in *Kunsthistorische Forschungen. Otto Pächt,* ed. A. Rosenauer and G. Weber (Salzburg: Residenz, 1972), 17–22.

22 C. Frick, "Review of Bauer and Strzygowski, *Eine Alexandrinische Weltchronik,*" *Byzantinische Zeitschrift* 16 (1907): 632–44.

23 M. Whitby and M. Whitby, *Chronicon Paschale 284–628 AD* (Liverpool: Liverpool University Press, 1989), ix–xxviii.

24 See *Hippolytus Werke, Vierter Band: Die Chronik,* ed. R. Helm (Berlin: Akademie, 1955). The *status quaestionis* of the Hippolytan corpus is set out in R. Heine, "Hippoytus, Ps.-Hippolytus and the Early Canons," in F. Young et al., eds., *The Cambridge History of Early Christian Literature* (Cambridge: Cambridge University Press, 2004), 142–51.

25 We have followed the fuller version appended to the *Chronicle* of Fredegar.

26 W. Adler and P. Tuffin, *The Chronography of George Synkellos: A Byzantine Chronicle of Universal History from the Creation* (Oxford: Oxford University Press, 2002), xxix–lxxv.

27 Procopius, *Bell.* 5.5.8–10; *Epistulae Austrasicae* 18–20, Corpus Christianorum Series Latina 117, ed. W. Gundlach (Turnhout: Brepols, 1957), 436–39.

28 Procopius, *Bell.* 6.25; cf. 6.28.7–23.

29 John Lydus, *De magistratibus* 3.56; cf. Isidore of Seville, *Etym.* 9.2.101.

30 Procopius, *Bell.* 8.33.3.

31 We should probably add to the narrative of Alexander, or the material taken from the same source, the notices on the original subjection of the

Romans to the eastern powers (1.6.6) and Nebuchadnezzar's conquests from the Caspian Gates to the Pillars of Hercules, including the land of the Romans (1.8.1).

32 Procopius, *Bell.* 3.2.6 (cf. 8.5.2), 5.1.9–12, 5.5.8–10.

33 Procopius, *Bell.* 7.33.5–6; Agathias, 1.4 (21B–23B).

34 Procopius, *Bell.* 5.25.9–10.

35 Malalas, 6.24, 25, 29, 7.1–2.

36 Malalas, 7.17–19, 8.1–5. See B. Garstad, "The Tyche Sacrifices in John Malalas: Virgin Sacrifice and Fourth-Century Polemical History," *Illinois Classical Studies* 30 (2005): 87–93.

37 Malalas, 1.8–15.

38 See E. Hardy, "The Egyptian Policy of Justinian," *Dumbarton Oaks Papers* 22 (1968): 21–41.

39 See Y. Hen, *Culture and Religion in Merovingian Gaul, AD 481–751* (Leiden: E. J. Brill, 1995), 175 and n. 121.

40 See Garstad, "Barbarian Interest in the *Excerpta Latina Barbari,*" *Early Medieval Europe* 19 (2011): 5–6, 14–24.

41 E. Lowe, *Codices Latini Antiquiores,* Part 5 (France: Paris) (Oxford: Clarendon, 1950), 13.

42 J. Hubert, J. Porcher, and W. F. Volbach, eds., *L'Europe des invasions, L'univers des formes* 12 (Paris: Gallimard, 1967), 202.

43 A. Dierkens, "Superstitions, christianisme et paganisme à la fin de l'époque mérovingienne: A propos de l'*Indiculus superstitionium et paganiarum,*" in *Magie, sorcellerie, parapsychologie,* ed. H. Hasquin (Brussels: Éditions de l'Université de Bruxelles, 1984), 9–26.

44 Homer, *Iliad* 19.404–18; Herodotus, 3.84–6; Tacitus, *Germ.* 10.3–5; Justin, *Epit.* 1.10.4–5.

45 Martin of Braga, *De correctione rusticorum* 3–14.

46 Boniface, *Epistula* 23.

47 Ermoldus Nigellus, *Carmen in honorem Hludowici* 4.1911–45.

48 Caesarius of Arles, *Sermo* 193.4.

49 Martin of Braga, *De correctione rusticorum* 7.

50 Ælfric, *De falsis deis;* Wulfstan, *De falsis deis.*

51 Gregory of Tours, *Historia Francorum* 2.29.

52 Boniface, *Epistula* 23.

53 See Garstad, "Barbarian Interest in the *Excerpta Latina Barbari,*" 13.

54 K. Hauck, *Goldbrakteaten aus Sievern* (Munich: W. Fink, 1970), 288–303.

THE APOCALYPSE
ATTRIBUTED TO
SAINT METHODIUS

Τοῦ ἐν ἁγίοις πατρὸς ἡμῶν Μεθοδίου
ἐπισκόπου Πατάρων τοῦ μάρτυρος λόγος
ἠκριβωμένος περὶ τῆς βασιλείας τῶν ἐθνῶν καὶ
εἰς τοὺς ἐσχάτους καιροὺς ἀκριβὴς ἀπόδειξις
ἀρχόμενος ἀπὸ Ἀδὰμ ἕως συντελείας κόσμου.

I

Ἰστέον ὅτι ἐξελθόντες ὅ τε Ἀδὰμ καὶ ἡ Εὔα ἐκ τοῦ παραδείσου παρθένοι ἐτύγχανον. Ἐν δὲ τῷ τριακοστῷ χρόνῳ
τῆς ἐξόδου αὐτῶν ἐκ τοῦ παραδείσου ‹Ἀδὰμ ἔγνω(κεν) Εὔ-
αν τὴν γυναῖκα αὐτοῦ καὶ συλλαβοῦσα›[1] τέτοκεν[2] Κάϊν τὸν
πρωτότοκον καὶ τὴν ἀδελφὴν[3] αὐτοῦ Καλμάναν· καὶ μετὰ
τριακοστὸν ἕτερον ἔτος ἐγέννησε τὸν Ἄβελ σὺν τῇ Δεβόρᾳ
τῇ ἀδελφῇ αὐτοῦ.

2   Τῷ δὲ ἑκατοστῷ τριακοστῷ χρόνῳ τῆς ζωῆς τοῦ Ἀδὰμ
ἀπέκτεινεν ὁ Κάϊν Ἄβελ τὸν ἀδελφὸν αὐτοῦ καὶ ἐποίησαν
κοπετὸν ἐπ’ αὐτὸν ὅ τε Ἀδὰμ καὶ ἡ Εὔα ἐπὶ χρόνους ἑκα-
τόν· τῷ δὲ διακοσιοστῷ τριακοστῷ ἔτει τῆς πρώτης χιλιάδος, ὅ[4] ἐστιν ὁ πρῶτος αἰών, ἐγεννήθη ὁ Σὴθ ἀνὴρ γίγας
ἐν ὁμοιώματι τοῦ Ἀδάμ. Τῷ δὲ τεντακοσιοστῷ χρόνῳ τῆς
πρώτης χιλιάδος οἱ υἱοὶ τοῦ Κάϊν κατεπόρνευον τὰς γυναῖκας τῶν ἀδελφῶν αὐτῶν.

3   Γνοὺς οὖν ταῦτα ὁ Ἀδὰμ ἐλυπήθη σφόδρα. Ἐν δὲ τῷ

AN ACCURATE RELATION OF OUR HOLY
FATHER METHODIUS, MARTYR BISHOP
OF PATARA, CONCERNING THE KINGDOM
OF THE HEATHEN NATIONS AND AN EXACT
DEMONSTRATION OF THE END TIMES
BEGINNING WITH ADAM AND LEADING
UP TO THE END OF THE WORLD.

Chapter 1

K now that when Adam and Eve left Paradise they were
virgins. In the thirtieth year after their departure from Paradise <Adam knew his wife Eve and she conceived and> bore
Cain their firstborn and his sister Calmana. And after another thirty years she gave birth to Abel along with his sister
Deborah.

In the hundred and thirtieth year of the life of Adam Cain 2
killed Abel his brother and Adam and Eve made lament over
him for a hundred years. In the two hundred and thirtieth
year of the first millennium, that is the first age, Seth was
born, a gigantic man in the likeness of Adam. In the five
hundredth year of the first millennium the sons of Cain
prostituted the wives of their brothers.

When Adam knew these things he was grieved very much. 3

ἑξακοσιοστῷ χρόνῳ τῆς αὐτῆς ‹πρώτης› χιλιάδος οἴστρῳ ἔρωτος πορνείας αἱ τούτων κατεσχέθησαν γυναῖκες καῖ εἰς μανίαν ἐτράπησαν καὶ τοῖς ἰδίοις ἄνδρασιν ὡς γυναιξὶν ἐκέχρηντο, καὶ γεγόνασιν ἀληθῶς προῦπτος αἰσχύνη τοῖς ὁρῶσι, καταπορνεύσασαι τὴν αἰδώ.

4   Τῷ δὲ ὀκτακοσιοστῷ⁵ χρόνῳ τῆς ζωῆς τοῦ Ἀδὰμ κατεπλάτυνε ἐν τῇ γῇ τὸ μύσος⁶ τῆς πορνείας ὑπὸ τῶν υἱῶν τοῦ ἀδελφοκτόνου Κάϊν.

5   Ἐτελεύτησε δὲ ὁ Ἀδὰμ τῷ ἐνακοσιοστῷ τριακοστῷ χρόνῳ τῆς πρώτης χιλιάδος· καὶ τηνικαῦτα ἐχωρίσθησαν ἀπ᾽ ἀλλήλων ἡ τοῦ Σὴθ γενεὰ ἐκ τῆς τοῦ Κάϊν συγγενείας, καὶ ἀνήνεγκε Σὴθ τὴν αὐτοῦ γενεὰν ἄνω ἐν ὄρει τινὶ παραπλησίῳ ὄντι τοῦ παραδείσου. Καὶ κατῴκουν ὅ τε Κάϊν καὶ ἡ τούτου συγγένεια ἐν τῷ πεδίῳ, ἐν ᾧ τὴν θεήλατον ἀδελφοκτονίαν εἰργάσατο. Τῷ δὲ τεσσαρακοστῷ χρόνῳ τοῦ Ἰάρεδ ἐπληρώθη ἡ πρώτη χιλιὰς ἤγουν ὁ πρῶτος αἰών.

2

Τῷ δὲ τριακοσιοστῷ τεσσαρακοστῷ χρόνῳ τοῦ Ἰάρεδ, ἤγουν τῆς δευτέρας χιλιάδος, ἐπανέστησαν κακότεχνοι ἄνδρες, πονηροὶ καὶ παράνομοι, πάσης ἀνομίας πλήρεις,⁷ ἐκ τῶν υἱῶν τοῦ Κάϊν, Ἰουβὴθ καὶ Θουλουκήλ, τέκνα τοῦ Λαμὲχ τοῦ τυφλοῦ, τοῦ καὶ τὸν Κάϊν ἀποκτείναντος· ὧν καὶ κυριεύσας ὁ διάβολος ἐτροπώσατο αὐτους ἅπαν εἶδος μουσικῶν⁸ κατασκευάσαι.

In the six hundredth year of this first millennium their women were possessed by the sting of the love of fornication and turned to madness and used their own men as women, and they became indeed a manifest shame to those who saw, prostituting their modesty.

In the eight hundredth year of the life of Adam the stain 4 of fornication spread abroad in the earth under the sons of the brother-slayer Cain.

Adam died in the nine hundred and thirtieth year of the 5 first millennium. And at that time they were severed from one another, the family of Seth from the kin of Cain, and Seth led his family up onto a mountain near Paradise. And Cain and his kin settled on the plain on which he committed his God-hunted[1] fratricide. In the fortieth year of Jared the first millennium was completed, that is to say the first age.

Chapter 2

In the three hundred and fortieth year of Jared, that is of the second millennium, evil-intentioned men rose up in insurrection, wicked and lawless, full of every outlawry, out of the sons of Cain, Ioubeth and Thouloukel, the offspring of blind Lamech, who killed Cain. The Devil controlled them, and turned them to composing every kind of music.[2]

2   Τῷ δὲ πεντακοσιοστῷ χρόνῳ τῆς δευτέρας χιλιάδος ἔτι μειζόνως ἐξεκαύθησαν ἐπὶ τῇ ἀθέσμῳ πορνείᾳ[9] πάντες οἱ ἄνθρωποι ἐν τῇ παρεμβολῇ Κάϊν τῆς προτέρας χείρονες γενόμενοι γενεᾶς, οἳ καὶ δίκην ἀλόγων ζῴων ἀλλήλοις ἐπέβαινον, ἐπὶ μὲν τοὺς ἄρρενας τὸ θῆλυ, ἐπὶ δὲ θῆλυ τὸ ἄρρεν.[10]

3   Τῷ δὲ ἑπτακοσιοστῷ ἔτει τῆς τοῦ Ἰάρεδ ζωῆς ἤτοι ἐν τῇ δευτέρᾳ χιλιάδι προσέθετο ὁ πονηρὸς καὶ ὀλέθριος διάβολος πόλεμον πορνείας προσάψαι τοῖς υἱοῖς Σὴθ εἰς τὰς θυγατέρας τοῦ Κάϊν καὶ ἐξωθήσας ἔρριψε τοὺς γίγαντας τοῦ Σὴθ ἐν βόθρῳ τῆς ἁμαρτίας. Καὶ ὀργισθεὶς κύριος ὁ θεὸς ἐν τῷ τέλει τῆς δευτέρας χιλιάδος ἐγένετο ὁ κατακλυσμὸς τῶν ὑδάτων καὶ ἠφανίσθη πᾶσα ἡ πρώτη δημιουργία καὶ διάπλασις.

3

Καὶ τῷ δὲ ἑξακοσιοστῷ δωδεκάτῳ ἔτει τῆς ζωῆς Νῶε ἐν χρόνῳ δωδεκάτῳ[11] τῆς τρίτης χιλιάδος μετὰ τὸ ἐξελθεῖν Νῶε τῆς κιβωτοῦ, ἔκτισαν οἱ υἱοὶ Νῶε νέον κτίσμα ἐν τῇ ἐξωτέρᾳ γῇ καὶ ἐπωνόμασαν τὸ ὄνομα τοῦ χωρίου Θαμνὼν ἐπὶ τῷ ὀνόματι τοῦ ἀριθμοῦ τῶν ἐξελθουσῶν ὀκτὼ ψυχῶν ἐκ τῆς κιβωτοῦ.

2   Τῷ δὲ ἑκατοστῷ χρόνῳ τῆς τρίτης χιλιάδος ἐγεννήθη τῷ Νῶε υἱὸς ἐν ὁμοιώματι αὐτοῦ καὶ ἐπωνόμασεν αὐτὸν

In the five hundredth year of the second millennium all 2 of the people in the camp of Cain were even more inflamed in their lawless fornication and became even worse than the previous generation. And they mounted one another after the manner of brute beasts, a female upon males here, a male upon a female there.

In the eight hundredth year of the life of Jared, that is in 3 the second millennium, the wicked and destructive Devil proceeded to afflict the war of fornication upon the sons of Seth; he drove them out to the daughters of Cain, and cast the giants of Seth into the pit of sin. The Lord God was angered, and at the end of the second millennium a flood of waters came and the whole first creation and fashioning disappeared.

Chapter 3

And in the six hundred and twentieth year of the life of Noah, in the twentieth year of the third millennium, after Noah left the ark, the sons of Noah established a new settlement in the outer earth and named the place Thamnon after the name of the number of the eight souls who left the ark.[3]

In the hundredth year of the third millennium a son was 2 born to Noah in his likeness and he named him Jonetos. In

Ἰώνητον· τῷ δὲ τριακοσιοστῷ χρόνῳ τῆς τρίτης χιλιάδος ἔδωκε Νῶε χαρίσματα ⟨Ἰωνήτῳ⟩ τῷ υἱῷ αὐτοῦ καὶ ἀπέστειλεν αὐτὸν ἐν τῇ γῇ τῆς ἑῴας.

3 Καὶ μετὰ τὴν τοῦ Νῶε τελευτὴν τῷ ἑξακοσιοστῷ ἐνενηκοστῷ ἔτει τῆς τρίτης χιλιάδος ἀνῆλθον οἱ υἱοὶ Νῶε ἐκ τῆς ἑῴας γῆς καὶ ἔκτισαν ἑαυτοῖς πύργον ἐν γῇ Σεναάρ· κἀκεῖ ἐφύρθησαν αἱ γλῶσσαι καὶ διεμερίσθησαν ἐπὶ προσώπου πάσης τῆς γῆς.

4 Ἰώνητος δὲ ὁ τοῦ Νῶε υἱὸς εἰσῆλθεν εἰς τὴν ἑῴαν μέχρι τῆς θαλάσσης τῆς ἐπιλεγομένης ἡλίου χώρας, ἔνθα ἡ ἀνατολὴ γίνεται τοῦ ἡλίου, καὶ κατῴκησεν ἐκεῖ.

5 Οὗτος δὲ ὁ Ἰώνητος ἔλαβε παρὰ θεοῦ χάρισμα σοφίας, ὃς πρῶτος ἀστρονομίας τὴν τέχνην ἐφεύρατο. Πρὸς τοῦτον δὲ κατελθὼν ὁ Νεβρὼδ ὁ γίγας καὶ παιδευθεὶς εἴληφε παρ' αὐτοῦ τὴν βουλὴν ἐφ' ᾧ βασιλεῦσαι αὐτόν. Νεβρὼδ δὲ οὗτος τῶν ἡρώων ἐτύγχανεν[12] τῶν τέκνων τοῦ Σὴμ καὶ αὐτὸς πρῶτος ἐβασίλευσεν ἐπὶ τῆς γῆς.

6 Τῷ δὲ ἑπτακοσιοστῷ ἐνενηκοστῷ ἔτει τῆς τρίτης χιλιάδος ἐκτίσθη ἡ Βαβυλὼν ἡ μεγάλη καὶ ἐβασίλευσεν ἐν αὐτῇ ὁ Νεβρὼδ, καὶ μετὰ ταῦτα ἐποίησαν ἑαυτοῖς υἱοὶ Χὰμ βασιλέα ἐξ αὐτῶν, οὗ τὸ ὄνομα Πόντιπος. Καὶ τῷ ἑπτακοσιοστῷ ἐνενηκοστῷ ἐνάτῳ χρόνῳ τῆς τρίτης χιλιάδος, τῷ τρίτῳ ἔτει τῆς βασιλείας Νεβρὼδ, ἔπεμψαν ἄνδρας δυνατοὺς ἐκ τῶν τέκνων τοῦ Ἰάφεθ, σοφοὺς πάνυ τεχνίτας καὶ ἀρχιτέκτονας, καὶ κατῆλθον εἰς τὴν ἑῴαν γῆν πρὸς Ἰώνητον τὸν υἱὸν Νῶε καὶ ᾠκοδόμησαν αὐτῷ πόλιν καὶ ἐπωνόμασαν αὐτὴν Ἰώνητον κατὰ τὴν προσηγορίαν αὐτοῦ.

the three hundredth year of the third millennium Noah gave gifts to <Jonetos> his son and sent him out into the land of the dawn.

And after the death of Noah in the six hundred and nine- 3 tieth year of the third millennium the sons of Noah went up out of the dawn land and built for themselves a tower in the land of Shinar. And there the tongues were confused and they were divided over the face of the earth.

Jonetos the son of Noah went to the east as far as the sea 4 and the place called the Country of the Sun, where the rising of the sun takes place, and he settled there.

This Jonetos received from God the gift of wisdom, and 5 he was the first to discover the practice of astronomy. Nimrod the giant came down to him, and was instructed and took from him the counsel by which he ruled. This Nimrod was of the heroes, of the children of Shem, and he was the first to rule as a king on the earth.[4]

In the seven hundred and ninetieth year of the third mil- 6 lennium Babylon the Great was founded and Nimrod ruled in it. And after these things the sons of Ham made a king for themselves out of their own number, whose name was Pontipos. And in the seven hundred and ninety-ninth year of the third millennium, in the third year of the reign of Nimrod, he sent strong and able men from the sons of Japheth, wise in regard to all aspects of craftsmanship and architecture, and they went down to the land of the dawn to Jonetos the son of Noah and built a city for him and called it Jonetos after his name.

7 Καὶ εἰρήνη πολλὴ γέγονεν ἐπὶ τῆς βασιλείας Ἰωνήτου
καὶ Νεβρὼδ ἄχρι τῆς ἄρτι. Ἐπὶ δὲ τῆς βασιλείας Νεβρὼδ
υἱοῦ Σὴμ καὶ Ποντίπου υἱοῦ Χὰμ οὐκ ἦν εἰρήνη· ἐν γὰρ
ταῖς ἡμέραις Νεβρὼδ ‹οἱ› υἱοὶ Χὰμ καὶ Ἰάφεθ κατ᾽ ἀλλήλων
ὡπλίζοντο.

8 Ἔγραψε δὲ Ἰώνητος ἐπιστολὴν πρὸς Νεβρὼδ οὕτως ὅτι
ἡ βασιλεία ‹τῶν υἱῶν› τοῦ Ἰάφεθ, αὕτη μέλλει ἐξαλείφειν
τὴν βασιλείαν τῶν τέκνων τοῦ Χάμ. Αὗται γὰρ πρῶται
βασιλεῖαι ἀνεδείχθησαν ἐπὶ τῆς γῆς καὶ μετὰ ταῦτα ἔμα-
θον πάντα τὰ ἔθνη καθιστᾶν ἑαυτοῖς βασιλεῖς.

4

Μετὰ δὲ τὴν βασιλείαν Νεβρὼδ, τελεσθείσης ἤδη τῆς
τρίτης χιλιάδος, τῷ ἑβδομηκοστῷ τετάρτῳ ἔτει, τουτέστι
τῷ τριακοστῷ ἑβδόμῳ ἔτει τῆς τετάρτης χιλιάδος, ἀεὶ
ἐπολέμησαν μετ᾽ ἀλλήλων ἀμφότεραι αἱ βασιλεῖαι· καὶ ἡτ-
τήθη ἡ τῶν Αἰγυπτίων βασιλεία ὑπὸ τῆς Νεβρὼδ βασιλείας. Καὶ περικρατὴς γέγονεν ἡ βασιλεία Βαβυλῶνος ἐν τῷ
σπέρματι Νεβρὼδ ἕως τοῦ Χουζιμιζδῆ· οὗτος ἔλαβεν ἑαυτῷ
γυναῖκα ἐκ τῶν τέκνων τοῦ Χάμ.

2 Τελευτήσαντος δὲ τοῦ Χουζιμιζδῆ ἔλαβεν Ἰζδὴ ὁ τούτου
ἀπόγονος τὴν ἑαυτοῦ μητέρα εἰς γυναῖκα καὶ ἐγέννησεν
ἑαυτῷ τὸν Ἐρεσδή. Οὗτος συνήγαγεν ἑαυτῷ δυνάμεις
πολλὰς καὶ ἐπανέστη κατὰ τῆς βασιλείας τῶν τέκνων τοῦ
Χὰμ καὶ αἰχμαλώτευσεν αὐτοὺς καὶ κατέφλεξε πάσας τὰς
χώρας τῆς δύσεως πυρί.

And a great peace reigned under the kingship of Jonetos 7 and Nimrod up to the present. But in the reign of Nimrod the son of Shem and Pontipos the son of Ham there was not peace. For in the days of Nimrod the sons of Ham and Japheth took up arms against one another.

Jonetos wrote a letter to Nimrod to the effect that "the 8 kingdom <of the sons> of Japheth itself intends to wipe out the kingdom of the children of Ham." For these were the first kingdoms to appear on the earth and after these things all peoples learned to appoint kings for themselves.

Chapter 4

After the reign of Nimrod, when the third millennium had already come to an end, in the seventy-fourth year,[5] that is in the thirty-seventh year of the fourth millennium, both kingdoms were constantly making war with one another. And the kingdom of the Egyptians was defeated by the kingdom of Nimrod. And the kingdom of Babylon became an imperial power in the posterity of Nimrod until Chouzimizdes. This man took a wife for himself from among the children of Ham.

When Chouzimizdes died his descendant Izdes took his 2 own mother to wife and she bore him Eresdes. This man gathered to himself many powers and rose up against the kingdom of the children of Ham and made them captives and consumed all the land of the west with fire.

3 Τῷ δὲ δευτέρῳ ἔτει τῆς βασιλείας Χοσδρῶ, υἱοῦ τοῦ
Ἐρεσδῆ, συνηθροίσθησαν οἱ υἱοὶ Χὰμ καὶ κατῆλθον ἐπὶ
τὴν ἑῴαν τοῦ πολεμῆσαι μετὰ τοῦ βασιλέως Χοσδρῶ.
Ἦσαν δὲ τριακόσιαι εἴκοσι χιλιάδες πεζῶν ῥάβδους μόνον
κατέχοντες ἐν ταῖς χερσὶν αὐτῶν.

4 Ἀκούσας δὲ Χοσδρῶ περὶ τούτων ἐμειδίασε καὶ παρ-
είασεν αὐτοὺς ἄχρις ἂν παρῆλθον τὸν Τίγριν ποταμόν.
Κἀκεῖ ἐξαπέστειλεν κατ᾽ αὐτῶν τὸν ἴδιον στρατὸν ἐπιβάν-
τας ἐπὶ ἐλεφάντων καὶ ἀπέκτεινεν ἅπαντας, καὶ οὐχ ὑπ-
ελείφθη ἀπ᾽ αὐτῶν οὐδὲ εἷς, καὶ οὐ προσέθηκαν ἔτι πολεμῆσαι υἱοὶ Χάμ. Ἔκτοτε παροξύνθησαν αἱ βασιλεῖαι κατ᾽
ἀλλήλων.

5

Καὶ ἐν τῷ τέλει τῆς τετάρτης χιλιάδος, ἤτοι τῷ εἰκοστῷ
πέμπτῳ χρόνῳ τοῦ Χοσδρώ, τῷ πέμπτῳ χρόνῳ τῆς πέμπτης
χιλιάδος, κατῆλθε Σαμψισανὼ ἐκ τῆς ἑῴας, ὅς ἐστιν ἐκ τῆς
συγγενείας Ἰωνήτου τοῦ υἱοῦ Νῶε, καὶ ἠρήμωσεν ἀπὸ τοῦ
Εὐφράτου ἕως τοῦ Ἐδροηγάν, τουτέστιν ἑξήκοντα ἑπτὰ
πόλεις καὶ τὰς χώρας αὐτῶν

2 καὶ ἐπέβη ἐπὶ τὰς τρεῖς βασιλείας τῶν Ἰνδῶν καὶ κατ-
έκαυσε πυρὶ καὶ ἠρήμωσε καὶ ἐξῆλθεν ἐπὶ τὴν ἔρημον
Σαβὰ καὶ κατέκοψε τὴν παρεμβολὴν τῶν τέκνων τοῦ
Ἰσμαὴλ τοῦ υἱοῦ τῆς Ἅγαρ τῆς Αἰγυπτίας, παιδίσκης

In the second year of the reign of Chosdro, the son of 3
Eresdes, the sons of Ham were assembled and went down
to the east to make war with Chosdro the king. They were
three hundred and twenty thousand foot soldiers, and had
only sticks in their hands.

When Chosdro heard about them he grinned and dis- 4
missed them until they crossed the Tigris River. And there
he sent out against them his own army mounted on elephants and he killed them all, and not one of them was left
alive. And the sons of Ham have not given up making war
yet. From that time the kingdoms have been stirred up
against one another.

Chapter 5

And at the end of the fourth millennium, that is in the
twenty-fifth year of Chosdro, in the fifth year of the fifth
millennium, Sampsisano, who was of the tribe of Jonetos
the son of Noah, came down from the east and laid waste
the country from the Euphrates to Edroega [Azerbaijan],
that is sixty-seven cities and their territories.

And he came upon the three kingdoms of the Indians and 2
burned them with fire and devastated them, and he came
out into the desert of Sheba and broke up the encampment
of the children of Ishmael the son of Hagar the Egyptian,

Σάρρας γυναικὸς Ἀβραάμ. Καὶ ἀπέδρασαν ἅπαντες καὶ ἀπέφυγον ἐκ τῆς ἐρήμου Αἰθρίβων καὶ εἰσῆλθον εἰς τὴν οἰκουμένην γῆν καὶ ἐπολέμησαν μετὰ τῶν βασιλέων τῶν ἐθνῶν καὶ ἠρήμωσαν καὶ αἰχμαλώτευσαν καὶ κατεκυρίευσαν τὰς βασιλείας τῶν ἐθνῶν τὰς ἐν τῇ γῇ τῆς ἐπαγγελίας·

3   καὶ ἐπλήσθη ἡ γῆ ἐξ αὐτῶν καὶ ἐκ τῆς παρεμβολῆς αὐτῶν· ἦσαν γὰρ ὡς ἀκρίδες καὶ ἐπορεύοντο γυμνοὶ καὶ ἤσθιον κρέα‹ς› καμήλων κατεσκευασμένον ἐν †βαφίοις† καὶ ἔπινον αἷμα κτηνῶν καὶ γάλα.

4   Ὅτε οὖν κατεκράτησαν οἱ υἱοὶ Ἰσμαὴλ πάσης τῆς γῆς καὶ ἠρήμωσαν πόλεις καὶ χώρας αὐτῶν καὶ κατεδυνάστευσαν ἐν ὅλαις ταῖς νήσοις, τὸ τηνικαῦτα κατεσκεύαζον ἑαυτοῖς ναῦς καὶ δίκην πετεινῶν ταύταις κεχρημένοι ἵπταντο ἐπὶ τῶν ὑδάτων ‹τῆς θαλάσσης›[13] καὶ ἀνῆλθον εἰς τὰς χώρας τῆς δύσεως μέχρι τῆς μεγάλης Ῥώμης καὶ τοῦ Ἰλλυρικοῦ καὶ τοῦ †Γιγήτου† καὶ Θεσσαλονίκης καὶ Σαρδανίας τῆς μεγάλης καὶ ἐπέκεινα Ῥώμης. Καὶ κατεκυρίευσαν τῆς γῆς ἐπὶ χρόνους ἑξήκοντα καὶ ἐποίησαν ἐν αὐτῇ ὅσα ἠθέλησαν.

5   Μετὰ δὲ ἑβδομάδας ὀκτὼ καὶ ἥμισυ τῆς αὐτῶν δυναστείας, δι᾽ ἧς κατεκράτησαν πάσας τὰς βασιλείας τῶν ἐθνῶν, ὑπερυψώθη αὐτῶν ἡ καρδία ἐν τῷ θεάσασθαι αὐτοὺς κυριεύσαντας καὶ κατακρατήσαντας ἅπαντας.

6   Ἐν δὲ τῷ καιρῷ ἐκείνῳ γεγόνασιν ἐν αὐτοῖς τύραννοι ἀρχιστράτηγοι τέσσαροι υἱοὶ τυγχάνοντες Οὐμαίας τῆς οὕτω παρ᾽ αὐτοῖς ὀνομαζομένης, ὧν τὰ ὀνόματα Ὀρὴβ καὶ Ζὴβ καὶ Ζεβαιὲ καὶ Σαλμανά· οὗτοι ἐπολέμησαν μετὰ

thc maidservant of Sarah the wife of Abraham. And they all ran away and fled out of the desert of Yathrib[6] and came into the inhabited world and made war with the kings of the nations and laid their lands waste and took them captive and gained dominion over the kingdoms of the heathen in the Promised Land.

And the land was filled with them and with their encamp- 3 ment. For they were like locusts and went about naked and ate the meat of camels prepared in skins[7] and drank the blood of cattle and milk.

So when the sons of Ishmael overcame the whole land 4 and laid waste cities and their territories and dominated the islands, they then built for themselves ships and used them in the manner of birds, flying over the waters <of the sea>, and they came up to all the lands of the West as far as Great Rome and Illyricum and †Gigetum†[8] and Thessalonica and Sardinia the Great and beyond Rome. And they were lords of the earth for sixty years and did whatever they pleased in it.

After eight and a half weeks of their dominion, during 5 which they prevailed over all the kingdoms of the nations, the heart was exalted within them at seeing that they were lords and conquerors of all.

In that time there arose among them four tyrants, chiefs 6 of the army, who were sons of Umaia (who was thus named by them), whose names [were] Oreb and Zeeb and Zebah and Zalmuna.[9] These men made war with the Israelites, and

τῶν Ἰσραηλιτῶν, καὶ καθ' ὃν τρόπον ἐποίησεν αὐτοῖς ὁ θεὸς λύτρωσιν ἐκ τῶν χειρῶν τῶν Αἰγυπτίων διὰ Μωσέως τοῦ θεράποντος αὐτοῦ, τὸν αὐτὸν δὴ τρόπον καὶ τῷ τότε καιρῷ ἐποίησεν μετ' αὐτῶν ἔλεος καὶ ἐλυτρώσατο αὐτοὺς ἐξ αὐτῶν διὰ τοῦ Γεδεὼν καὶ ἠλευθερώθη ὁ Ἰσραὴλ ἐκ τῆς δουλείας τῶν τέκνων τοῦ Ἰσμαήλ.

7 Οὗτος γὰρ ὁ Γεδεὼν κατέκοψε τὰς παρεμβολὰς αὐτῶν καὶ ἐκδιώξας ἐξήνεγκεν αὐτοὺς ἐκ τῆς οἰκουμένης γῆς εἰς τὴν ἔρημον Ἐθρίβ, ἐξ ἧς ἐτύγχανον.

8 Καὶ οἱ ὑπολειφθέντες δέδωκαν συνθήκας εἰρήνης τοῖς υἱοῖς Ἰσραὴλ καὶ ἐξῆλθον ἐπὶ τὴν ἔρημον τὴν ἐξωτέραν ἐννέα φυλαί· μέλλουσι δὲ ἐξιέναι ἄλλο ἅπαξ καὶ ἐρημῶσαι τὴν γῆν καὶ κατακρατῆσαι τὴν οἰκουμένην καὶ τὰς χώρας ἐν εἰσόδῳ εἰρήνης ἀπὸ τῆς Αἰγύπτου ἕως Αἰθιοπίας καὶ ἀπὸ τοῦ Εὐφράτου μέχρι Ἰνδίας καὶ ἀπὸ τοῦ Τίγριδος ἕως τῆς εἰσόδου Νὼδ βασιλείας Ἰωνήτου υἱοῦ Νῶε καὶ ἀπὸ Βορρᾶ ἕως Ῥώμης καὶ τοῦ Ἰλλυρικοῦ καὶ Γιγήτου καὶ Θεσσαλονίκης καὶ Ὀβοίας[14] καὶ ἕως τῆς θαλάσσης τοῦ Πόντου, καὶ ἐν διπλότητι ἔσται ὁ ζυγὸς αὐτῶν ἐπὶ τραχήλου πάντων τῶν ἐθνῶν.

9 Καὶ οὐκ ἔσται ἔθνος ἢ βασιλεία ὑπὸ τὸν οὐρανὸν οἳ ἰσχύσουσι πολεμῆσαι αὐτοὺς ἄχρι ἀριθμοῦ χρόνων ἑβδομάδων ἑπτά. Καὶ μετὰ ταῦτα ἡττηθήσονται ὑπὸ τῆς βασιλείας τῶν Ῥωμαίων καὶ ὑποταγήσονται αὐτῇ· καὶ γὰρ αὐτὴ μεγαλυνθήσεται ὑπὲρ πάσας τὰς βασιλείας τῶν ἐθνῶν καὶ οὐ μὴ ἐξαλειφθῇ ὑπ' οὐδεμιᾶς αὐτῶν εἰς τὸν αἰῶνα· ἔχει γὰρ ὅπλον ‹ἀνίκητον›,[15] δι' οὗ πάντες αὐτῇ ἡττηθήσονται.

just as God brought about for them deliverance out of the hands of the Egyptians through his servant Moses, thus at that time he had mercy on them and delivered them from them through Gideon and freed Israel from slavery to the sons of Ishmael.

For this Gideon broke up their camps and pursued them 7 and drove them out of the inhabited world into the desert of Yathrib, out of which they came.

And those who were left made peace treaties with the 8 sons of Israel and went out into the outer desert as nine tribes. But they will surely come out once again and lay waste the land and prevail over the inhabited world and the regions at the entrance of peace[10] from Egypt to Ethiopia and from the Euphrates as far as India and from the Tigris to the entrance of Nod,[11] the kingdom of Jonetos the son of Noah, and from the north to Rome and Illyricum and †Gigetum† and Thessalonica and Oboia[12] and to the sea of Pontus, and doubly will their yoke be upon the neck of all the nations.[13]

And there will not be a nation or kingdom under the 9 heaven that will be able to fight them until the completion[14] of seven weeks of years. And after these things they will be defeated by the kingdom of the Romans and subjected to it. For that kingdom will be exalted over all the kingdoms of the heathen nations and it will not be wiped out by any one of them unto eternity. For it has an <invincible> weapon, through which all will be defeated by that kingdom.[15]

6

Ἀπ' ἐντεῦθεν οὖν κατανοήσατε ἐκ τῶν κυκλικῶν χρόνων τῶν βασιλέων καὶ αὐτὴ ἡ ἀλήθεια τῶν πραγμάτων δείκνυσιν ἑαυτὴν φανεράν, ἄνευ πλάνης ἢ ἀπάτης τινός.

2 Ἀπὸ Νεβρὼδ γὰρ τοῦ ἥρωος μέχρι τοῦ Περουσδὲκ ἡ βασιλεία τῶν γιγάντων κατεκράτει τῆς γῆς Βαβυλῶνος καὶ ἀπὸ τοῦ Περουσδὲκ ἕως Σῆς τοῦ γέροντος ἐκ τῆς Ἰδρουηγὰν ἐβασίλευον Πέρσαι καὶ ἐκ τοῦ Σῆς ἕως Περουσδὲκ ἐβασίλευον ‹οἱ› ἐκ τῆς ‹Σ›λὲκ καὶ Κτησοῦν, καὶ ἐκ τῆς Περουσδῆ ἕως Σενερὴβ οἱ ἐκ Βαβυλῶνος ἐβασίλευον.

3 Καὶ ἔλαβεν Σενερὴβ γυναῖκαν τὴν Ἰεκνὰδ ἐκ τῆς Ἀραρὰτ καὶ ἐγέννησεν αὐτῷ Ἀρδεμέλεχ καὶ Τζαρατζὰρ καὶ οὗτοι ἀπέκτειναν τὸν ἑαυτῶν πατέρα καὶ ἔφυγον εἰς τὴν γῆν Ἀραρὰτ.

4 Καὶ ἐβασίλευσεν ἐκεῖ Σαραδὼν εἰς Βαβυλῶνα ἀντὶ τοῦ πατρὸς αὐτοῦ Σενερήβ, καὶ Ναβουχοδονόσορ ὁ ἐκ πατρὸς γενόμενος Λουζία καὶ ἐκ μητρὸς βασιλίσσης Σαβᾶ.

5 Ἡνίκα οὖν εἰσῆλθε Σενερὴβ τοῦ πολεμῆσαι μετὰ τοῦ βασιλέως Ἰνδίας καὶ ἕως Σαβᾶ καὶ ἐρήμωσε πολλὰς χώρας, συνεξῆλθεν αὐτῷ Ναβουχοδονόσορ, ἐκείνου δηλονότι συνεξαγαγόντος αὐτὸν μεθ' ἑαυτοῦ, καὶ κατέστησεν αὐτὸν ἀρχιστράτηγον αὐτοῦ, καὶ διὰ τὴν ἐν αὐτῷ σοφίαν καὶ δυναστείαν ἐδόθη αὐτῷ ἡ βασιλεία Βαβυλῶνος.

6 Καὶ ἔλαβεν ἑαυτῷ γυναῖκα ἐκ τῶν Μήδων τὴν Ἐρουσδούμ, καὶ μετὰ τὴν τελευτὴν Ναβουχοδονόσορ καὶ Βαλ-

Chapter 6

From what follows ponder and learn from the circling years of kings, and the very truth of things shows itself clearly, without any error or deceit.

For from Nimrod the hero until Perousdec the kingdom ² of the giants prevailed over the land of Babylon and from Perousdec to Ses, the old man from Idrouegan (i.e., Azerbaijan), the Persians ruled and from Ses to Perousdec <those> from <S>lec and Ctesphon ruled, and from Perousdec to Sennacherib those from Babylon ruled.

And Sennacherib took as his wife Iecnad from Ararat and ³ she bore him Ardemelech and Tzaratzar and these men killed their own father and fled to the land of Ararat.[16]

And then Saradon reigned in Babylon in the place of his ⁴ father Sennacherib, and Nebuchadnezzar who was born of Louzia, his father, and the queen of Sheba, his mother.

So when Sennacherib came to make war with the king ⁵ of India as far as Sheba and devastated many countries, Nebuchadnezzar went with him, that is to say Sennacherib brought him out with him, and appointed him the general of his army, and because of the wisdom within him and his sovereignty the kingdom of Babylon was granted to him [i.e., Nebuchadnezzar].

And he took a wife for himself from the Medes, Erous- ⁶ doum, and after the death of Nebuchadnezzar and Belshaz-

τάσαρ τοῦ υἱοῦ αὐτοῦ ἐβασίλευσεν Δαρεῖος ὁ Μῆδος ὁ ἀπέγγονος τῆς Ἐρουσδούμ. Δαρεῖος δὲ ἔγημεν τὴν Δωροὺμ Πέρσισσαν οὖσαν, ἐξ ἧς τίκτεται Χώρης ὁ Πέρσης.

7

Ἄκουε τοίνυν πῶς συνήφθησαν οἱ βασιλεῖς οὗτοι ἀλλήλοις, οἱ μὲν τῆς Βαβυλῶνος τοῖς Μήδοις, Πέρσαις δὲ Μῆδοι, καὶ περικρατεῖς γεγόνασιν οἱ ἐκ Βαβυλῶνος τῆς τε Αἰθιοπίας καὶ Σαβᾶ καὶ τῶν βασιλέων τῶν ἐθνῶν ἀπὸ θαλάσσης ἕως τοῦ Εὐφράτου ποταμοῦ, ἔτι δὲ καὶ τῆς βασιλείας τοῦ Δαβὶδ διὰ τοῦ Ναβουχοδονόσορ, ἔτι δὲ καὶ τῶν Ἀρράβων[16] καὶ τῶν Αἰγυπτίων.

2 Δαρεῖος δὲ ὁ Μῆδος κατεκυρίευσε τῆς τε βασιλείας τῶν Ἰνδῶν καὶ Λιβύων, Χώρης δὲ ὁ Πέρσης κατεκράτησε Θράκης καὶ ἀπελυτρώσατο τοὺς υἱοὺς Ἰσραὴλ καὶ ἀπέστειλεν αὐτοὺς εἰς τὴν γῆν τῆς ἐπαγγελίας προστάξας ἀνοικοδομῆσαι τὸν ναὸν τοῦ θεοῦ τὸν ὑπὸ Ναβουχοδονόσορ καταπτωθέντα καὶ διὰ τοῦτο γέγονεν κατὰ τὴν διάταξιν τοῦ βασιλέως Χώρου.

zar his son, Darius the Mede, the descendant of Erousdoum, reigned. Darius married Daroum, who was a Persian, from whom Chores the Persian was born.

Chapter 7

Hear now how these kings were united to one another, those of Babylon with the Medes on the one hand, and the Medes with the Persians on the other, and those of Babylon came to have power over Ethiopia and Sheba and the kings of the nations from the sea to the Euphrates River, and even over the kingdom of David through Nebuchadnezzar, and even over the Arabs and the Egyptians.

Darius the Mede gained dominion over the kingdom of the Indians and Libyans, and Chores the Persian prevailed over Thrace and delivered the sons of Israel and sent them back to the Promised Land with orders to rebuild the temple of God which was destroyed by Nebuchadnezzar. And because of this things turned out according to the command of King Chores.

8

Ἄκουε τοίνυν αὖθις σὺν ἀκριβείᾳ, πῶς αἱ τέσσαρες βασιλεῖαι ἀλλήλαις συνήφθησαν, οἱ Αἰθίοπες Μακεδόσι, Ῥωμαίοις‹ καὶ Ἕλληνες· αὗταί εἰσιν οἱ τέσσαρες ἄνεμοι τῆς ὑπ᾽ οὐρανόν, οὓς ἐθεάσατο ὁ Δανιὴλ συσσείοντας τὴν μεγάλην θάλασσαν.

2 Φίλιππος γὰρ ὁ Ἀλεξάνδρου πατὴρ Μακεδὼν ἦν καὶ ἔγημε τὴν Χουσὴθ θυγατέρα τοῦ βασιλέως Φὸλ τῆς Αἰθιοπίας, ἐξ ἧς οὗτος Ἀλέξανδρος τίκτεται Ἑλλήνων τύρρανος γεγονώς.

3 Οὗτος κτίζει Ἀλεξάνδρειαν τὴν μεγάλην καὶ βασιλεύει ἐν αὐτῇ χρόνους δέκα καὶ ἐννέα· οὗτος κατελθὼν εἰς τὴν ἑῴαν ἀπέκτεινε Δαρεῖον τὸν Μῆδον καὶ κατεκυρίευσε χωρῶν πολλῶν καὶ πολέων καὶ περιενόστησε τὴν γῆν καὶ κατήχθη ἕως τῆς ‹ἑῴας καὶ τῆς› θαλάσσης τῆς ἐπονομαζομένης ἡλίου χώρας, ἔνθα καὶ ἑώρακεν ἔθνη ἀκάθαρτα καὶ δυσειδῆ.

4 Εἰσὶ δὲ ἐκ τῶν υἱῶν Ἰαφὲθ ἀπόγονοι, ὧν τὴν ἀκαθαρσίαν θεασάμενος ἐμυσάχθη· ἤσθιον γὰρ ἅπαντες αὐτῶν κανθαροειδῶς μυσαρά τε καὶ κίβδηλα· κύνας, μύας, κάτας, ὄφεις, νεκρῶν σάρκας, ἀμβλώματα, ἐκτρώματα, ἔμβρυα μήπω τελείως ἀπαρτισθέντα ἤ τινα τῆς διαπλάσεως ἀποσῴζοντα χαρακτῆρα καὶ ταῦτα κτηνῶν, οὐ μὴν ἀλλὰ καὶ ἅπαν εἶδος θηρίων ἀκαθάρτων, τοὺς δὲ νεκροὺς οὐκ ἔθαπτον, ἀλλ᾽ ἤσθιον αὐτούς.

5¹ Ταῦτα ὁ Ἀλέξανδρος ἰδὼν γινόμενα ὑπ᾽ αὐτῶν τά τε

22

Chapter 8

Now hear again precisely how the four kingdoms were united with one another, the Ethiopians with the Macedonians, and the Greeks with the Romans. These are the four winds under heaven, which Daniel saw disturbing the great sea.[17]

For Philip, the father of Alexander, was a Macedonian 2 and he married Chouseth, the daughter of King Phol of Ethiopia, and out of her was born this Alexander, who became tyrant of the Greeks.

This man founded Alexandria the Great and ruled in it 3 for nineteen years. He went down to the east and slew Darius the Mede and gained dominion over many countries and cities and he went round the earth and went down as far as the <dawn and the> sea, called the Country of the Sun, where he saw unclean and ugly nations.

These are the descendants of the sons of Japheth, whose 4 uncleanness when he saw it disgusted him. For all of them eat in the manner of beetles what is loathsome and debased: dogs, mice, cats,[18] snakes, dead bodies, abortions, miscarriages, fetuses not completely formed or some preserving the marks of formation,[19] and these of unclean animals. And they do not bury the dead, but eat them.

Alexander saw these things done by them as hateful and 5[1]

μυσαρὰ καὶ ἀθέμιτα, δεδιὼς μήποτε μιάνωσι πᾶσαν τὴν
γῆν ἐδεήθη τοῦ θεοῦ περὶ αὐτῶν καὶ προστάξας συνήγαγεν
ἅπαντας αὐτούς τε καὶ τὰς γυναῖκας αὐτῶν καὶ τὰ τέκνα
αὐτῶν καὶ πάσας τὰς παρεμβολὰς αὐτῶν.

5²   Ταῦτα δὲ πάντα θεασάμενος ὁ Ἀλέξανδρος ὑπ᾽ αὐτῶν
ἐναγῶς καὶ μυσαρῶς γενόμενα,[17] δεδοικὼς μήπως ἀφίκνοιτο
ἐν τῇ ἁγίᾳ γῇ καὶ μιάνωσιν αὐτὴν ἐκ τῶν μιαρῶν αὐτῶν
ἐπιτηδευμάτων, ἐδεήθη τοῦ θεοῦ ἐκτενῶς καὶ προστάξας
συνήγαγεν αὐτοὺς ἅπαντας καὶ ‹τὰς› γυναῖκας αὐτῶν καὶ
τὰ τέκνα καὶ ἁπαξαπλῶς πάσας τὰς παρεμβολὰς αὐτῶν.

6¹   Καὶ ἐξαγαγὼν αὐτοὺς ἐκ τῆς ἑῴας γῆς κατεδίωξεν
ὀπίσω αὐτῶν, ἕως οὗ εἰσήχθησαν ἐν τοῖς πέρασιν τοῦ
Βορρᾶ, καὶ οὐκ ἔστιν εἴσοδος οὔτε ἔξοδος ἀπὸ ἀνατολῶν
μεχρὶ δυσμῶν, δι᾽ ἧς τις πρὸς αὐτοὺς περάσαι ἢ εἰσελθεῖν
οὐκ εἶχεν.

6²   Καὶ ἐξήγαγεν αὐτοὺς ἐκ τῆς ἑῴας γῆς καὶ κατεδίωξεν
ὀπίσω αὐτῶν, ἕως οὗ εἰσήχθησαν ἐν τοῖς πέρασι τοῦ
Βορρᾶ, καὶ οὐκ ἔστιν οὔτε εἴσοδος οὔτε ἔξοδος αὐτῶν ἀπὸ
ἀνατολῶν μεχρὶ δυσμῶν, δι᾽ ἧς τις πρὸς αὐτοὺς ἢ εἰσέλθῃ
ἢ ἐξέλθῃ.

7   Εὐθὺς[18] οὖν παρακαλέσας[19] τὸν θεὸν ὁ Ἀλέξανδρος, καὶ
ἐπήκουσεν αὐτοῦ τῆς δεήσεως καὶ προσέταξε Κύριος ὁ
Θεὸς τοῖς δύο ὄρεσιν, οἷς ἐστι προσηγορία οἱ Μαζοὶ τοῦ
Βορρᾶ, καὶ ἐπλησίασαν ἀλλήλοις ἄχρι πηχῶν δυοκαί-
δεκα.

8   Καὶ κατεσκεύασε πυλὰς χαλκᾶς καὶ ἐπέχρισεν αὐτὰς
ἀσυγκίτῃ, ἵνα εἰ καὶ βούλοιντο ἀνοῖξαι αὐτὰς ἐν σιδήρῳ
μὴ δύνανται ἢ διαλῦσαι αὐτὰς πυρὶ μὴ ἰσχύσουσιν, ἀλλ᾽

lawless, and fearing lest they should at some time pollute the whole earth he entreated God in prayer concerning them, and issuing commands he gathered all of them together, and their wives and their children and all of their camps.

Alexander looked at all these things accursed and hate- 5^2 fully arisen of themselves, and he feared lest they should somehow reach the Holy Land and pollute it with their abominable practices, and he earnestly supplicated God and issuing commands he gathered all of them together, and their wives and their children and all of their camps.

And driving them out of the land of the dawn he pursued 6^1 close behind them, until they were brought into the lands beyond the north, and there is neither way in nor way out from east to west, through which one could go over or come in to them.

And he drove them out of the land of the dawn and pur- 6^2 sued close behind them, until they were brought into the lands beyond the North, and there is neither a way in nor a way out for them from east to west, through which one might come in to them or might go out.

As soon, therefore, as Alexander called upon God, the 7 Lord God heard his prayer and commanded two mountains, whose name is the Paps of the North, and they drew as close as twelve cubits to one another.

And he prepared brazen gates and covered them with 8 asyncite,[20] so that if they should want to open them with iron they would not be able or to dissolve them with fire

αὐτίκα τὸ πῦρ ὑπαντῶν[20] σβέννυται· τοιαύτη γὰρ ἡ φύσις τοῦ ἀσυγκίτου ἐστίν, ὅτι οὔτε σιδήρου ὑφίσταται τὴν κατάκλασιν[21] οὔτε πυρὸς τὴν διάλυσιν· πάσας γάρ τὰς περινοίας τῶν δαιμόνων καὶ ἐπινοίας ἑώλους τε καὶ κενὰς ἀπεργάζεται.

9 Ταῦτα τοίνυν τὰ ἐναγῆ τε καὶ κίβδηλα καὶ μυσαρώτατα ἔθνη πάσαις ταῖς μαγικαῖς κακοτεχνίαις κέχρηνται, καὶ ἐν τούτοις αὐτῶν τὴν ῥυπαρὰν καὶ ἀπάνθρωπον, μᾶλλον δὲ λέγειν μισόθεον, κατήργησε γοητείαν, ὥστε μὴ δύνασθαι αὐτοὺς μήτε πυρὶ μήτε σιδήρῳ ἢ τινι ἑτέρᾳ ἐπινοίᾳ τὰς τοιαύτας ἀναμοχλεῦσαι πύλας καὶ ἀποδρᾶσαι.

10 Ἐν δὲ τοῖς ἐσχάτοις καιροῖς κατὰ τὴν τοῦ Ἰεζεκιὴλ προφητείαν τὴν λέγουσαν· ἐν τῇ ἐσχάτῃ ἡμέρᾳ τῆς συντελείας τοῦ κόσμου ἐξελεύσεται Γὼγ καὶ Μαγὼγ εἰς τὴν γῆν τοῦ Ἰσραήλ, οἵ εἰσιν ἔθνη καὶ βασιλεῖς οὓς καθεῖρξεν Ἀλέξανδρος ἐν τοῖς πέρασι τοῦ Βορρᾶ· Γὼγ καὶ Μαγὼγ καὶ Ἀνοὺγ καὶ Ἁγὴγ καὶ Ἀχενὰζ καὶ Δηφὰρ καὶ Φωτιναῖοι καὶ Λίβιοι καὶ Εὔνιοι καὶ Φαριζαῖοι καὶ Δεκλημοὶ καὶ Ζαρματαὶ καὶ Θηβλαῖοι καὶ Ζαρματιανοὶ καὶ Χαχώνιοι καὶ Ἀμαζάρθαι καὶ Γαρμίαρδοι καὶ ἀνθρωποφάγοι οἱ λεγόμενοι Κυνοκέφαλοι καὶ Θάρβιοι καὶ Ἄλανες καὶ Φισολονίκιοι καὶ Ἄρκναιοι καὶ Ἀσαλτήριοι. Οὗτοι οἱ εἴκοσι καὶ δύο βασιλεῖς καθεστήκασιν ἐμφρούριοι ἔνδον τῶν πυλῶν, ὧν ὁ Ἀλέξανδρος ἔπηξεν.

they would not prevail, rather straightaway the fire when it made contact would be quenched. For the nature of asyncite is such that it does not submit to the destruction of iron or the dissolution of fire. For he made all of the thoughts and designs of the demons stale and empty.

So these accursed, false, and foul nations employed all kinds of magical intrigues, and in these things he rendered their sordid and inhuman, or to put it more strongly, godless sorcery ineffectual, so that they were not able by fire or iron or any other device to force open gates such as these and make their escape. 9

In the end times, according to what the prophecy of Ezekiel says, in the last day of the consummation of the world Gog and Magog, who are the nations and kings which Alexander shored up in the extremities of the north, will come out into the land of Israel.[21] Gog and Magog and Anug and Ageg and Ashkenaz and Dephar and the Photinaeans and Libians and Eunians and Pharizaeans and Declemans and Zarmats and Theblaeans and Zarmatians and Chachonians and Amazarthans and Garmiardans and the cannibals called Cynocephalans (Dog-heads) and Tharbians and Alans and Phisolonicians and Arcnaeans and Asalterians.[22] These are the twenty-two kings set under guard within the gates which Alexander fixed. 10

9

Τελευτήσαντος τοιγαροῦν Ἀλεξάνδρου τοῦ ‹πρώτου›[22] βασιλέως ‹Ἑλλήνων›[23] ἐβασίλευσαν ἀντ᾿ αὐτοῦ οἱ τέσσαρες παῖδες αὐτοῦ· οὐ γὰρ ἔγημε ποτέ. Χουσὴθ δὲ ἡ μήτηρ αὐτοῦ ἀνέλυσεν ἐν τῇ οἰκείᾳ πατρίδι εἰς τὴν Αἰθιοπίαν.

2 Βύζας οὖν ὁ κτίσας τὸ Βυζάντιον ἀπέστειλεν ἐν τῇ θαλάσσῃ πρὸς τὸν Φὸλ βασιλέα τῆς Αἰθιοπίας Γερμανικὸν τὸν αὐτοῦ στρατηγὸν καὶ εἰρήνευσε μετ᾿ αὐτοῦ, γράψας αὐτῷ περὶ Χουσὴθ τῆς μητρὸς Ἀλεξάνδρου, ὅπως ἂν αὐτὴν λάβῃ ἑαυτῷ εἰς γυναῖκα καὶ βασιλεύσῃ αὐτήν.

3 Δεξάμενος οὖν Φὸλ ὁ βασιλεὺς τὰ γράμματα παρὰ τοῦ Γερμανικοῦ καὶ ἑωρακὼς τὰς παρ᾿ αὐτοῦ φιλοτιμίας καὶ δεξάμενος ἄγαν εὐφράνθη· ἀνέστη οὖν καὶ αὐτὸς καὶ συναγαγὼν ἐξ ὅλων τῶν εἰδῶν Αἰθιοπίας,[24] λαβὼν δὲ ἅμα καὶ τὴν θυγατέρα αὐτοῦ Χουσὴθ ἐπορεύθη εἰς Βύζαν ἔχων μεθ᾿ ἑαυτοῦ τριάκοντα χιλιάδας Αἰθιόπων. Καὶ ἐδεξιώθη ὑπὸ τοῦ Βύζα ἔξω ‹πέραν›[25] τῆς θαλάσσης ἐν Χαλκηδόνι μετὰ πλείστης θυμηδίας. Δέδωκε δὲ καὶ δωρήματα[26] πάμπολλα τοῖς συνοῦσιν αὐτῷ, καὶ εἰσῆλθε Φὸλ εἰς Βύζαν καὶ δέδωκε καὶ αὐτὸς φιλοτιμίας μεγάλας καὶ δωρεὰς μεγίστας κατὰ βασιλικὴν μεγαλοψυχίαν.

4 Καὶ ἔλαβεν Βύζας ὁ βασιλεὺς τὴν Χουσὴθ τὴν θυγατέρα Φὸλ βασιλέως Αἰθιοπίας, ἐξ ἧς ἐτέχθη αὐτῷ θυγάτηρ, ἣν καὶ ὠνόμασεν ἐπ᾿ ὀνόματι τῆς πολέως Βυζαντίαν, ἣν καὶ ἔγημε Ῥωμύλος Ἀρμέλαος βασιλεὺς Ῥώμης· καὶ διὰ τὴν ὑπερβάλλουσαν αὐτῆς ὡραιότητα ἠγάπησεν αὐτὴν

Chapter 9

So then when Alexander the <first> king of <the Greeks> died, his four servants reigned in his stead.[23] For he never married. Chouseth his mother returned to her own country, Ethiopia.

Byzas, therefore, after he established Byzantium, sent his 2 general Germanicus by sea to Phol, the king of Ethiopia, and made peace with him, and wrote to him concerning Chouseth, the mother of Alexander, how he would take her as his wife and appoint her queen.

So when King Phol took the letter from Germanicus and 3 observed the honors paid by him and received them, he was quite delighted. Accordingly he himself arose, gathered together <examples> of all the sights of Ethiopia,[24] and taking along his daughter Chouseth as well, made his way to Byzas, bringing thirty thousand Ethiopians with him. And he was welcomed by Byzas with much gladness of heart outside <across> the sea at Chalcedon. And he gave numerous presents to those who were with him, and Phol approached Byzas and himself gave him great honors and very great gifts in keeping with kingly magnanimity.

And King Byzas took Chouseth the daughter of Phol, the 4 king of Ethiopia, and from her a daughter was born to him, whom he named Byzantia after the name of the city, and Romulus Armelaus, the king of Rome, married her. And because of her youthful beauty he loved her very much. He

σφόδρα. Ἦν δὲ καὶ αὐτὸς ἄγαν ἁπλοῦς καὶ μεγαλόδωρος, ὅθεν καὶ ἐν τοῖς προικῴοις αὐτοῦ ἐδωρήσατο αὐτῇ τὴν Ῥώμην· ἀκούσαντες δὲ οἱ μεγιστᾶνες αὐτοῦ ἠγανάκτησαν κατ᾽ αὐτοῦ.

5 Τέτοκεν οὖν αὐτῷ ἡ Βυζαντία τρεῖς υἱούς, ὧν τὸν μὲν ἕνα ἐπωνόμασε κατὰ τὴν τοῦ πατρὸς προσηγορίαν Ἀρμέλαον, τὸν δὲ ἕτερον Οὐρβανόν, τὸν δὲ ἄλλον Κλαύδιον.

6 Ἐβασίλευσαν οὖν ἑκάτεροι, ὁ μὲν Ἀρμέλαος εἰς Ῥώμην ἀντὶ Ἀρμελάου τοῦ πατρὸς αὐτοῦ, Οὐρβανὸς δὲ εἰς Βύζαν πόλιν τῆς μητρὸς αὐτοῦ, Κλαύδιος δὲ ἐν Ἀλεξανδρείᾳ.

7 Κατεκράτησεν οὖν τὸ σπέρμα τῆς Χουσὴθ θυγατρὸς Φὸλ βασιλέως Αἰθιοπίας τήν τε[27] τῶν Μακεδόνων καὶ τῶν Ῥωμαίων καὶ Ἑλλήνων ἕως αἰῶνος· τοίνυν ἡ βασιλεία τῶν Ἑλλήνων, ἥτις ἐστι τῶν Ῥωμαίων, ἐκ σπέρματος τῶν Αἰθιόπων κατάγεται· αὕτη "προφθάσει χεῖρα αὐτῆς τῷ θεῷ" ἐν τῇ ἐσχάτῃ ἡμέρᾳ κατὰ τὴν προφητικὴν ἐκφαντορίαν. Προθεωρήσας γὰρ ὁ μακάριος Δαβὶδ ἐν τοῖς τοῦ πνεύματος ὄμμασι καὶ προειδὼς ὅτι Χουσὴθ Φὸλ θυγάτηρ βασιλέως Αἰθιοπίας μέλλει ἐξαναστήσεσθαι τὴν βασιλείαν τῶν Ῥωμαίων, προεφήτευσε λέγων· "Αἰθιοπία προφθάσει χεῖρα αὐτῆς τῷ θεῷ." Τινὲς οὖν διενοήθησαν ὅτι διὰ τὴν τῶν Αἰθιόπων βασιλείαν αἰνιττόμενος ὁ ἅγιος Δαβὶδ ταῦτα εἴρηκεν, ἀλλ᾽ ἐψεύσθησαν τῆς ἀληθείας οἱ ταῦτα νοήσαντες·

8 ἡ γὰρ ἐκ σπέρματος Αἰθιοπίσσης[28] συνισταμένη βασιλεία αὕτη κέκτηται τὸ μέγα τε καὶ σεβάσμιον ξύλον τοῦ τιμίου καὶ ζωοποιοῦ σταυροῦ τοῦ ἐν τῷ μέσῳ τῆς γῆς

was himself, moreover, very frank and generous, wherefore among the goods of his dowry he made a present to her of Rome. And when his grandees heard, they were vexed with him.

So Byzantia bore three sons to him, one of whom was 5 named Armelaus after his father's name, the next Urbanus, and the other Claudius.

Accordingly they each ruled as king, Armelaus in Rome 6 in the place of his father, Urbanus in Byzas the city of his mother, and Claudius in Alexandria.

Therefore the seed of Chouseth, the daughter of King 7 Phol of Ethiopia, gained mastery over the Macedonians and the Romans and Greeks forever. Accordingly, the kingdom of the Greeks, that is of the Romans, is derived from the seed of the Ethiopians, which "shall stretch out her hands unto God" according to the prophetic disclosure.[25] For the blessed David looked ahead with the eyes of the spirit and foresaw that Chouseth, the daughter of Phol king of Ethiopia, was going to raise up the kingdom of the Romans, and he prophesied, saying, "Ethiopia shall stretch out her hands unto God." So some have supposed that the holy David spoke in riddles through [the metaphor of] the kingdom of the Ethiopians when he said these things, but they play false with the truth who think this,

For the very kingdom established from the seed of the 8 Ethiopian maiden has acquired the great and awesome wood of the honorable and life-giving cross fixed in the midst of

προσπαγέντος, [οὗ ἐκρεμάσθη τὸ κυριακὸν καὶ ἄχραντον σῶμα διὰ τὰς ἁμαρτίας ἡμῶν][29] ὅθεν εἰκότως αὐτὸς ὁ θεοπάτωρ Δαβὶδ ἀπεφήνατο· "Αἰθιοπία προφθάσει χεῖρα αὐτῆς τῷ θεῷ" οὐκ ἔστι γὰρ ἔθνος ἢ βασιλεία ὑπὸ τὸν οὐρανὸν δυνάμενον καταδυναστεῦσαι τῆς βασιλείας τῶν χριστιανῶν,

9   ‹ἕως›[30]—ὃ γὰρ εἰπόντες ἔφαμεν ἄνω τὸ ἐν μέσῳ τῆς γῆς ἐμπαγέντα—τῷ ζωοποιῷ ὀχύρωται σταυρῷ, ὑφ᾿ οὗ καὶ τὰ τῆς οἰκουμένης πέρατα λίαν πανσόφως περιγράφονται κατά τε πλάτος καὶ μῆκος καὶ ὕψος καὶ βάθος. Ποία γὰρ ἰσχὺς ἢ τίς δυναστεία ἐξισχύσει πώμοτε τὴν τοῦ σταυροῦ περιδράξασθαι δύναμιν, οὗ τῷ κράτει καὶ τῷ σεβάσματι ἡ τῶν Ῥωμαίων τεθωράκισται βασιλεία διὰ τοῦ ἐν αὐτῷ προσπαγέντος δεσπότου ἡμῶν Ἰησοῦ Χριστοῦ;

IO

Ἀκούσωμεν οὖν τί Παῦλος ὁ θεσπέσιος προηγόρευσεν περὶ τῆς ἐσχάτης ἡμέρας καὶ τῆς τῶν Ῥωμαίων βασιλείας. Φησὶ γὰρ ἐν τῇ δευτέρᾳ πρὸς Θεσσαλονικεῖς ἐπιστολῇ· "ἐρωτῶμεν ὑμᾶς, ἀδελφοί, ὑπὲρ τῆς παρουσίας τοῦ κυρίου ἡμῶν Ἰσοῦ Χριστοῦ καὶ ὑμῶν[31] ἐπισυναγωγῆς ἐπ᾿ αὐτόν, εἰς τὸ μὴ ταχέως σαλευθῆναι ὑμᾶς ἀπὸ τοῦ νοὸς μήτε θροηθέντας μήτε διὰ πνεύματος μήτε διὰ λόγου μήτε δι᾿ ἐπιστολῆς ὡς δι᾿ ἡμῶν, ὡς ὅτι ἐφέστηκεν ἡ παρουσία τοῦ

the earth, [on which was hung the lordly and undefiled body by reason of our sin] which is why the very father of God, David, reasonably declared, "Ethiopia shall stretch out her hands unto God." For there is no nation or kingdom under heaven able to lord it over the kingdom of the Christians,

<So long as> it gathers strength from the life-giving cross, 9 which we said above is fixed in the midst of the earth, the cross by which in exceeding and completely wise manner the ends of the earth are circumscribed according to breadth and length and height and depth. For what manner of force or what lordship has sufficient strength ever to grasp the power of the cross, by whose might and holiness the kingdom of the Romans has been covered with a breastplate through the one who was hung upon it, our Lord Jesus Christ?

Chapter 10

So let us listen to what the divinely eloquent Paul foretold concerning the last day and the kingdom of the Romans. For he said in the second letter to the Thessalonians: "We beseech you, brethren, by the coming of our Lord Jesus Christ, and by *your* gathering together unto him, that ye be not soon shaken in mind, or be troubled, neither by spirit, nor by word, nor by letter as from us, as that the *coming of the Lord* is

κυρίου· μή τις ὑμᾶς ἐξαπατάτω κατὰ μηδένα τρόπον. Ὅτι, ἐὰν μὴ ἔλθῃ ἡ ἀποστασία πρῶτον καὶ ἀποκαλυφθῇ ὁ ἄνθρωπος τῆς ἀνομίας,³² ὁ υἱὸς τῆς ἀπωλείας, ὁ ἀντικείμενος καὶ ὑπεραιρόμενος ἐπὶ³³ πάντα λεγόμενον θεὸν ἢ σέβασμα, ὥστε αὐτὸν εἰς τὸν ναὸν καθίσαι ἀποδεικνύντα ἑαυτὸν ὅτι ἐστὶ θεός," καὶ μετὰ βραχέα· "μόνον ὁ κατέχων ἄρτι ἕως ἐκ μέσου γένηται, καὶ τότε ἀποκαλυφθήσεται ὁ ἄνομος."

2   Τίς οὖν ἐστιν ὁ ἐκ μέσου εἰ μὴ ἡ τῶν Ῥωμαίων βασιλεία; Πᾶσα γὰρ ἀρχὴ καὶ ἐξουσία τοῦ κόσμου τούτου καταργηθήσεται ἄνευ ταύτης·

3   καὶ γὰρ αὐτὴ πολεμεῖται καὶ οὐχ ἡττᾶται καὶ πάντα τὰ ἔθνη τὰ συγκρούοντα μετ' αὐτῆς ἀναλωθήσονται ὑπ' αὐτῆς καὶ αὐτὴ κατακρατήσει, ἕως οὗ φθάσει ἡ ἐσχάτη ὥρα καὶ τότε "προφθάσει χεῖρα αὐτῆς τῷ θεῷ" καὶ κατὰ τὸν ἀπόστολον τὸν λέγοντα· "ὅταν καταργηθῇ πᾶσα ἀρχὴ καὶ πᾶσα ἐξουσία," τότε καὶ αὐτὸς ὁ υἱὸς "παραδώσει τὴν βασιλείαν τῷ θεῷ καὶ πατρί." Ποίαν βασιλείαν; Δηλονότι τῶν χριστιανῶν.

4   Ποῦ γὰρ ἐστιν ἢ ἔσται βασιλεία ἢ ἑτέρα δυναστεία ταύτης ὑπερφανεῖσα; εἰ βούλει γὰρ σοπῆσαι τὸ ἀκριβές, λάβε μοι τὸν Μωσέως λαὸν τὸν τοσούτοις σημείοις καὶ τέρασι καὶ βυθῷ θαλάσσης τοὺς Αἰγυπτίους ἐκτίλαντα·³⁴ ἴδε μοι καὶ Ἰησοῦν τὸν τοῦ Ναυῆ, ὑφ' οὗ καὶ ὁ ἥλιος κατὰ Γαβαὼ ἵσταται καὶ ἡ σελήνη κατὰ φάραγγα ‹Ἐλώμ,³⁵ καὶ ἄλλα τινὰ ἐξαίσια θαύματα γίνεται, καὶ ἁπλῶς ἅπαν τὸ τῶν Ἑβραίων νόησον κράτος πῶς ὑπὸ τῆς τῶν Ῥωμαίων ἐξήλειπτε βασιλείας· οὐ Τίτος καὶ Οὐεσπασιανὸς κατέκοψαν ἅπαντας; οὐκ ἀρότρῳ τὸν ναὸν ἐκπορθήσας Ἀδριανὸς

at hand. Let no man deceive you by any means: for that day shall not come, except there come a falling away first, and that man of *lawlessness* be revealed, the son of perdition; who opposeth and exalteth himself above all that is called God or that is worshipped; so that he sitteth in the temple, showing himself that he is God," and after a few words, "only he who now letteth will let, until he be taken out of the midst, and then shall that wicked be revealed."[26]

Which then is the one "out of the midst" if not the kingdom of the Romans? For all rule and authority of this world are rendered null and void apart from her;[27] 2

For war is also made upon her and she is not overcome, and all the nations which dash themselves against her will be destroyed by her and she will prevail, until the last hour will arrive and then she "shall stretch out her hands unto God" and, as the apostle says, "when all rule and all authority shall have *been* put down," and the Son himself "will deliver up the kingdom to God, even the Father."[28] What manner of kingdom? Quite clearly that of the Christians! 3

For where is, or will there be, a kingdom or another power that excels her? Now if you wish to look into the accuracy [of what I say], take as my proof the people of Moses who by so many signs and wonders and the depth of the sea wiped out the Egyptians. Look for me also to Joshua the son of Nun, under whom the sun stood still at Gibeon and the moon at the valley of <Elom> (i.e., Ajalon),[29] and to what other wondrous miracles occurred. And simply think how all the power of the Hebrews was wiped out by the kingdom of the Romans. Did not Titus and Vespasian cut them all down? Did not Hadrian plunder the temple and plow it 4

ἠροτρίασεν;³⁶ τίς οὖν ἄρα γέγονεν ἢ γενήσεται κατ᾽ αὐτὴν ἑτέρα βασιλεία; ἀλλ᾽ οὐδεμίαν εὑρήσομεν, εἴπερ τῆς ἀληθείας φροντίζομεν.

5 Οὐ χίλια ἔτη ἐβασίλευσαν οἱ Ἑβραῖοι; Καὶ ἐξεκόπη ἡ βασιλεία αὐτῶν! Αἰγύπτιοι τρισχίλια· καὶ αὐτοὶ ὡσαύτως ἀπώλοντο. Βαβυλώνιοι τετρακισχίλια ἐβασίλευσαν, ἀλλὰ καὶ αὐτοὶ ἐκόπησαν.³⁷ Ἐκκοπείσης τοιγαροῦν τῆς τῶν Μακεδόνων βασιλείας, ἤτοι τῶν Αἰγυπτίων, καθοπλισθεῖσα κατὰ τῆς τῶν Ῥωμαίων βασιλείας ἡ τῶν βαρβάρων βασιλεία, τουτέστι Τοῦρκοι καὶ Ἄβαρεις,³⁸ ‹καὶ›³⁹ οὗτοι κατεπόθησαν ὑπ᾽ αὐτῆς.

6 Εἶτα ἀναλωθείσης τῆς βασιλείας τῶν Περσῶν ἐπαναστήσονται ἀντ᾽ αὐτῆς κατὰ τῶν Ῥωμαίων οἱ υἱοὶ τοῦ Ἰσμαὴλ υἱοῦ τῆς Ἄγαρ, ὃν ἡ Γραφὴ "βραχίονα τοῦ νότου" ἐκάλεσεν, ἤγουν ὁ Δανιήλ, καὶ ἀντιτάξονται τῇ βασιλείᾳ τῶν Ῥωμαίων ἐπ᾽ ἀριθμῷ κυκλουμένων ἑβδοματικῶν ἑβδόμῳ χρόνῳ, διότι ἤγγικεν ἡ συντέλεια καὶ οὐκ ἔσται μῆκος χρόνων ἔτι.

II

Ἐν γὰρ τῇ ἐσχάτῃ χιλιάδι, ἤτοι τῇ ἑβδόμῃ, ἐν αὐτῇ ἐκριζοῦται ἡ τῶν Περσῶν βασιλεία, καὶ ἐν αὐτῇ ἐξελεύσεται τὸ σπέρμα τοῦ Ἰσμαὴλ ἐκ τοῦ ἐρήμου τοῦ Ἐθρίβου⁴⁰ καὶ ἐξιόντες συναχθήσονται ὁμοθυμαδὸν εἰς Γαβαὼθ τὴν μεγάλην.

under with a plow? So what other kingdom has arisen or will arise against her? We shall surely find none at all, if we take thought for truth.

Did not the Hebrews reign for a thousand years? And 5 their kingdom was cut off! The Egyptians three thousand, and they were likewise utterly destroyed! The Babylonians reigned four thousand, but these were cut down as well! And when the kingdom of the Macedonians, indeed of the Egyptians, was accordingly cut off, the kingdom of the barbarians, that is the Turks and the Avars, armed itself against the kingdom of the Romans, <and> the latter were swallowed up by it.

Then when the kingdom of the Persians is destroyed, in 6 its place against the Romans will rise up the sons of Ishmael, the son of Hagar, whom the scripture, that is Daniel, called "the arm of the south,"[30] and they will range themselves in battle against the kingdom of the Romans in terms of the number of circling weeks in the seventh year, since the end has come and the length of time will go no further.

Chapter 11

For in the last millennium, that is the seventh, in that time the kingdom of the Persians will be uprooted, and in that time the seed of Ishmael will come out of the desert of Yathrib and having come out they will be gathered together in one accord at Gabaoth the Great.[31]

2 Κἀκεῖ πληρωθήσεται τὸ λεχθὲν διὰ τοῦ προφήτου Ἰεζε-
κιήλ· "υἱὲ ἀνθρώπου, κάλεσον τὰ θηρία τοῦ ἀγροῦ καὶ τὰ
πετεινὰ τοῦ οὐρανοῦ καὶ πρότρεψον αὐτὰ λέγων· "συν-
αθροίσθητε καὶ δεῦτε, διότι θυσίαν μεγάλην θύσω ὑμῖν·
φάγετε σάρκας δυναστῶν καὶ πίετε αἷμα γιγάντων."

3 Ἐν ταύτῃ τοίνυν τῇ Γαβαὼθ πεσοῦνται ἐν στόματι
μαχαίρας πάντες οἱ δυνάσται τῶν Ἑλλήνων, τουτέστι τῶν
Ῥωμαίων· καθὼς γὰρ καὶ αὐτοὶ ἀπέκτειναν τοὺς δυνάστας
τῶν Ἑβραίων καὶ τῶν Περσῶν, οὕτω καὶ αὐτοὶ πεσοῦνται
ἐν στόματι μαχαίρας ὑπὸ τοῦ σπέρματος Ἰσμαήλ, ὃς ἐπι-
κέκληται ὄναγρος,⁴¹ διότι ἐν θυμῷ καὶ ὀργῇ ἀποσταλήσον-
ται ἐπὶ πρόσωπον πάσης τῆς γῆς ἐπί τε τοὺς ἀνθρώπους
καὶ τὰ κτήνη καὶ τὰ θηρία καὶ ἐπὶ τὰ ἄλση καὶ τὰ φυτὰ καὶ
ἐπὶ τὰς λόχμας καὶ ἐπὶ πᾶν εἶδος κάρπιμον.

4 Καὶ ἔσται ἡ παρουσία αὐτῶν παιδεία ἀνίλεως·⁴² καὶ
προπορεύσονται αὐτῶν ἐπὶ τὴν γῆν τέσσαρες πληγαί·
ὄλεθρος καὶ ἀπώλεια, φθορὰ καὶ ἐρήμωσις.

5 Λέγει γὰρ ὁ θεὸς τῷ Ἰσραὴλ διὰ Μωσέως· "οὐχ ὅτι
ἀγαπᾷ ὑμᾶς Κύριος ὁ θεὸς εἰσάγει ὑμᾶς εἰς τὴν γῆν τῆς
ἐπαγγελίας τοῦ κληρονομῆσαι αὐτήν, ἀλλὰ διὰ τὰς
ἁμαρτίας τῶν κατοικούντων ἐν αὐτῇ." Οὕτω καὶ τοὺς
υἱοὺς Ἰσμαήλ· οὐχ ὅτι ἀγαπᾷ αὐτοὺς Κύριος ὁ θεὸς δίδωσιν
αὐτοῖς δυναστείαν κρατῆσαι τῆς γῆς τῶν χριστιανῶν,
ἀλλὰ διὰ τὴν ἁμαρτίαν καὶ τὴν ἀνομίαν τὴν ὑπ᾽ αὐτῶν
γινομένην· ὁμοία γὰρ αὐτῶν οὔτε ἐγένετο οὐδ᾽ οὐ μὴ
γενήσεται ἐν ὅλαις ταῖς γενεαῖς.

6 Τί γάρ; Ἐνεδιδύσκοντο οἱ ἄνδρες ἐκ τῶν μοιχαλίδων

38

And then will be fulfilled what was said through the ʾ prophet Ezekiel: "Son of man, summon the beasts of the field and the birds of the heaven, and urge them on, saying, 'Gather yourselves together and come, since I will offer a great sacrifice for you. Eat the bodies of lords and drink the blood of giants.'"[32]

In that time, therefore, at Gabaoth all the lords of the 3 Greeks, that is of the Romans, will fall at the mouth of the sword. For just as they themselves slew the lords of the Hebrews and of the Persians, so they also will fall at the mouth of the sword by the hand of the seed of Ishmael, who has been called a wild ass,[33] because in wrath and anger they will be sent over the face of the whole world against the men and the stock animals and the wild beasts and to the groves and the trees and to the copses and to every kind of fruitful thing.

And their arrival will be a chastisement without mercy.[34] 4 And four disasters will go before them on the earth, death and destruction, ruin and desolation.

For God says to Israel through Moses, "Not because the 5 Lord God loves you does he bring you into the Land of Promise to inherit it, but because of the sins of those who dwell in it."[35] Just so with the sons of Ishmael. Not because the Lord God loves them does he give them power to conquer the land of the Christians, but because of the sin and the lawlessness which have been brought into being by them. For nothing like their sin has arisen nor will arise in all generations.

Why? Men put on the apparel of adulterous and wanton 6

γυναικῶν καὶ προϊσταμένων ἐσθῆτας καὶ καθάπερ γυναῖκες ἑαυτοὺς ἐξωράϊζον καὶ ἵσταντο ἐν ταῖς πλατείαις καὶ
ἀγοραῖς τῶν πόλεων φανερῶς καὶ "μετήλλατον τὴν φυσικὴν χρῆσιν εἰς τὴν παρὰ φύσιν," καθὼς φησιν ὁ ἱερὸς
ἀπόστολος. Ὡσαύτως καὶ αἱ γυναῖκες ταῦτα ἅπερ καὶ οἱ
ἄνδρες ἔπραττον.

7   Συνεγίνοντο οὖν μιᾷ γυναικὶ πατὴρ ἅμα τῷ υἱῷ αὐτοῦ
καὶ ἀδελφῷ καὶ παντὶ τῷ τῆς συγγενείας προσψαύοντι·
ἠγνοοῦντο γὰρ ὑπὸ τῶν ἑταιρίδων. Διὸ ὁ σοφώτατος
Παῦλος πρὸ χρόνων εἰκότως ἀνέκραξεν· "διὰ τοῦτο γάρ,"
φησιν, "παρέδωκεν αὐτοὺς ὁ θεὸς εἰς πάθη ἀτιμίας· αἱ γὰρ
θήλειαι αὐτῶν μετήλλαξαν τὴν φυσικὴν χρῆσιν εἰς τὴν
παρὰ φύσιν· ὁμοίως καὶ οἱ ἄρρενες ἀφέντες τὴν φυσικὴν
χρῆσιν τῆς θελείας ἐξεκαύθησαν ἐν τῇ ὀρέξει αὐτῶν εἰς
ἀλλήλους ἄρσενες ἐν ἄρσεσι τὴν ἀσχημοσύνην κατεργα-
ζόμενοι καὶ τὴν ἀντιμισθίαν τῆς πλάνης αὐτῶν ἐν ἑαυτοῖς
ἀπολαμβάνοντας."

8   Διὰ τοῦτο τοίνυν παραδίδωσιν αὐτοὺς ὁ θεὸς εἰς χεῖρας
βαρβάρων, ὑφ' ὧν πεσοῦνται εἰς ἀκαθαρσίαν καὶ δυσωδίαν,
καὶ μιανθῶσιν αὐτῶν αἱ γυναῖκες ὑπὸ τῶν μεμιασμένων.
Καὶ ἐπιθήσουσι κλήρους οἱ υἱοὶ Ἰσμαὴλ

9   καὶ παραδοθήσεται ἡ γῆ Περσίδος εἰς φθορὰν καὶ
ἀπώλειαν καὶ οἱ κατοικοῦντες ἐν αὐτῇ εἰς αἰχμαλωσίαν καὶ
εἰς σφαγὴν ἀχθήσονται. Ἀρμενία καὶ οἱ κοικοῦντες ἐν
αὐτῇ ἐν αἰχμαλωσίᾳ καὶ μαχαίρᾳ παραδοθήσονται.[43] Καπ-
παδοκία εἰς φθορὰν καὶ ἐρήμωσιν, καὶ οἱ ταύτης οἰκήτορες
ἐν αἰχμαλωσίᾳ καὶ σφαγῇ καταποθήσονται.

10   Σικελία ἔσται εἰς ἐρήμωσιν καὶ οἱ ἐν αὐτῇ οἰκοῦντες εἰς

women and adorned themselves as women and stood in the streets and squares of the cities openly and "did change the natural use into that which is against nature" as the Holy Apostle says.[36] Likewise women also did the same things as the men.

Accordingly a father along with his son and brother and every near member of his kin have intercourse with a single woman. For they were not recognized by the prostitutes. For which reason the exceeding wise Paul before these times quite naturally decried them: "*Since* for this cause," he says, "God gave them up unto vile affections: for even their women did change the natural use into that which is against nature: And likewise also the men, leaving the natural use of the woman, burned in their lust one toward another; men with men working that which is unseemly, and receiving in themselves that recompense of their error."[37]

And now for this reason God delivers them into the hands of barbarians, by which they will fall into impurity and foul stench, and their women will be stained by their defilements.[38] And the sons of Ishmael will cast lots [over them].

And the land of Persia will be handed over to ruin and destruction and those who dwell in it will be driven into captivity and slaughter. Armenia and those who dwell in it will be handed over to captivity and sword. Cappodocia to perdition and desolation, and her inhabitants will be swallowed up in captivity and destruction.

Sicily will become a desolation and those who dwell in it

σφαγὴν καὶ αἰχμαλωσίαν παραδοθήσονται. Ἡ γῆ Συρίας ἔσται ἔρημος καὶ διεφθαρμένη καὶ οἱ κατοικοῦντες ἐν αὐτῇ ἀπολοῦνται μαχαίρᾳ. Κιλικία[44] ἐρημωθήσεται καὶ οἱ κατοικοῦντες ἐν αὐτῇ ἀπολοῦνται ἐν μαχαίρᾳ καὶ εἰς αἰχμαλωσίαν ἔσονται.

11 Ἑλλὰς εἰς διαφθοράν, καὶ οἱ κατοικοῦντες ἐν αὐτῇ εἰς αἰχμαλωσίαν καὶ εἰς μάχαιραν ἔσονται· Ῥωμανία εἰς φθορὰν ‹καὶ εἰς σφαγὴν ἔσται›[45] καὶ ‹οἱ κατοικοῦντες ἐν αὐτῇ›[46] εἰς φυγὴν τραπήσονται, καὶ αἱ νῆσοι τῆς θαλάσσης εἰς ἐρήμωσιν καὶ οἱ κατοικοῦντες ἐν αὐταῖς ἀπολοῦνται μαχαίρᾳ καὶ αἰχμαλωσίᾳ.

12 Αἴγυπτος ἑῴα τε καὶ Συρία ὑπὸ ζυγὸν καὶ ‹εἰς›[47] θλῖψιν ἄμετρον ἀχθήσονται καὶ ἀγγαρευθήσονται ἀφειδῶς καὶ ἀπαιτηθήσονται ὑπὲρ τῶν ψυχῶν αὐτῶν χρυσίου ὁλκὴν ὑπὲρ τὴν ἰσχὺν αὐτῶν, καὶ ἔσονται οἱ κατοικοῦντες Αἴγυπτον καὶ Συρίαν ἐν στενοχωρίᾳ καὶ θλίψει ἑπταπλασίονι[48] τῶν ἐν αἰχμαλωσίᾳ.

13 Καὶ πλησθήσεται ἡ γῆ τῆς ἐπαγγελίας ἀνθρώπων ἐκ τῶν τεσσάρων ἀνέμων τῶν ὑπὸ τὸν οὐρανὸν καὶ ἔσονται "ὡς ἀκρὶς τὸ πλῆθος," ἥτις συναθροίζεται ὑπὸ ἀνέμου, καὶ ἔσται ἐν αὐταῖς λιμὸς καὶ λοιμὸς καὶ ὑψωθήσεται ἡ καρδία αὐτῶν τῶν ὀλοθρευτῶν καὶ εἰς ὑπερηφανίαν ἀρθήσεται· καὶ λαλήσουσιν ὑπέρογκα ἕως καιροῦ τοῦ τεταγμένου αὐτοῖς καὶ κατακρατήσουσιν τήν τε εἴσοδον καὶ ἔξοδον τοῦ βορρᾶ καὶ τῆς ἑῴας καὶ δυσμῶν[49] τῆς θαλάσσης καὶ ἔσονται πάντα ὑπὸ τὸν ζυγὸν αὐτῶν· ἄνθρωποι, κτήνη, πετείνά. Καὶ τὰ ὕδατα τῆς θαλάσσης ὑπακούσωσιν αὐτοῖς.

will be handed over to slaughter and captivity. The land of Syria will be a desert and ruined, and those who dwell in it will die by the sword. Cilicia will be desolated, and those who dwell in it will die at sword edge and will go into captivity.

Greece will go to destruction, and those who dwell in it to captivity and to sword. Romania[39] <will go> to perdition <and to slaughter>, and <those who dwell in it> will be turned to flight, and the islands of the sea will become a desolation and those who dwell on them will be destroyed by sword and captivity.

Eastern Egypt and Syria will be driven under the yoke and into boundless affliction and will be pressed into unsparing service, and a weight of gold will be demanded of them above their spirits and beyond their strength, and those who inhabit Egypt and Syria will be in distress and affliction seven times worse than that of those in captivity.

And the Promised Land will be filled with men from the four winds under heaven and they will be "like grasshoppers for multitude,"[40] and it will be gathered by a wind, and there will be famine and pestilence in their midst and the heart of the destroyers will be exalted and raised to arrogance. And they will speak "great swelling words"[41] until the time appointed to them and they will prevail over the entrance and the exit of the North and of the East and West, [and] of the sea, and all will come under their yoke, men and beasts and birds. And the waters of the sea will obey them.

14 Καὶ αἱ ἔρημοι πόλεις αἱ χηρωθεῖσαι⁵⁰ τῶν οἰκητόρων
αὐτῶν, ἔσονται αὐτοῖς· καὶ ἀπογράψονται τὰ ὄρη ἑαυτοῖς
καὶ τὰς ἐρήμους· καὶ οἱ ἰχθύες τῆς θαλάσσης καὶ τὰ ξύλα
τοῦ δρυμοῦ καὶ ὁ χοῦς τῆς γῆς καὶ οἱ λίθοι καὶ ἡ εὐφορία
τῆς γῆς ἔσται ἐν ταῖς εἰσόδοις αὐτῶν· καὶ οἱ πόνοι καὶ οἱ
ἱδρῶτες τῶν γεωργῶν τῆς γῆς καὶ ἡ κληρονομία τῶν
πλουσίων καὶ τὰ προσφερόμενα τοῖς ἁγίοις, κἄν τε χρυσὸς
κἄν τε ἄργυρος κἄν τε λίθοι τίμιοι ἢ χαλκὸς ἢ σίδηρος, τὰ
τε ἐνδύματα ἱερά τε καὶ ἔνδοξα, καὶ τὰ βρώματα πάντα καὶ
πᾶν ὅ, τι τίμιον αὐτοῖς ἔσονται. Καὶ ὑπεραρθήσεται⁵¹ αὐτῶν
ἡ καρδία ἕως ἂν ἀπαιτήσωσι καὶ αὐτοὺς τοὺς νεκροὺς
κατ᾽ ἰσότητα τῶν ζώντων. Ὡσαύτως ἔκ τε τῶν χηρῶν καὶ
ὀρφανῶν καὶ ἐκ τῶν ἁγίων

15 καὶ οὐκ ἐλεήσουσι πένητα καὶ πτωχόν· ἀτιμάσουσιν δὲ
πᾶσαν γερουσίαν καὶ ἐκθλίψουσι τοὺς πένητας καὶ οὐ μὴ
σπλαγχνισθήσονται οὔτε ἐπὶ τοῖς ἀσθενέσι καὶ ἀδυνάτοις,
ἀλλ᾽ ἐμπαίξουσι καὶ διαγελάσουσι τοῖς τε ἐν σοφίᾳ λάμ-
πουσιν καὶ τοῖς ἐν πολιτικοῖς καὶ δημοσίοις διαπρέπουσι
πράγμασι. Καὶ κατασχεθήσονται ἅπαντες σιγῇ καὶ φόβῳ,
μὴ ἰσχύοντες ἐλέγξαι ἢ ἀποφθέγξασθαι "τί τοῦτο"; ἢ "τί
ἐκεῖνο" καὶ ἔσονται ἔκθαμβοι ‹καὶ ἔμφοβοι⁵² πάντες οἱ
κατοικοῦντες τὴν γῆν· καὶ ἔσται ἡ σοφία αὐτῶν καὶ ἡ παί-
δευσις αὐτοφυὴς αὐτοῖς μὴ αὐξανομένη μήτε κατ᾽ ἐπίδοσιν
αὐτοῖς προστιθεμένη καὶ οὐκ ἔστιν ὁ δυνάμενος ἀλλοιῶσαι
ἢ ἐπιμέμψασθαι⁵³ αὐτῶν τοὺς λόγους.

16 Καὶ ἔσται ἡ ὁδὸς αὐτῶν ἀπὸ θαλάσσης ἕως θαλάσσης
καὶ ἀπὸ ἀνατολῶν ἕως δυσμῶν καὶ ἀπὸ βορρᾶ ἕως τῆς
ἐρήμου τῆς Ἐθρίβου. Καὶ κληθήσεται ἡ ὁδὸς αὐτῶν ὁδὸς

And the desolate cities bereft of their inhabitants will be- 14
long to them. And they will claim title to mountains and
deserts. And the fish of the sea and the timber of the forest
and the dust of the earth and the stones and the produce of
the land will be in their revenue.[42] And the labors and sweat
of the tillers of the soil and the inheritance of the wealthy
and the tithes to the holy, be it gold or silver or precious
gems or bronze or iron, and the splendid sacred garments
and all of the food and everything which is of any value will
belong to them. And their hearts will be exalted until they
demand as much from the dead themselves as from the living.[43] Likewise from widows and orphans and from the consecrated.

And they will not have pity on the poor and the needy; 15
they will show no respect at all to old age and they will op-
press the paupers and show no compassion toward the weak
and the powerless, but will mock and laugh to scorn those
who are illustrious in wisdom and those who are preeminent
in the affairs of the city and the state. And everyone will
be overcome with silence and fear, having no power to question or openly demand, "What is this?" or "What is that?"
And everyone who dwells on the earth will be amazed <and
fearful>. And their wisdom and natural education will not
be increased nor added to according to their increase[44] and
no one will be able to alter or to fault their words.

And their road will go from sea to sea and from east to 16
west and from the north to the desert of Yathrib. And their
road will be called a road of anguish, and old men and old

στενοχωρίας καὶ ὁδεύσωσιν ἐν αὐτῇ πρεσβῦται καὶ πρεσβύ-
τιδες, πτωχοί τε καὶ πλούσιοι, πεινῶντες καὶ διψῶντες,
δέσμιοι, καὶ μακαρίσουσι τοὺς νεκρούς.

17 Ἡ γὰρ ὑπὸ τοῦ ἀποστόλου λεχθεῖσα παιδεῖα—ἤτοι
ἀποστασία—αὕτη ἐστί· φησὶ γὰρ ὅτι "ἐὰν μὴ ἔλθῃ ἡ
ἀποστασία πρῶτον καὶ ἀποκαλυφθῇ ὁ ἄνθρωπος τῆς
ἀνομίας, ὁ υἱὸς τῆς ἀπωλείας·" ἡ γὰρ ἀποστασία παιδεία
ἐστὶ καὶ παιδευθήσονται πάντες οἱ κατοικοῦντες τὴν γῆν.
Καὶ ἐπειδὴ ὄνον ἄγριον ἐκάλεσεν ὁ θεὸς τὸν Ἰσμαὴλ τὸν
πατέρα αὐτῶν, διὰ τοῦτο οἱ ἄγριοι ὄνοι καὶ αἱ δορκάδες
τῆς ἐρήμου καὶ ἅπαν εἶδος θηρίων ἀτιθάσων τε καὶ ἡμέρων[54] λιμώξουσι καὶ ὀλιγωθήσονται, καὶ ἐκδιωχθήσονται
οἱ ἄνθρωποι καὶ τὰ θηρία ἀναλωθήσονται, καὶ κόψουσι
πάντα τὰ ξύλα τοῦ δρυμοῦ καὶ τὸ κάλλος τῶν ὀρέων
ἀφανισθήσεται· καὶ ἐρημωθήσονται αἱ πόλεις καὶ ἔσονται
αἱ χῶραι ἄβατοι διὰ τὸ ὀλιγωθῆναι τὴν ἀνθρωπότητα καὶ
μιανθήσεται ἡ γῆ ἐν αἵματι καὶ ἀποκρατήσει τοὺς καρποὺς
αὐτῆς· οὐ γὰρ εἰσιν [οἱ] ἄνθρωποι οἱ τυραννικῶς κρατοῦν-
τες βάρβαροι, ἀλλὰ τέκνα τῆς ἐρήμου εἰσὶ καὶ εἰς ἐρήμωσιν
ἥξουσιν· ἐφθαρμένοι εἰσὶ καὶ εἰς φθορὰν ἀποσταλήσονται·
ἐβδελυγμένοι εἰσὶν καὶ τὸ μύσος ἀσπάζονται. Καὶ ἐν τῇ
ἀρχῇ τοῦ καιροῦ τῆς ἐξόδου αὐτῶν τῆς ἐξ ἐρήμου γενο-
μένης ῥομφαιᾳ τὰς ἐν γαστρὶ ἐχούσας κεντήσωσι καὶ τὰ
βρέφη ἐκ τῶν μητρικῶν ἀγκαλῶν ἁρπάζοντες πατάξωσι,
καὶ ἔσονται τοῖς θηρίοις εἰς βρῶσιν.

18 Τοὺς δὲ ἱερεῖς ἔνδον τῶν ἁγίων μολύνοντες κατασφά-
ξουσι καὶ συγκοιτασθῶσιν ταῖς γυναῖξιν ἐν τοῖς σεπτοῖς
καὶ ἱεροῖς τόποις, ἐν οἷς ἡ μυστικὴ καὶ ἀναίμακτος θυσία

women will travel along it, rich and poor, hungry and thirsty, bound captives, and they will think the dead happy.

For this is the chastisement, that is a "falling away," spoken of by the apostle; for he says that "except there come a falling away first, and that man of *lawlessness* be revealed, the son of perdition."[45] For the falling away is a chastisement, and all those who dwell on the earth will be chastised. And since God called their father Ishmael a wild ass, for this reason the wild asses and the gazelles of the desert and every kind of beast, both wild and tame, will starve and grow less, and the men will be driven away and the animals will be wasted, and they will cut down all the trees of the forest and the beauty of the mountains will disappear. The cities will be made desolate, and the fields will be impassable because of the diminishment of humanity, and the earth will be stained with blood and will withhold her fruits. For these men are not barbarians who rule like tyrants, but children of the desert and they will have come to desolation. They are loathsome and they embrace abomination. And when the time comes when they begin to leave the desert they will stab the pregnant women with a sword and snatch babies from their mothers' arms and smash them, and they (sc. the babes) will be meat for the beasts.

They will slaughter the priests after defiling them within the sanctuaries and go to bed with women in the venerable and holy places, in which the mystic, bloodless sacrifice is

ἐκτελεῖται· καὶ τὰς ἱερὰς στολὰς ἐπενδύσονται αἱ γυναῖκες αὐτῶν καὶ οἱ υἱοὶ καὶ αἱ θυγατέρες αὐτῶν· καὶ ἐπιθήσουσιν αὐτὰς ἐπὶ τοὺς ἵππους αὐτῶν καὶ ἐν ταῖς κλίναις ἐφαπλώσουσιν, καὶ τὰ κτήνη αὐτῶν ἐν ταῖς λάρναξι τῶν ἁγίων δεσμήσουσι, καὶ ἔσονται φονεῖς διεφθαρμένοι, ὅτι πῦρ δοκιμασίας ἐστὶ τῷ γένει τῶν χριστιανῶν.

12

Φησὶ γὰρ ὁ ἱερὸς ἀπόστολος· "οὐχὶ πάντες οἱ ἐξ Ἰσραὴλ οὗτοι Ἰσραήλ·" οὐκοῦν οὐ πάντες ὅσοι χριστιανοὶ λέγονται χριστιανοὶ τυγχάνουσιν. "Ἑπτὰ γὰρ," καθὼς φησιν ἡ Γραφή, "χιλιάδες ἐσώθησαν τῶν υἱῶν Ἰσραήλ, οἵτινες οὐκ ἔκαμψαν γόνυ τῇ Βάαλ," καὶ ἅπας ὁ λαὸς τοῦ Ἰσραὴλ δι' αὐτῶν ἐσώθη.

2 Οὕτω καὶ τότε ἐν τῷ καιρῷ τῆς τε ἀποστασίας καὶ τῆς παιδείας τῶν υἱῶν Ἰσμαὴλ ὀλίγοι εὑρεθήσονται χριστιανοὶ ἀληθεῖς, καθάπερ ὁ σωτὴρ ἡμῶν ἐν τοῖς ἁγίοις εὐαγγελίοις ἔλεγεν· "ἆρα ἐλθὼν ὁ υἱὸς τοῦ ἀνθρώπου εὑρήσει πίστιν ἐπὶ τῆς γῆς"; Ὀλιγωθήσεται δὲ ἐν τῷ καιρῷ ἐκείνῳ τὸ πνεῦμα τῶν τελείων.

3 Καὶ πολλοὶ ἀπαρνήσονται τὴν ἀληθῆ[55] πίστιν τόν τε ζωοποιὸν σταυρὸν καὶ τὰ ἅγια μυστήρια, καὶ χωρὶς βίας καὶ[56] κολάσεως ἢ αἰκισμῶν ἀπαρνήσονται τὸν Χριστὸν καὶ ἀκολουθήσωσι τοῖς ἀποστάταις.

carried out. Their wives and sons and daughters will put on the sacred robes over their clothes. And they will put them on their horses and spread them over their beds. They will stable their flocks in the tombs of the saints. And there will be corrupt murders, inasmuch as the fire of testing comes to the race of the Christians.

Chapter 12

For the Holy Apostle says, "They are not all Israel, which are of Israel."[46] So not all those who are called Christians are indeed Christians. As scripture says, "For seven thousand of the sons of Israel were preserved who have not bowed the knee to Baal,"[47] and the whole people of Israel was preserved through them.

Thus also then in the time of the falling away and of the chastisement of the sons of Ishmael few will be found true Christians, just as Our Savior said in the Holy Gospels, "When the Son of Man cometh, shall he find faith on the earth?"[48] and in that time the spirit of the perfect will be diminished. 2

And many will deny the true faith and the life-giving cross and the holy mysteries, and without violence or punishment or ill-treatment they will deny the Christ and follow the apostates. 3

4 Προλαβὼν γὰρ ὁ θεῖος ἀπόστολος ἐκήρυξεν εἰπών, ὅτι
"ἐν ὑστέροις καιροῖς ἀποστήσονταί τινες τῆς πίστεως,
προσέχοντες πνεύμασι πλάνης καὶ διδασκαλίαις τῶν δαιμόνων ἐν ὑποκρίσει ψευδολόγων κεκαυστηριασμένων τὴν
ἰδίαν συνείδησιν."

5 Καὶ αὖθις ὁ αὐτός·[57] "ἐν ταῖς ἐσχάταις ἡμέραις ἐνστή-
σονται καιροὶ χαλεποί· ἔσονται γὰρ οἱ ἄνθρωποι φίλαυτοι,
φιλάργυροι, ἀλαζόνες, ὑπερήφανοι, βλάσφημοι, γονεῦσιν
ἀπειθεῖς, ἄχρηστοι,[58] ἀνόσιοι, ἄστοργοι, ἄσπονδοι, διάβολοι, ἀκρατεῖς, ἀνήμεροι, ἀφιλάγαθοι, προδόται, προπετεῖς,
τετυφωμένοι, φιλήδονοι μᾶλλον ἢ φιλόθεοι, ἔχοντες μόρφωσιν εὐσεβείας, τὴν δὲ δύναμιν αὐτῆς ἠρνημένοι."

6 Καὶ πάντες οἱ ἀσθενεῖς τῇ πίστει ἐν τῇ παιδείᾳ ἐκείνῃ
φανερωθήσονται καὶ αὐτοὶ ἑαυτοὺς ἀφορίσουσι[59] τῶν
ἁγίων ἐκκλησιῶν ἰδίᾳ προαιρέσει· αὐτὸς γὰρ ὁ καιρὸς
προσκαλεῖται[60] αὐτοὺς ἐπὶ τὴν πλάνην· ταπεινόφρονες δὲ
καὶ ἥσυχοι, χρηστοὶ καὶ ἀληθινοί, ἐλεύθεροι καὶ ἐπίλεκτοι[61]
οὐ ζητηθήσονται ἐν τῷ καιρῷ ἐκείνῳ,

7 ἀλλ᾽ ἀντὶ τούτων[62] ζητηθήσονται, οἵτινές εἰσι φίλαυτοι,
φιλάργυροι, ἀλαζόνες, ὑπερήφανοι, βλάσφημοι, ἅρπαγες,
πλεονέκται, μέθυσοι, ἀνελεήμονες, ἀποστάται, ἄσπονδαι,
ἄστοργοι, ἀχάριστοι,[63] ἀνόσιοι, διάβολοι, ἀκρατεῖς, ἀνήμεροι, ἀτίθασοι,[64] προδόται, προπετεῖς, τετυφωμένοι, φιλήδονοι μᾶλλον ἢ φιλόθεοι, πόρνοι, μοιχοί, κλέπται, ἐπίορκοι,
ψεῦσται, ἀνδραποδισταί, ἔχοντες μόρφωσιν εὐσεβείας,
τὴν δὲ δύναμιν αὐτῆς ἠρνημένοι.

8 Οὗτοι ἔσονται ὑπηρέται τῶν ἡμερῶν ἐκείνων καὶ πάντα
τὰ ὑπ᾽ αὐτῶν αὐτοῖς προστασσόμενα εὐχέρως ἐκτελέσωσι.

For anticipating these things the godly apostle preached 4
and said that "in the latter times some shall depart from the
faith, giving heed to spirits *of seduction,* and doctrines of devils, speaking lies in hypocrisy, having their conscience seared
with a hot iron."[49]

And again the same said, "In *the* last days perilous times 5
shall come. For men shall be lovers of their own selves, covetous, boasters, proud, blasphemers, disobedient to parents,
useless, unholy, without natural affection, truce-breakers,
false accusers, incontinent, fierce, despisers of those that
are good, traitors, heady, high-minded, lovers of pleasures
more than lovers of God; having a form of godliness, but denying the power thereof."[50]

And all those who are weak in the faith will be made 6
known in that chastisement and they will separate themselves from the holy churches by their own choice. For the
time itself summons them to error. The humble and quiet,
useful and trusty, frank and select will not be sought out in
that time.

But in their place those will be sought out who are lovers 7
of their own selves, money-loving, boasters, proud, blasphemers, extortioners, covetous, drunkards, unmerciful,
apostate, truce-breakers, without natural affection, un-
thankful, unholy, false accusers, incontinent, fierce, *wild,*
traitors, heady, high-minded, lovers of pleasures more than
lovers of God, fornicators, adulterers, thieves, perjured persons, liars, men-stealers, *those* having a form of godliness, but
denying the power thereof.[51]

These will be the servants of those days, and all of the or- 8
ders given to them will be carried out with ease by them.

Καὶ οἱ φοβούμενοι τὸν κύριον εἰς οὐδὲν λογισθήσονται
ἐνώπιον τῶν ὀφθαλμῶν αὐτῶν, ἀλλ᾽ ἐν ἀτιμίᾳ ἔσονται ὃν
τρόπον⁶⁵ καταπεπατημένη κόπρος.

13

Γενήσονται γὰρ οἱ ἄνθρωποι ἐν τῇ παιδείᾳ ἐκείνῃ τῶν
υἱῶν Ἰσμαὴλ καὶ ἐλεύσονται ἐν ἀνάγκαις ἕως ἂν ἀπελπίσω-
σιν τὴν ζωὴν ἑαυτῶν. Καὶ ἀρθήσεται ἡ τιμὴ ἐκ τῶν ἱερέων
καὶ ὑπείξει⁶⁶ ἡ λειτουργία τοῦ θεοῦ καὶ παύσει πᾶσα θυσία
ἀπὸ τῶν ἐκκλησιῶν, καὶ ἔσονται οἱ ἱερεῖς ὡς ὁ λαός.

2   Καὶ ἐν τῷ καιρῷ ἐκείνῳ, ἤτοι τῷ ἑβδοματικῷ ἑβδόμῳ
χρόνῳ, ἡνίκα πληροῦται ὁ ἀριθμὸς τῶν ἐτῶν τῆς δυναστείας αὐτῶν, ‹δι᾽›ἧς⁶⁷ κατεκράτησαν τῆς γῆς, πληθυνθήσε-
ται καὶ ἡ θλῖψις ἐπὶ τοὺς ἀνθρώπους καὶ ἐπὶ τὰ κτήνη καὶ
ἔσται λιμὸς καὶ λοιμὸς καὶ φθαρήσονται καὶ ῥιφήσονται οἱ
ἄνθρωποι ἐπὶ προσώπου τῆς γῆς ὥσπερ χοῦς καὶ καθ᾽
ἑκάστην ἡμέραν ἐν τῷ καιρῷ ἐκείνῳ ἔτι μία πληγὴ προσ-
τεθήσεται τοῖς ἀνθρώποις.

3   Καὶ κοιτάσει ὁ ἄνθρωπος τῇ ἑσπέρᾳ καὶ ἀναστήσεται
τὸ πρωῒ καὶ εὑρήσει ἐπὶ τῆς φλιᾶς⁶⁸ τῆς θύρας αὐτοῦ τοὺς
ἀπαιτοῦντας αὐτὸν ὅλκην χρυσίου ἢ ἀργυρίου⁶⁹ καὶ ἀγγα-
ρεύοντας αὐτόν, καὶ ἐκδαπανηθήσεται πᾶσα δοσοληψία⁷⁰
χρυσίου καὶ ἀργυρίου. Καὶ πωλήσει ἄνθρωπος πᾶσαν τὴν
χρείαν αὐτοῦ καὶ τὰ ὀργανικὰ σίδηρα καὶ τὰ ἐντάφια
αὐτοῦ.

And those who fear the Lord will be esteemed as nothing in their eyes; they will be held in dishonor, in the way dung is trampled underfoot.

Chapter 13

For people will be born in that chastisement of the sons of Ishmael and they will go in such straits that they will despair of their life. And honor will be taken away from the priests and the ministry of God will depart and every sacrifice will cease from the churches, and the priests will be as the laity.

And in that time, that is in the period of the seventh 2 week, when the number of the years of their dominion will be fulfilled, during which they controlled the earth, the affliction will be increased for men and for beasts and there will be famine and plague, they will perish and men will be thrown upon the face of the earth like dust, and every day in that time yet one more blow will be laid upon men.

And a man will go to bed in the evening and wake up in 3 the morning and find at his doorpost men who demand of him a weight of gold or silver and press him into service, and his entire ready supply of gold and silver will be exhausted. And the man will offer for sale all his necessary equipment[52] and his iron tools and his burial shroud.

4 Καὶ ἐν αὐτῷ τῷ ἑβδοματικῷ χρόνῳ πωλήσωσιν οἱ ἄνθρωποι τὰ τέκνα αὐτῶν. Τίνος οὖν χάριν παρορᾷ ὁ θεὸς τοὺς πιστοὺς ὑπενεγκεῖν τὰς θλίψεις ταύτας, ἀλλ᾽ ἵνα δειχθῶσιν οἱ πιστοί τε καὶ ἄπιστοι καὶ ἀφορισθήσονται τὰ ζιζάνια ἀπὸ τοῦ σίτου, διότι πῦρ δοκιμασίας ἐστὶν ὁ καιρὸς ἐκεῖνος;

5 Καὶ μακροθυμήσει ὁ θεὸς ἐπὶ ταῖς θλίψεσι τῶν δικαίων καὶ πιστῶν, ἵνα φανῶσιν οἱ ἐκλεκτοί· προεῖπε γὰρ ἡμῖν ὁ κύριος οὕτως· "μακάριοί ἐστε, ὅταν ὀνειδίσωσιν ὑμᾶς καὶ διώξουσι[71] καὶ εἴπωσι πᾶν πονηρὸν ῥῆμα καθ᾽ ὑμῶν ψευδόμενοι ἕνεκεν ἐμοῦ. Χαίρετε καὶ ἀγαλλιᾶσθε, ὅτι ὁ μισθὸς ὑμῶν πολὺς ἐν τοῖς οὐρανοῖς· οὕτως γὰρ ἐδίωξαν τοὺς προφήτας τοὺς πρὸ ἡμῶν," "ὁ δὲ ὑπομείνας εἰς τέλος, οὗτος σωθήσεται."

6 Καὶ μετὰ τὴν θλῖψιν τὴν ὑπὸ τῶν Ἰσμαηλιτῶν γινομένην, ἡνίκα κινδυνεύσωσιν οἱ ἄνθρωποι θλιβόμενοι, μὴ ἔχοντες ἐλπίδα σωτηρίας ἢ ἀπολυτρώσεως ἐκ τῶν χειρῶν τῶν Ἰσμαηλιτῶν, διωκόμενοι, θλιβόμενοι, κακουχούμενοι, ἐν πείνῃ καὶ δίψῃ καὶ γυμνότητι, οἱ δὲ βάρβαροι οὗτοι ἔσονται τρώγοντες καὶ πίνοντες καὶ καυχώμενοι ἐν ταῖς νίκαις αὐτῶν καὶ ἐν ταῖς ἐρημώσεσιν αἷς ἐρήμωσαν Περσίδα τε καὶ Ῥωμανίαν, Κιλικίαν τε καὶ Συρίαν, Καππαδοκίαν τε καὶ Ἰσαυρίαν καὶ Ἀφρικὴν καὶ Σικελίαν καὶ τοὺς κατοικοῦντας πλησίον Ῥώμης καὶ τὰς νήσους, ἐνδιδυσκόμενοι καθάπερ νυμφίοι, καὶ βλασφημοῦντες λέγουσιν ὅτι "οὐκ ἔχουσιν ἀνάρρυσιν οἱ χριστιανοὶ ἐκ τῶν χειρῶν ἡμῶν,"

7 [τότε αἰφνίδιον[72] ἐλεύσονται ἐν ἅρμασι καὶ ἐν ἵπποις μυριοπλασίως· ἐξελεύσεται γὰρ τῷ πρώτῳ μηνὶ τῆς ἐνάτης

And in this time of the week men will sell their children. 4
For what reason would God take no notice of the faithful
enduring these afflictions, except that the faithful and the
unfaithful might be made known and the tares separated
from the wheat, because that time is a fire of testing?

And God waits patiently over the tribulations of the just 5
and faithful, so that the elect will be revealed. For the Lord
has already spoken to us in this manner: "Blessed are ye,
when men shall revile you, and persecute you, and shall say
all manner of evil against you falsely, for my sake. Rejoice,
and be exceeding glad: for great is your reward in heaven: for
so persecuted they the prophets which were before you, but
he that endureth to the end shall be saved."[53]

And after the tribulation under the Ishmaelites has come 6
about, when men will be in peril and afflicted, having no
hope of salvation or redemption out of the hands of the Ishmaelites, hunted, afflicted, and tormented with hunger and
thirst and nakedness, these barbarians will be eating and
drinking and boasting of their victories and of the desolations to which they have reduced Persia and Romania, Cilicia and Syria, Cappadocia and Isauria and Africa and Sicily
and those living near Rome and the islands, dressing up like
bridegrooms, and blaspheming they say, "The Christians
have no rescue from out of our hands."[54]

Then all of a sudden they will come in chariots and on 7
horses ten thousandfold. For this horde[55] will come out in
the first month of the ninth indiction and will overwhelm[56]

ἐπινεμήσεως καὶ συλλαβέτω⁷³ τὰς πόλεις τῆς ἀνατολῆς κατακλύζων πάσας, μερισθήσεται δὲ εἰς ἀρχὰς τρεῖς·⁷⁴ καὶ τὸ μὲν ἓν μέρος χειμάσει εἰς Ἔφεσον, τὸ δὲ ἕτερον εἰς Πέργαμον, καὶ τὸ τρίτον εἰς τὰ Μαλάγινα.

8 Καὶ οὐαί σοι χῶρα Φρυγία καὶ Παμφυλία καὶ Βιθυνία· ὅταν γὰρ παχνίσῃ, ὁ Ἰσμαὴλ παραλαμβάνει σε· ἐλεύσεται γὰρ ὥσπερ πῦρ κατεσθίον ἅπαντας καὶ οἱ ναῦται αὐτοῦ ἑβδομήκοντα χιλιάδες, καὶ ἐρημώσουσιν τὰς νήσους καὶ τοὺς τὴν παραλίαν οἰκοῦντας.

9 Οὐαί σοι, Βύζα, ὅτι ὁ Ἰσμαὴλ παραλαμβάνει σε· περάσει γὰρ πᾶς ἵππος Ἰσμαὴλ⁷⁵ καὶ στήσει ὁ πρῶτος αὐτῶν τὴν σκηνὴν αὐτοῦ κατέναντί σου, Βύζα, καὶ ἄρξηται πολεμεῖν καὶ συντρίψει τὴν πύλην Ξυλοκέρκου καὶ εἰσελεύσεται ἕως τοῦ Βοός· τότε Βοῦς βοήσει σφόδρα καὶ Ξηρόλαφος κραυγάσει, συγκοπτόμενοι ὑπὸ τῶν Ἰσμαηλιτῶν.

10 Τότε φωνὴ ἔλθῃ ἐκ τοῦ οὐρανοῦ λέγουσα· "ἀρκεῖ μοι ἡ ἐκδίκησις αὕτη," καὶ ἀρεῖ κύριος ὁ θεὸς τότε τὴν δειλίαν τῶν Ῥωμαίων καὶ βάλῃ εἰς τὰς καρδίας τῶν Ἰσμαηλιτῶν καὶ τὴν ἀνδρείαν τῶν Ἰσμαηλιτῶν βάλῃ εἰς τὰς καρδίας τῶν Ῥωμαίων καὶ στραφέντες ἐκδιώξουσιν αὐτοὺς ἐκ τῶν ἰδίων συγκόπτοντες ἀφειδῶς. Τότε πληρωθήσεται τὸ γε-γραμμένον· "εἷς διώξεται χιλίους καὶ δύο μετακινήσουσι μυριάδας." Τότε συντελεσθήσονται καὶ οἱ πλωτῆρες αὐτῶν καὶ εἰς ἀφανισμὸν γενήσονται.]

11 τότε αἰφνίδιον ἐπελεύσονται ἐπ' αὐτοὺς θλῖψις καὶ στε-νοχωρία,⁷⁶ καὶ ἐξελεύσεται ἐπ' αὐτοὺς βασιλεὺς Ἑλλήνων, ἤτοι Ῥωμαίων, μετὰ μεγάλου θυμοῦ καὶ ἐξυπνισθήσεται καθάπερ ἄνθρωπος ἀπὸ ὕπνου πιὼν οἶνον πολύν, ὃν

all of the cities of the east and seize them. Then it will be divided into three commands. And the one part will turn the land to winter barrenness[57] as far as Ephesus, the other as far as Pergamum, and the third as far as Malagina.[58]

And woe to you, land of Phrygia and Pamphylia and 8 Bithynia! For when it becomes frosty with cold,[59] Ishmael will overtake you. For he will come like a fire devouring everyone, and he and his seventy thousand sailors will devastate the islands and those who live along the coast.

Woe to you, Byzas, because Ishmael overtakes you. For 9 every horse of Ishmael will pass through and the first among them will pitch his tent before you, Byzas, and he will begin to make war and will break down the gate of Xylokerkos and will proceed as far as "the cow."[60] Then the cow will low loudly and Xerolaphos[61] will bay, since they were thrashed by the Ishmaelites.

Then a voice will come out of the heavens saying, "This 10 same punishment suffices for me." And the Lord God will then snatch the cowardice of the Romans and thrust it into the hearts of the Ishmaelites and take the manliness of the Ishmaelites and cast it into the hearts of the Romans; they will turn and drive them from their homes and crush them without mercy. Then that which was written will be fulfilled: "One *shall* chase a thousand, and two put ten thousand to flight."[62] Then their sailors also will be exhausted and will come to destruction.

Then all of a sudden affliction and trouble will come to 11 them, and the king of the Greeks, that is of the Romans, will go out to them with great anger and he will be aroused like a man roused from sleep after drinking much wine,[63] whom

ἐλογίζοντο οἱ ἄνθρωποι ὡσεὶ νεκρὸν ὄντα καὶ εἰς οὐδὲν χρησιμεύοντα· οὗτος ἐξελεύσεται ἐπ᾽ αὐτοὺς ἐκ τῆς θαλάσσης Αἰθιοπίας καὶ βάλῃ ῥομφαίαν καὶ ἐρήμωσιν εἰς τὴν Ἔθριβον, ἥτις ἐστὶ πατρὶς αὐτῶν, καὶ αἰχμαλωτεύσει τὰς γυναῖκας καὶ τὰ τέκνα αὐτῶν. Ἐπὶ δὲ τοὺς κατοικοῦντας τὴν γῆν τῆς ἐπαγγελίας κατέλθωσιν οἱ υἱοὶ τοῦ βασιλέως καὶ ἐν ῥομφαίᾳ ἐκκόψουσιν αὐτοὺς ἀπὸ τῆς γῆς.

12 Καὶ ἐπιπέσῃ ἐπ᾽ αὐτοὺς φόβος πάντοθεν· καὶ αὐτοὶ καὶ αἱ γυναῖκες αὐτῶν καὶ τὰ τέκνα αὐτῶν καὶ αἱ τιθηνούμεναι τὰ βρέφη αὐτῶν καὶ πᾶσαι αἱ παρεμβολαὶ αὐτῶν αἱ οὖσαι ἐν τῇ γῇ τῶν πατέρων αὐτῶν εἰς τὰς χεῖρας τοῦ βασιλέως τῶν Ῥωμαίων παραδοθήσονται ἐν ῥομφαίᾳ καὶ αἰχμαλωσίᾳ καὶ θανάτῳ καὶ φθορᾷ.

13 Καὶ ἔσται ὁ ζυγὸς τοῦ βασιλέως τῶν Ῥωμαίων ἐπ᾽ αὐτοὺς ἑπταπλασίων οὗ ἦν ὁ ζυγὸς αὐτῶν ἐπ᾽ αὐτούς. Καὶ καταλάβῃ αὐτοὺς στενοχωρία μεγάλη· πεῖνα καὶ δίψα καὶ θλῖψις. Καὶ ἔσονται δοῦλοι αὐτοὶ καὶ αἱ γυναῖκες αὐτῶν καὶ τὰ τέκνα αὐτῶν καὶ δουλεύσουσι τοῖς δουλεύσασιν αὐτοῖς καὶ ἔσται ἡ δουλεία αὐτῶν πικροτέρα τε καὶ ὀδυνηροτέρα ἑκατονταπλασίονα.

14 Καὶ εἰρηνεύσει ἡ γῆ ἡ ὑπ᾽ αὐτῶν ἐρημωθεῖσα, καὶ ἐπανέλθῃ ἕκαστος εἰς τὴν γῆν αὐτοῦ καὶ εἰς τὴν κληρονομίαν τῶν πατέρων αὐτοῦ—Ἀρμενία, Κιλικία, Ἰσαυρία, Ἀφρική, Ἑλλάς, Σικελία—καὶ πᾶς ὁ ὑπολιμπασθεὶς[77] ἐκ τῆς αἰχμαλωσίας ἐπανελεύσεται εἰς τὰ ἴδια καὶ τὰ πατρικὰ αὐτοῦ.

15 Καὶ πληθυνθήσονται οἱ ἄνθρωποι ἐπὶ τῆς γῆς τῆς ἐρημωθείσης ὡσεὶ ἀκρίς· ἡ Αἴγυπτος ἐρημωθήσεται, Ἀραβία ἐν πυρὶ καυθήσεται, ἡ γῆ τοῦ Ἀβρανοῦς ἐρημωθήσεται

58

men have reckoned to be dead and good for nothing. This man will come out against them from the sea of Ethiopia and plunge a sword and desolation into Yathrib, which is their homeland, and he will take captive their women and children. The sons of the king will descend upon those who dwell in the Promised Land and with the sword cut them off from the land.

And a fear will fall upon them from every side. And they 12 and their women and their children and the nurses suckling their babies and all the encampments which are in the land of their fathers will be delivered up into the hands of the king of the Romans with sword and captivity and death and ruin.

And the yoke of the king of the Romans upon them will 13 be sevenfold what their yoke was upon the Romans. And a great distress will overtake them, hunger and thirst and affliction. And they themselves will be slaves, and their wives and their children, and they will serve those who once served them and their servitude will be a hundred times more bitter and painful.[64]

And the country devastated by them will be at peace, and 14 each man will go up to his land and to the inheritance of his fathers—Armenia, Cilicia, Isauria, Africa, Greece, Sicily— and every man left behind out of captivity will come up to his own and his patrimony.

And men will be multiplied on the desolated earth like 15 the locust. Egypt will be devastated, Arabia will be burned with fire, the land of Abran[65] will be desolate, and the seacoast will be at peace. And all of the wrath and the anger of

καὶ ἡ παράλιος εἰρηνεύσει. Καὶ πᾶς ὁ θυμὸς καὶ ἡ ὀργὴ
τοῦ βασιλέως τῶν Ῥωμαίων ἐπὶ τοὺς ἀρνησαμένους τὸν
κύριον ἡμῶν Ἰησοῦν Χριστὸν ἐκκαυθήσεται καὶ εἰρηνεύσει
ἡ γῆ· καὶ ἔσται εἰρήνη καὶ γαλήνη ἐπὶ τῆς γῆς μεγάλη, οἵα
οὐ γέγονεν οὐδὲ μὴ γενήσεται καθὼς ὅτι ἐσχάτη ἐστὶ καὶ
ἐν τῷ τέλει τῶν αἰώνων.

16   Ἔσται δὲ εὐφροσύνη ἐπὶ τῆς γῆς καὶ κατοικήσουσιν οἱ
ἄνθρωποι ἐν εἰρήνῃ καὶ ἀνοικοδομήσουσιν τὰς πόλεις καὶ
ἐλευθερωθήσονται οἱ ἱερεῖς ἐκ τῶν ἀναγκῶν αὐτῶν καὶ
ἀναπαύσονται οἱ ἄνθρωποι ἐν τῷ καιρῷ ἐκείνῳ τῶν θλί-
ψεων αὐτῶν.

17   Καὶ αὕτη ἐστὶν ἡ εἰρήνη, ἣν ὁ θεῖος ἀπόστολος διη-
γόρευσεν ὅτι "ὅταν εἴπωσιν· εἰρήνη καὶ ἀσφάλεια, τότε
ἐπιπεσεῖται ἐπ᾽ αὐτοὺς αἰφνίδιος ὄλεθρος," καὶ αὖθις ὁ
κύριος ἐν τοῖς εὐαγγελίοις, οὕτως φάσκων· "ὥσπερ γὰρ ἐν
ταῖς ἡμέραις τοῦ Νῶε ἦσαν οἱ ἄνθρωποι τρώγοντες καὶ
πίνοντες, γαμοῦντες καὶ ἐκγαμίζοντες, οὕτως ἔσται καὶ ἐν
τῇ ἐσχάτῃ ἡμέρᾳ."[78]

18   Ἐν ταύτῃ τοιγαροῦν τῇ εἰρήνῃ καθίσουσιν οἱ ἄνθρωποι
ἐπὶ τῆς γῆς μετὰ χαρᾶς καὶ εὐφροσύνης τρώγοντες καὶ
πίνοντες, γαμοῦντες καὶ ἐκγαμίζοντες, σκιρτῶντες καὶ
ἀγαλλιώμενοι, καὶ οἰκοδομήσουσιν οἰκοδομὰς καὶ οὐκ
ἔσται ἐν τῇ καρδίᾳ αὐτῶν φόβος ἢ μέριμνα.

19   Τότε ἀνοιχθήσονται αἱ πύλαι τοῦ βορρᾶ καὶ ἐξελεύσονται
αἱ δυνάμεις τῶν ἐθνῶν, αἵ εἰσιν καθειργμέναι ἔσωθεν, καὶ
σαλευθήσεται πᾶσα ἡ γῆ ἀπὸ προσώπου αὐτῶν καὶ θρο-
ηθήσονται οἱ ἄνθρωποι καὶ φύγωσιν καὶ κρύψουσιν[79] ἑαυ-

the king of the Romans against those who denied our Lord Jesus Christ will be burned up and the land will be at peace. And there will be a great peace and quiet upon the earth such as has not been nor will be until the last [day] at the end of the ages.[66]

There will be gladness upon the earth and men will settle 16 down in peace and they will rebuild the cities and the priests will be freed from their constraints and men will rest at that time from their afflictions.[67]

And this is the peace of which the godly apostle declared 17 that "when they shall say, Peace and safety; then sudden destruction *falleth* upon them,"[68] and moreover the Lord speaks thus in the gospels: "For as in the days of Noah there were men eating and drinking, marrying and giving in marriage, so it will be *at the last day*."[69]

In that peace, therefore, men will sit down upon the earth 18 with joy and gladness, eating and drinking, marrying and giving in marriage, jumping for joy and rejoicing, and they will build buildings and there will be no fear or worry in their hearts.[70]

Then the gates of the North will be opened up and out 19 will come the powers of the nations which were enclosed within, and the whole earth will reel from their face, and men will cry aloud and flee and hide themselves in the moun-

τοὺς ἐπὶ τὰ ὄρη καὶ ἐπὶ τὰ σπήλαια καὶ ἐν τοῖς μνημείοις. Καὶ νεκρωθήσονται φόβῳ καὶ φθαρήσονται πολλοὶ καὶ οὐκ ἔσται ὁ θάπτων τὰ σώματα.

20 Τὰ γὰρ ἔθνη τά ἐρχόμενα ἀπὸ βορρᾶ ἐσθίουσι σάρκας ἀνθρώπων καὶ πίνουσιν αἵματα[80] θηρίων ὥσπερ ὕδωρ καὶ ἐσθίουσι τὰ ἀκάθαρτα καὶ τοὺς ὄφεις καὶ σκορπίους καὶ πάντα τὰ μυσαρὰ καὶ βδελυκτὰ θηρία καὶ τὰ ἑρπετὰ τὰ ἕρποντα ἐπὶ τὴν γῆν τά τε κτηνώδη καὶ τὰ νεκρὰ σώματα καὶ τὰ ἐκτρώματα τῶν γυναικῶν. Καὶ σφάξουσι νήπια καὶ παράσχωνται[81] ταῖς μητράσιν αὐτῶν καὶ ἑψήσουσι τὰ κρέα αὐτῶν καὶ κατέδονται αὐτὰ καὶ φθεροῦσι τὴν γῆν καὶ μιάνωσιν αὐτὴν καὶ ἀφανίσωσιν αὐτὴν καὶ οὐδεὶς ἔσται ὁ δυνάμενος στῆναι ἐναντίον αὐτῶν.

21 Μετὰ οὖν ἑβδομάδα χρόνων, ἡνίκα καταλάβωσι τὴν πόλιν Ἰόππην, ἀποστελεῖ κύριος ὁ θεὸς ἕνα τῶν ἀρχιστρατήγων αὐτοῦ καὶ πατάξει αὐτοὺς ἐν μίᾳ ῥοπῇ καιροῦ. Καὶ μετὰ ταῦτα καταβήσεται ὁ βασιλεὺς τῶν Ῥωμαίων καὶ κατοικήσει ἐν Ἰερουσαλὴμ ἑβδομάδα χρόνων καὶ ἥμισυ καὶ ἐν τῷ πληρώματι τῶν δέκα καὶ ἥμισυ χρόνων φανήσεται ὁ υἱὸς τῆς ἀπωλείας.

14

Οὗτος γεννᾶται εἰς Χωραζὶν καὶ ἀνατρέφεται εἰς Βηθσαϊδὰ καὶ βασιλεύσει εἰς Καπερναούμ. Καὶ εὐφρανθήσεται Χωραζὶν διότι ἐγεννήθη ἐν αὐτῇ, καὶ Βηθσαϊδὰ διότι

tains and in the caves and among the gravestones. And they will be deadened with fear and many will perish and there will be none to bury the bodies.[71]

For the nations coming from the North eat the flesh of 20 men and drink the blood of beasts like water[72] and eat unclean things: snakes and scorpions and all abominable and disgusting beasts and the reptiles that creep upon the earth and brutal things and dead bodies and the aborted fetuses of women. And they will slaughter infants, even producing them from their wombs, and they will boil the meat and eat it. And they will corrupt the earth and befoul it and deface it, and there will be no one able to stand before them.

So after a week of years, when they seize the city of Joppa, 21 the Lord God will send out one of the chief commanders of his army and he will smite them in a single moment of time. And after these things the king of the Romans will come down and he will dwell in Jerusalem for a week and a half of years, and upon the completion of ten and a half years the son of perdition will appear.

Chapter 14

This man is born at Chorazin and raised at Bethsaida and rules at Capernaum. And Chorazin will be glad because he was born in her, and Bethsaida because he was raised in her,

ἀνετράφη ἐν αὐτῇ, καὶ Καπερναοὺμ διότι ἐβασίλευσεν ἐν αὐτῇ. Τούτου χάριν ἐν τοῖς εὐαγγελίοις ὁ κύριος ἐκ τρίτου δέδωκε τὸ οὐαὶ εἰπών· "οὐαί σοι, Χωραζί, οὐαί σοι, Βηθσαϊδά· καὶ σύ, Καπερναούμ, ἡ ἕως τοῦ οὐρανοῦ ὑψωθεῖσα, ἕως τοῦ Ἅιδου καταβήσει."

2 Καὶ ἐπὰν φανερωθῇ ὁ υἱὸς τῆς ἀπωλείας, ἀναβήσεται ὁ βασιλεὺς τῶν Ῥωμαίων ἄνω εἰς Γολγοθᾶ, ἔνθα ἐπάγη τὸ ξύλον τοῦ σταυροῦ εἰς τὸν τόπον, ἐν ᾧ ὑπέμεινεν θάνατον Χριστὸς ὁ θεὸς ἡμῶν.

3 Καὶ ἀρεῖ ὁ βασιλεὺς τῶν Ῥωμαίων τὸ στέμμα αὐτοῦ καὶ ἐπιθήσει αὐτὸ ἐν τῷ σταυρῷ καὶ ἐκπετάσει τὰς χεῖρας αὐτοῦ εἰς τὸν οὐρανὸν καὶ παραδώσει τὴν βασιλείαν τῶν χριστιανῶν τῷ θεῷ καὶ πατρί.

4 Καὶ ἀναληφθήσεται ὁ σταυρὸς εἰς τὸν οὐρανὸν ἅμα τῷ στέμματι τοῦ βασιλέως, διότι ὁ σταυρός, ἐν ᾧ ἐκρεμάσθη ὁ κύριος ἡμῶν Ἰησοῦς Χριστὸς διὰ τὴν κοινὴν πάντων σωτηρίαν, αὐτὸς μέλλει φανήσεσθαι ἔμπροσθεν αὐτοῦ ἐν τῇ παρουσίᾳ αὐτοῦ εἰς ἔλεγχον τῶν ἀπίστων.

5 Καὶ πληροῦται ἡ προφητεία τοῦ Δαβὶδ λέγουσα ἐπ᾽ ἐσχάτου τῶν ἡμερῶν· "Αἰθιοπία προφθάσει χεῖρα αὐτῆς τῷ θεῷ," διότι ἐκ σπέρματος τῶν υἱῶν Χουσὴθ θυγατρὸς Φὸλ βασιλέως τῶν Αἰθιόπων αὐτοὶ ἐσχάτως προφθάσωσι χεῖρα αὐτῶν τῷ θεῷ.

6 Καὶ ἅμα[82] ὑψωθήσεται ὁ σταυρος εἰς τὸν οὐρανόν, καὶ παραδώσει τὸ πνεῦμα αὐτοῦ ὁ τῶν Ῥωμαίων βασιλεύς· τότε καταργηθήσεται πᾶσα ἀρχὴ καὶ ἐξουσία. Καὶ ὅτε ἐμφανῶς γένηται ὁ υἱὸς τῆς ἀπωλείας—ἔστι δὲ οὗτος ἐκ

and Capernaum because he ruled in her. For this reason in the gospels the Lord three times uttered the word "woe," saying, "Woe unto thee, Chorazin! Woe unto thee, Bethsaida! And then, Capernaum, which art exalted unto heaven, shalt be brought down to hell."[73]

And when the son of perdition will be revealed, the king 2 of the Romans will go up to Golgotha, where the wood of the cross was fixed at the place in which Christ our God endured death.

And the king of the Romans will take his wreath[74] and 3 place it on the cross and spread out his hands to heaven and deliver the kingdom of the Christians to God, even the Father.[75]

And the cross will be taken up to heaven along with the 4 wreath of the king because the cross, on which Our Lord Jesus Christ was hanged for the sake of the common salvation of all, itself is destined to appear in front of him at his coming as a refutation of unbelievers.

And the prophecy of David will be fulfilled which says at 5 the end of days "Ethiopia shall stretch out her hands unto God,"[76] because from the seed of the sons of Chouseth, the daughter of Phol king of the Ethiopians, these men will in the end stretch out their hands unto God.

And as soon as the cross is lifted up to heaven, the king of 6 the Romans will surrender his spirit; then all rule and authority will be abolished.[77] And this is when the son of perdition will be revealed—this is the man from the tribe of Dan

τῆς φυλῆς τοῦ Δὰν κατὰ τὴν προφητείαν τοῦ πατριάρχου Ἰακὼβ τὴν λέγουσαν· "Δάν, ὄφις ἐφ' ὁδοῦ ἐγκαθήμενος, ἐπὶ τρίβου δάκνων πτέρναν ἵππου καὶ πεσεῖται ὁ ἱππεὺς εἰς τὰ ὀπίσω περιμένων τὴν σωτηρίαν τοῦ κυρίου,"

7 ἵππος τοίνυν ἐστὶν ἡ ἀλήθεια καὶ ἡ εὐσέβεια τῶν δικαίων, πτέρνα δὲ ἡ ἐσχάτη ἡμέρα—καὶ οὗτοι οἱ ἅγιοι οἱ ἐν τῷ τότε χρόνῳ ἐπὶ τῷ ἵππῳ, ἤγουν ἐπὶ τῆς ἀληθοῦς ἐπιβεβηκότες πίστεως, δηχθήσονται ὑπὸ τοῦ ὄφεως, ἤτοι τοῦ υἱοῦ τῆς ἀπωλείας, ἐν τῇ πτέρνῃ, ἤγουν ἐν τῇ ἐσχάτῃ ἡμέρᾳ, εἰς τὰς φαντασίας καὶ εἰς τὰ ψευδοποιὰ αὐτοῦ σημεῖα.

8 Ποιήσει γὰρ τότε σημεῖα καὶ τέρατα πολλὰ ἐπὶ τῆς γῆς ἀδρανῆ καὶ ἐξίτηλα· τυφλοὶ γὰρ ἀναβλέψουσι, χωλοὶ περιπατήσωσι, κωφοὶ ἀκούσονται καὶ δαιμονιῶντες ἰαθήσονται. Μεταστρέψει τὸν ἥλιον εἰς σκότος καὶ τὴν σελήνην εἰς αἷμα καὶ ἐν τούτοις τοῖς ψευδοσημείοις καὶ φαντασιώδεσι τέρασι πλάνης πλανήσει, εἰ δυνατόν, καὶ τοὺς ἐκλεκτούς, καθὼς ὁ κύριος προηγόρευσεν.

9 Ἀτενίσας γὰρ ὁ πατριάρχης Ἰακὼβ τῷ τῆς διανοίας ὄμματι κατενόησεν τὴν μέλλουσαν ὑπὸ τοῦ ἀλιτηρίου ὄφεως, ἤτοι τοῦ υἱοῦ τῆς ἀπωλείας, γίνεσθαι ἐπὶ τοῖς ἀνθρώποις θλῖψιν τε καὶ στενοχωρίαν, καὶ προηγόρευσεν οὕτως ἐκ προσώπου τοῦ ἀνθρωπίνου γένους τὴν φωνὴν ποιησάμενος· "τὴν σωτηρίαν σου περιμένομεν, κύριε," ὁ δὲ κύριος αὖθις προαπεφήνατο λέγων· "εἰ δυνατὸν πλανῆσαι καὶ τοὺς ἐκλεκτούς."

10 Εἰσελεύσεται γὰρ οὗτος ὁ υἱὸς τῆς ἀπωλείας εἰς τὰ

according to the prophecy of the patriarch Jacob, which says, "Dan *is* a serpent by the way, besetting the path, that biteth the horse heels, so that his rider shall fall backward, waiting for the salvation of the Lord."[78]

The horse then is the truth and righteousness of the just, and the heel the last day—and these holy ones who are at that time on the horse, that is to say mounted upon the true faith, will be bitten by the serpent, that is the son of perdition, in the heel, that is to say in the last day, by his showy parades and deceptive signs. 7

For at that time he will perform many signs and wonders, powerless and fading, over the earth. For the blind will receive their sight, the lame will walk, the deaf will hear, and the demon-possessed will be healed. He shall turn the sun into darkness, and the moon into blood, and in these false signs and fantastic wonders of deceit he will deceive, if possible, the very elect, just as the Lord foretold.[79] 8

For peering with the eye of his understanding the patriarch Jacob perceived what would happen under the wicked serpent, that is the son of perdition, that a tribulation and distress will come upon men, and he foretold in this manner employing the voice issuing from the face[80] of mankind, "We have waited for thy salvation, O Lord,"[81] and again the Lord prophesied, saying "if possible, to deceive the very elect."[82] 9

For this son of perdition will go to Jerusalem and sit in 10

Ἱεροσόλυμα καὶ καθίσει εἰς τὸν ναὸν τοῦ θεοῦ ἴσα θεῷ ἄνθρωπος ὑπάρχων σάρκινος ἐκ σπέρματος ἀνδρὸς καὶ ἐκ μήτρας γυναικὸς ἐκ φυλῆς τυγχάνων τοῦ Δάν· [καὶ Ἰούδας γὰρ ὁ Ἰσκαριώτης ὁ καὶ προδοὺς τὸν κύριον ἐκ φυλῆς ἐστὶ καὶ αὐτὸς τοῦ Δάν.]⁸³

11 Πληθυνομένης οὖν τῆς θλίψεως τῶν ἡμερῶν ἐκείνων ὑπὸ τοῦ υἱοῦ τῆς ἀπωλείας οὐ φέρει τὸ θεῖον καθορᾶν τὴν ἀπώλειαν τοῦ γένους τῶν ἀνθρώπων, ὧν ἐξηγόρασεν τῷ οἰκείῳ αἵματι, καὶ ἐξαποστελεῖ οὖν εὐθὺς τοὺς ἰδίους αὐτοῦ καὶ γνησίους θεράποντας Ἐνώχ τε καὶ Ἡλίαν εἰς ἔλεγχον τοῦ ἀντικειμένου. Παρουσίᾳ οὖν πάντων τῶν ἐθνῶν ἐλέγξουσιν αὐτοῦ τὴν πλάνην καὶ ἀναδείξουσιν αὐτὸν ψεύστην ἐπὶ παντὸς ἀνθρώπου καὶ μηδὲν ὄντα καὶ ὅτι δι᾽ ἀπώλειαν καὶ πλάνην τῶν πολλῶν ἐξῆλθεν

12 τὰ οὖν ἔθνη ὁρῶντα αὐτὸν αἰσχυνθέντα τήν τε πλάνην αὐτοῦ ἐλεγχθεῖσαν ὑπὸ τῶν τοῦ θεοῦ θεραπόντων ἐάσωσιν αὐτὸν καὶ φεύξονται ἀπ᾽ αὐτοῦ καὶ προσκολληθήσονται τοῖς δικαίοις ἐκείνοις. Ὁρῶν οὖν αὐτὸς ἑαυτὸν δεινῶς ἐλεγχόμενον καὶ ὑπὸ πάντων περιφρονούμενον θυμῷ καὶ ὀργῇ ὑπερζέσας ἀναιρεῖ τοὺς ἁγίους ἐκείνους.

13 Τότε φανήσεται τὸ σημεῖον τῆς παρουσίας τοῦ υἱοῦ τοῦ ἀνθρώπου καὶ ἥξει ἐπὶ τῶν νεφελῶν τοῦ οὐρανοῦ μετὰ δόξης οὐρανίου⁸⁴ καὶ "ἀνελεῖ αὐτὸν κύριος τῷ πνεύματι τοῦ στόματος αὐτοῦ," κατὰ τὴν ἀποστολικὴν ἐκφαντορίαν.

14 Τότε λάμψουσιν οἱ δίκαιοι "ὡς φωστῆρες ἐν κόσμῳ, λόγον ζωῆς ἐπέχοντες," οἱ δὲ ἀσεβεῖς ἐκδιωχθήσονται καὶ ἀποστραφήσονται εἰς τὸν Ἅιδην, ἐξ οὗ ῥυσθείημεν ἅπαντες

the temple of God, equal to God, being a man of flesh from the seed of a man and from a mother who is a woman of the tribe of Dan.[83] [*interpolation:* For Judas Iscariot who betrayed the Lord is also from the tribe of Dan.]

So when the tribulation of those days is increased[84] by the son of perdition, the Divinity will not endure to look down on the perdition of the race of men, whom he redeemed with the blood of his own household, and so he will at once send forth his familiar and trusted servants, Enoch and Elijah, for the refutation of the opposition. So in the presence of all the nations they will expose his deceit and reveal him to be a liar to every man and a nobody and that he issued forth for the perdition and deception of many. 11

So the nations will see him put to shame and his deceit exposed by the servants of God, and they will abandon him and flee from him and join those just men. Then seeing that he has been decisively convicted and is despised by all, boiling over with wrath and anger this man will kill those holy ones. 12

Then will appear the sign of the Coming of the Son of Man and he will arrive on the clouds of heaven with heavenly glory and "the Lord shall consume *him* with the spirit of his mouth," according to the apostolic revelation.[85] 13

"Then shall the righteous shine" "as lights in the world, holding forth the word of life"[86] and the impious will be driven out and turned away to hell, out of which let all of 14

οἱ θεὸν ζῶντα λατρεύοντες, χάριτι καὶ φιλανθρωπίᾳ τοῦ κυρίου καὶ θεοῦ καὶ σωτῆρος ἡμῶν Ἰησοῦ Χριστοῦ, μεθ᾽ οὗ τῷ πατρὶ ἅμα τῷ ἁγίῳ καὶ ζωοποιῷ πνεύματι τίμη, δόξα, κράτος, μεγαλωσύνη τε καὶ μεγαλοπρέπεια, νῦν καὶ ἀεὶ καὶ εἰς τοὺς αἰῶνας τῶν αἰώνων, ἀμήν.

us who worship the living God be delivered by the grace and love for mankind of our Lord and God and Savior Jesus Christ,[87] with whom to the Father along with the Holy and life-giving Spirit be honor, glory, dominion, majesty, and sublimity, now and always and unto the ages of ages. Amen.

THE APOCALYPSE
ATTRIBUTED TO
SAINT METHODIUS

Praefacivncvla Petri Monachi

Amor est karitatis et amiculum pacis, que nostrum circa vestrum sepius inflammat dissiderium cordis. Nam hanc nullus ambigat esse dilectio minime vera, quae illud Decalocum implet effectum:[1] "Diliges," inquid, "proximum tuum, sicut te ipsum." Hunc nos quoque tam divini carminis meditantis versiculum optamusque vocare ipsius sanctae caritatis consortis.

Unde amore conpulsi dilectione vestrae fraternitatis, non quasi doctiores, sed ut viri[2] in virtutum tramite valde minores et in lege divina multumque inperitioris, sed, ut prefatus sum, amor inperat quod amatur, instat ut maneat, amans vero oboediendo cervicem subponit, obtemperans propter subiectionem sacrificio meliore. Caretas ergo urget nostra humilitas aliquos vobis apices de Scripturis sanctis intimare ob animae vestrae desiderio rogati. Quod nos propter oboedientiam caritatis respondemus esse futurus, si vita tamen fuerit in Dei arbitrio, impliturus. Nunc vero, non ut temere arbetremur a quibusdam quasi nostrum aliquid inferamus, quia non desunt qui carnaliter sapientes insultent, etiam

The Brief Preface of Peter the Monk

It is the love of charity and the garment of peace that often inflames the desire of my heart with regard to yours. For no one should doubt that this is, at the very least, the true love, which fulfills this pronouncement of the Decalogue: "Thou shalt love," it says, "thy neighbor as thyself."[1] And contemplating this little verse of such a divine song we long to be called partners in this same holy charity.

For which reason we have been compelled by love and esteem of your brotherhood, not as if we were more learned, but as men just setting out on the path of virtues and very inexperienced in the divine law, but, as I said before, love commands what is loved, it pursues so that it may remain, indeed the lover bows his neck in obedience and yields in subjection to a better sacrifice. Love, therefore, urges my humility to press upon you a few writings from the sacred scriptures, on account of the express wish of your spirit. Because of the obedience of love we answer that we will fulfill this request, if, that is, life enough will have been allotted by the judgment of God. Now then, lest we be rashly thought by some to be adding something of our own (for there is no lack of those who, wise according to the flesh, would ridi-

si eorum auribus aliorumque proficiat veritatis auditus, et maxime his temporibus, quibus nos conspicimus et factis viciisque constringi, presentibus auribus praecipue contemptorum melius vel conpetentius preteritorum doctorum seu priscorum patrum dormientumque iam dudum in Christo sensibus insinuavi[3] doctrinam.

Beati igitur Methodii episcopi et martyris dicta de Greco in Latino transferre sermone curavi, et quoniam nostri<s> sunt aptius prophetata temporibus, "in quos finis saeculorum," sicut apostolos inquid Paulus, "pervenerunt," ut iam[4] per ipsa que nostris cernimus oculis, vera esse credamus ea, quae predicta sunt a patribus nostris. Propter quod magis arbitratus sum hunc libellum de Greco in Latinum vertere †laboravi.†

cule [us], even if it would benefit their ears and those of others to hear the truth, especially in these times in which we can see ourselves fettered both by [evil] deeds and vices) to the ears of those present, and of the disdainful in particular, or better or more appropriately into their thoughts I have imparted the teaching of the departed doctors and the ancient fathers who have long been asleep in Christ.

So I have undertaken to translate the sayings of the blessed Methodius, bishop and martyr, from the Greek into the Latin language, also because what was prophesied is more relevant to our own times, "upon whom the ends of the world," as the Apostle Paul says, "are come,"[2] so that now through those very things which we discern with our own eyes we may believe to be true what was foretold by our fathers. For which reason I thought it all the more important to work[3] at translating this little book from Greek into Latin.

Caput 1

Sciendum namque est, quomodo exeuntes Adam quidem et Eva de paradyso virgines fuisse. In anno autem XXX^{mo} expulsionis eorum de paradyso genuerunt Cain primogenitum et sororem eius Calmanan et post XXX^{mo} alium annum pepererunt Abel cum sororem eius Debboram.

2 Anno autem treginsimo et centisimo vitae Adae occidit Cain fratrem suum Abel et fecerunt planctum super eum Adam quoque et Eva in annis C. CC^{mo} autem et XXX^{mo} anno primi miliari, quod est primum seculum, natus est Sedh vir gigans in similitudinem Adae. Quingentisimo vero anno in eadem primi chiliadem fili Cain abutebantur uxores fratrum suorum in fornicationibus nimis.

3 <. . .> Sexscentesimo autem anno ipsius primi miliarii stuprum amoris fornicationis istorum mulieres conlapsae sunt vel defusae et in vesaniam verse sunt: nam suis viris tamquam mulieribus supergressae utebantur, et facti sunt viri,

Chapter 1

Surely it ought to be known that when they left paradise Adam himself and Eve were virgins. In the 30th year, however, of their expulsion from paradise they bore Cain their firstborn and his sister Calmana. And after another 30 years they gave birth to Abel along with his sister Deborah.

In the hundred and thirtieth year of the life of Adam Cain 2 killed his brother Abel and Adam and also Eve lamented over him for 100 years. In the 230th year of the first millennium, that is also the first age, Seth was born, a gigantic man in the likeness of Adam. In the five hundredth year in the same first millennium the sons of Cain abused the wives of their own brothers in excessive fornications.

In the six hundredth year of this first millennium their 3 women fell into the defilement of the love of fornication, or rather they were poured out[4] and turned to madness, for they went on top and used their own men as if they were

clarius ut dicam, confusio videntibus et in fornicationem suam inverecundae apparentibus.

4   DCCC^{mo} autem anno vitae Adae dilatatum est super terram fornicationis inmunditiam a filiis fratricidae Cain.

5   Mortuus est autem Adam anno DCCCC et XXX vitae suae in primo miliario. Et tunc disiuncti sunt ab invicem, hoc est generatio Seth a cognatione Cain. Et abstulit Seth suam cognationem sursum in quendam montem, proximus paradyso qui erat. Habitabant quoque Cain et huius cognatio in campo, in quo et nefandum fratris homicidium perpetravit. XL vero anno temporis Iared pertransivit primum miliarium seu prima generatio.

Caput 2

Anno autem CCCXL Iared secundo miliario surrexerunt viri malae artis, inventores iniqui et omni nefariae pleni, ex filiis Cain, id est Iobeth et Tholucel, filii Lamech, qui fuit caecus, qui et Cain interfecit. Quos et[5] dominatus diabolos convertit eos post omnem speciem musicam conponendi.

2   Anno autem D secundi miliarii adhuc etiam maius[6] exarserunt in obscinissimam fornicationem omnes homines in castris Cain, peius facti priori generationis. Qui et in more animalium in alterutrum convenientes insurgebant, et

women, and they became men, or if I might speak more clearly, a confusion to those who saw and shameless in their own fornication to those who came in sight.

In the 800th year of the life of Adam the filth of fornica- 4 tion was spread over the earth by the sons of the brother-slayer Cain.

Adam died in the 930th year of his life in the first millen- 5 nium. And then they were divided from each other, that is the family of Seth from the kin of Cain. And Seth took away his kin up to a certain mountain, which was near paradise. And Cain and his kin dwelled on the very plain in which he committed the wicked murder of his brother. In the 40th year of the time of Jared the first millennium, or first generation, passed away.

Chapter 2

In the 340th year of Jared in the second millennium men of evil art rose up, inventors of wickedness and full of every outlawry, out of the sons of Cain, that is Ioubeth and Thouloukel, the sons of Lamech, who was blind, and who killed Cain. The Devil mastered them and turned them after the composing of every kind of music.[5]

In the 500th year of the second millennium all of the 2 people in the camp of Cain were even more inflamed in their most abominable fornication, and they became worse than the previous generation.[6] And they mounted one another in the manner of animals, and even onto the male [or] female

quidem in virilem muliebrem sexum <. . .>. Similiter isdem turpissimis et incestis actibus hi, qui erant de cognatione Cain, utebantur.

3   DCC autem tempore Iared vitae suae anno, quod est in secunda chiliadeam, apposuit malignus et infestus diabolos bellum fornicationis adiungere filiis Seth, ut concupiscerent filias Cain et proiciens apparuerunt gigantes super terra[7] de Seth, qui in peccati foveam conlapsi atrocissimi facti sunt. Et iratus dominus Deus in explicionem secundi milarii factum est dilluvium aquarum et omnis creatura prima deleta est vel absorta. Deperiit generatio primi hominis figmenti.

Caput 3

Et DCXII anno vitae Noe, iam in <. . .> trium milium annorum, postquam exivit Noe de arca, aedificaverunt filii Noe novam possessionem in exteriora terra et appellaverunt nomen regionis illius Thamnon secundum noncupationem numeri, qui exierunt de archa, id est VIII.

2   C autem anno de tercia chiliadea natus est Noe filius secundum ipsius similitudinem et vocavit nomen eius Ionitum. CCC vero tempore de trium milium annorum dedit Noe donationes filio suo Ionito et demisit eum in terram Eoam.

3   Et post obitum Noe DCXC anno in eosdem[8] trium milium annorum ascenderunt filii Noe de terra Eoam et

[indiscriminately] <. . .> Likewise those who were of the kin of Cain practiced these same most base and unchaste deeds.

In the 700th year of the life of Jared, that is in the second millennium, the spiteful and troublesome Devil applied himself to bringing the war of fornication to the sons of Seth, so that they should desire the daughters of Cain, and, as he pushed them on, there appeared giants in the earth,[7] [the sons] of Seth, who fell into the pit of sin and became altogether dreadful. And the Lord God was angered at the outcome of the second millennium; a flood of waters came about and all of the first creation was wiped out or swallowed up. The generation of the first man formed perished.

Chapter 3

And in the 612th year of the life of Noah, already in the <. . .> of the third millennium, after Noah left the ark, the sons of Noah built a new estate in the outer earth and they called the name of this region Thamnon after the name of the number of those who left the ark, that is 8.[8]

In the 100th year of the third millennium a son was born to Noah according to his likeness and he called his name Jonitus. In the 300th year of the third millennium Noah gave gifts to his son Jonitus and sent him away into the land of Eoa.[9]

And after the death of Noah in the 690th year into the same third millennium the sons of Noah went up from the land of the East and built for themselves a tower in the land

aedificaverunt sibi turrem in terra Sennahar. Et illuc divisi sunt linguae; et dispersae⁹ sunt super faciem totius terrae.

4 Ionitus autem, filius Noe, introovit in Eoam usque ad mare, qui vocatur "Hiliu Chora," id est "Regio Solis," in quo solis ortum fit, et habitavit ibidem.

5 Hic Ionitus accipit a Deo donum sapientiae, qui non solum hoc tantum, sed et omnem astronomiae articulum¹⁰ factusque inventor. Ad hunc discendens Nebroth, qui fuit gigans, et eruditus ab eo accipit ab illo consilium, in quibus regnare coepisset. Hi<c> autem Nebroth ex filiis discendebat hiroum; qui fuit filius Sem et ipse primus regnavit super terram.

6 DCC vero et XC <anno> terciae chiliadae, quod agebatur trium milium annorum, aedificata est Babillon magnam et regnavit in ea Nebroth. Et post haec faecerunt sibi filii Cham regem ex ipsis, cui nomen est Pontipus. Et iam DCCXC et nono anno temporis trium millium annorum, anno tertio regni Nebroth, miserunt viros potentes ex filiis Iapheth, sapientes [et] artifices <et> arte tectonicam constructores, et discenderunt in Eoam terram ad Ionitum, filium Noe, et aedificaverunt ei civitatem, quam nuncupaverunt Ionitum iuxta nominis illius noncupationem.

7 Et pax multa erat in regno Ioniti et Nebroth usque in praesentem diem. In regno autem Nebroth, filii Sem, et Pontipum, filii Cham, <non erat pax. In diebus enim Nebroth filii Cham>¹¹ et Iapheth contra invicem rebellabant.

8 Scripsit ergo Ionitus epistolam ad Nebroth ita quia "Regnum filiorum Iaphedi, hic incipiet delere regnum filiorum

of Shinar. And there the tongues were divided and they were scattered over the face of the whole earth.[10]

Jonitus, the son of Noah, entered into Eoa as far as the 4 sea, which is called "Hiliu Chora," that is "the Country of the Sun," in which the rising of the sun takes place, and he lived there.

This Jonitus received from God the gift of wisdom; not 5 only this alone, but he also became the inventor of every division of astronomy. Nimrod, who was a giant, came down to him and learned from him and received from him the counsel by which[11] he might begin to rule. This Nimrod was descended from the sons of heroes; he was a son of Shem and he was the first to rule as a king over the earth.

In the 790th <year> of the third millennium, which is the 6 passing of three thousand years, Babylon the Great was built and Nimrod ruled in it. And after these things the sons of Ham made a king for themselves out of their own number, whose name was Pontipus. And in the 790th and ninth year of the time of the third millennium, in the third year of the reign of Nimrod, they sent strong men from the sons of Japheth, wise craftsmen and builders with skill in architecture, and they went down into the land of Eoa to Jonitus the son of Noah and built a city for him, which they named Jonitus after the form of his name.

And there was a great peace in the reign of Jonitus and 7 Nimrod up to the present day. But in the reign of Nimrod the son of Shem and Pontipus the son of Ham <there was not peace. For in the days of Nimrod the sons of Ham> and of Japheth made war[12] against each other.

So Jonitus wrote a letter to Nimrod thus, that "this king- 8 dom of the sons of Japheth will begin to wipe out the

Cham." Haec autem regna primo apparuerunt in terra et post haec dedicerunt omnes gentes constituere sibi regnum.

Caput 4

Post regnum igitur Nebri, expletam[12] iam tertiam[13] chiliadem † annorum <. . .> anno VIII† quartae chiliadis, semper pugnabant ad invicem utrumque regna. Et divictum est regnum Aegyptiorum a regno Nebroth. Et optinuit potentatum regnum Babillonis in semine Nebroth usque ad Chuzimisdem. Hic accipit sibi uxorem de filiis Cham.

2   Defuncto autem Chuzimisdem sumpsit Ezdem,[14] huius nepus, matrem eius in uxorem et genuit ei Eresdem. Hic congregavit sibi virtutes multas et surrexit adversus regnum *<filiorum>* Cham et captibavit et concremavit igni omnes regiones, quae erant ab Occidente.

3   In secundo anno regni Chosdri, filii Eresdim, congregati sunt autem filii Cham et descenderunt in terram Eoam, ut praeliarent cum regem[15] Chosdron. Fuerunt autem trecenta et viginti milia peditum, virgas solummodo manibus contenti.

4   Audiens autem de his Chosdro subrisit et dimisit eos, usque dum transissent fluminem Tigrem. Et illuc mittens contra eos exercitum suum super elephantos ascendentes, omnes eos interfecit, et non est relictus ex eis quisquam.

kingdom of the sons of Ham." These were the first kingdoms to appear on the earth and after these all peoples learned to establish kingdoms for themselves.

Chapter 4

So after the reign of Nimrod, when the third millennium had already been completed, †in the eighth <. . .> year† of the fourth millennium, both kingdoms were constantly fighting against one another. And the kingdom of the Egyptians was defeated by the kingdom of Nimrod. And the kingdom of Babylon gained dominion in the posterity of Nimrod until Chuzimizdes. This man took a wife for himself from among the sons of Ham.

When Chuzimizdes died, his descendant Ezdes took his 2 own mother to wife and she bore him Eresdes. This man gathered to himself many powers and rose up against the kingdom <of the sons> of Ham and he captured and burned with fire all the lands which are from the west.[13]

In the second year of the reign of Chosdro, the son of 3 Eresdes, the sons of Ham were assembled and went down to the land of Eoa so that they might make war with King Chosdro. They were three hundred and twenty thousand foot soldiers, armed with only sticks in their hands.

When Chosdro heard about them he grinned and dis- 4 missed them until they crossed the Tigris River. And there he sent against them his own army mounted on elephants and he killed them all, and not one of them was left alive.

Et amplius non adposuerunt filii Cham, ut pugnarent cum eis. Et ex tunc inamaricatae sunt regna contra invicem.

Caput 5

Et in fine quattuor milium annorum, sive in XXV adhuc temporis <. . .> chiliades, discendit Sampsisahib[16] de Eoam, qui fuit de cognatione Ioniti, filii Noe, et depopulatus est ab Eufraten usque ad Edroigan, id est LXVII civitates et regionis earum.

2   Et pertransivit in tribus regnis Indorum et incendit et desolavit. Et exiit in desertum Saba et concidit castra filiorum Ismahel, filii Agar Aegyptiae, ancillae Sarrae, uxoris Abrahae. Et expulsi sunt omnes et fugierunt de solitudinem Ethribum et introierunt in terra inhabitabilem et pugnaverunt cum reges gentium. Et depopulati sunt et captivaverunt et dominati sunt regna gentium, quae erant in terra promissionis.

3   Et repleta est ex eis et de castra illorum. Erant autem quasi locustae et incedebant nudo corpore et edebant carnes camellorum conposite in utribus et bibebant sanguinem iumentorum in lacte mixto.

4   Cumque igitur obtenuissent filii Ismael universam terram et desolassent urbes et regiones eorum et dominassent in omnibus insulis, tunc illoque tempore construxerunt sibi

And the sons of Ham have not given up[14] fighting against them yet. And since then the kingdoms have been in enmity against one another.

Chapter 5

And at the end of the fourth millennium, or in the 25th year of the <. . . > millennium, Sampsisahib, who was of the kin of Jonitus the son of Noah, came down from the East and laid waste the country from the Euphrates to Edroiga, that is 67 cities and their territories.

And he passed through the three kingdoms of the Indians and burned them and devastated them. And he came out into the desert of Sheba and broke up the encampment of the sons of Ishmael the son of Hagar the Egyptian, the maidservant of Sarah the wife of Abraham. And they were all driven out and fled from the desert of Yathrib and came into the inhabited world and fought with the kings of the nations. And they laid them waste and took them captive and gained dominion over the kingdoms of the nations which were in the Promised Land. 2

And [the land] was filled with them and with their encampment. They were like locusts[15] and went about naked and ate the meat of camels prepared in skins and drank the blood of cattle with milk mixed in. 3

So when the sons of Ishmael overcame the whole land and laid waste cities and their territories and dominated the islands, they then built for themselves ships and using them 4

navigia et in modum volucrum his utentibus advolabant super aquas maris. Ascenderunt igitur et in regionibus Occidentis usque ad magnam Romam et Illyrico et Gigitum et Thesalonica et Sardiniae magnae, quae est trans illa Romam. Et dominati sunt terrae in annis LX et fecerunt in ea quecumque voluerunt.

5   Post vero ebdomadas octo et dimidiam eorum potentatus, per quem obtinuerunt universarum regnum gentium, superexaltatum est cor eorum, dum se viderent obtenuisse et dominasse omnia.[17]

6   In tempore autem illo facti sunt eis tyrranni, principes militiae quattuor, qui fuerunt filii Umeae, quae ab eis sic vocabatur, quorum nomina sunt haec: Oreb et Zeb et Zebee et Salmana. Hi pugnaverunt cum Israhelitae et, quem ad modum fecit eis Deus redemptionem de manu[18] Aegyptiorum per Moysen famulum suum, eodem vero modo etiam tunc illo tempore operatus est cum eis misericordiam et redimit eos ex eis per Gedeon. Et liberatus est de servitute filiorum Ismahel.

7   Hic enim Gedeon concidit castra eorum et persequens eiecit eos de terra inhabitabilem in solitudinem Ethribum, de qua et prodierant.

8   Et qui relicti sunt, dederunt foedera pacis filiis Israhel. Et exierunt in desertum exteriorem novem tribus. Futuri sunt autem, ut exeant aliud semel et destitutam faciant terram et obtinere orbem terrae et regionis in introitu pacis a terra Aegypti usque Aethiopia et ab Euphraten usque Indias et a Tigren usque ad introitum Naod regni Ioniti, filii Noe, et ab aquilone usque Romam et Ilirico et Gigitu et Thesalonicam

in the manner of birds they flew forth over the waters of the sea. So they came up to all the lands of the West as far as Great Rome and Illyricum and Gigitum and Thessalonica and Sardinia the Great, which is across from Rome. And they were lords of the earth for 60 years and did whatever they pleased in it.

After eight and a half weeks of their dominion, through- 5 out which they prevailed over the kingdom of all the nations, the heart was exalted within them when they saw that they were conquerors and lords of all.

In that time there arose among them tyrants, four chiefs 6 of the army, who were sons of Umaia (who was thus called by them), whose names were Oreb and Zeeb and Zebah and Zalmuna.[16] These men fought with the Israelites, and just as God brought about for them deliverance out of the hand of the Egyptians through his servant Moses, so also at that time he had mercy on them and delivered them from them through Gideon. And he was freed from slavery to the sons of Ishmael.[17]

For this Gideon broke up their encampment and pursued 7 them and drove them out of the inhabited world into the desert of Yathrib, from which they had come.

And those who were left made peace treaties with the 8 sons of Israel. And nine tribes went out into the outer desert. It will come about that they will come out once again and make the land desolate and prevail over the whole world and the regions at the entrance of peace[18] from the land of Egypt to Ethiopia and from the Euphrates to India and from the Tigris to the entrance of Nod,[19] the kingdom of Jonitus the son of Noah, and from the north to Rome and Illyricum and Gigitum and Thessalonica and Olbania and as far as the

et Olbaniae et usque ad mare, quae Ponto mittit. Et erit iugum eorum duplex super cervices omnium gentium.

9 Et non erit gens aut regnum sub caelo, qui possint eos expugnare usque ad numerum temporum ebdomadarum VII. Et post haec devincuntur a regno caelesti et Romanorum, etiam subiciuntur ei. Etenim hoc regnum magnificabitur, id est Romanorum, super omnia regna gentium et nequaquam delebitur a nullo eorum in aeternum. Habent enim arma inexpugnabilem, per quem omnes deiciuntur adversarii eius.

Caput 6

Abhinc igitur considerate a circumgyrantium temporum regnantium, et haec est veritas rerum, que se ipsa clarius ostendit, absque ullo errorem caligines vel aliquam seductionem.

2 A Nebroth enim, qui fuit irous, usque ad Perrusdec regna gigantium obtenuit terra Babyllonia. Et a Perusdec usque ad Ses seniores, qui fuit de Hidruhigam, regnabant Persi. Et a Ses usque ad Perusdech regnaverunt de Lec et a Phun. Et a Perusdec usque ad Seneribec et Babylloniae regnabant.

3 Et accepit Seneribec uxorem Iecnad de Ararat. Et peperit ei Ardemelech et Tzaratzar. Et hi interfecerunt patrem suum et fugierunt in terra Ararat.

4 Et regnavit illuc Saradon in Babyllonem pro patre suo Seneribech, et Nabucchodonossor, qui erat ex patre Luzia et ex matre reginae Saba.

sea which gives onto Pontus. And their yoke will be double on the necks of all the nations.

And there will not be a nation or a kingdom under heaven 9 which will be able to overcome them until the completion of 7 weeks of years. And after these things they will be defeated by the kingdom of heaven and of the Romans and subjected to it. For this kingdom, that is of the Romans, will be exalted over all the kingdoms of the nations and it will by no means be destroyed by any of them unto eternity. For they have an invincible weapon, through which all of its enemies will be defeated.

Chapter 6

From this time onward, therefore, ponder from the circling years of kings, and this is the truth of things which shows itself clearly without any obscure error or misleading.

For from Nimrod, who was a hero, until Perusdec the 2 kingdom of the giants prevailed over the land of Babylon.[20] And from Perusdec until Ses the old man, who was from Hidruhiga, the Persians ruled. And from Ses until Perusdec those from Lec and Phun ruled. And from Perusdec until Seneribec[21] they ruled in Babylon.

And Seneribec took as his wife Iecnad from Ararat. And 3 she bore him Ardemelech and Tzaratzar. And these men killed their own father and fled to the land of Ararat.[22]

And then Saradon reigned in Babylon in the place of his 4 father Seneribec, and Nebuchadnezzar, who was born of his father Luzia and his mother the queen of Sheba.

5   Cumque igitur introisset Seneribech ad pugnandum cum rege Indiae et usque Saba et desolasset quamplurimas regiones, convenit cum eo exisse Nabuchodonossor, illo videlicet educens eum simulque secum, et constituit eum principem militiae suae. Et propter sapientiam, que in illo erat, et potentiam datum est ei regnum Babylloniae.

6   Et sumpsit sibi uxorem de Medis, nomine Erusdem. Et post obitum Nabocchodonossor et Baltasar, filii eius, regnavit Darius Medus, nepus Erusdem. Darius autem duxit uxorem Dorun, Persissa genere, de qua natus est Chores Persus.

Caput 7

Audi nunc igitur, quomodo conmixti sunt hi reges cum invicem sibi, et hi quidem Babyllonis Mediis et Perses vero cum Medis. Et obtenuit[19] et potentior factum est regnum Babyllonis[20] quam Aethiopiae et Saba et omnium regum gentium a mare usque ad Euphraten flumine. Adhuc autem et Daviticum regnum per Nabuchodonossor devinctum est, etiam et Arabeorum et Aegyptorum.

2   Darius ergo Medus supergressus est regnum Indorum et Aethiopum. Chores autem Persus obtenuit[21] Thraciam et redimet[22] filios Israhel et misit in terra[23] promissionis praecipiens eis aedificare templum Dei, quod destructum erat ab Nabuchodonossor. Et propter hoc factum est secundum imperium Chores regis.

So when Seneribec came to fight with the king of India 5
even as far as Sheba and devastated many countries, it was
fitting that Nebuchadnezzar go out with him; that is to say
[Seneribec] brought him out along with him, and appointed
him the general of his army. And because of the wisdom that
was in him, and the power, the kingdom of Babylon was
granted to him [Nebuchadnezzar].

And he took a wife for himself from the Medes, Erusdem 6
by name. And after the death of Nebuchadnezzar and of
Belshazzar his son, Darius the Mede,[23] the descendant of
Erusdem, reigned. Darius married Dorun, a Persian by na-
tionality, from whom Chores the Persian was given birth.

Chapter 7

So hear now how these kings were joined with one another, those of Babylon with the Medes, and the Persians
with the Medes. And the kingdom of Babylon prevailed and
became more powerful than Ethiopia and Sheba and all the
kings of the nations from the sea to the Euphrates River. It
went so far that even the kingdom of David, as well as that
of the Arabs and the Egyptians, was defeated through Nebuchadnezzar.

Darius the Mede defeated the kingdom of the Indians 2
and Ethiopians. Chores the Persian prevailed over Thrace
and delivered the sons of Israel and sent them to the Promised Land with orders to build the temple of God which had
been destroyed by Nebuchadnezzar. And because of this it
happened according to the command of King Chores.

Caput 8

Audi igitur nunc certisseme, quomodo quatuor haec regna convenierunt sibi: Aethiopes enim Macedonis et Romanis Greci. Haec sunt quattuor venti <...> cummoventes mare magnum.

2   Philippus namque pater Alexandri quidem Macedon fuit et accepit in coniugium[24] Cuseth,[25] filia regis Phol Aethiopiae, de qua hic natus est Alexander, Gregorum tyrranus factus.

3   Hic condedit Alexandriam magnam et regnavit in ea annis XVIIII. Iste discendens in Eoam occidit Darium Medorum et dominatus est multarum regionum et civitatum et demultavit terram et discendit usque ad mare, qui vocatur "Regio Solis," ubi conspexit gentes inmundas et aspectu orribilis.

4   Sunt autem ex filiis Iapeth nepotes, quorum inmunditiam videns exorruit.[26] Commendebant enim hi omnes cantharo speciem omnem coinquinabilem vel spurcebilem, id est canes, mures, serpentes, morticinorum carnes, aborticia, informabilia corpora et ea, que in alvo necdum † per leniamenta † coaculata sunt vel ex aliqua parte † membrorum producta conpago † formam figmenti possit perficere vultum vel figuram expremere et haec iumentorum, necnon etiam et omnem speciem ferarum inmundarum.[27] Mortuos autem nequaquam sepeliunt, sed sepe commedent eos.

5   Haec vero universa contemplatus Alexander ab eis

Chapter 8

So now hear most certainly how these four kingdoms came together among themselves, the Ethiopians with the Macedonians and the Greeks with the Romans. These are the four winds <. . .> disturbing the great sea.[24]

For Philip, the father of Alexander, was a Macedonian 2 and he received in marriage Chuseth, the daughter of King Phol of Ethiopia, and from her was born this Alexander, who became tyrant of the Greeks.

This man founded Alexandria the Great and ruled in it 3 for 19 years. He went down to Eoa and slew Darius of the Medes and gained dominion over many countries and cities and he subdued the earth and went down to the sea, which [place] is called the Country of the Sun, where he caught sight of unclean and ugly nations.

These are the descendants of the sons of Japheth, whose 4 uncleanness he saw and he shuddered at. For all of them eat in the semblance of the beetle[25] every polluted and filthy thing, dogs, mice, snakes, carrion, abortions, miscarriages, and those which in the womb †because of softening† had not yet formed a solid from a liquid or a structure made of any part of the limbs which might in form and figure produce an appearance or imitate a shape,[26] and the miscarriages of animals, as well as every kind of unclean animal. They never bury their dead, but often eat them.[27]

Alexander considered all of these things, that they were 5

inmunditer et sceleriter fieri, timens ne quando eant exilientes in terra sancta et illa contaminent a pollutis suis iniquissimis affectionibus, depraecatus est Deum inpensius. Et praecipiens congregavit eos omnes mulieresque eorum et filius et omnia scilicet castra illorum.

6   Et eduxit eos de terra orientale et conclusit minans[28] eos, donec introissent in finibus Aquilonis. Et non est introitus nec exitus ab Oriente usque in Occidentem, [quis] per quod *<quis>*[29] possit ad eos transire vel introire.

7   Continuo ergo supplicatus est Deum Alexander, et exaudivit eius obsecrationem et praecipit Dominus Deus duobus montibus, quibus est vocabulum "Ubera Aquilonis," et adiuncti proximaverunt invicem usque ad duodecem cubitorum.

8   Et construxit portas aereas et superinduxit eas asincitum, ut, si voluerint eas patefacere in ferro, non possunt aut dissolvere per igne nec valeant utrumque, sed statim ignis omnis extinguitur. Talis enim est natura asinciti, quia neque ferro confringitur ictus[30] ferientes[31] neque igne suscipit resolutionem. Universas enim adinventiones daemonum et calliditates mortiferas vel supervacuas opera[n]tur.[32]

9   Haec obscinissime et deforme vel sordidae gentes cuncta[33] [que] magicae artis malorum abuttuntur inmunditer. Etiam in his illorum sordidam et inhumanam, magis autem, ut conpetenter dicitur, Deo odibilem distructa est maleficia, ita ut non possint neque ferro neque per igne vel quodcumque libet aliud astuciam easdem reserare vel aperire portas et fugire.

being done by them in an unclean and wicked manner, and he feared lest they ever leave and go to the Holy Land and pollute it with their defiled and unjust state of body and mind, and so he earnestly supplicated God. And issuing commands he gathered all of them together, and their wives and their sons and, of course, all of their camps.

And he led them out of the eastern land and hemmed 6 them in and drove them on until they came to the furthest regions of the North. And there is neither a way in nor a way out from east to west, through which one might be able to cross over or go in to them.

Therefore Alexander immediately called upon God, and 7 the Lord God heard his prayer and commanded two mountains, whose name is the Paps of the North, and they were joined together and drew as close as twelve cubits to one another.

And he constructed brazen gates and covered them with 8 asincitum, so that if they should want to open them with iron they would not be able or to dissolve them with fire they would not prevail either, rather straightaway all the fire would be quenched. For the nature of asincitum is such that neither is it broken by the striking blows of iron nor does it undergo dissolution by fire. For it is effective with all the inventions of the demons and deadly and useless contraptions.

These filthy and misshapen or vile nations employed in 9 unclean fashion all of the evils of magical art. And in these things too their sordid and inhuman, or, to put it more strongly, hateful to God, sorcery was undone, so that they were not able by fire or iron or any other conceivable cunning to unlock or open these same gates and make their escape.

10 In novissimis vero temporibus secundum Ezechielis prophetiam, que dicit: "In novissimo die consummationes mundi exiet Gog et Magog in terra Israel," qui sunt gentes et reges, quos retrusit Alexander in finibus Aquilonis. Gog et Magog et Anog et Ageg et Achennaz et Dephar et Putinei et Libii et Eunii et Pharizei et Declemi et Zarmathae[34] et Theblei et Zarmatiani et Chachonii et Amazarthe et Agrimardii et Anuphagii, qui dicuntur Cynocephali, et Tharbei et Alanes et Physolonicii et Arcnei et Asalturii. Hi viginti duo reges consistunt reclusi intrinsecus portarum, quas confixit Alexander.

Caput 9

Defuncto igitur namque Alexandro, primus rex Gregorum, regnaverunt pro eo quattuor pueri eius: non enim coniunctus est matrimonio aliquando. Chuseth vero mater eius regressa est in propriam patriam Aethyopiam.

2   Byzas igitur, qui Byzantium condedit, misit per mare ad Phol, regem Aethiopiae, Germanicum, sui exercitus principem, et pacificavit cum eo, scribens ei de Chuseth, matrem Alexandri, qualiter eam sibi accipiat in uxorem et regnificet eam.

3   Suscipiens ergo Phol rex litteras a Germanico et videns que detulerat largissima dona, et accipiens nimis laetatus est. Surrexit igitur et ipse et congregans ex omnibus speciorum[35] Aethiopiae sumensque pariter et filiam suam Chuseth

In the end times, according to what the prophecy of Eze- 10
kiel says, in the last day of the consummation of the world
will come out into the land of Israel Gog and Magog,[28] who
are the nations and kings that Alexander hid in the ends of
the North. Gog and Magog and Anog and Ageg and Achennaz and Dephar and the Putinaeans and Libians and Eunians and Pharizeans and Declemans and Zarmats and The-
bleans and Zarmatians and Chachonians and Amazarthans
and Agrimardians and Anuphagians, who are called Cyno-
cephalians, and the Tharbeans and Alans and Physoloni-
cians and Arcneans and Asalturians. These twenty-two kings
reside shut up within the gates that Alexander fixed.

Chapter 9

So then, when Alexander, the first king of the Greeks,
died, his four servants reigned in his stead, for he was never
joined in marriage. Chuseth his mother returned to her own
homeland, Ethiopia.

Therefore Byzas, who founded Byzantium, sent German- 2
icus, the chief of his army, by sea to Phol, the king of Ethiopia, and made peace with him, and wrote to him concerning
Chuseth, the mother of Alexander, [and] how he might take
her as a wife for himself and make her queen.

So when King Phol took the letter from Germanicus and 3
noticed what exceedingly bountiful gifts he had brought, he
received them and was quite delighted. Accordingly he himself arose, gathered together samples of all the fair sights of
Ethiopia, and taking along his daughter Chuseth as well, he

profectus est in Byzantium abens secum XXX milia Aethiopum in comitatu. Et susceptus est a Byzas protinus foras[36] trans mare in Calcidonum cum multa nimiaque alacritate animi. Dedit autem et dona cupiosa valde his, qui cum eo fuerant. Et introivit Phol in Byzantem et dedit munera magna et dona maxima secundum regalem magnanimitatem.

4   Et accipit rex Byzas Chuseth, filiam Phol regis Aethiopiae, ex qua ei nata est filia, quam et nuncupavit in nomine civitatis Byzanteam, quam et nuptus est Romyllus,[37] qui et Armaleus, rex Romae. Propter nimiam autem pulchritudinem eius dilexit eam valde. Erat quippe et ipse nimis simplex et magnanimus, unde et in dotalibus eius, ut sunt matrimonialia, donavit ei Romam. Audientes autem optimatis eius indignati sunt contra eum.

5   Peperit vero ei Bizantea filios tres, quos et nuncupavit, primogenitum quidem secundum appellationem patris Armaleum, secundum autem Urbanum, tertium denominavit Claudium.

6   Regnaverunt igitur uterque, et quidem Armaleus in Romam pro patri suo Armaleo, Urbanus vero in Byzam civitatem matris suae, Claudius autem in Alexandria.

7   Optinuit igitur semen Chuseth, filiae Phol regis Aethiopiae, Macedonumque et Romanorum <. . .> ex semine Aethiopum. Haec "praeveniet manus eius Deo" in novissimo die secundum propheticam expositionem. Providens autem beatus David spiritalibus oculis et praenoscens, quomodo Chuseth, filia Phol regis Aethiopiae, incipiet exsuscitare regnum Romanorum, praefatus est dicens: "Aethiopia praeveniet manus eius Deo." Quidam igitur consideraverunt,

set out for Byzantium taking with him thirty thousand Ethiopians in his train. And he was welcomed directly by Byzas with much and great gladness of heart outside [the city] across the sea at Chalcedon. And he gave very numerous presents to those who were with him. And Phol approached Byzas and gave him great honors and very great gifts according to kingly magnanimity.

And King Byzas took Chuseth, the daughter of Phol the 4 king of Ethiopia, from whom a daughter was born to him, whom he called Byzantea after the name of the city, and Romulus, who is also Armeleus, the king of Rome, married her. Because of her exceeding beauty he loved her very much. He was himself certainly very frank and generous, wherefore also among the goods of her dowry, which are the marriage gifts, he made a present to her of Rome. And when his grandees heard, they were vexed with him.

Byzantea bore three sons to him, and she named them, 5 the firstborn Armeleus after his father's name, the second Urbanus, and the third she called Claudius.

Accordingly they each ruled as king, Armeleus in Rome 6 in the place of his father Armeleus, Urbanus in Byzas his mother's city, and Claudius in Alexandria.

Therefore the seed of Chuseth, the daughter of Phol the 7 king of Ethiopia, gained <mastery> over the Macedonians and the Romans . . . from the seed of the Ethiopians. This one "shall stretch out her hands unto God" at the last day according to the word of the prophet. The blessed David looked ahead with the eyes of the spirit and foreknew that Chuseth, the daughter of Phol king of Ethiopia, would begin to rouse the kingdom of the Romans, and he prophesied saying, "Ethiopia shall stretch out her hands unto God."[29]

quia propter Aethiopum regnum conpulsus beatus David haec locutus est, sed mentiti sunt veritate, qui haec ita existimant,

8   siquidem etenim ex semine Aethiopisse constituto regno hoc constructum est magnum et venerabilem lignum sanctae et honorificum et vivificatoriae crucis, <quod> in medio terrae confixum est: unde fortassis, ut conpetet, ipse effatus est antiquus pater David, ita pronuntians: "Aethiopia praeveniet manus eius Deo." Non est enim gens aut regnum sub caelo, quae praevalere possunt superare regnum christianorum,

9   sicuti iam enim praefati locuti sumus superius —, quod in medio terrae vivificans confixa et solidata est crux, a quo et orbis terrae fines valde sapienterque discribuntur constare secundum latitudo quoque et longitudo et altitudo vel profundum. Qualisve possit vel quis poterit[38] virtutem superare umquam sanctae crucis <vel> adpraehendere potentiam? Sic enim obtinet venerationem Romani imperii dignitas, pollens per eum, qui in ea pependit, dominum nostrum Iesum Christum.

Caput 10

Audiamus igitur, quid praedicatur divinorum Paulus edocuit significans de novissimo die et Romanorum regnum. In quibusdam enim secundam ad Thesalonicensis epistolam ita inquid: "Rogamus itaque vos, fratres, per adventum Domini

So some have supposed that the blessed David was constrained by the kingdom of the Ethiopians when he said these things, but they play false with the truth who think thus,

Since in fact the great and venerable and honored wood ⁸ of the life-giving cross has been set up by the kingdom established from the seed of the Ethiopian lady, <which wood> is fixed in the midst of the earth: which is why—perhaps, as is fitting, the ancient father David himself made the statement, thus declaring, "Ethiopia shall stretch out her hands unto God." For there is no nation or kingdom under heaven which is able to prevail and overcome the kingdom of the Christians,

for just as we have already said above—, because the life- ⁹ giving cross has been fixed and made firm in the midst of the earth, by which the ends of the earth are very wisely described to be fixed according to breadth and length and height or depth. What manner of man or who would ever be able to overcome the strength of the Holy Cross <or> to grasp its power? For thus the grandeur of the Roman Empire gains respect, being powerful through him who was hanged upon it, our Lord Jesus Christ.

Chapter 10

So let us listen to what Paul, the preacher of the divine words,³⁰ taught, indicating the last day and the kingdom of the Romans. For in some of the same [passages], in the second letter to the Thessalonians, he spoke thus: "*Therefore*

nostri Iesu Christi et vestro conventui in id ipsum, ut non cito moveamini a senso vestro neque terreamini neque per spiritum neque per verbum neque per epistolam tamquam per nos missa, quasi instet adventus Domini; ne quis vos seducat ullomodo, quia nisi venerit discessio primum et revelatus fuerit homo iniquitatis, filius qui est perditionis, qui est adversarius et extollens se super omnem quod dicitur Deum aut quod colitur, ita ut in templo Dei sedeat ostendens se, quasi sit Deus," et post posillum: "Solummodo nunc," inquid, "qui tenet, teneat, donec e medio fiat, et tunc revelabitur iniquus."

2   Quis igitur est "e medio," nisi Romanorum imperium? Omnis enim principatus et potestas huius mundi distruetur[39] absque hunc.

3   Namque hic oppugnatur et non superabitur, et omnes gentes, quae cum eo confligunt, conterentur vel consumentur ab eo. Et obtenebit, donec ultima hora perveniet, et haec "preveniet manus eius Deo," etiam secundum apostolum dicentem: "cumque distruetur omnis principatus et potestas universa et ipse Filius tradederit regnum Deo et Patri." Qualem regnum? Scilicet Christianorum.

4   Ubi enim umquam erit vel fuit aut est regnum sive alia potentia, que super hunc emineat? Si volueris enim mihi, quod certum est, pertractare, accipe, quaeso te, mihi Mosaicum plebemque tantis signis et portentis et in profundum maris etiam Aegyptios excucientem. Vide mihi et Iesum

we beseech you, brethren, by the coming of our Lord Jesus Christ, and by *your coming together* unto *it,* that ye be not soon shaken in mind, or be troubled, neither by spirit, nor by *word,* nor by letter as from us, as that the *coming* of Christ is at hand. Let no man deceive you by any means: *because* that day shall not come, except there come a falling away first, and that man of *lawlessness* be revealed, the son *who is* of perdition; who *is an adversary* and exalteth *himself* above all that is called God, or that is worshipped; so that he as God sitteth in the temple of God, showing himself *as if he were* God," and after a little bit, "*only* he who now letteth will let, until he be taken out of the way [*or* midst], and then shall that wicked be revealed."[31]

Who then is the one "out of the midst," if not the empire of the Romans? For all rule and authority of this world will be ruined apart from her. 2

For it is also besieged and will not be overcome, and all the nations that dash themselves against it are ground up and spent by it. And it will prevail until the last hour will arrive and she "shall stretch out her hands unto God" and as the Apostle says, "when all rule and *all* authority" will be ruined and the Son himself "shall have delivered up the kingdom to God, even the Father."[32] What manner of kingdom? Quite clearly that of the Christians. 3

For when will there ever be or has there been or is there a kingdom or another power that could surpass it? Now if you should wish to examine what is certain to me, take as my proof, I ask you, the people of Moses who by so many signs and wonders cast even the Egyptians into the depth of the 4

Nave, sub quem etiam sol circa Gabaon stetit et luna circa vallem Hiericho. Et alia quam pluriora et stupenda Deo miracula fiunt et, ut verius clareque[40] dicam, omnem Hebreorum considera fortitudinem, quomodo sub Romanorum imperio deleta et contrita est. Titus igitur et Vespasianus conciserunt universus.[41] Numquid templum in aratro expugnans Adrianus non aravit? Quis ergo igitur fuit vel erit secundum hunc aliud regnum? Sed nullum vidilicet invinimus, <si> pro veritate curam geramus.

5   Nonne mille anni regnaverunt Hebrei? Et abscisum est regnum eorum! Aegyptii autem trium milium annorum, et ipse[42] nihilominus ita perierunt. Babyllonitae quattuor milium regnant annorum, sed et ipse similiter abscidentur. Concisione igitur Macedoniorum regnum sive Aegyptiorum conflixerunt armis adversus regnum Romanorum seu barbarorum regnum, id est Turcorum, et Abares, qui simul universi absorti ab eo sunt.

6   Itaque postquam absortum fuerit regnum Persarum, consurgent[43] pro illis adversus Romanorum imperium filii Hismahel, filii Agar, quos scriptura commemorans "australem brachium" appellavit, Danihel quoque hoc praedicens. Et contradicunt regno Romanorum in numero circumeuntium temporum, septimo ipso tempore annorum, id est in septemilium annorum mundi, eo quod adpropinquavit consumatio saeculi et non erit longitudo temporum amplius.

sea. Look, if you please, also to Joshua the son of Nun, under whom the sun stood still at Gibeon and the moon at the valley of Jericho.[33] And think of how many and how marvelous were the other miracles done by God, and, if I may speak truly and clearly, consider all the strength of the Hebrews, and how it was wiped out and ground down under the empire of the Romans. Titus and Vespasian then cut them all down. Did not Hadrian reduce the temple and plow it under with a plow? So what other kingdom has arisen or will arise after it? We shall surely find none at all, <if> we take care for truth.

Did not the Hebrews reign for a thousand years? Yet their 5 kingdom was cut off! And the Egyptians for three thousand years, nonetheless they perished even so. The Babylonians reigned for four thousand years, but they will be cut off likewise. So at the breaking up of the kingdom of the Macedonians, or the Egyptians, the kingdom of the barbarians, that is of the Turks, and the Abares clashed in arms with the kingdom of the Romans, and these were all swallowed up by it at once.[34]

And so after the kingdom of the Persians is swallowed up, 6 in their place against the empire of the Romans will rise up the sons of Ishmael, the son of Hagar, whom the scripture mentions, calling them "the arm of the south,"[35] and Daniel predicts this too. And they oppose the kingdom of the Romans in the number of the circling times, in the seventh time of years, that is in the seventh millennium of the world, because the end of the age has come and there will be no more length of time.

Caput 11

In novissimum enim miliarium,[44] seu septimo tunc agentem, in ipso eradicabitur regnum Persarum. Et in ipso septimo miliario incipient exire semin Ismahel de deserto Ethribum et, cum exierint, congregabuntur unanimes in magnam Gabaot.

2   Et illic conplebitur, quod dictum est per Ezechielem prophetam: "Fili hominis," inquid, "voca bestias agri et volatilia caeli et exhortare illa, dicens: Congregamini et venite eo quod sacrificium magnum immolo vobis. Manducate carnes fortium et bibite sanguinem excelsorum."

3   In hac itaque Gabaoth cadent in ore gladii <...> a semine Ismaheles, qui appellatus est "onager," eo quod in ira et furore mittuntur super faciem totius terrae, super homines quoque et iumenta et bestias silve et super omnem saltum et plantariam et super omnem nemorum et in omnem speciem fructiferam.

4   Et erit adventus eorum castigatio sine misericordia et praehibunt eis super terra quattuor iste plage, id est: interitus et perditio, corruptio quoque et desolatio.

5   Dicit enim Deus ad Israel per Moysen: "Non quia diligit[45] vos dominus Deus, introducit vos in terram promissiones, ut hereditemini eam, sed propter peccata inhabitantium in eam." Sic etenim filios Ismahel, non quod eos diligat dominus Deus, dabit eis potentiam hanc, ut obteneant terram

Chapter II

For in the last millennium, or the seventh which will then be under way, in that time the kingdom of the Persians will be uprooted. And in that seventh millennium the seed of Ishmael will begin to come out of the desert of Yathrib and when they will have come out they will be gathered together in one accord at Gabaoth the Great.

And there will be fulfilled what was said through the 2 prophet Ezekiel: "Son of man," he said, "call the beasts of the field and the birds of heaven, and urge them on, saying, 'Gather yourselves together and come, since I will offer a great sacrifice for you. Eat the flesh of the mighty and drink the blood of the lofty.'"[36]

At that place Gabaoth, therefore, they will fall at the 3 mouth of the sword <. . .> by the seed of Ishmael, who has been called a wild ass,[37] because in wrath and anger they are sent over the face of the whole world, over men and stock animals and the beasts of the wood and over every grove and sapling and over all the copses and against every kind of fruitful thing.

And their arrival will be a chastisement without mercy 4 and these four blows will go before them over the earth, that is, death and destruction, and ruin and desolation.

For God says to Israel through Moses, "Not because the 5 Lord God loves you does he bring you into the Land of Promise, that you should inherit it, but because of the sins of those who dwell in it."[38] Just so with the sons of Ishmael, it is not because the Lord God loves them will he give them this power that they should conquer the land of the

christianorum, sed propter peccatum et iniquitatem, quae ab eis committitur. Similia eis non sunt facta, sed neque fiunt in omnebus generationibus.

6 Namque igitur induentur viri adulterinis muliercolis et meretricum indumenta et quemadmodum muliercolas semetipsos exornabant stantes in plateis et in foribus civitatum palam omnibus et "inmutaverunt naturalem usum in eum, qui est contra natura," sicuti beatus quoque et sacratissimus apostolus inquid. Similiter et mulieres haec, quod et viri, agentes.

7 Convenerunt itaque uni muliere pater simul et filius illius et frater et universi, qui cognatione adiunti videntur. Ignorabantur enim a meretricibus. Propter quod sapientissimus Paulus ante temporum seriem fortassis exclamans ait: "Propter hoc enim" inquit, "tradedit illos Deus in passiones ignominiae, nam faeminae eorum conmutaverunt naturalem usum in eum usum, qui est extra naturam, similiter vero et masculi eorum demittentes naturalem usum faeminae exarserunt in desideriis suis in invicem, masculi in masculos turpitudinem operantes et retributionem mercidis[46] erroris sui in semetipsos recipientes."

8 Propter hoc igitur tradentur a Deo in manus barbarorum, a quibus cadent in omni[47] inmunditiam et fetorem pollutionis, et contaminantur mulieres eorum a pollutis barbaris. Et mittunt sortes filii Ismahel super filios et filias eorum.

9 Et traditur terra Persarum in corruptionem et perdictionem, et habitatores eius in captivitatem et occisionem abducentur, Armeniam quoque et eos, qui habitant in ea, in captivitatem et gladio corruent. Capadociam in

Christians, but because of the sin and lawlessness that are committed by them. For nothing like these things has been done nor will be done in all generations.

For indeed men arrayed themselves like adulterous 6 women in the apparel of harlots and adorned themselves as women standing in the streets and squares of the cities openly before all and they "did change the natural use into that which is against nature" as the blessed and most hallowed Apostle says.[39] Likewise women also did the same things as the men.

Accordingly a father along with his son and brother and 7 everyone who appears to be joined to him by kinship had intercourse with a single woman. For they were ignored by the prostitutes. For which reason the exceeding wise Paul before these times quite naturally decried them when he spoke: "*Since* for this cause God gave them up unto vile affections: for even their women did change the natural use into that which is *outside of* nature: *indeed* likewise also *their* men, *repressing* the natural use of the woman, burned in their lust one toward another; men with men working that which is unseemly, and receiving in themselves that *retribution* and recompense of their error."[40]

Therefore for this reason they are delivered by God into 8 the hands of barbarians, by which they will fall into all uncleanness and filth of pollution, and their women will be stained by the polluted barbarians. And the sons of Ishmael cast lots over their sons and their daughters.

And the land of the Persians will be handed over to ruin 9 and destruction and those who dwell in it will be led off into captivity and slaughter. Armenia and those who dwell in it will collapse into captivity and the sword. Cappadocia [will

corruptionem et in desolationem, et eius habitatores in captivitate et iugulationem absorbentur.

10 Sicilia erit in desolationem et eos, qui habitant in ea, in occisionem et captivitatem ducuntur. Terra Syriae erit in solitudinem et corrupta, et commorantes in ea in gladio perient. Cilicia desolabitur et, qui inhabitant in ea, erunt in corruptionem et in captivitatem ducentur.

11 Grecia in occisione gladii et perditionem vel corruptionem et, qui sunt eius habitatores, in captivitate ducuntur. Romania corrumpitur et in occisione erit et convertuntur in fugam. Et insulas maris in desolationem erunt et, qui in eis habitant, peribunt in gladio et in captivitate.

12 Aegyptus quoque et Oriens vel Siriam sub iugo erunt et in tribulationes inmensas coartantur. Angariabuntur enim sine misericordia et appetuntur super vires animarum suarum pondus auri vel argenti. Et erunt habitatores Aegypti vel Syriae in angustia et afflictionem septies tantum his, qui in captivitate sunt.

13 Et replebitur terra promissionis hominum a quattuor ventis, qui sub caelo sunt. Et erunt tamquam locustae in multitudinem, que congregabitur a vento, et erit in eis pestilentia et fames. Et exaltabitur cor eorum exterminatorum et in superbiam el<ev>abitur[48] et loquentur excelsa usque ad tempus constitutum eis et obtenebunt[49] introitumque et exitum aquilonis et eoam, occasum et a maritimo, et erunt omnia sub iugo eorum: homines quoque et iumenta, volatilia vel pisces mari natantia, etiam et aquis maris obaudient eis.

fall] into ruin and desolation, and her inhabitants will be swallowed up in captivity and murder.

Sicily will become a desolation and those who dwell in it 10 will be led into slaughter and captivity. The land of Syria will be [turned] into a desert and ruined and the inhabitants in it will die by the sword. Cilicia will be desolated and those who dwell in it will go to ruin and be led into captivity.

Greece will go to the slaughter of the sword and destruc- 11 tion or ruin and those who dwell in it will be led into captivity. Romania[41] will be ruined and go to slaughter and they will be turned to flight. And the islands of the sea will become a desolation and those who dwell on them will perish by the sword and in captivity.

Egypt, the East, and Syria will be under the yoke and will 12 be constrained into boundless afflictions. For they will be pressed into unsparing service, and a weight of gold or silver will be demanded of them above and beyond the strength of their spirits. And the inhabitants of Egypt or Syria will be in distress and affliction seven times worse than that of those in captivity.

And the Promised Land will be filled by men from the 13 four winds which are under heaven. And they will be like locusts for multitude,[42] which will be gathered by the wind, and there will be pestilence and famine in their midst. And the heart of those destroyers will be exalted and raised to arrogance and they will speak haughty words until the time appointed to them and they will prevail over the entrance and the exit of the North and Eoa, the West and from the seacoast, and all will come under their yoke, men and animals, birds or fish swimming in the sea, and even the waters of the sea will obey them.

14 Et destitute civitates, quae viduate ab eis de habitatoribus suis fuerunt, erunt illorum. Et scribent sibi terminos per solitudinem. Et ligna silvarum et pulverem terrae et lapides et ubertas terrae et pisces maris erunt in introitum eorum. Et labores vel sudores agricultorum terrae et hereditas divitum et, que inferuntur sanctis, sive aurum sive argentum sive lapides praetiosae seu aeramentum vel ferrum sit, omnia illorum erit. Indumenta etiam sacrata vel praeclara et escas omnes et omnem, quicquid praetiosum est, illorum erunt. Et exaltabitur cor eorum usque adeo, ut et mortuos appetant secundum aequalitatem vivorum. Similiter autem et ex pupillis et viduis et ex sanctorum exigentes.

15 Et non miseribuntur inopem et pauperem, omnem enim maiorem natum inhonorant et affligunt egenus et non habebunt viscera misericordiae neque super inbecillis et infirmos, sed inludent et derident omnes, qui in sapientia fulgebunt, et eos, qui in rebus rei publice magnificantur.[50] Et conticiscent universi silentio vel timore, non valentes arguere vel proloqui: "quid est hoc?" aut: "<quid> illud?," et obstupescent omnes pre timore, qui inhabitant terram. Et erit sapientia eorum et disciplina prodiens a semet ipsam[51] eis, non subcrescens neque †addendum vel adiciendum ad eam† et non erit, qui possit inmutare aut quirillare sermones eorum.

16 Et erit iter eorum a mari usque ad mari, et ab ortu solis usque ad occasum, et ab aquilone usque ad desertum Ethribum. Et vocabitur iter eorum viam angustiae et gradiuntur in ea senes et seniores sue, inopesque et divites, esurientes et sicientes, compediti, et beatificant eos, qui iam mortui sunt.

And the desolate cities which have been bereft of their [14] inhabitants by them will be theirs. And they will inscribe boundary markers for themselves through the desert.[43] And the timber of the forest and the dust of the earth and the stones and the produce of the land and the fish of the sea will be in their revenue.[44] And the work and the sweat of the tillers of the soil and the inheritance of the wealthy and the tithes to the holy, be it gold or silver or precious stones or bronze or iron, all will be theirs. Even the splendid sacred garments and all the food and everything which is of any value will be theirs. And their heart will be exalted until they demand as much from the dead as from the living.[45] Likewise they will exact dues from orphans and widows and from the consecrated.

And they will have no pity on the poor and needy, they [15] fail to revere every elder and crush the destitute and they will not have the bowels of compassion for the weak or for the feeble, but they will mock and laugh at all those who are illustrious in wisdom and those who are preeminent in the affairs of the republic. And everyone will become quiet in silence and fear, having no power to accuse or demand, "What is this?" or "<What> is that?" And everyone who dwells on the earth will be astounded with fear. And their wisdom and education will proceed from themselves to them, not increasing, nor added to, nor having addition to it, and there will be no one able to alter or to fault their speech.

And their road will go from sea to sea and from the rising [16] of the sun to its setting and from the north to the desert of Yathrib. And their road will be called a way of hardship, and old men and their older women will travel along it, rich and poor, hungry and thirsty, bound captives, and they will consider them happy who are already dead.

17   Etiam namque ab apostolo praedicta disciplina—seu discessio—haec est. Qui [ut] enim inquid: "nisi cum vinerit discessio primum et revelatus fuerit homo peccati, filius perditionis." Siquidem discessio est disciplina vel correptio et corripiuntur universi habitatores terrae. Et quoniam onager appellavit Deus Ismahelem patrem illorum, propter hoc onagri et capriae a deserto et omnem speciem bestiarum supergredien<*tum*> raviem et mansuetorum conterentur ab eis et paucitabunt sub eis et persequentur homines et bestias silvae famae interibunt eo, quod distituti sunt regiones terrae, et abscident omnem lignum saltui et speciem montium disperiet, et desolabuntur urbes et erunt regiones sine via, eo quod deminuta est humanitas, et polluetur terra a sanguine et continebit fructos suos. Non enim sunt homines qui tyrannico morae barbaricae nationes obtenentes, sed filii sunt a deserto exilientes et ideo in desolationem prodiunt. Corrupti sunt et in corruptionem mittentur, et odibiles sunt atque abhominabiles et ideo odium amplectuntur. Et in principio exitus eorum incipientes ab heremo habentibus in utero gladio perforabunt et fetum conpungent simul cum matribus, et infantes ab umeris nutricum rapientes percutient, et erunt bestiis in escam.

18   Sacerdotes autem intrensecus sanctorum locorum coinquinantes interficient et concumbent cum mulieribus intus in venerabilibus vel sacratis locis, in quibus mysticum et incontaminatum sacrificium perficitur caelebrandum. Et

For this is even the chastisement, that is the "falling 17
away," foretold by the Apostle. For he says, "except there
come a falling away first, and that man of sin be revealed, the
son of perdition."[46] Then indeed the falling away is a chastisement or a reproof, and all the inhabitants of the earth
are reproved. And since God called their father Ishmael a
wild ass, for this reason the wild asses and the wild goats
from the desert and every kind of beast, both those that live
in the wild[47] and the tame, will be ground down by them and
they will grow fewer under them and men will hunt [them],
and the beasts of the wood will perish in hunger because the
lands of the earth are forsaken, and they will cut down all
the timber of the woodland and the beauty of the mountains
will be undone, and cities will be made desolate and their
territories impassable because humanity is diminished,[48]
and the earth will be stained with blood and hold back her
fruits. For these are not men who rule the nations in tyran-
nical manner, in a barbaric fashion, but they are sons burst-
ing forth from the desert and so they proceed into desolation. They are corrupt and will be sent into corruption, and
they are hateful and detested and so they embrace what is
hateful. And at the beginning of their departure when they
set out from the desert they will stab the pregnant women
with a sword and pierce the unborn child along with their
mothers and snatch babies from the shoulders of their
nurses and smash them, and they will become food for the
beasts.

They will slaughter the priests within the sanctuaries af- 18
ter defiling them and go to bed with women in the venerable
and holy places, in which the mystic and uncontaminated
sacrifice that ought to be celebrated is carried out. And their

sacratas stolas superinduentur mulieres eorum et super filios suos inponent ea et super filias suas. Et in equis suis et
super lectis expandent ea et iumenta sua ad sepulchra sanctorum colligant tamquam ad praesipia. Et erunt homicidae
et percorrupti[52] et ignis probationis genere christianorum.

Caput 12

Sacratissimus enim apostolus inquid: "Non enim omnes,
qui ex Israhel, hi sunt Israhel." Itaque non omnes, qui dicuntur christiani, ipsi christiani sunt. "Septe enim," sicut dicit
Scriptura, "virorum milia salvati sunt filiorum Israhel, qui
non curvaverunt genua sua ante Baal," et omnis populus Israhel per eos salvi facti sunt.

2   Sic et in ipso tempore discessionis et eruditionis filiorum
Ismahel pauci inveniuntur christiani viri, quemadmodum
ipse Salvator noster in sanctis evangeliis dicit: "Utique veniens Filius hominis, putas, inveniet fidem in terram?" Mi-
nuetur vero in tempore illo spiritus perfectorum.[53]

3   Et multi abnegabunt viram fidem, vivificatoriam vero
crucem Christi et sancta mysteria. Etiam sine aliqua vim vel
tormenta[54] aut flagellis abnegant Christum et adsecuntur
transgressoribus.

4   Praecidens[55] enim divinitus plenus Apostolus praedicavit,
dicens quia "in temporibus illis recidunt quid<a>m a fidem,

wives will be clothed with the sacred robes and they will put them over their sons and over their daughters. And they will [put] them on their horses and spread them over their beds, and they will tie up their draft animals at the tombs of the saints as if at mangers.[49] And there will be murderers and the thoroughly corrupt and the fire of testing for the race of the Christians.

Chapter 12

For the most holy Apostle says, "For they are not all Israel, which are of Israel."[50] So not all those who are called Christians are indeed Christians. Just so the scripture says, "for seven thousand men of the sons of Israel have been preserved alive who have not bowed their knees before Baal,"[51] and the whole people of Israel was preserved through them.

Thus also in the time of the falling away and of the instruction[52] of the sons of Ishmael few will be found true Christians, just as Our Savior himself says in the Holy Gospels, "when the Son of Man cometh, *do you think that*[53] he shall find faith on the earth?"[54] Indeed in that time the spirit of the perfect will be diminished. 2

And many will deny the true faith, the life-giving cross of Christ, and the holy mysteries. And without any force or torture or whips they deny Christ and follow the transgressors. 3

For anticipating these things and full of inspiration from heaven the Apostle preached and said that "in *those* times 4

adtendentes spiritibus erroris et demonium doctrinas in infidelitate et dolo mendacibus sermonibus et cauteriantium suam conscientiam."

5 Et continuo adiciens idem dicit: "In novissimis diebus insurgunt tempora saevissima. Erunt enim homines semetipsos amantes, amatores pecuniae, elati, superbi, blasphemi, parentibus non oboedientes, inutilis, inmundi, sine affectionem, absque foedere, delatores, incontenentes, inmoderati, malorum amatoris, proditores, susorrones, inflati, luxuriosi magis quam amatores Dei, habentes quidem pietatis formam, virtutem autem eius negantes."

6 Et omnes inbicillis et infidelis in illa correptionem manifestabuntur et semetipsos segregabunt ab ecclesiis sanctis propria voluntate. Idem enim tempus advocat eos in errorem. Humiliter vero sentientes et quieti suavisque et verissimi, liberi quoque vel sapientes, etiam et electi vel utiles non queruntur in tempore illo,

7 sed propter hos inquiruntur, quicumque tales sunt: semetipsos diligentes, cupidi pecuniae, elati, superbi, blasphematores, raptores, plurium possessores, circumventores, ebriosi, inmisericordes, transgressores, sine affectionum, sine vinculo[56] caritatis, insuaviles, inmundi, damnatores, incontinentes, inmansueti, furibundi, proditores, susurrones, protervi, inflati, luxoriosi, lenocinio amatores magis quam amatores Dei, fornicatores, adulteri, fures, periuratores, mendaces, plagiarii, habentes speciem quidem pietatis, virtutem autem eius negantes.

8 Isti tales erunt ministri dierum illorum et omnia, que ab

some shall *withdraw* from the faith, giving heed to seducing spirits and lying *speeches with the* doctrines of devils *in unfaithfulness and deceit and searing* their conscience with a hot iron."[55]

And immediately, adding further, the same one said, "In the last days *most savage* times shall *arise.* For men shall be lovers of their own selves, *lovers of money,* boasters, proud, blasphemers, disobedient to parents, *useless, unclean,* without natural affection, implacable, *denouncers,* incontinent, *extravagant,* lovers of *evils,* traitors, whisperers, *puffed up, given to luxury* more than lovers of God, having a *kind* of godliness, but denying the power thereof."[56] 5

And all the weak and faithless will be made known in that reproach and they will separate themselves from the holy churches by their own choice. For the time itself summons them to error. The humble-minded and the quiet, the pleasant and the undoubtedly trusty, the frank as well as the wise, even the elect and the useful will not be sought out in that time, 6

But because of these those will be sought out, whoever are such as these: lovers of their own selves, covetous of money, boasters, proud, blasphemers, robbers, owners of excessive goods, cheaters, drunkards, unmerciful, transgressors, without natural affection, without the bond of charity, unpleasant, unclean, given to condemnation, incontinent, wild, frenzied, traitors, whisperers, insolent, puffed up, given to luxury, lovers of pandering more than lovers of God, fornicators, adulterers, thieves, perjured persons, liars, men-stealers, those having a form of godliness, but denying the power thereof.[57] 7

Such as those will be the servants of those days and 8

eis imperantur, facile perficiunt. Timentes vero Deum in nihilo reputabuntur in conspectu oculorum eorum, sed erunt in vituperationem,[57] quemadmodum conculcatur stercore.

Caput 13

Erunt enim homines in illa correptionem filiorum Ismahel et veniunt in necessitatibus usque quo desperant vitam suam. Et tollitur honor a sacerdotibus et subpraemitur ministerium Dei et quiescit omnis sacrificium ab ecclesiis, et erunt sacerdotes sicut et populus.

2   Et in eodem tempore, seu in septimo ebdomatico tempore, cumque conplebitur numerus annorum potentatui eorum, per quod obtenuerunt terram, multiplicabitur etiam et tribulatio super homines et super iumenta, et erit fames et pestilentia et corrumpentur homines et proicientur homines super faciem terrae sicut pulvis, et per singulos dies in tempore illo adhuc plagam unam adicietur hominibus.

3   Etiam dormiens adcuvabit[58] homo ad vesperum et exsurget mane et reperiet ad limen ianuae domus suae, qui eum exigunt[59] pundus auri vel argenti et angariantes se, et expenditur omnes acceptio auri et argenti. Et venundabit homo omnem utensilium suum et feramenta sua operaturia et mortalia vestimenta sua.

everything that is commanded by them they will carry out with ease. And those who fear God will be esteemed as nothing in their eyes, but they will be objects of abuse, in the way dung is trampled underfoot.[58]

Chapter 13

For there will be people in that rebuking from the sons of Ishmael and they will come in such straits that they will despair of their life. And honor will be taken away from the priests and the ministry of God will be ended and every sacrifice will cease from the churches, and the priests will be just as the laity.

And in that time, that is in the period of the seventh 2 week,[59] when the number of the years of their dominion will be fulfilled, during which they controlled the earth, even the affliction too will be increased over men and over animals, and there will be famine and plague and people will be destroyed and people will be cast forth over the face of the earth like dust, and every day in that time one more blow will be laid upon men.

And a man will lie down to sleep in the evening and wake 3 up in the morning and find at the threshold of the door of his house men who demand of him a weight of gold or silver and press him into service, and his whole supply[60] of gold and silver will be exhausted. And the man will offer for sale all his necessary equipment and his iron tools[61] and his burial sheets.

4   Et in ipso ebdomatico tempore vendunt homines natos suos. Cuius itaque rei gratia dispexerit Deus fidelis ut sufferant has tribulationes, sed ut monstrentur qui sunt fidelissimi quoque vel infidelis et ut separentur lollia a tritico mundo, eo quod ignis probationis est tempus illud?

5   Et longanimiter f<e>ret Deus super tribulationes iustorum et fidelium, ut manifesti appareant electi. Praedixit enim nobis Deus ita: "Beati," inquid, "estis, cum exprobraverint vos et persecuti vos fuerint et dixerint omnem verbum malum adversum vos propter me mentientes. Gaudite et exultate, quoniam mercis vestra copiosa est in caelis. Sic enim persecuti sunt prophetas, qui fuerunt ante vos." "Qui autem sustinuerunt usque in finem, hic salvus erit."

6   Et post tribulationem, quae fit a filiis Ismahel, cumque periculati fuerint homines tribulatione passi, nequaquam habentes spem salutis aut redemptionem aliquam de manibus eorum, persecuti et tribulati ab eis, afflicti, qui fuerint in famem et sitem et nuditatem, barbaris[60] vero nationes erunt hi commedentes et bibentes et iocundantes, in victoriis eorum gloriantes et in desolationibus, quibus desolaverunt Persidamque et Romaniam, Ciliciam quoque et Syriam, Cappadotiamque et Isauriam, Africam quoque vel Siciliam et eos, qui habitant proximae Romam et insulas, circumamicti quemadmodum sponsi, et blasphemantes dicunt quia: "Nequaquam habebunt christiani ereptionem de manibus nostris."

11   Tunc subito insurgent super eos tribulatio et angustia, et exiliet super eos rex Gregorum, sive Romanorum, in furore

And in this very time of the week men will sell their own 4
children. For what reason then would God simply despise
the faithful so that they endure these tribulations, except
that[62] so those who are truly faithful and those who are unfaithful may be made known, and so that the tares may be
separated from the clean wheat, because that time is the
time of the testing of fire?

And God will wait patiently over the tribulations of the 5
just and faithful, so that the elect may appear clearly. For
God has already spoken to us in this manner: "Blessed," he
said, "are ye, when men shall accuse you, and persecute you,
and shall say all manner of evil words against you falsely, for
my sake. Rejoice and be exceeding glad: for great is your reward in heaven: for so persecuted they the prophets which
were before you." "But those that endure to the end shall be
saved."[63]

And after the tribulation that comes about at the hands 6
of the sons of Ishmael, when men will be in peril and suf-
fer tribulation, having no hope at all of salvation nor any
redemption out of their hands, hunted and oppressed by
them, tormented inasmuch as they will have come into hunger and thirst and nakedness, these barbarian nations will be
eating and drinking and joking, boasting of their victories
and of the desolations to which they have reduced Persia
and Romania, Cilicia as well as Syria, Cappadocia and Isauria, Africa as well as Sicily and those who live near Rome and
the islands, dressed up like bridegrooms and speaking blas-
phemy they say that "the Christians will have no rescue at all
out of our hands."[64]

Then all of a sudden affliction and trouble will come to 11
them, and the king of the Greeks, that is, of the Romans,[65]

magno et expergiscitur tamquam homo a somno vini, quem exaestimabant homines tamquam mortuum esse et in nihilo utilem. Proficisse hic exiet super eos a mare Aethiopiae et mittit gladium et desolationem in Ethribum, que est eorum patria, et captivabit mulieres eorum et filios illorum. Super habitantes autem terram promissionis discendent filii regis in gladio et concidunt eos a terra.

12 Et inruet super eos timor et tremor undique, et ipse et uxores et filii eorum et lugebunt infantes suos, flentes super eos, et omnia castra eorum, que sunt in terra patrum illorum; in manus regis Romanorum tradentur in gladio et captivitatem et mortem et corruptionem.

13 Et erit rex Romanorum inponens iugum suum super eos septiens tantum, quod erat iugum eorum super terra.[61] Et conpraehendit eos angustia magna, famem et sitem et tribulatio. Et erunt servi ipsi et mulieres et filii eorum, et servient eis, qui sibi serviebant, et erit servitus eorum amarissimi et durissime centuplo.

14 Et tunc pacificabitur terra, que ab eis fuerat destituta, et rediet unusquisque in terram suam et in hereditatem patrum suorum, Armeniam, Ciliciam, Isauriam, Africam, Greciam, Siciliam, et omnis, qui de captivitate relictus est, revertetur in propria et in paterna sua.

15 Et multiplicabuntur homines super terra, que desolata fuerat, sicut locustae in multitudinem. Aegyptus vero desolabitur, Arabia igne concremabitur, terra Auraniae[62] cremabitur et maritime pacificantur. Et omnis indignatio et furor regis Romanorum super eos, qui abnegaverunt dominum

will spring upon them in great anger and he will be aroused like a man from a drunken sleep,[66] whom men reckoned to be dead and good for nothing. This man will march out to proceed against them from the sea of Ethiopia and send a sword and desolation into Yathrib, which is their homeland, and he will take captive their wives and their sons. The sons of the king will descend upon those living in the Promised Land with the sword and cut them off from the land.

And fear and trembling will rush upon them from every side, and they themselves[67] and their wives and their sons and their babies will mourn, weeping over them, and all the encampments which are in the land of their fathers; they will be delivered into the hands of the king of the Romans with the sword, and into captivity and death and ruin. 12

And the king of the Romans will set upon them his yoke which is sevenfold what their yoke was upon the earth. And a great distress will seize them, hunger and thirst and affliction. And they themselves will be slaves, and their wives and sons, and they will serve those who used to serve them, and their servitude will be a hundred times more bitter and hard.[68] 13

And then the land will be at peace, which had been devastated by them, and each man will return to his own country and to the inheritance of his fathers, to Armenia, Cilicia, Isauria, Africa, Greece, and Sicily, and every man left from captivity will come back to his own and to his patrimony. 14

And, like locusts in number, men will be multiplied over the earth which was devastated. Egypt will be devastated, Arabia will be burned up with fire, the land of Aurania will be burned, and the seacoasts will be pacified. And all the displeasure and the anger of the king of the Romans against 15

nostrum Iesum Christum, exardiscit et sedebit terra in pace. Et erit pax et tranquillitas magna super terra, qualis nondum est facta, †sed† neque fiet similis illa eo quod novissima est et in fine saeculorum.

16 Erit enim laetitiam super terram et commorabuntur hominis in pace et reaedificabunt civitates et liberabuntur sacerdotes de necessitatibus suis et requiescent homines in tempore illo a tribulationibus suis.

17 Et haec est pax, quam beatus Apostolus exposuit, quia "cum dixerint: "pax et securitas," tunc eis superveniet subito interitus," et continuo Dominus in evangelio sic inquiens: "sicut enim in diebus Noe erant homines manducantes et bibentes, nubentes et nuptui tradentes, ita erit et in novissimo die."

18 In hac igitur pacem sedebunt homines super terra[63] cum gaudio et laetitia, commedentes et sese potantes, nubentes et dantes ad nuptias, exsultantes et gaudentes, et aedificationes construentes, et non erit in corde eorum timor vel solicitudo.

19 Tunc reserabuntur portae aquilonis et egredientur virtutes gentium illarum, quas conclusit intus Alexander, et concutietur omnis terra a conspectu earum et expaviscent homines et fugientes conterriti abscondent se in montibus et in speluncis et in munumentis.[64] Et mortificabuntur a timore et corrumpentur prae pavore quamplurimi, et non erit, qui corpora sepeliat.

20 Gentes namque, que exient ab aquilone, comedent carnes hominum et bibent sanguinem bestiarum sicut aqua et comedent inmunda[s],[65] serpentes et scorpiones et omnem sord<i>dissimum et abominabilem genus bestiarum et rep-

those who denied Our Lord Jesus Christ will be kindled[69] and the earth will rest at peace. And there will be a great peace and quiet over the earth, the like of which has not yet been nor will be until the last day at the end of the ages.[70]

For there will be gladness over the earth and men will 16 dwell in peace and rebuild the cities and the priests will be freed from the compulsions they were under and men will rest at that time from their afflictions.[71]

And this is the peace of which the blessed Apostle ex- 17 plained that "when they shall say, Peace and safety; then *all of a sudden* destruction cometh upon them,"[72] and moreover the Lord speaks thus in the Gospel: "For as in the days of Noah there were men eating and drinking, marrying and giving in marriage, so it will be *at the last day.*"[73]

In that peace, therefore, men will sit upon the earth with 18 joy and gladness, eating and drinking to themselves,[74] marrying and giving in marriage, jumping for joy and rejoicing, and constructing buildings, and there will be no fear or worry in their hearts.[75]

Then the gates of the North will be unbarred and out will 19 come the powers of the nations which Alexander enclosed within, and the whole earth will be struck by their appearance and men will become terrified and flee, and, fleeing in terror, they will hide themselves in the mountains and in caves and among the tombs. And they will be deadened with fear and many will be wasted with terror, and there will be none to bury the bodies.[76]

For the nations which will come out from the North will 20 eat the flesh of men and drink the blood of beasts like water[77] and eat unclean things: snakes and scorpions and every utterly filthy and detestable kind of beast and

tilia, que repunt super terram,[66] iumentorum autem et corpora mortua et abortitia mulierum. Etiam occidunt parvulus et cedunt eos suis matribus <. . .> et edunt eos. Et corrumpent terram et contaminabunt eam <. . .>, et nullus erit, qui poterit stare coram eis.

21   Post ebdomada vero temporis, cumque [iam][67] conpraehenderint[68] civitatem Ioppen, emittit dominus Deus unum ex principibus militiae suae et percutiet eos in uno momento temporis. Et post haec discendit rex Romanorum et demorabitur in Hierusalem septimana temporum et dimedia, quod est X anni et dimidium,[69] et, cum suplebuntur decim et demedium anni, apparebit filius perditionis.

Caput 14

Hic nascitur in Chorozaim et nutrietur in Bethsaidam et regnavit in Gapharnaum. Et laetabitur Chorozaim eo quod natus est in ea, et Bethsaida, propter quod nutritus est in ea, et Capharnaum ideo, quod regnaverit in ea. Propter hanc causam in evangelio Dominus tertio sententiam dedit "Vae," dicens: "Vae tibi, Chorozaim; vae tibi, Bethsaida, et tibi, Capharnaum, si usque in caelum exultaveris, usque ad infernum discendes!"

2   Et cum apparuerit filius perditionis,[70] ascendit rex Romanorum sursum in Golgotha, in quo confixum est lignum sanctae crucis, in quo loco pro nobis Dominus mortem sustenuit.

reptiles, which creep upon the earth, and the carcasses of animals and the aborted fetuses of women. They even slay young children and slaughter[78] them at their mothers <...> and eat them. And they will corrupt the earth and befoul it <...>, and there will be no one who will be able to stand before them.

After a week of time, when they seize the city of Joppa, 21 the Lord God will send out one of the commanders of his army and he will smite them in a single moment of time. And after these things the king of the Romans will come down and he will stay in Jerusalem for a week and a half of times, which is 10 and a half years, and, when ten and a half years are completed, the son of perdition will appear.

Chapter 14

This man is born at Chorazin and will be raised at Bethsaida and will rule at Capernaum. And Chorazin will be glad because he was born in her, and Bethsaida because he was raised in her, and Capernaum because he will have ruled in her. For this reason in the Gospel the Lord three times passed a sentence of 'Woe,' saying, "Woe unto thee, Chorazin! woe unto thee, Bethsaida! And *unto thee* Capernaum, *if* thou hast been exalted unto heaven, shalt be brought down to hell."[79]

And when the son of perdition shows himself, the king of 2 the Romans will go up to Golgotha, where the wood of the holy cross was fixed at the place in which the Lord underwent death for our sakes.

3　Et tollet rex coronam de capite suo et ponet eam super crucem et expandit manus suas in caelum et tradet regnum christianorum Deo et patri.

4　Et adsumetur crux in caelum simul cum corona regis, propter quod [quia] crux, in qua pependit dominus noster Iesus Christus propter communem omnium salutem, ipsa crux incipiet apparere ante eum in adventum ipsius ad arguendum perfidiam infidelium.

5　Et complebitur prophetia David, que dicit in novissimis diebus: "Aethiopia praeveniet manus eius Deo," eo quod ex semine filiorum Chuseth, filiae Phol regis Aethiopiae, ipsi novissimi praeveniunt manus sua<s> Deo.

6　Et cumque exaltabitur crux in caelum sursum, etiam tradet continuo spiritum suum Romanorum rex. Tunc distruetur omnem principatum et potestatem, ut appareat manifestus filius perditionis. Est autem hic de tribu Dan secundum prophetiam patriarchae Iacob, que dicit: "Dan, serpens in via et accubans in semitam, momordens calcaneum equi, et cadet ascensor retrorsum, salutarem Domini sustenens."

7　Equus igitur est veritas et pietas iusturom, calcaneum vero novissima dies. Et hi sancti, qui in eodem tempore super aequo, scilicet super veram fidem, aequitantes, persequuntur a serpente, sive filio perditionis; in calcaneo mordentur, vidilicet in ultima die, in phantasmatis et in mendacibus signis, que fiunt ab eo.

8　Faciet etenim[71] tunc signa et prodigia multa super terra,[72] inercia vel invicillia.[73] Caeci namque respiciunt, claudi

And the king will take the crown from his head and place 3
it on the cross and spread out his hands to the heaven and
deliver the kingdom of the Christians to God, even the Father.[80]

And the cross will be taken up into heaven along with the 4
king's crown, because the cross on which Our Lord Jesus
Christ was hanged for the sake of the common salvation of
all, the cross itself will commence to appear before him at
his coming as a refutation of the treachery of unbelievers.

And the prophecy of David will be fulfilled which says 5
in the last days "Ethiopia shall stretch out her hands unto
God"[81] because from the seed of the sons of Chuseth, the
daughter of Phol king of Ethiopia, these last will stretch out
their hands unto God.

And as soon as the cross will be raised up into heaven, the 6
king of the Romans will also immediately surrender his
spirit. Then all rule and authority will be demolished,[82] so
that the son of perdition may show himself openly. This man
is from the tribe of Dan according to the prophecy of the
patriarch Jacob, which says, "Dan shall be a serpent by the
way, lying near the path, that biteth the horse heel, so that
his rider shall fall backward, maintaining the salvation of the
Lord."[83]

The horse, therefore, is the truth and sense of duty of the 7
just, and the heel the last day. And these holy ones, who are
at that time on the horse, that is to say mounted upon the
true faith, are pursued by the serpent, or the son of perdition; they are bitten in the heel, manifestly in the last day in
the apparitions and deceptive signs which are made by him.

Then indeed he will perform many signs and wonders, 8
powerless and frail, over the earth. For the blind see again,

ambulant, surdi audiunt et daemoniosi curantur. Convertit enim sol in tenebris et lunam in sanguinem et in his eius mendacibus signis et deceptionis prodigia seducit, si potest fieri, etiam electus, secuti Dominus explanavit.

9 Aspiciens enim patriarcha Iacob cordis oculis consideravit, que futura esset a venenoso serpente, vel filio perditionis, facienda in hominibus tribulatio seu angustiam, <*et*> exposuit, sicut ex persona generis humani vocem emittens: "Salutarem tuum expectabo, Domine." Dominus autem continuo praefatus est dicens: "Si fieri potest etiam in errorem inducere electos."

10 Ingredietur enim hic filius perditionis in Hierusolimam et sedebit in templo Dei sicut Deus, homo cum sit carnalis ex semine viri et ex utero mulieris, de tribu Dan discendens. Etiam nam et Iudas Scariothes, traditur Domini, de tribu Dan existebat et ipse.

11 Cumque multiplicata fuerit tribulatio dierum illorum a filio perditionis, non ferit divinitas aspicere perditionem generis humani, quem redimit proprio sanguine[74] <*et*> mittit continuo suos famulos sincerissimusque carissimus, id est Enoch et Helian, ad arguendum inimicum. Palam omnium ergo gentium corripient eius seductionem et ostendunt eum mendacem coram omnem hominem et nihil esse, et quia propter interitum et perditionem multorum exiet.

12 Itaque gentes videntes illum confusum et eius seductionem arguendam a famulis Dei, sinent eum et fugient ab illo et adherebunt iustis illis. Videns igitur seductor semet ipsum

the lame walk, the deaf hear, and the demon-possessed are healed. For he turns the sun into shadows and the moon into blood and through these false signs of his and portents of deceit he leads astray, if possible, the very elect, just as the Lord stated.[84]

For examining them with the eyes of the heart the Patri- 9 arch Jacob contemplated the things that would happen at the hand of the poisonous serpent, that is the son of perdition, that a tribulation and a distress would come upon men, and he set this forth, issuing his voice as if from a human being,[85] "I will await thy salvation, O Lord,"[86] immediately the Lord prophesied saying, "if it were possible, to deceive the very elect."[87]

For this son of perdition will enter Jerusalem and sit in 10 the temple of God as God, although he is a man of flesh from the seed of a man and from the womb of a woman, a descendant of the tribe of Dan.[88] For Judas Iscariot also, the betrayer of the Lord, was himself from the tribe of Dan.

And when the tribulation of those days is increased[89] by 11 the son of perdition, the Divinity will not endure to look on the perdition of the race of men, whom he redeemed with the blood of his own household, and he will at once send forth his most honest and well-beloved servants, Enoch and Elijah, to denounce the enemy. Therefore in the presence of all the nations they will attack his deceit and show him to be a liar before every man and to be nothing, and that he will issue forth for the ruin and perdition of many.

And so when the nations see him put to shame and his 12 deceit to be refuted by the servants of God, they will abandon him and flee from him and cling to those just men. Then when the seducer sees that he has been rebuked to scorn

dirissime increpatum et ab omnibus contemptum furor<e> et ira fervens[75] interficiet sanctos illos.

13 Tunc apparebit signum adventus Filii hominis, et veniet in nubibus caeli cum gloria caeleste et "interficiet eum Dominus spiritu oris sui" secundum expositionem apostolicam.

14 "Tunc fulgebunt iusti" "tamquam stelle in mundo verbum vitae in se contenentes," impii autem proicientur in infernum, ex quo eripiamur per gratiam et humanitatem domini Dei et Salvatoris nostri Iesu Christi, cum quo est Patri una cum Spiritu sancto omnis honor et gloria, potestas, magnitudo et imperium, nunc et semper et in saecula saeculorum. Amen

EXPLICIT SERMO SANCTI METHODII

EPISCOPI DE FINE MUNDI.

DEO GRACIAS.

and is despised by all, boiling over with wrath and anger he will kill those holy ones.

Then will appear the sign of the Coming of the Son of 13 Man, and he will come on the clouds of heaven with heavenly glory and "the Lord shall consume *him* with the spirit of his mouth," according to the apostolic revelation.[90]

"Then shall the righteous shine" "*as stars* in the world, 14 holding forth *in themselves* the word of life,"[91] but the impious will be cast forth into hell, out of which let us be delivered through the grace and kindness of our Lord God and Saviour Jesus Christ,[92] with Whom to the Father along with the Holy Spirit is all honour and glory, power, greatness and dominion, now and always and unto the ages of ages. Amen.

THIS ENDS THE DISCOURSE OF SAINT
METHODIUS THE BISHOP CONCERNING THE
END OF THE WORLD.
THANKS BE TO GOD.

AN ALEXANDRIAN
WORLD CHRONICLE

Caput I[1]

Primus homo factus est a deo cui nomen erat Adam, uxor autem eius Aeva. Ab Adam usque ad dilivium Noe generationes X, anni autem duo milia ducenti quadraginta duo.[2]

Adam factus est annorum ducentorum treginta et sic genuit Seth. Mortuus est autem Adam annorum noningentorum treginta.

Seth autem vixit annos CCV:[3] fiunt simul anni quadringenti XXXV, et genuit Enos. Mortuus est autem Seth annorum noningentorum duodecim.

Enos autem vixit annos CXC: fiunt simul anni sexcenti viginti[4] quinque, et genuit Cainan. Mortuus est autem Enos annorum noningentorum quinque.

Cainan autem vixit annos CLXX: fiunt simul anni DCC nonaginta quinque, et genuit Malelehel. Mortuus est autem Cainan annorum noningentorum XC.[5]

Malelehel autem vixit annos centum sexaginta quinque: fiunt simul anni noningenti sexaginta, et genuit Iared. Mortuus est autem Malelehel annorum octingentorum nonaginta.[6]

Iared autem vixit annos centum sexaginta duos: fiunt simul anni mille centum viginti duo, et genuit Enoch. Mortuus est autem Iared annorum noningentorum LXII.

Enoch autem vixit annos centum sexaginta V: fiunt simul anni mille ducenti octuaginta VII, et genuit Mathusalam. Placuit autem Enoch deo factus annorum tricentorum sexaginta quinque et translatus est.[7]

BOOK I

Chapter 1

The first man was made by God;[1] his name was Adam, and his wife was Eve. From Adam to the flood of Noah there are 10 generations, or 2,242 years.[2]

Adam was 230 years old when he begat Seth. Adam died at 930 years of age.

Seth lived 205 years (altogether this makes 435 years), and begat Enos. Seth died at 912 years.

Enos lived 190 years (altogether this makes 625[3] years), and begat Cainan. Enos died at 905 years.

Cainan lived 170 years (altogether this makes 795 years), and begat Maleleel. Cainan died at 990 years.

Maleleel[4] lived 165 years (altogether this makes 960 years) and begat Jared. Maleleel died at 890 years.

Jared lived 162 years (altogether this makes 1,122 years), and begat Enoch. Jared died at 962 years.

Enoch lived 165 years (altogether this makes 1,287 years), and begat Methuselah. Enoch pleased God, and when he was 365 years old he was translated.

Mathusalam autem vixit annos CLXVII: fiunt simul anni mille quadringenti LIIII et genuit Lamech. Mortuus est autem Mathusalam annorum noningentorum LXVIIII. Lamech autem vixit annos CLXXXVIII: fiunt simul anni mille DCXLII, et genuit Noe. Mortuus est autem Lamech annorum septingentorum.[8]

2   Factus est autem Noe annorum quingentorum: fiunt simul anni duo milia CXLII, et genuit Noe tres filios, Sem, Cham et Iafeth. Et factum est cum homines multiplicarentur super terram et filias procreassent. Videntes autem angeli dei filias hominum quod essent pulchrae, acceperunt sibi uxores ex omnibus quas elegerant. Et dixit dominus deus:[9] Non permanebit spiritus meus in hominibus istis in aeternum quia caro sunt, eruntque[10] dies eorum annorum CXX. Gigantes autem erant super terram in diebus illis et ultra. Cumque introissent angeli dei ad filias hominum, illeque[11] genuerunt, illi fuerunt gigantes, a seculo homines nominati. Corrupta est autem terra coram deo et repleta est terra iniquitate. Et vidit dominus deus terram quia[12] corrupta erat: omnis quippe caro corruperat viam suam super terram. Et dixit dominus deus ad Noe: Tempus omnium rerum[13] venit coram me. Et quia repleta est terra iniquitates eorum, et ecce corumpam[14] eos et terram. Fac autem tibi arcam de lignis quadratis[15] et linies eam intrinsecus et extrinsecus asfalto bitumini. Et quod sequitur.

Et fecit Noe[16] omnia quae praeceperat illi dominus deus. Et erat Noe annorum sexcentorum: fiunt autem simul anni duo milia ducenti quadraginta duo, et diluvium aquarum factum est super terram quadraginta diebus et quadraginta noctibus. Et mortua est omnis caro quique habuit spiritum

Methuselah lived 167 years (altogether this makes 1,454 years), and begat Lamech. Methuselah died at 969 years.

Lamech lived 188 years (altogether this makes 1,642 years), and begat Noah. Lamech died at 700 years.[5]

Noah[6] came to be 500 years old (altogether this makes 2,142 years), and Noah begat three sons, Shem, Ham, and Japheth. And it came about that when men were multiplied over the earth and produced daughters, the angels of God saw the daughters of men that they were fair, and they took wives for themselves of all whom they chose. And the Lord God said, "My spirit will not endure in those men forever since they are flesh, and their days will be one hundred and twenty years." 2

There were giants upon the earth in those days and later.[7] Whenever the angels[8] of God went in to the daughters of men, and they gave birth to children, they were giants, men well known by the age.[9] The earth was corrupt before God and the earth was filled with iniquity.[10] And the Lord God saw the earth, that it was corrupt; for all flesh had corrupted its way upon the earth. And the Lord God said to Noah, "The time of all things has come before me. For the earth is filled with their injustice, and behold I shall destroy them and the earth. Make for yourself an ark from squared timbers and you will coat it inside and outside with asphalt pitch."[11] And what follows.[12]

And Noah did all the things which the Lord God commanded him. And Noah was 600 years old[13] (altogether this makes 2,242 years), and a flood of waters came to be over the earth for 40 days and 40 nights.[14] And all flesh died,

vitae in semet ipso super terram, ab homine usque ad pecus et reptile et ferarum et omnium quod erat super terram habens spiritum uitae in semet ipso.

3   Post haec autem in sexcentesimo primo anno exiit Noe et omnes qui cum eo erant de arca. Fiunt autem simul ab Adam usque ad diluvium Noe anni duo milia ducenti quadraginta duo.[17] Et a diluvio Noe usque ad turris aedificationem et confusione linguarum generationes sex, anni autem quingenti quinquaginta octo.

Hii sunt autem filii Noe, Sem, Cham et Iafeth <...>[18] post diluvium[19] sic. Sem factus est annorum CI: fiunt simul anni duo milia trecenti quadraginta tres, et genuit Arfaxad.

Arfaxad autem vixit annos centum treginta V: fiunt simul anni duo milia quadringenti septuaginta octo, et genuit Cainan.

Cainan autem vixit annos centum treginta: fiunt simul anni duo milia sexcenti octo, et genuit Salam.

Salam autem vixit annos centum treginta: fiunt simul anni duo milia septingenti treginta octo, et genuit Eber.

Eber autem vixit annos centu XXXIIII: fiunt simul anni duo milia octingenti septuaginta duo,[20] et genuit Falech et Ragau fratrem eius.[21] Sub ipso factum est dispersio.

Et fuit omnis terra labia et vox una omnibus.[22] Et factum est dum moverent ab oriente, invenerunt Paneum, quod est terra fructifera, in terra Sennaar et habitaverunt ibi. Et dixit homo ad proximum suum: Venite, faciamus nobis lateres et coquamus eas igne. Et facta est eis ipsa latera quasi lapis, et bitumen erat illis lutus.[23] Et dixerunt: Venite, aedificemus nobis civitatem et turrem, cuius capud[24] sit usque ad caelum, et faciamus nobis nomen, antequam dispersi fuerimus

whatever had the spirit of life in itself upon the earth, from man to cattle and creeping things and wild beasts and everything on the earth which had the spirit of life in itself.[15]

After these things, in his 601st year, Noah and all who were with him left the ark.[16] Altogether this makes from Adam to the flood of Noah 2,242 years. And from the flood of Noah to the building of the tower and the confusion of languages there are six generations, or 558 years. 3

These are the sons of Noah: Shem, Ham, and Japheth <. . .> After the Flood [the genealogical chronology continues] thus:[17] Shem was 101 years old[18] (altogether this makes 2,343 years), and begat Arphaxad.

Arphaxad lived 135 years (altogether this makes 2,478 years), and begat Cainan.[19]

Cainan lived 130 years (altogether this makes 2,608 years), and begat Salah.

Salah lived 130 years (altogether this makes 2,738 years), and begat Eber.

Eber lived 134 years (altogether this makes 2,872[20] years), and begat Peleg[21] [and his brother[22] Reu]. In his time[23] the dispersion occurred.

And there was in the whole world one language and one voice for all.[24] And it came about that when they moved from the east, they found Paneum, which is a fertile land,[25] in the land of Shinar and they lived there. And a man said to his neighbor, "Come, let us make bricks and bake them with fire." And these bricks were made by them as stone, and bitumen was for them mud. And they said, "Come, let us build for ourselves a city and a tower, whose top will be all the way to heaven, and let us make a name for ourselves, before we shall have been scattered over the whole face of the

super omnem faciem terrae. Et descendit[25] dominus deus videre civitatem et turrem, quam aedificaverant filii hominum. Et dixit dominus deus: Ecce labia et vox omnibus una, et hoc initiarunt facere. Et nunc non minuitur ex ipsis omnia, quaecumque proposuerunt facere. Venite, descendentes dispersas faciamus ibi eorum linguas, ut non obaudiat unusquisque vocem proximi sui. Et dispersit illos dominus deus inde super faciem omnis terrae, et cessaverunt aedificantes[26] civitatem et turrem. Propter hoc vocatum est nomen eius Confusio, quia ibi confudit dominus labia omnis terrae et exinde dispersit eos dominus deus super omnem faciem terrae.

Fiunt autem simul ab Adam usque ad turris aedificationem et dispersionem terrae generationes quindecim, anni duo milia octingenti LXXVIII.

Caput II[27]

Terrae divisiones tres filios Noe post diluvio factum est sic. Sem, Cham et Iafeth, trium fratrum,[28] secundum tribum partiti sunt super terram. Et Sem primo genito a Persida et Bactrium usque in India longitudo, latitudo autem ab India usque Rinocorurum. Cham autem secundo ab Rinocorurum usque Garirum, Iafeth autem tertio a Midia usque Garirum

earth." And the Lord God came down to see the city and the tower, which the sons of men had built.[26] And the Lord God said, "Behold, there is one language and one voice for all, and this is what they have begun to do. And now nothing at all, of whatever they have proposed to do, will be diminished. Come, let us go down and there make their tongues scattered, so that each one may not comprehend the voice of his neighbor." And the Lord God scattered them from that place over the face of the whole earth, and they stopped building the city and the tower. On account of this the name of it was called Confusion (i.e., Babel), because there the Lord confused the language of the whole earth and the Lord God scattered them out from there over the whole face of the earth.

Altogether there are from Adam to the building of the tower and the scattering of the earth fifteen generations, 2,878 years.

Chapter 2

The division of the earth among the three sons of Noah after the Flood was made as follows. [The descendants] of Shem, Ham, and Japheth, the three brothers, were divided across the earth according to their tribes. And for Shem, the firstborn, the length [of his territory][27] is from Persia and Bactria as far as India, and the breadth from India to Rhinocorura.[28] For Ham, the second-born, from Rhinocorura as far as Gadeira; for Japheth, the third-born, from Media as

ad aquilonem. Habet autem Iafeth fluvium Tigrem, qui dividet Midiam et Babyloniam in terra Assyriorum, Cham autem habet fluvium Geon qui vocatur Nilus, Sem autem Eufraten.

Confusae sunt autem linguae super terram post diluvium. Fuerunt autem quae confusae sunt linguae septuaginta duo, qui autem turrem aedificabant fuerunt gentes septuaginta duo,[29] qui in linguis[30] super faciem terrae divisae sunt. Nebrod autem gigans,[31] filius Chus Ethiopu iste, pro cibaria eorum venando porrigebat eis feras. Nomina autem septuaginta duo[32] sunt haec.

Filii Iafeth filio Noe tertio iuniori.

Gamer, a quo Cappadoci, et Magog, a quo Chaldei et Galates, et Made, a quo Midi, et Yoias,[33] a quo Greci et Hiones, et Thobail, a quo Thettali, et Mosoch, a quo Illyrici, et Thiras, a quo Thraci, et Chattaim, a quo Macedoni.

Et filii Gamer filio Iafeth tertio filio Noe.

Aschanath, a quo Sarmati, et Erisfan, a quo Rodii, et Thorgaman, a quo Armenii.

Et filii filiorum Iafeth filii Noe.

Elisa, a quo Siculi, et Thareis, a quo Iberi qui et Tyrannii, et Cittei,[34] a quo Romei qui et Latini.

far as Gadeira, and north from there. Japheth has the Tigris River, which divides Media and Babylon in the land of the Assyrians, Ham has the River Gihon, which is called the Nile, and Shem has the Euphrates.

The languages were confused across the earth after the Flood. There were 72 languages that were confused, and there were 72 peoples who were building the tower, and who were scattered over the face of the earth according to their languages. Nimrod was a giant, that son of Cush the Ethiopian,[29] and by hunting he offered them wild beasts for their food.[30] The names of the 72 [peoples] are these.

The sons of Japheth, the third and youngest son
of Noah

Gomer, from whom [are descended] the Cappadocians, and Magog, from whom the Chaldeans, and Galatians,[31] and Madai, from whom the Medes, and Javan, from whom the Greeks and the Ionians, and Tubal, from whom the Thessalians, and Meshech, from whom the Illyrians, and Tiras, from whom the Thracians, and Chattaim,[32] from whom the Macedonians.

And the sons of Gomer the son of Japheth the
third son of Noah

Ashkenaz, from whom the Sarmatians, and Ersifan,[33] from whom the Rhodians, and Togarmah, from whom the Armenians.

And the sons of the sons of Japheth the son of
Noah

Elishah, from whom the Sicels, and Tarshish, from whom the Iberians, who are also known as the Tyrannians, and Kittim,[34] from whom the Romans, who are also known as the Latins.

2   Omnes isti filii Iafeth tertio filio Noe. Ex istis dispersae sunt insulae gentium.[35] Sunt autem et Cyprii ex Citteis ex filiorum Iafeth. Simul gentes quindecim. Invenimus autem qui ab aquilone sunt ex ipsis ex tribu Citteis. Est autem de Elladii gentes omnes ex ipso, excepto his qui habitaverunt[36] in postero ibi Essaitei, qui habitaverunt circa mare honorabilem civitatem quae vocatur Athenas, simul autem et Thibas, qui Sidonii sunt acolae[37] de Cathmo Aginoru. Chalcedonii autem Tyranni peregrini fuerunt, et alii simili modo qui posthac in Ellada migraverunt.

Haec sunt autem gentes Iafeth tertio filio Noe a Midia usque ad Speriam[38] a parte Oceani adtendens ad aquilonem sic: Midii, Albani, Gargani, Errei, Armeni, Amazoni, Coli, Corzini, Dennagi, Cappadoci, Paflagoni, Mariandini, Tabarini, Challyri,[39] Mossonici, Sarmati, Saurobati, Meoti, Scythi, Taurinii, Thraci, Bastarni, Illyrici, Macedoni, Greci, Ligyrii, Istrii, Hunni, Dauni, Iapygii, Colabri, Oppici, Latini qui et Romei, Tyranni, Calli qui et Celtei,[40] Ligistini, Celtibirii, Ibirii, Galli Aquitanii, Illyrici, Basantii, Cyrtanii, Lysitani, Huaccai, Cynii, Brittani qui in insulis habitant.

Qui autem sapiunt ex ipsis litteris hii sunt: Ibirii, Latini qui utuntur[41] Romei, Spani, Greci, Midi, Armenii.

3   Sunt autem termina eorum a Midia usque Garirum quod ad aquilonem, laterae autem a fluvio et fluvium[42] usque Mastusias contra solem.[43]

All of these are sons of Japheth the third son of Noah. 2
The islands of the nations were divided among them. The
Cyprians too are [descended] from Kittim, [one] of the sons
of Japheth. Altogether there are 15 peoples.
We find that those who are from the north are of those
of the tribe of Kittim. All of the peoples of Greece are [de-
scended] from him, except those who lived there later: the
Saites, who lived around the sea in the notable city called
Athens,[35] and likewise [the inhabitants of] Thebes, who are
the Sidonian settlers of Cadmus, son of Agenor. The Chalcedonians were Tyrian colonists,[36] and [there are] others
who in like manner afterward traveled to Greece.

These are the peoples of Japheth, the third son of Noah,
from Media as far as the west, from the region of the Ocean
stretching to the north, thus: Medes, Albanians, Garganians,
Erraeans, Armenians, Amazons, Colians, Corzinians, Den-
nagians, Cappadocians, Paphlagonians, Mariandinians,
Tabarinians, Challyrians, Mossonicians, Sarmatians, Sauro-
batians, Maeotians, Scythians, Taurians, Thracians,
Bastarnians, Illyrians, Macedonians, Greeks, Ligurians,
Istrians, Huns,[37] Daunians, Iapygians, Calabrians, Oscans,
Latins who are also called Romans, Tyrannians, Gauls who
are also called Celts, Lygistinians, Celtiberians, Iberians,
Aquitanian Gauls, Illyrians, Basantians, Cyrtanians, Lusita-
nians, Huaccaians, Cynians, Britons who live in the islands.

Those of them who know letters are these: Iberians, Latins whose letters the Romans use, Spaniards, Greeks, Medes,
Armenians.

Their borders are from Media to Gadeira, including all 3
the territory to the north.[38] The sides[39] are from the river
and the river[40] to Mastousia in the east.[41]

Provintiae autem eorum sunt haec: Midia, Albania, Amazonia, Armenia parva et magna, Cappadocia, Paflagonia, Galatia, Colchus, India, Achaia, Bosporina, Meotia, Derris, Sarmatia, Tauriannia, Bastarnia, Scythia, Thracia, Macedonia, Dermatia, Molchia, Thettalia, Lucria, Byotia, Etolia, Attica, Achaia, Pelepponissus, Acarnia, Ipirotia, Illyria lucidissima,[44] Adracia a quo Hadriaticum pelagus, Gallia, Tuscinia, Lysitania, Messalia, Italia, Celtica, Spanogallia, Ibiria, Spania magna. Simul provintiae Iafeth quadraginta duae[45] usque ad Brittaniacas insulas quae ad aquilonem respiciunt.

Sunt autem eis et insulae commune autem Sicilia, Eubya, Rodus, Chius, Lesbus, Cythira, Zacynthus, Cefalinia, Thaci, Corcyra, et qui in circuitu sunt, parte Asiae qui vocatur Ionia.[46]

Fluvius autem est eis Tigris dividens Midiam et Babiloniam. Haec sunt termini tertio filio Noe.

4   Genealogia Cham secundo filio Noe.

Filii autem Cham secundo filio Noe: Chus primo genitus, ex quo Ethiopi, et Mestreim, ex quo Egyptii, et Fud, ex quo Troglodyti, et Chanaan, ex quo Afri et Punici.

Filii autem Chus Ethiopu filio Cham secundo filio Noe Sabat et Eugilat et Sabascatha et Regma et Secathath.

Et filii Regma filio Chus filio Cham secundo filio Noe Sabat et Iudadad.

Et Chus genuit Nebrod Ethiopem et venatorem et gigantem.

Their provinces are these: Media, Albania, Amazonia, Lesser and Greater Armenia, Cappadocia, Paphlagonia, Galatia, Colchis, India,[42] Achaea,[43] Bosporina, Maeotis, Derris, Sarmatia, Tauriannia, Bastarnia, Scythia, Thrace, Macedonia, Dalmatia, Molchia,[44] Thessaly, Locris, Boeotia, Aetolia, Achaea, the Peloponnese, Acarnia, Epirus, Illyria "the Brightest,"[45] Adracia after which the Adriatic Sea is named, Gaul, Tuscany, Lusitania, Messalia, Italy, Celtica, Spanogallia,[46] Iberia, Greater Spain. Altogether these are 42 provinces of Japheth all the way to the British Isles, which face to the north.

There are also the islands which belong to them: Sicily, Euboea, Rhodes, Chios, Lesbos, Cythera, Zacynthos, Cephalenia, Ithaca, Corcyra, and those lying in a circle around the part of Asia that is called Ionia (i.e., the Cyclades).

The River Tigris, which divides Media and Babylon, belongs to them. These are the borders of the third son of Noah.

The genealogy of Ham the second son of Noah   4

The sons of Ham, the second son of Noah:[47] Cush, the firstborn, from whom [are descended] the Ethiopians, and Mizraim, from whom the Egyptians, and Phut, from whom the Troglodytes, and Canaan, from whom the Africans and the Phoenicians.

The sons of Cush the Ethiopian, the son of Ham, the second son of Noah, were Seba and Havilah and Sabtah and Raamah and Sabtecha.

And the sons of Raamah, the son of Cush, the son of Ham, the second son of Noah, were Sheba and Dedan.

And Cush begat Nimrod the Ethiopian, both a hunter and a giant.

Et Aegyptiorum patrias cum Mestreim patre eorum octo. Dicit autem sic: Et Mestreim genuit illus[47] Lydiim, ex quo facti sunt Lydii, et illus Enemigim, ex quo Pamphyli, et illus Labiim, ex quo Libii, et illus Nefthabiim, ex quo Fygabii,[48] et illus Patrosoniim, ex quo <Criti, et illus Chaslomiim ex quo>[49] Licii, et illus Cafthoriim, ex quo Cilicii.

Chananeorum autem patrias cum Chanahan patre eorum sunt duodecim. Dicit enim sic: Et Chanahan genuit Sidona primogenitum, et Chetteum, et Amorreum, et Gergeseum, et Aeggeum,[50] et Aruceum,[51] ex quo Tripolitani, et Asethneum, ex quo Orthosiasti, et Arudium, ex quo Aradii, et Samareum, et Ferezeum, et Amathium.

Est autem habitatio eorum ab Rinocorurum usque Garirum aspiciente ad septentrionem[52] longitudo. Quae autem ex ipsis natae sunt gentes Ethiopi, Troglodyti, Aggei, Gagarini,[53] Isabini,[54] Piscescomeduli, Ellaini, Aegyptii, Finici, Libyi, Marmaridii, Carii, Psylliti, Myssi, Mososini,[55] Fygadii, Maconii, Bythynii, Nomadii, Lycii, Mariandini, Pamphyli, Mososini,[56] Pissidii, Autalei, Cilicii, Maurisii, Criti, Magartei, Numidii, Macarii, Nasamonii.

Hii possident ab Egypto usque ad septentrionalem oceanum,[57] gentes XXXII. Qui autem ex ipsis sciunt litteras sunt haec: Fynici, Egyptii, Pamphyli, Frygii.

And the nations[48] of the Egyptians with Mizraim their father are eight. As it says:[49] And Mizraim begat the Ludim, from whom come the Lydians, and the Anamim, from whom the Pamphylians, and the Lehabim, from whom the Libyans, and the Naphtuhim, from whom the Phrygians, and the Pathrusim, from whom <the Cretans, and the Casluhim, from whom> the Lycians, and the Caphtorim, from whom the Cilicians.

The nations of the Canaanites with Canaan their father are 12. For as it says:[50] And Canaan begat Sidon his firstborn, and the Hethite, and the Amorite, and the Girgasite, and the Hivite, and the Arkite, from whom the Tripolitanians,[51] and the Sinite, from whom the Orthosiastians, and the Arvadite, from whom the Aradians, and the Zemarite, and the Perizzite,[52] and the Hamathite.

Their dwelling is from Rhinocorura to Gadeira in length, and [all the territory] to the south[53] of this line. The peoples who are sprung from them (i.e., the sons of Ham) are: the Ethiopians, the Troglodytes, the Angaeans, the Ganginians, the Isabinians, the Fish-Eaters (i.e., Ichthyophagi),[54] the Ellainians, the Egyptians, the Phoenicians, the Libyans, the Marmaridae, the Carians, the Psyllitians,[55] the Mysians, the Mosynaeci, the Phrygians, the Macones, the Bithynians, the Nomades, the Lycians, the Mariandynians, the Pamphylians, the Mossynians, the Pisidians, the Autalaeans, the Cilicians, the Maurusians [Moors], the Cretans, the Magartaeans, the Numidians, the Macarians,[56] the Nasamones.

These 32 peoples possess [the land] from Egypt to the [southern] ocean. Those of them who know letters are these: the Phoenicians, the Egyptians, the Pamphylians, the Phrygians.

5   Est autem terminum Cham ab Rinocorurum qui extendit a Syria[58] et Ethiopia usque Garirum. Nomina autem provintiarum sunt haec: Egyptus cum omnibus qui in circuitu eius sunt, Ethiopia quae aspicit ad Indos, et alia Ethiopia unde egreditur Ethioporum fluvius Geon qui vocatur Nilus, Rubra qui aspicit ad[59] orientem, Thebaida, tota Libya qui extendit usque Corcyna,[60] Marmaria, et omnia quae in circuitu eius sunt, Syrta habens gentes tres, Nasamona, Macas, Tautameus, Libya alia qui respicit et extendit[61] usque ad minorem Syrtiam, Numeda, Massyris,[62] Mauritania, qui extendit usque Eracleoticum terminum contra Gararitum. Habet qui aspicit ad aquilonem qui circa mare sunt, Ciliciam, Pamphyliam, Pissidiam, Myssiam, Lygdoniam,[63] Frygiam, Camiliam, Lyciam, Cargam,[64] Lydiam, Troadam, Eoliam, Bithyniam antiquam qui vocatur Frygia. Simul provintias XIII.[65]

    Sunt autem eis et insulas communae Corsula, Lapanduoa, Gaula,[66] Melitia, Cercina, Minna, Taurana,[67] Sardana, Galata, Gorsuna, Crita, Gauloroda, Thira, Cariatha, Astavetera, Chius, Lesbus, Teneda, Iambra, Iasa,[68] Samus, Cous, Cnidus, Nisyra magna, Cyprus. Simul insulas XXV.[69]

    Habet enim et fluvium Geon qui vocatur Nilus, qui circuit Egyptum et Ethiopiam. Dividet inter Cham et Iafeth ab ore occidui maris.

    Haec est genealogia Cham secundo filio Noe.

The border of Ham is from Rhinocorura, which extends 5 from Syria and Ethiopia[57] to Gadeira. The names of its provinces are these: Egypt with all [of the lands] round about, Ethiopia which looks to the Indians, and the other Ethiopia from which flows the river of the Ethiopians, the Gihon which is called the Nile, Erythraea,[58] which looks to the east, the Thebaid, all of Libya which extends as far as Cyrene, Marmarica and all [of the lands] round about, Syrtis which has three peoples: the Nasamones, the Macae, the Tautamaeans, the other Libya which faces and extends to Syrtis Minor, Numidia, Massouris, Mauritania which extends to the Pillars of Hercules opposite Gadeira. [The territory of Ham] has [these lands] which look to the north and lie around the sea: Cilicia, Pamphylia, Pisidia, Mysia, Lycaonia, Phrygia, Camilia, Lycia, Caria, Lydia, the Troad, Aeolia, ancient Bithynia which is called Phrygia. Altogether these are 13 provinces.

There are also the islands which belong to them: Corsula, Lampedusa, Gozo, Malta, Cercina, Meninx, Taurana, Sardinia, Galata, Gorsyne, Crete, Gauloride, Thera, Carpathos, Old Cities (i.e., Astypalaea),[59] Chios, Lesbos, Tenedos, Imbros, Thasos, Samos, Cos, Cnidos, Nisyros the great,[60] Cyprus. In all 25 islands.

For [the territory of Ham] also has the River Gihon which is called the Nile, which encompasses Egypt and Ethiopia.[61] The mouth of the western sea divides between Ham and Japheth.[62]

This is the genealogy of Ham the second son of Noah.

6   Genealogia Sem primo genito filio Noe.[70]
De Sem autem primo genito filio Noe sunt tribus viginti quinque. Hii contra orientem habitaverunt. Elam, unde Elimei, et Asur, unde Assyrii, et Arfarad, unde Chaldei, et Lud, unde Alazonii,[71] et Futh, unde Persi,[72] et Aram, unde Yantii.

Et filius[73] Aram filii Sem filio Noe qui et Hul,[74] ex quo nascuntur Lydii, et Gather, unde Gasfinii, et Mosoch, unde Mossinii. Et Arfaxad genuit Cainan, unde fiunt qui ab oriente Samaritae. Cainan autem genuit Salathee, unde fiunt Salathii. Et Salathee genuit Eber, unde fiunt Ebrei. Eber autem nati sunt ei filii duo,[75] Falec, unde ascendit generatio Abrahae, et Ectam fratrem eius.

Ectam autem genuit Ermodad, unde nascuntur Indii, et Saleph, unde nascuntur Bactrianii, et Aram, unde et Arabii, et Iduram, unde et Milii,[76] et Ethil, unde Arrianii, et Abimeil, unde Yrcanii, et Declam, unde Cedrysii, et Gebal, unde Scythii, et Sabal, unde Adamosynii,[77] et Huir, unde Armenii, et Eugee, unde Nudisapientes. Hii omnes de Sem primogenito Noe.

Omnium filiorum Sem est habitatio a Bactriona[78] usque Rinocorurum qui pertinet usque ad Syriam et Egyptum et mare Rubrum et ab orae quae est Arsinoita India.[79]

The genealogy of Shem the firstborn son   6
of Noah

From Shem the firstborn son of Noah there are 25 tribes.[63] These lived toward the east. Elam, whence [came] the Elymaeans, and Asshur, whence the Assyrians, and Arphaxad, whence the Chaldaeans, and Lud, whence the Alazonians, and Futh,[64] whence the Persians, and Aram, whence the Yantians.[65]

And the sons of Aram, the son of Shem, the son of Noah are [Uz] and Hul,[66] from whom the Lydians arose, and Gether, whence the Gasphenians, and Mash, whence the Mossinians.

And Arphaxad begat Cainan, whence come, from the east, the Samaritans.[67] Cainan begat Salathee (i.e., Sala),[68] whence come the Salathians.[69] And Salathee begat Heber, whence come the Hebrews. Two sons were born to Heber, Peleg, whence arises the lineage of Abraham, and Joktan his brother.

Joktan begat[70] Elmodad, whence the Indians are born, and Sheleph, whence the Bactrians are born, and Aram,[71] whence also the Arabs, and Hadoram, whence also the Carmelians,[72] and Uzal, whence the Arians, and Abimael, whence the Hyrcanians, and Diklah, whence the Cedrusians,[73] and Ebal, whence the Scythians, and Sheba, whence the Adamosynians, and Ophir, whence the Armenians, and Havilah, whence the Naked Sages (i.e., Gymnosophists). These are all from Shem the firstborn of Noah.

The dwelling of all the sons of Shem is from Bactria to Rhinocorura, which stretches as far as Syria and Egypt and the Red Sea and from the outlet, which is Arsinoite India.[74]

Haec autem quae ex ipsis factas sunt gentes: Ebrei qui et Iudei, Persi, Midi, Peoni, Ariani, Assyrii, Yrcani, Indii, Magardi,[80] Parthi, Germani, Elymei, Cossei, Arabi antiqui, Cedrusii, Arabi primi, Nudi Sapientes. Extendit autem habitatio eorum usque Rinocorurum et usque Cilicia. Qui autem noverunt ex ipsis litteras sunt Ebrei qui et Iudei, Persi, Midi, Chaldei, Indii, Assyrii.

7   Est autem habitatio filiorum Sem primo genito filio Noe in longitudine ab[81] India usque Rinocorurum, latitudo autem a Persida et Bactrium usque in inferiore India.

Nomina autem provintiarum filiorum Sem sunt haec: Persida cum omnibus subiacentibus gentibus, Bactriana, Yrgania, Babilonia, Cordilia,[82] Assyria, Mesopotamia, Arabia antiqua, Elymea, India, Arabia famosa, Cylisyria, Commagenia, et Funice quae est filiorum Sem.

8   Omnes isti ex trium filiorum Noe tribus LXXII.[83]

Gentes autem, quas dispersit dominus deus super faciem omnis terras[84] secundum linguas eorum in diebus Falec et Ectam fratrem eius in turris aedificatione quando confusas sunt linguas eorum, sunt autem haec:

i Ebrei qui et Iudei.	vi Arabi primi et secundi.
ii Assyrii.	vii Madiani primi et
iii Chaldei.	secundi.
iv Midi.	viii Adiabini.
v Persi.	viiii Taiani.

These are the peoples who were produced from them: the Hebrews or Jews, the Persians, the Medes, the Peonians,[75] the Arians, the Assyrians, the Hyrcanians, the Indians, the Macardians, the Parthians, the Germans,[76] the Elymaeans (i.e., Elamites), the Cossaeans,[77] the ancient Arabs, the Cedrusians, the first Arabs, the Naked Sages. Their dwelling extends as far as Rhinocorura and as far as Cilicia. Those of them who know letters are the Hebrews or Jews, the Persians, the Medes, the Chaldaeans, the Indians, the Assyrians.

The dwelling of the sons of Shem the firstborn son of 7 Noah extends in length from India to Rhinocorura, in breadth from Persia and Bactria to lower India.

The names of the provinces of the sons of Shem are these: Persia with all of its subject peoples, Bactria, Hyrcania, Babylon, Cordilia, Assyria, Mesopotamia, ancient Arabia, Elymaea (i.e., Elam), India, Arabia Felix, Coele-Syria, Commagene, and Phoenicia which belongs to the sons of Shem.[78]

All these 72 tribes descend from the three sons of 8 Noah.[79]

The peoples which the Lord God scattered over the face of the whole earth according to their languages in the days of Peleg and Joktan his brother at the building of the tower, when their languages were confused, are these:

1. Hebrews or Jews
2. Assyrians
3. Chaldaeans
4. Medes
5. Persians

6. First and Second Arabs
7. First and Second Midianites.
8. Adiabenes
9. Taeni[80]

x Salamossini.[85]
xi Sarracini.
xii Magi.
xiii Caspiani.
xiv Albani.
xv Indi primi et secundi.
xvi Ethiopi primi et secundi.
xvii Egyptii et Thibei.
xviii Libyi.
xviiii Chotthei.
xx Chananei
xxi Ferezei.
xxii Eugei.
xxiii Amorrei.
xxiv Gergesei.
xxv Iebusei.
xxvi Idomei.
xxvii Samarei.
xxviii Fynici.
xxviiii Euri.[86]
xxx Cilicii qui et Tharsi.
xxxi Cappadoci.
xxxii Armenii.
xxxiii Ibiri.
xxxiv Bibrani.[87]
xxxv Scythi.
xxxvi Colchi.
xxxvii Sanni.

xxxviii Bosporani.
xxxviiii Asiani.
xl Issaurii.
xli Lycaonii.
xlii Pissidii.
xliii Galatas.
xliv Pamflagoni.
xlv Flygii.
xlvi Greci qui et Achei.
xlvii Thessali.
xlviii Macedonii.
xlviiii Thraci.
l Myssi.
li Bessi.
lii Dardani.
liii Sarmati.
liv Germani.
lv Pannonii.
lvi Norici.
lvii Delmatii.
lviii Romei qui et Cittei.
lxviiii Lygurii.[88]
lx Galli qui et Celtei.
lxi Aquitanii.
lxii Brittani.
lxiii Spani qui et Tyranni.
lxiv Mauri.
lxv Macuaci.
lxvi Getuli.
lxvii Afri.

10. Alamossynians[81]
11. Saracens
12. Magi
13. Caspians
14. Albans
15. First and Second Indians
16. First and Second Ethiopians
17. Egyptians and Thebans
18. Libyans
19. Hethites
20. Canaanites
21. Perizzites
22. Hivites
23. Amorites
24. Girgasites
25. Jebusites
26. Idumaeans (i.e., Edomites)
27. Samaritans
28. Phoenicians
29. Syrians
30. Cilicians or Tharsians[82]
31. Cappadocians
32. Armenians
33. Iberians
34. Bibrani
35. Scythians
36. Colchians
37. Sanni[83]

38. Bosporans
39. Arians
40. Isaurians
41. Lycaonians
42. Pisidians
43. Galatians
44. Paphlagonians
45. Phrygians
46. Greeks or Achaeans
47. Thessalians
48. Macedonians
49. Thracians
50. Mysians
51. Bessi[84]
52. Dardanians
53. Sarmatians
54. Germans
55. Pannonians
56. Norici[85]
57. Dalmatians
58. Romans or Cittaeans
59. Ligurians
60. Gauls or Celts
61. Aquitanians
62. Britons
63. Spaniards or Tyrannians
64. Moors
65. Macuaci[86]
66. Getulians
67. Africans

LXVIII Mazici.

LXVIIII Tarantii[89]
exteriores.

LXX Boradii.[90]

LXXI Celtionii.[91]

LXXII Taramantii exteriores
qui usque in Ethiopia
extendunt.

Fiunt simul tribus LXXII.
Istas gentes dispersit dominus deus super faciem omnis terrae secundum linguas eorum. Fiunt simul tribus LXXII.

Caput III

E t hoc studui significare tibi quales sunt et acolae ignotas gentes et interpretationes eorum et fines et habitationes eorum et quae vicinas regiones eorum. Initiamus scribere ab oriente usque in occidente secundum ordinem.

Persi et Midi acolae facti sunt Parthi et quae in circuitu gentes Pacis usque media Syria.

Arabi autem acolae facti sunt Arabi famosi: isto autem nomine nominatur Arabia ab omnibus famosa.

Chaldei autem acolae facti sunt Mesopotamite.

Madianite acolae facti sunt Cinedocolpitas et Troglodytas et Piscescomeduli.

Grecorum autem gentes et nomina eorum sunt quinque: Hionii, Arcadii, Biotii, Eolii, Laconii. Istorum autem acolae facti sunt Pontici et Bithynii, Troii et Asiani, Carii et Lycii, Pamphyli, Cyrinei, et insulae multae quae vocantur

68. Mazices[87]

69. Outer Garamantes

70. Borades

71. Celtiones

72. Outer Garamantes, who stretch to Ethiopia.[88]

Altogether 72 tribes.

The Lord God scattered those peoples over the face of the whole earth according to [their] languages. Altogether 72 tribes.

Chapter 3

And I have endeavored to indicate this to you:[89] what sort of colonists the unknown peoples are, their identities, their borders and dwellings, and which the regions adjacent to their own. We shall begin to set them down from the east to the west in order.[90]

The Persian and Median colonists[91] became the Parthians and the peoples around Peace (i.e., Eirene—?)[92] as far as the middle of Syria.[93]

The Arabian colonists became the "Renowned Arabs": from that name Arabia is called "Renowned" by all.[94]

The Chaldean colonists became the Mesopotamians.

The Midianite colonists became Cinedocolpitae,[95] the Troglodytes, and the Fish-Eaters (i.e., Ichthyophagi).

The peoples of the Greeks and their names are five: Ionians, Arcadians, Boeotians, Aeolians, Laconians. Their colonists became the Ponticans and Bithynians, the Trojans and Asians, the Carians and Lycians, the Pamphylians, the Cyreneans,[96] and [the inhabitants] of the many islands which

Cycladas XI, qui Myrtium pelagum habent. Sunt autem haec: Andrus, Tinus,[92] Tio, Naxus, Ceus, Curus, Dilus, Sifnus, Nirea,[93] Cyrnus, Marathrum.[94]

Sunt et alias insulas magnas duodecim, qui etiam et civitates plures habent quae vocantur Esporadas, in quas habitaverunt Greci. Sunt autem haec: Eubia, Crita, Sicilia, Cyprus, Cous, Tamus,[95] Rodus, Chius, Thassus, Limnus, Lesbus, Samothraci.[96]

Est[97] autem ab Biotes[98] Eubia sicut ab Hiones[99] Ionidis civitates sedecim nominatas. Sunt autem haec: Clazomena, Mitilina, Focea, Priinna, Erythra, Samus, Teus, Colofa, Chius, Efesus, Smyrna, Perinthus, Byzantius, Chalcedona, Pontus, Amissus eleuthera.[100]

2   Romanorum autem qui et Cittei gentes et acolae sunt septem: Tuscii, Emillisui, Sicinii, Campani, Apulisii, Calabrii, Lucanii.

Afrorum autem gentes et acolae sunt V: Nebdini,[101] Cnithi,[102] Numidii, Sii,[103] Nassamonii. Sunt autem eis et insulas V civitates habentes: Sardinia,[104] Corsica, Girba, Cercina, Galata.[105]

Maurorum autem gentes et acolae sunt tres: Mosulami, Tiggitanii, et Sarinei.

Spanorum autem qui et Tyrinniorum, vocantur autem Paraconnisii,[106] gentes et acolae sunt quinque: Lysitanii, Beticii, Autrigonii, Vuascones, Callaici qui et Aspores[107] vocantur.

Tallorum[108] autem qui et Narbudisii vocantur gentes et acolae sunt quattuor: Lugdunii, Bilici, Sicanii, Ednii.

Germanorum autem gentes et acolae sunt quinque: Marcomallii, Bardunii, Cuadrii, Berdilii, Ermunduli.

are called the 11 Cyclades, which lie in the Myrtoan Sea.[97] These are: Andros, Tenos, Tio,[98] Naxos, Ceos, Curos, Delos, Siphnos, Neraea,[99] Cyrnos,[100] Marathon.

There are also 12 other large islands, which also have several cities, which are called the Sporades,[101] which the Greeks have settled.[102] These are: Euboea, Crete, Sicily, Cyprus, Cos, Samos, Rhodes, Chios, Thasos, Lemnos, Lesbos, Samothrace.

Euboea is named after the Boeotians, just as there are 16 cities called Ionides after the Ionians. These are: Clazomenae, Mytilene, Phocaea, Priene, Erythrae, Samos, Teos, Colophon, Chios, Ephesus, Smyrna, Perinthus, Byzantium, Chalcedon, Pontus,[103] free Amissus.[104]

The peoples and the colonists of the Romans, or Cittaeans, are seven: the Etruscans, Aemilians,[105] Sicanians,[106] Campanians, Apulians, Calabrians, Lucanians. 2

The peoples and the colonists of the Africans are five:[107] the Nebdini, Cnethi,[108] Numidians, Saei,[109] Nasamones. Five islands which have cities belong to them: Sardinia, Corsica, Girba,[110] Cercina, Galata.

The peoples and the colonists of the Moors are three: the Mosulami,[111] Tingitanians,[112] and Sarinaeans.[113]

The peoples and the colonists of the Spaniards, or Tyrinnians (also called the Taraconenses),[114] are five: the Lusitanians, Baeticans, Autrigonians, Vascones, Callaicans who are also called Asturians.

The peoples and the colonists of the Gauls,[115] who are called Narbonenses, are four: the Lugdunenses, Belgians,[116] Sicanians,[117] Ednians.[118]

The peoples and the colonists of the Germans are five:[119] the Marcomanni, Bardunians, Quadi, Berdilians, Hermunduri.[120]

Sarmatorum autem gentes et acolae sunt II: Amaxobii et Grecosarmates.

Istas gentes et peregrinationes eorum sicut dispersas sunt super terram.

Et hoc[109] mihi studium fuit significare tibi de ignotas gentes et oppidos eorum et nominatos montes et illos principales fluvius, ut ne de hoc inmemor sis.

Initiemus autem dicere de illas ignotas gentes ab oriente usque ad occiduum solis quomodo habitant.

Illi Adiabeni habitant ultra Arabia interiore, Tainaii[110] autem ultra illos, Alamosyni[111] autem ultra Arabes in inferiore Arabia, Saccini[112] autem ultra Taones,[113] Albani autem ultra Caspianorum portas, Madinii fortiores, qui expugnati sunt a Moyse, in Rubro maris. Illa autem modica Madian[114] est ultra de illa Rubra mare, ubi regnavit Raguel et Iothor socer Moysi.

Et ultra Cappadocia in dextera Armenii et Birri[115] et Birrani,[116] in leva autem Scythi et Colchi et Bosporani, Sanni autem qui dicuntur Sanniggii, qui et usque Pontum extendunt, ubi est congregatio Apsari[117] et Sebastopolis et Causolimin[118] et Fasis fluvius. Usque ad Trapezuntum extendunt istas gentes. In leva autem parte Nauthi et Labooti.

3   Montes[119] autem sunt nominati duodecim in terra excepto illum deo spiratum montem Sina sic: Libanus in Syria inter Biblo et Biryto, Caucasus in Scythia, Taurus in Cilicia et Cappadocia, Aulas[120] in Libya, Parnasus in Focida, Citherus in Byotia, Elicus in Teumiso, Parthenius in Eubya,

The peoples and the colonists of the Sarmatians are two: the Hamaxobians[121] and Graecosarmatians.[122]

These are the peoples and their migrations as they were dispersed over the earth.

And I have been at pains to indicate to you the unknown peoples and their towns and the famous mountains and the most important rivers, so that you should not be unmindful of all of this.

Let us begin to speak of those unknown peoples[123] from the rising to the setting of the sun,[124] [telling] where [or how] they live.[125]

The Adiabenians live beyond inner Arabia, the Taiani live beyond them, the Alamosyni live beyond the Arabs in lower Arabia, the Saracens[126] live beyond the Taeni,[127] the Albanians live beyond the Caspian Gates, the Greater Midianites,[128] who were conquered by Moses, live on the Red Sea. Lesser Midian is beyond the Red Sea, where Reuel or Jethro,[129] the father-in-law of Moses, ruled.

And beyond Cappadocia on the right[130] [live] the Armenians and Iberians and Birrani, on the left Scythians and Colchians and Bosporans, the Sanni, who are also called Sanningi,[131] who stretch as far as Pontus, where the assemblage (i.e., fort) of Apsarus[132] is and Sebastopol and Causolimin (i.e., the harbor of Issus)[133] and the River Phasis. These peoples stretch as far as Trebizond. On the left, moreover,[134] are the Nauthians and Labootians.[135]

There are 12 famous mountains in the world—apart from the one upon which the Spirit of God descended[136]—they are: Lebanon in Syria, between Byblos and Beirut, Caucasus in Scythia, Taurus in Cilicia and Cappadocia, Atlas in Libya, Parnassus in Phocis, Cithaeron in Boeotia, Helicon

3

Nysseusin in Arabia, Lycabantus in Italia et Gallia, Pinnius in Chio qui et Mimas,[121] Olympius autem in Macedonia.[122] Significantes[123] autem nomina montium terrae necesse est de illos principales fluvios nuntiare tibi.

Fluvii autem sunt nominati quadraginta: Indus qui vocatur Fison, et Nilus qui vocatur Geon, Tigris et Eufrates, Iordanis, Cifissus, Taneus, Isminius, Erymanthus, Alyus, Assopus, Thermodus, Erasimus, Rius, Borysthenus, Alfius, Taurus, Eurotus, Meandrus, Axxius, Pyramus, Orentus, Danubius, Ebrus, Saggarius, Achelmus, Pinnius, Euginus, Sperchius, Gaustrus, Semoius, Scamandrus, Styramus, Parthenius, Istrus, Rinus, Betus, Rodanus, Eridanus, Beus, Thubiris qui nunc vocatur Thubiris. Fiunt simul flumina currentes[124] XL.[125]

Caput IIII

Significantes autem his omnibus tempus advenit ad textum chronicae currere annos. Sicut prius demontravimus dicentes, ab Adam usque ad diluvium Noe generationes quidem X, anni duo milia ducenti quadraginta duo, et a diluvio Noe usque ad turris edificationem et confusione divisarum linguarum generationes quidem sex, anni autem quingenti quinquaginta octo. Fiunt simul anni duo milia octingenti.

in Telmissus, Parthenius on Euboea, Nysaeus in Arabia,[137] Lycabantus in Italy and Gaul,[138] Pelinion or Mimas on Chios,[139] and Olympus in Macedonia.

Having indicated the names of the mountains of the world, it is necessary to report to you the most important rivers.

There are 40[140] famous rivers:[141] the Indus, which is called the Pison,[142] and the Nile, which is called the Gihon,[143] the Tigris and the Euphrates,[144] the Jordan, the Cephissus, the Tanais (i.e., Don), the Ismenus, the Erymanthus, the Halys, the Asopus, the Thermodon, the Erasinus, the Rius,[145] the Borysthenes, the Alpheus, the Taurus, the Eurotas, the Meander, the Axius, the Pyramus, the Orontes, the Danube, the Hebrus, the Sangarius, the Achelous, the Pinnius, the Evenus, the Sperchius, the Caÿster, the Simoeis, the Scamander, the Strymon, the Parthenius, the Ister (i.e., Danube), the Rhine, the Baitis,[146] the Rhodanus (i.e., Rhone), the Eridanus (i.e., Po), the Baeus, the Thouberis, which is now called the Tiber. Altogether there are 40 flowing rivers.

Chapter 4

Having indicated all these things the time has come to run through the years according to the text of the chronicle. As we showed before from Adam to the flood of Noah there are 10 generations, 2,242 years, and from the flood of Noah to the building of the tower and the confusion of the different tongues there are 6 generations, or 558 years. Altogether this makes 2,800 years.[147]

Et a divisione terrarum usque dum genuit Abraham Isaac generationes quidem sex, anni autem sexcenti tres[126] sic.

Post divisionem terrarum factus est Falec annorum C: fiunt simul anni duo milia noningenti, et genuit Ragau. Sub isto divisio facta est. Falec enim inpraetatur divisio.

2   Vixit autem Ragau annos centum treginta II: fiunt simul anni trea milia treginta II, et genuit Seruch.

Vixit autem Seruch annos centum treginta duos: fiunt simul anni trea milia CLXIIII, et genuit Nachor.

Vixit autem Nachor annos septuaginta nouem: fiunt simul anni trea milia CCXLIII, et genuit Tharam.

Vixit autem Thara annos LXX: fiunt simul anni trea milia CCCXIII, et genuit Abraham.

Factus est autem Abraham annorum LXXV: fiunt simul anni trea milia CCCLXXXVIII, quando praecepit illi deus exire de domo patris sui et venire in terram Chanaan.

Habitavit autem Abraham in terra Chanaan alios annos XXV: fiunt anni centum, et sic genuit Isaac. Fiunt simul ab Adam usque quod genuit Abraham Isaac omnes anni trea millia quadringenti XIII.[127]

Temporibus vere Abrahae quando genuit Isaac Syrorum primus regnavit Bilus annos LXII, Sicyoniorum autem regnavit Egialeus, in Egyptios regnavit Arouth Farao.

Fiunt simul ab Adam usque dum genuit Abraham Isaac generationes XXI, anni trea milia quadringenti XIII, et ab Abraham usque ad exitum filiorum Israhel per Moysen generationes quidem VI, anni autem quadringenti[128] tres.

3   Abraham autem erat annorum centum, quando genuit Isaac: fiunt simul ab Adam anni trea milia quadringenti XIII.

And from the division of the lands to when Abraham begat Isaac there are six generations, or 603 years, thus: After the division of the lands Peleg was 100 years old (altogether this makes 2,900 years), and begat Reu. In his time the division occurred. For Peleg is translated as "division."

Reu lived 132 years (altogether this makes 3,032 years), 2 and begat Serug.

Serug lived 132 years (altogether this makes 3,164 years), and begat Nahor.

Nahor lived 79 years (altogether this makes 3,243 years), and begat Terah.

Terah lived 70 years (altogether this makes 3,313 years), and begat Abraham.

Abraham was 75 years old (altogether this makes 3,388 years), when God commanded him to leave the house of his father and go to the land of Canaan.

Abraham lived in the land of Canaan for another 25 years (this makes 100 years), and then begat Isaac. Altogether this makes from Adam to when Abraham begat Isaac in all 3,413 years.

In the time of Abraham, when he begat Isaac, Belus reigned over the Syrians as their first king for 62 years, Aegialeus ruled the Sicyonians, and Arouth reigned as pharaoh among the Egyptians.

Altogether this makes from Adam to when Abraham begat Isaac 21 generations, or 3,413 years, and from Abraham to the exodus of the sons of Israel through Moses 6 generations, or 403 years.

Abraham was 100 years old when he begat Isaac: alto- 3 gether this makes from Adam 3,413 years.

Vixit autem Isaac annos sexaginta: fiunt anni trea milia quadringenti septuaginta tres, et genuit Iacob.

Vixit autem Iacob annos octuaginta tres: fiunt simul anni trea milia quingenti quinquaginta sex, et genuit Levi et fratres eius.

Vixit autem Levi annos XLV: fiunt simul anni trea milia DCI, et sic genuit Caath.

Vixit autem Caath annos LX: fiunt simul anni trea milia DCLXI, et genuit Ambram.

Vixit autem Ambram annos LXXV, fiunt simul anni trea milia septingenti XXXVI, et genuit Moysen et Aaron et Mariam sororem eorum.

Factus est autem Moyses annorum LXXX (fiunt simul anni trea milia octingenti XVI) quando intravit ad Faraonem regem Egypti. Et fecit dominus deus signa et prodigia per manum Moysi, mittens decem plagas in Egypto. Et eduxit filios Israhel de Egypto in manu forte, et transierunt mare Rubrum pedibus sicut aridam.[129]

Fecerunt[130] autem <. . .>[131] et in herimo Sinai filii Israhel comedentes manna annos XL: fiunt simul anni trea milia octingenti LVI. Fiunt ab Adam usque ad mortem Moysi anni trea milia octingenti LVI.

In diebus autem Moysi Froneus Argion regnavit cum Inachum, Leucyppus autem Siceis regnavit, Eretheus Athineis regnavit, Hilochus autem Assyriis regnavit, Petessonsius autem Farao in Egypto. Occiduum enim sine regno erat.

Fiunt simul ab Adam usque ad mortem Moysi generationes quidem XXVI, anni autem trea milia octingenti LVI, et a morte Moysi usque ad mortem Hiesu Nave et Finees sacerdotis anni LIIII sic.

Isaac lived 60 years (altogether this makes 3,473 years), and begat Jacob.

Jacob lived 83 years (altogether this makes 3,556 years), and begat Levi and his brothers.

Levi lived 45 years (altogether this makes 3,601 years), and then begat Kohath.

Kohath lived 60 years (altogether this makes 3,661 years), and begat Amram.

Amram lived 75 years (altogether this makes 3,736 years), and begat Moses and Aaron and Miriam, their sister.

Moses was 80 years old (altogether this makes 3,816 years) when he went to Pharaoh, the king of Egypt. And the Lord God performed signs and wonders by the hand of Moses, sending ten plagues on Egypt. And he led the sons of Israel out from Egypt in his mighty hand, and they crossed the Red Sea on foot as if through dry land.

The sons of Israel were in the wilderness of Sinai eating manna for 40 years: altogether this makes 3,856 years. This makes from Adam to the death of Moses 3,856 years.

In the days of Moses Phoroneus ruled the Argives with Inachus,[148] Leucippus ruled the Sicyonians, Erechtheus ruled the Athenians, Belochus ruled the Assyrians, and Petissonius was pharaoh in Egypt. For there was no kingdom in the regions of the west.

Altogether this makes from Adam to the death of Moses 26 generations, or 3,856 years, and from the death of Moses to the death of Joshua the son of Nun and Phinehas the priest 54 years, thus:

Caput V

Post mortem autem Moysi et Aaron suscitavit dominus deus spiritum suum super Hiesu filium Nave, et transmeavit populum filiorum Israhel Iordanis fluvium, et ceciderunt muri Hiericho. Et exterminavit a facie filiorum Israhel Chananeum et Chetteum et Eugeum et Ferezeum et Amorreum et Gergeseum et Hiebuseum, et fecit in terram quam invasit annos XXXI sic: pugnando fecit annos sex et possidens alios viginti quinque annos terram illam, fiunt simul anni treginta unum. Fiunt simul ab Adam anni trea milia octingenti octuaginta septem.

Et post obitum Hiesu filii Nave praefuit populo Finees sacerdos annos XXIII, fiunt anni LIIII. Fiunt simul ab Adam usque ad obitum Hiesu filii Nave et Finees sacerdotis omnes anni trea milia noningenti decem.[132]

Et ab obito Hiesu et Finees usque ad initium Heli sacerdotis, finis autem iudicum filiorum Israhel, anni sunt quadragenti XLV[133] sic.

Post obitum Hiesu et Finees peccavit populus filiorum Israhel ad deum, et tradidit illos deus Chusateri regi Mesopotamiae, et servierunt illi annos novem. Fiunt simul anni trea milia noningenti XVIIII. Et clamaverunt ad dominum, et suscitavit illis dominus deus principem Gothonial, fratrem Chaleb iuvenem, de tribu Iuda. Iste pugnavit cum Chusather in bello et interfecit eum. Et iudicavit Gothonial populum annos XXXIIII. Fiunt simul anni trea milia noningenti LIII.

Chapter 5

After the death of Moses and Aaron the Lord God raised up his spirit upon Joshua the son of Nun, and the people of the sons of Israel crossed the River Jordan, and the walls of Jericho fell down. And he drove out from before the face of the sons of Israel the Canaanite, and the Hittite, and the Hivite, and the Perizzite, and the Amorite, and the Girgashite, and the Jebusite. And he was in the land which he invaded for 31 years, thus: he was fighting for 6 years and for a further 25 years he was in possession of this land; altogether this makes 31 years. Altogether this makes from Adam 3,887 years.

And after the death of Joshua the son of Nun Phinehas the priest was in charge of the people for 23 years; this makes 54 years. Altogether this makes from Adam to the death of Joshua the son of Nun and Phinehas the priest in all 3,910 years.

And from the death of Joshua and Phinehas to the beginning of the priesthood of Eli, that is, the end of the judges of the sons of Israel, there are 445 years, thus:

After the death of Joshua and Phinehas the people of the sons of Israel sinned before God, and God handed them over to Cushan-rishataim, the king of Mesopotamia, and they served him for nine years. Altogether this makes 3,919 years. And they cried to the Lord, and the Lord God raised up for them a leader, Othniel, Caleb's younger brother, from the tribe of Judah. This man fought with Cushan-rishataim in war and slew him. And Othniel judged the people for 34 years. Altogether this makes 3,953 years.

2   Et iterum peccavit populus ad deum et traditi sunt a domino Eglom regi Moab, et servierunt illi filii Israhel annos XVIII. Fiunt simul anni trea milia noningenti LXXI. Convertentes autem iterum ad deum suscitavit illis principem Naoth, virum de tribu Efraim, et interfecit Eglom. Et praefuit populo annos LV. Fiunt simul anni quattuor milia XXVI.

Post Naoth autem iudicavit populum filiorum Israhel Semegas filius eius, et ipse iudicavit Israhel annos viginti V. Fiunt simul anni quattuor milia LI.

In diebus Naoth et Semega filium eius iudicum in ipsis scribuntur fuisse Promitheus et Epimitheus et Atlas et providens Algus, item Deucalios, et post eos diluvius sub Gregorum. Memoratur[134] Promitheus plasmare homines sicut phittonissae,[135] non autem sic, sed quia sapiens fuit valde inperitos homines quasi parvulos plasmabat. Atlas autem, Promitheus frater, amabilis astrologus fulgebat: per disciplinam eius et caelum illi fertur deponi. Euripidus autem poeta super nubes dixit Atlatum esse. Epimitheus autem dicitur inventor lyrae et omne organa musica.

3   Et post obitum Naoth et Semega iudicum iterum peccavit populus coram domino deo, et tradidit illos dominus deus Iabi regi Assyriorum, et servierunt ei annos XX. Fiunt simul anni quattuor milia LXXI.

Sub isto prophetavit Deborra, uxor Lafiu, et per ipsam tenuit principatum filiorum Israhel Barach, ille de Aminoem, de tribu Neptalim. Iste pugnavit contra Sisara principe Iabis et superavit eum. Et regnavit super filios Israhel

And again the people sinned before God, and they were 2 handed over by the Lord to Eglon the king of Moab, and the sons of Israel served him for 18 years. Altogether this makes 3,971 years. But when they turned back to God, he raised up for them a leader *Naoth*,[149] a man from the tribe of Ephraim, and he slew Eglon. And he was in charge of the people for 55 years. Altogether this makes 4026 years.

After *Naoth* his son Shemgar judged the people of the sons of Israel, and he judged Israel for 25 years. Altogether this makes 4,051 years.

In the days of the judges *Naoth* and Shemgar his son it is recorded that Prometheus and Epimetheus lived, and Atlas and Foreseeing Argos,[150] as well as Deucalion, and after them was the flood in the time of the Greeks. It is related that Prometheus molded men[151] as witches[152] do, but it was not like this, rather because he was an exceedingly wise man he molded ignorant men as if they were little children. Atlas, the brother of Prometheus, shone as an admirable[153] astrologer, and it is said that by his learning the very sky was brought down to him.[154] Euripides the poet said that Atlas was above the clouds.[155] Epimetheus is called the inventor of the lyre and every kind of musical instrument.

And after the death of the judges *Naoth* and Shemgar the 3 people sinned again before the Lord God, and the Lord God handed them over to Jabin the king of the Assyrians,[156] and they served him for 20 years. Altogether this makes 4,071 years.

In his time Deborah, the wife of Lapidoth, prophesied and through her Barak the son of Abinoam from the tribe of Naphtali held the leadership of the sons of Israel. This man fought against Sisera, Jabin's captain, and overcame him.

iudicans eos Deborra cum Barach annos XL. Fiunt simul anni quattuor milia CXI.

In diebus autem Deborra et Barach omnes de Dena[136] scribuntur esse, Athineorum autem tunc regnavit Cecrops qui vocabatur Dipsyis[137] annos L: Dipsyis autem vocabatur, quia statura procerus erat.[138]

Post mortem autem Deborra et Barach iterum peccavit populus coram deo, et tradidit illos dominus deus Orib <et Zeb>[139] Madianitis, et servierunt eis annos VII. Fiunt simul anni quattuor milia CXVIII.

Post haec suscitavit deus Gedeon habentem tricentos viros, et interfecit Oreb et Zeb et duodecim milia Allofylorum. Et iudicavit Gedeon Israhel annos XL. Fiunt simul anni quattuor milia CLVIII.

In diebus autem Gedeoni principis Zethus et Afius filii Zini scribuntur, et illa Ganymidis et Persea et Dionysu. Amfius autem Cadmu nepus Thibeis regnavit et condidit mura Thibeae.[140]

4   Et post Gedeon praefuit filios Israhel filius Abimelech, et ipse iudicavit Israhel annos III. Fiunt simul anni quattuor milia CLXI.

Et post istum iterum rexit filios Israhel Thola filius Fila filio Charram quem de tribu Efraim, et ipse iudicavit Israhel annos XXIII. Fiunt simul anni quattuor milia CLXXXIIII.

In diebus autem his illas de Lycurgum et Acteum et Pelopum scribuntur.

Et post mortem Tholae filio Fila surrexit Iaher ille Galadita de tribu Manasse. Et ipse iudicavit Israhel annos XXII. Fiunt simul anni quattuor milia CCVI.[141]

And Deborah, with Barak, reigned over the sons of Israel, judging them, for 40 years. Altogether this makes 4,111 years.

In the days of Deborah and Barak all those things concerning Zeus are recorded as having taken place. Cecrops, who was called *Diphyes,* then ruled the Athenians for 50 years; he was called *Diphyes* because he was tall in stature.[157]

After the death of Deborah and Barak the people sinned again before God, and the Lord God handed them over to Oreb <and Zeeb>[158] the Midianites, and they served them for seven years. Altogether this makes 4,118 years.

After these things God raised up Gideon, who had three hundred men, and he slew Oreb and Zeeb and twelve thousand of the Gentiles.[159] And Gideon judged Israel for 40 years. Altogether this makes 4,158 years.

In the days of Gideon the leader are recorded Zethus and Amphion the sons of Zeus,[160] and the affairs of Ganymede and Perseus and Dionysus. Amphion, the descendant of Cadmus,[161] ruled the Thebans and built the walls of Thebes.

And after Gideon his son Abimelech was in charge of the sons of Israel, and he judged Israel for three years. Altogether this makes 4,161 years. 4

And after him Tola the son of Puah the son of Charram, who was from the tribe of Ephraim, again ruled the sons of Israel, and he judged Israel for 23 years.[162] Altogether this makes 4,184 years.

In these days are recorded the events to do with Lycurgus and Actaeon and Pelops.

And after the death of Tola the son of Puah Jair, a Gileadite from the tribe of Manasseh, arose. And he judged Israel for 22 years. Altogether this makes 4,206 years.

Et post mortem Iaher principis iterum peccaverunt filii Israhel coram deo, et traditi sunt Amanitis, et servierunt illos[142] annos XVIII. Fiunt simul anni quattuor milia CCXXIIII. Et clamaverunt iterum ad deum, et suscitavit eis principem Iefthe illum Galaditam de tribu Manasse, et liberavit eos, et praefuit populo annos sex. Fiunt simul anni quattuor milia CCXXX. Et post iudicavit Eglom ille Zabulonita annos X. Fiunt simul anni quattuor milia CCXL. Et post istum iudicavit Esbal ille Bethlemita de tribu Iuda, et ipse iudicavit Israhel annos VII. Fiunt simul anni quattuor milia CCXLVII. Et post istum praefuit populo Abdon filius Ella ille Farathonita de tribu Efraim, et ipse iudicavit Israhel annos VIII. Fiunt simul anni quattuor milia CCLV.

5 Et post istum iterum peccavit populus coram domino, et tradidit illos deus Fylisteis et alienigenis, et servierunt illis annos XL. Fiunt simul anni quattuor milia ducenti XCV.

In diebus autem illis solis aedificatus est, et mura Dardani scribuntur esse aedificata, in quo regnavit Darius et post istum Laomedus et Sarpidus et Siamus scolasticus rex.

Postquam autem reuersi sunt filii Israhel ad dominum suscitavit illis deus Sampson filium Manoe de tribu Dan. Iste expugnavit Allofylos et iudicavit Israhel annos XX. Fiunt simul anni quattuor milia CCCXV.

In diebus autem Sampson iudicis illa qui Dedela et Atrea[143] et Thyesten scribuntur, item autem Orfeus et

And after the death of Jair, the leader, the sons of Israel sinned again before God, and they were handed over to the Ammonites, and they served them for 18 years. Altogether this makes 4,224 years. And again they cried out to God, and he raised up for them a leader, Jephthah the Gileadite from the tribe of Manasseh, and he freed them, and he was in charge of the people for six years. Altogether this makes 4,230 years.

And afterward Elon the Zebulonite judged for 10 years. Altogether this makes 4,240 years.

And after him Ibzan the Bethlehemite of the tribe of Judah was judge, and he judged Israel for seven years. Altogether this makes 4,247 years.

And after him Abdon the son of Hillel, the Pirathonite from the tribe of Ephraim, was in charge of the people, and he judged Israel for eight years. Altogether this makes 4,255 years.

And after him the people sinned again before the Lord, 5 and God handed them over to the Philistines and the foreigners, and they served them for 40 years. Altogether this makes 4,295 years.

In these days Sun City (i.e., Ilium)[163] was built, and it is recorded that the walls of Dardanus were built, in which Darius ruled[164] and after him Laomedon and Sarpedon and Priam,[165] the scholarly[166] king.

Afterward the sons of Israel turned back to the Lord, and God raised up for them Samson the son of Manoah from the tribe of Dan. This man defeated the Gentiles and judged Israel for 20 years. Altogether this makes 4,315 years.

In the days of the judge Samson are recorded those things which concern Daedalus and Atreus and Thyestes, in the

Museus cognoscebantur et qui ad Eraclem pertinent et opus illorum, de quo Apollonius historiografus scripsit.[144]

Et post[145] obitum Sampson sine principem et pacem per annos XL. Fiunt simul anni quattuor milia CCCLV.

Et post haec Heli sacerdos iudicavit Israhel: quo tempore ille solis confixus est ab Acheis et Dardana mura confracta sunt.

Huc usque iudices Israhel constaverunt.[146]

Iudices enim Israhel secundum proprias eorum generationes finierunt, de illos autem qui sine genealogia manifestatio haec est.

Caput VI

Temporibus uero iudicum recensuimus dicendo in ispsis fuerunt qui ec Diu depinguntur; unde: Picus ille Cronu pronepus partibus occasu ipsis temporibus imperavit. Cronus quidem propater eius in divisione terrae fuit occidentales partes tenens, sicut sine urbes et sine reges essent: de quo multus est sermo et sine interpraetatione sunt.

Post Cronis autem perditionem secundum successiones[147] annorum Picus pronepus eius per tempora regnavit in Italia primus, quem et Serafin quidam interpraetaverunt, alii autem Dia Olympium, ceteri autem Plutea Aidonium, et alii Chthonium Posidona. Istorum autem nominum ei pertinuit

same [time] Orpheus and Musaeus were known, and [the things] which pertain to Heracles and their work,[167] about which Apollonius the historian wrote.[168]

And after the death of Samson [the people were] without a leader and without peace throughout 40 years. Altogether this makes 4,355 years.

And after these things Eli the priest judged Israel, in which time Sun City (i.e., Ilium) was razed by the Achaeans and the Dardanian walls were broken down.

Up to this point the judges remained in Israel.

For the judges of Israel ceased according to their proper generations, but this is the disclosure concerning those without a genealogy.

Chapter 6

In the time of the judges, we have mentioned, were those who are portrayed as the children of Zeus. So [we include here this narrative of him]: Picus, the son[169] of Cronus, ruled in the regions of the west in those times. Cronus, his father, obtained the western regions in the division of the earth,[170] as they were without cities and without kings (much is said concerning this, and it is not translated).

After the death of Cronus according to the passing of years Picus his son ruled, through time, the first in Italy, whom some have understood as Serapis, but others as Olympian Zeus, and still others as Pluto lord of Hades, and others as Chthonian Poseidon. But these names were his because

pro eo quod ille multa potuisset super omnes. Iste autem in Assyrios in iuventute regnans Ninus ibi vocabatur et condidit Ninivem civitatem Assyriorum. Uxor autem eius Semimaris mulier fuit maligna et praesumens et inpudica, quem Ream vocaverunt, alii autem Iram Zygiam, et alii Nemesim multiformem, ceteri autem Ecatin Chtonicam propter innumeram eius atrocitatem. Iste quidem relinquens uxori imperium occidentis partibus veniens imperavit. Erant enim omnes partes illas sine urbes et sine regem secundum quod narrat historia. In illis vero temporibus Picus Croni pronepus inveniens terram illam spaciosam manentem imperavit in illam annos LXXX patrias possidens. Et illas nobilissimas feminas per magicas et ingenia maligna convertens et avortivos faciebat, et sic mulieres, quae ab ipso deludebantur, domos et sedes praeparabant ei et sculptilia[148] multa multa illi configebant sicut placebat eis, et quasi deo eas conmiscuisset et in deum eum esse gloriabantur.[149]

2   Post istius autem perditionem Faunus filius eius regnavit in Italiam annos XXXV. Hic factus est vir impius et strenuus valde. Tunc descendit in Egyptum et ibidem demoratus est inperialem vestem indutus. Et sapiens videbatur ab Egyptios, per magicas et maleficia eos decipiebat, et suspitiones et divinationes illos dicebat,[150] avium narrationes et opupas adnuntiationes et equorum hinnos discebat et mortuorum divinationes et alia plura mala. Et dum conputatorem illum cernerent et valde loquacem sapientes Aegyptiorum, Hermem terbeatissimum illum glorificabant pro eo quod linguas eorum bene novisset ubique, simul autem et polyolbum et multoditatum et deorum illum ministrum

he had great power over all. He reigned among the Assyrians in his youth, and was there called Ninus, and founded Nineveh, the city of the Assyrians. His wife, Semiramis, was a spiteful and brazen and shameless woman, whom they called Rhea, and some Hera, patroness of marriage, and others Nemesis of many forms, still others Chthonian Hecate because of her numberless outrages. Picus surrendered his kingdom to his wife, and going to the regions of the west, ruled there. For all those parts were without cities and without a king according to what the history says. In those times Picus, the son of Cronus, finding that land still open and broad, ruled there and occupied the land[171] for 80 years. He also turned the heads of the most noble women through magic arts and malign contrivances and corrupted them.[172] So the women who were enchanted by him prepared houses and seats for him and made many, many statuettes of him since he was pleased with these things.[173] And as a god he had sexual relations with them, and they honored him as if he were a god.

After his death Faunus his son reigned in Italy for 35 years. 2 He became an impious and very busy man.[174] Then he went down to Egypt and stayed there wearing the royal robe. And he seemed wise to the Egyptians; he deceived them through magic arts and evil deeds. He spoke his "suspicions"[175] and prophesied to them, and learned the speech of birds and the pronouncements of the hoopoe and the neighing of horses and the divination of the dead and many other evils. And since the wise men of the Egyptians perceived him to be a mathematician and quite a talker they honored him as Hermes Trismegistus, because he knew their languages everywhere so well; they also admired him as a rich and wealthy

suspicabant. Regnavit autem ibi annos XXXV. Fiunt autem ab Adam usque ad initium regni Picu qui interpraetatur Serapidus pronepus Croni anni quattuor milia C.

3 Tunc Eraclius ab Spanorum partibus rediens arma sua posuit in Roma, in Boarium forum, in templo clausit. Dicunt enim Eraclium in Latothibis fuisse ec Dius[151] et Alminius. Et fugiens Erysthea, regem Thibeorum, cum omnia sua navigavit et regnavit occidentis partibus: unde immagines auro vestitos sibi conposuit in novissimis occidentales partibus, qui et usque hodie stant: pro quo et Eurypidus ille poeta memoravit.

Fecit autem et filium ex ipsa neocorum Aleu filia Telefonum et Latinum eum vocauit. Regnavit autem Eraclius annos XXXVIII.

Post mortem autem Eraclii Telefus filius eius qui et Latinus vocatus est regnavit in ipsa provintia annos XVIII, et de eius nomine Romeos qui et Cittei vocantur Latinos nominavit, qui et usque hodiernum diem Latini vocantur.

Temporibus illis Frygius Eneas, Anchisso et Afroditis filius, venit de Lybia et cum Latino se coniunxit et fecit pugna cum illos Rutullos. Et in ipsa pugna Latinus occisus est, et imperium eius sumpsit Eneas et condidit Libyniam civitatem in nomine Dido illa Libyssa. Regnavit autem Eneas post solis desolationem, annos XVIIII a solis vastatione, et vixit in regno annos XXXVIII.

4 Post autem Eneae mortem Ascanius filius eius regnavit ibi annos XXXV et condidit Albaniam et regnum Albanis inposuit.

Post autem Ascanii mortem regnavit Albas Postumius ille

man[176] and a servant of the gods. He reigned there for 35 years. This makes from Adam up to the beginning of the reign of Picus (who is understood to be Serapis), the son of Cronus, 4,100 [or 4,200] years.[177]

Then Heracles, coming back from Spain, set up his arms 3 in Rome, in the Forum Boarium, and shut them in a temple. For they say that Heracles was born in *Latothibae,*[178] the child of Zeus and Alcmene.[179] Fleeing Eurystheus, the king of Thebes, he sailed away with his household[180] and reigned in the regions of the west. So he made images of himself clothed in gold in the furthest western regions, which stand even to this day (for which achievement even the great poet Euripides mentioned [him]).

He also had a son by Auge, the daughter of Aleus the temple servant [?],[181] Telephus,[182] whom he also called Latinus. Heracles reigned for 38 years.

After the death of Heracles, Telephus his son, who was also called Latinus, reigned in this province for 18 years. From his name he named the Romans (who are also called Cittaeans) Latins, and they are called Latins to this very day.

In these times Aeneas the Phrygian, the son of Anchises and Aphrodite, came from Libya and joined himself with Latinus and made war with the Rutulians. And in this war Latinus was killed, and Aeneas assumed his power and founded the city of Libynia in the name of Dido the Libyan.[183] Aeneas reigned after the desolation of Sun City [Ilium], for 19 years[184] from the destruction of Sun City [Ilium],[185] and he lived in his kingdom for 38 years.

After the death of Aeneas Ascanius his son reigned there 4 for 35 years and he founded Albania[186] and imposed his kingly power upon the Albans.

After the death of Ascanius Albas Postumus, the grandson

Eneae nepus annos XXXVI, et condidit Silvem. Ab isto qui postea reges Silvani vocati sunt.

Reges autem qui regnaverunt ab Alba in occiduum sunt isti.

Albas Silvius	Eneae nepus	annos XXXVI.
Tittus Silvius	regnavit	annos XXXVIII.
Francus Silvius	regnavit	annos LIII.
Latinus Silvius	regnavit	annos LVI.
Procnax Silvius	regnavit	annos XLVI.
Tarcyinius Silvius	regnavit	annos XVIII.
Cidenus Silvius	regnavit	annos XXXII.[152]
Abintinus Silvius	regnavit	annos XXI.
Rimus Silvius	regnavit	annos XXVIIII.[153]

5   Post istos regnavit Romulus in Roma, et condidit Romam et leges Romanis inposuit et causas edocuit. Fiunt vero simul ab Adam usque ad initium regni Romuli qui et Romam condidit omnes anni IIII milia octingenti XX.

1.[154] Primus quidem regnavit in Roma Romulus, a quo Romani dicti sunt, qui et Romam condidit. Et regnavit olympius annos VIIII et dimidium: fiunt anni XXXVIII. Fiunt simul anni IIII milia octingenti LVIII.

II. Post istum regnavit Nummas Pompius ann. XLI: fiunt anni IIII milia octingenti XCVIIII. Iste primum nummum adinvenit, pro quo usque hodie nummus dicitur ille dinarius.

of Aeneas, reigned for 36 years, and he founded Silvis.[187] From him the kings who came afterward were called Silvani.

The kings who ruled from Alba in the west are these:

Albas Silvius	the grandson of Aeneas	36 years
Titus Silvius	reigned	38 years
Francus Silvius	reigned	53 years
Latinus Silvius	reigned	56 years
Procnax Silvius	reigned	46 years
Tarquinius Silvius	reigned	18 years
Cidenus Silvius	reigned	32 years
Aventinus Silvius	reigned	21 years
Remus Silvius	reigned	29 years

After these men Romulus reigned in Rome, and founded 5 Rome and bestowed laws upon the Romans and taught them about lawsuits. There are altogether from Adam up to the beginning of the kingdom of Romulus who founded Rome in all 4,820 years.[188]

1. The first to reign in Rome was Romulus, from whom the Romans are named, who also founded Rome. And he reigned for nine and a half Olympiads: this makes 38 years. Altogether this makes 4,858 years.

2. After him Numa Pompilius reigned for 41 years: this makes 4,899 years. He invented the first coin *(nummus),* and to this day the denarius is called a nummus for him.[189]

III. Post istum regnavit in Roma Tullius Servilius annos XXXII: fiunt simul anni IIII milia noningenti XXXI.

IIII. Post istum regnavit in Roma Lucius Tarcynius annos XXIII: fiunt simul anni IIII millia noningenti LIIII.

V. Post istum regnavit in Roma Titus Superbus annos XXXVIII: fiunt anni IIII milia noningenti XCII.

VI. Post hunc regnavit in Roma Iulius Serugius annos XLIIII: fiunt anni V milia XXXVI.

VII. Post hunc regnavit in Roma Cyintus Tarcyniu annos XXXV: fiunt anni V milia LXXI.

Simul reges Romanorum a Romulo VII permanserunt annos CCLI,[155] et ab initio Latini qui fuit filius Eraclii anni DCLXXI.[156]

Isti reges, qui regnaverunt in Romam et in omnem occidentalis parte terram.

6   Post haec tradidit dominus deus regnum terrae Romanorum in manus Assyriorum, Chaldeorum, et Persarum, et Midorum. Et tributaria facta est terra illa Assyriis, et mansit Roma sine regnum, usque dum suscitavit deus Alexandrum Macedonem et conditorem. Iste quidem pugnavit contra regem Persarum et superavit eum. Et tradidit dominus in manum eius regnum Assyriorum, et introivit in potestate regnum eorum, et concussit civitates Persarum et Medorum, et liberavit omnem terram Romanorum et Grecorum et Egyptiorum de servitute Chaldeorum, et leges posuit mundo.

Fiunt simul ab Adam usque ad initium Romuli qui et Romam condidit anni IIII milia octingenti XX, et ab initio Romuli usque Cyinto Tarcinio anni CCLI.[157]

3. After him Tullius Servilius reigned in Rome for 32 years: altogether this makes 4,931 years.

4. After him Lucius Tarquinius reigned in Rome for 23 years: altogether this makes 4,954 years.

5. After him Titus Superbus reigned in Rome for 38 years: this makes 4,992 years.

6. After him Julius Serugius[190] reigned in Rome for 44 years: this makes 5,036 years.

7. After him Quintus the son of Tarquinius reigned in Rome for 35 years: this makes 5,071 years.

Altogether the seven kings of the Romans from Romulus endured for 251 years, and from the beginning [of the reign] of Latinus, who was the son of Heracles, there are 671 years.

These are the kings who ruled in Rome and in all the western part of the earth.

After these things the Lord God delivered the kingdom   6
of the land of the Romans into the hands of the Assyrians, Chaldeans, and Persians, and Medes. And the land was made tributary to the Assyrians, and Rome remained without dominion until the time when God raised up Alexander of Macedon, the Founder. He fought against the king of the Persians and defeated him. And the Lord delivered into his hand the kingdom of the Assyrians, and he entered their kingdom in power, and he overthrew the cities of the Persians and the Medes, and he freed the whole country of the Romans and the Greeks and the Egyptians from slavery to the Chaldeans, and he bestowed laws upon the world.

Altogether this makes from Adam up to the beginning [of the reign] of Romulus, who also founded Rome, 4,820 years, and from the beginning [of the reign] of Romulus to Quintus Tarquinius 251 years.

Caput VII

Ecce nunc manifestavimus quidem aedificationes Romanorum et quomodo quod annos regnaverunt. Necesse enim est ad historiam currere chronografum annos per Ebreorum regna, quis et clarior manifestat tempora singillatim et annos secundum ordinem.

Sicut prius manifestauimus, ab Adam usque ad finem iudicum Israhel ab initio Heli sacerdotis fiunt anni IIII milia CCCLV. Ecce nunc regnum primum.

Post iudices Israhel iudicauit filios Israhel Heli sacerdos, et ipse iudicavit Israhel annos XX: fiunt simul ab Adam anni IIII milia CCCLXXV, et tradidit dominus deus arcam in manus alienigenorum.

In diebus autem Heli sacerdotis solis exterminatio facta est ab Acheis, in quibus memorantur Agamomnus et Menelaus et Achilleus et quanti alii Danei, de quo historiam posuit Omirus litterator et scriba.

Post mortem autem Heli sacerdotis iudicavit Samuhel propheta filios Israhel. Et reduxit ab alienigenis arcam domini et introduxit eam in domo Aminadab. Et mansit ibi annos XX. Fiunt simul anni IIII milia CCCXCV.

Post haec unxit Samuhel Sahulem filium Cis regem super Israhel. Iste primus regnavit in Iuda annos XX. Fiunt simul anni ab Adam IIII milia CCCCXV.

2   Post mortem autem Sahul regis regnavit David filius Iesse

Chapter 7

As you see, we have shown which were the houses[191] of the Romans and how [and] for how many years they ruled. For it is necessary in regard to history for the chronographer to run through the years according to the kingdoms of the Hebrews, which also show more clearly the times one by one and the years in order.

Accordingly we have already shown,[192] from Adam up to the end of the judges of Israel, at the beginning of the rule of Eli the priest, there are 4,355 years. Now observe the first kingdom.[193]

After the judges of Israel Eli the priest judged the sons of Israel, and he judged Israel for 20 years: altogether this makes from Adam 4,375 years, and the Lord God delivered the ark into the hands of the Gentiles.[194]

In the days of Eli the priest the ruin of Sun City (i.e., Ilium) was accomplished by the Achaeans, among whom are mentioned Agamemnon and Menelaus and Achilles and all the other Danaans, concerning whom Homer, the scholar and writer, set out the history.

After the death of Eli the priest Samuel the prophet judged the sons of Israel. And he took the ark of the Lord back from the Gentiles and brought it into the house of Abinadab. And it remained there for 20 years.[195] Altogether this makes 4,395 years.

After these things Samuel anointed Saul the son of Kish king over Israel. He was the first to reign in Judah, for 20 years. Altogether this makes 4,415 from Adam.

After the death of Saul the king, David the son of Jesse 2

de tribu Iuda annos XL et menses sex, sic: in Chebron annos septem et dimidium, et in Hierusalem annos XXXIII: fiunt anni XL et dimidium. Simul anni IIII milia quadringenti LV et menses sex.

Iste reduxit arcam domini a domo Aminadab, et dum duceret eam declinavit vitulus et <. . . et Dominus>[158] obpressit Ozam, et mortuus est. Et timuit David et introduxit eam in domo Abdede Chettei, et fecit ibi menses V.

Prophetaverunt autem sub David Caath et Nathan. Fuit autem archistratigus David Moab filius Saruae sorori David. Iste dinumeravit tribus Israhel et invenit milia CLXX: Levi autem et Beniamin non dinumeravit. Numerum autem de his qui ceciderunt in Israhel milia LXX, pro eo quod dinumerati sunt et probare voluerunt dominum.

Post David autem regem regnavit Solomon filius eius annos XL: fiunt simul anni IIII milia quadringenti XLV.[159]

Iste aedificavit in Hierusolymis templum duodecimo anno regni sui. Et prophetaverunt sub Salomon Nathan et Achias ille Silonita et Sameus et Abdeus. Princeps autem sacerdotum fuit super eos Sadoc.

Post Salomon autem regnavit Roboam filius eius annos septem:[160] fiunt simul anni IIII milia quingenti XII[161] et dimidium.[162]

Sub isto divisum est regnum. Et regnavit Hieroboam servus Salomonis de tribu Efraim in Samaria. Iste fecit scandalum in Israhel, duas dammulas aureas. Prophetavit autem et Hieroboam et Achias ille Silonita et Sammeus filius Ellamei.

3   Post istum regnavit Abiu filius eius annos III: fiunt simul anni IIII milia quingenti XV et dimidium. Prophetaverunt autem ipsi prophetas.

from the tribe of Judah reigned for 40 years and 6 months, thus: in Hebron for seven and a half years, and in Jerusalem for 33 years; this makes 40 years and a half. Altogether 4,455 years and 6 months.

He brought the ark of the Lord back from the house of Abinadab, and while the calf[196] was pulling it he faltered and <. . . and the Lord> smote Uzzah and he died. And David was afraid and brought it into the house of Obed-edom the Gittite, and it spent five months there.[197]

Gad and Nathan prophesied under David. The commander of David's army was Joab the son of Zeruiah, David's sister.[198] He numbered the tribes of Israel and found 170,000 men, but he did not number Levi and Benjamin. The number of these who died in Israel was 70,000, because they had been numbered and wished to put the Lord to the test.[199]

After David the king Solomon his son reigned for 40 years; altogether this makes 4,445 years.

He built a temple in Jerusalem in the 20th year of his reign. And Nathan and Ahijah the Shilonite and Shemaiah and Iddo prophesied under Solomon.[200] The chief of priests over them was Zadok.

After Solomon Rehoboam his son reigned for seven years: altogether this makes 4,512 and a half years.

In his time the kingdom was divided. And Jeroboam the servant of Solomon from the tribe of Ephraim reigned in Samaria. He created a temptation to sin in Israel, two golden heifers.[201] And Jeroboam prophesied, as well as Ahijah the Shilonite and Shemaiah the son of Ellamei.[202]

After him Abijam his son reigned for three years: altogether this makes 4,515 and a half years. The same prophets prophesied. 3

Post hunc regnavit Asa filius Abiu annos XLI: fiunt simul anni IIII milia quingenti LVI et dimidium. Iste in senectute sua podalgivus factus est. Prophetavit autem sub ipso Annanias. Post hunc regnavit Iosafat filius eius annos XXV: fiunt simul anni IIII milia quingenti LXXXI et dimidium. Sub isto prophetavit Helias ille Thesbita et Micheas filius Embla et Abdeus filius Ananei. Sub Michea autem fuit pseudopropheta Sedecias ille de Chanaan. Post istum regnavit filius eius Ioram annos VIII: fiunt simul anni IIII milia quingenti LXXXVIIII et dimidium. Et sub ipso prophetavit Helias, post hunc Heliseus.

Sub istum autem et filium eius Ochoziam populus in Samaria stercora columborum comederunt, quando oravit Helias ut non plueret super terram, et non pluit caelum per annos tres et menses sex.

Post istum regnavit filius eius Ochozias annum unum et dimidium: fiunt simul anni IIII milia quingenti XCI. Et sub isto prophetavit Heliseus et Abdoneus.

Post hunc regnavit[163] Godolia, mater Ochoziae, uxor Ioram, annos VII: fiunt simul anni IIII milia quingenti XCVIII. Haec surgens interfecit filios filiorum suorum, quia erat de genere Achab regis Samariae uxor Ochozie filii eius. Soror autem Ochoziae filii Iosabe dum esset uxor Iodae principis sacerdotum rapuit Ioham filium Ochoziae, et hunc inposuit Iodae in regnum. Prophetavit enim et sub Godolia Elisseus et Abdias et Hiiu.

4 Post haec autem regnavit Iohas filius Ochoziae annos XL: fiunt simul anni IIII milia sexcenti XXXVIII. Iste occidit Zachariam filium Iodae sacerdotis inter templum et altare.

After him Asa the son of Abijam reigned for 41 years: altogether this makes 4,556 and a half years. In his old age he became gouty.[203] Hanani prophesied in his time.

After him Jehoshaphat his son reigned for 25 years: altogether this makes 4,581 and a half years. In his time Elijah the Tishbite prophesied, as well as Micaiah the son of Imla and Obadiah the son of Hanani.[204] In the time of Micaiah there was the false prophet Zedekiah from Canaan.[205]

After him Jehoram his son reigned for eight years: altogether this makes 4,589 and a half years. And in his time Elijah prophesied, and after him Elisha.

In his time and that of his son Ahaziah the people in Samaria ate the dung of doves, when Elijah prayed that it might not rain upon the earth, and the sky did not rain for three years and six months.[206]

After him Ahaziah his son reigned for a year and a half: altogether this makes 4,591 years. And in his time Elisha prophesied, as well as Jehonadab.[207]

After him Athaliah, the mother of Ahaziah, the wife of Jehoram, reigned for seven years: altogether this makes 4,598 years. She arose and killed the sons of her sons,[208] because she was of the family of Ahab the king of Samaria, the wife of Ahaziah her son.[209] But the sister of Ahaziah the son, Jehosheba, since she was the wife of Jehoiada the chief priest, snatched up Joash the son of Ahaziah and entrusted him to Jehoiada in anticipation of his kingdom. For Elisha prophesied even in the time of Athaliah, as well as Obadiah and Jehu.

After these things[210] Joash the son of Ahaziah reigned for 4 40 years: altogether this makes 4,638 years. He killed Zechariah the son of Jehoiada the priest between the temple and the altar.[211]

Post Iohas autem regnavit filius eius Amasias annos XXVIII: fiunt simul anni IIII milia sexcenti LXVI.

Post Amasiam autem regnavit filius eius Ozias annos LII: fiunt simul anni IIII milia septingenti XVIII. Hic fuit leprosus usque dum mortuus est. Iudicabat pro eo Ioatham filius eius, quem non sinebat sedere in solium regni. Prophetizaverunt autem sub Ozia Amos et Esaias filius eius et Osee Ebrei et Ionas Amathei de Gomor.

Post[164] Oziam autem regnavit Ioatham filius eius annos XVI: fiunt simul anni IIII milia septingenti XXXIIII. Et sub isto similiter prophetaverunt Esaias et Osee et Micheas ille Morathita et Iohel Bathueli.

Et post istum regnavit Achas filius eius annos XVI: fiunt simul anni IIII milia septingenti L. Et sub isto similiter prophetaverunt Esaias et Micheas, fuit autem princeps sacerdotum super eos Hurias.

Sub istius regno anno undecimo illa prima olympiada venit ad Grecis. Fiunt uero simul ab Adam usque initium olympiade omnes anni IIII milia septingenti XLV. Est autem olympiada anni IIII.

Sub istius regno anno XVI[165] surrexit Salbanasar rex Assyriorum et venit in Iudeam et transmigravit qui in Samaria erant in Midia et in Babylonia. Duo solummodo tribus remanserunt in Hierusalem qui fuerunt ex genere David regnaturi.[166]

Post Achas autem regnavit Ezechias filius eius annos XXV:[167] fiunt simul anni IIII milia septingenti LXXV. Et sub istum iterum prophetaverunt Esaias et Oseae et Micheas.

Sub istius regno Romulus qui Romam condidit regnavit olympiadas VIIII et dimidiam. Fiunt anni XXXVIII.

After Joash his son Amaziah reigned for 28 years: altogether this makes 4,666 years.

After Amaziah his son Uzziah reigned for 52 years: altogether this makes 4,718 years. This man was a leper until he died. Jotham his son acted as judge in the place of him whom he did not permit to sit on the throne of the kingdom.[212] In the time of Uzziah Amos and Isaiah his son and Hosea the son of Beeri and Jonah the son of Amittai from Gomor[213] prophesied.

After Uzziah his son Jotham reigned for 16 years: altogether this makes 4,734 years. And in his time likewise Isaiah and Hosea and Micah the Morashite and Joel the son of Pethuel prophesied.

And after him Ahaz his son reigned for 16 years: altogether this makes 4,750 years. And in his time likewise Isaiah and Micah prophesied, but Urijah was high priest[214] over them.

In the time of his kingship, in the 11th year, the first Olympiad came to the Greeks.[215] All the years, in fact, from Adam to the beginning of the Olympiad make up altogether 4,745 years. An Olympiad is four years.

In the time of his kingship, in the 16th year, Shalmaneser the king of the Assyrians arose and came to Judea and deported those who were in Samaria into Media and Babylon. Only two tribes remained in Jerusalem, who were from the people of David who was destined to rule.[216]

After Ahaz his son Hezekiah reigned for 25 years: altogether this makes 4,775 years. And again in his time Isaiah and Hosea and Micah prophesied.

In the time of his kingship Romulus who founded Rome reigned for nine and a half Olympiads. This makes 38 years.

5   Post istum Ezechiam regnavit Manasses filius eius annos LV: fiunt anni IIII milia octingenti XXX [sic].[168] Iste interfecit Esaiam prophetam: serrans eum divisit in duas partes, eo quod arguebat eum propter sacrificia idolorum.

Post regnum autem Manasse regnavit filius eius Amos annos II: fiunt simul anni IIII milia octingenti XXXII.[169]

Post Amos autem regnavit Iosias filius eius annos XXXI: fiunt simul anni IIII milia octingenti LXIII. Iste est Iosias, qui subposuit membra hominum sub membra idolorum sicut scriptum est. Sub isto et[170] pascha inventa est in Israhel anno XVIII regni Iosiae. A quo enim obiit Hiesu Nave, non servata est pascha sic nisi tunc.

Chelcheus sacerdos invenit in templo illum librum legis absconditum octavo decimo anno Iosiae.

Prophetaverunt autem et sub Iosia Elibasillim, qui fuit vesterarius sacerdotum, et Sofonias et Heremias et Oldad et Baruch. Fuit autem pseudopropheta Annanias Lurdus.

Post Iosiam autem regnavit Ioacham filius eius annos IIII et menses III: fiunt anni IIII milia octingenti LXVII. Istum ligavit Sennachaoch[171] rex Aegyptiorum ferreis vinculis et duxit in Aegyptum, fratrem autem eius Eliachim ordinavit pro eo. Et sub istum iterum prophetaverunt Hieremias et Buzzi et Baruch et Hurias filius Samiae de Cariathiarim.

Sub isto regnavit Eleachim pro Ioacham fratrem suum annos XI: fiunt simul anni IIII milia octingenti LXXVIII.[172]

Sub istius regno surrexit Nabuchodonosor rex Assyriorum et translatavit qui in Samaria erant in Midia et in Baby-

After this Hezekiah his son Manasseh reigned for 55 ⁵
years: this makes 4,830 years. He killed Isaiah the prophet;
he divided him into two parts with a saw, because he had
been censuring him on account of his sacrifices to idols.
After the kingship of Manasseh his son Amon reigned for
two years: altogether this makes 4,832 years.

After Amon his son Josiah reigned for 31 years: altogether
this makes 4,863 years. This was the Josiah who put the
limbs of men in the place of the limbs of idols, just as it is
written.[217] In his time the Passover too was discovered in Israel, in the 18th year of the reign of Josiah. For since the
death of Joshua the son of Nun the Passover was not observed in this way, except then.

Hilkiah the priest found the book of the law hidden in
the temple in the 18th year of Josiah.

And in the time of Josiah Elibasillim,[218] who was keeper
of the priests' wardrobe, and Zephaniah and Jeremiah and
Huldah and Baruch prophesied. But there was also the false
prophet Hananiah Lurdus ["the Bent"].[219]

After Josiah his son Jehoahaz reigned for four years and
three months: this makes 4,867 years. Sennachaoch[220] the
king of the Egyptians bound him in iron fetters and brought
him to Egypt, while he arranged for his brother Eliakim [to
rule] in his place. And in his time again Jeremiah and Buzi[221]
and Baruch and Urijah the son of Shemaiah from Kirjath-
jearim prophesied.

In his time Eliakim reigned in the place of his brother Jehoahaz for 11 years: altogether this makes 4,878 years.

In the time of his kingship Nebuchadnezzar the king of
the Assyrians arose and deported those who were in Samaria

Ionia, et Eleachim regem ligans aereis ligaminis duxit in Babyllonia. Prophetaverunt autem Hieremias et Baruch et Hurias.[173]

6 Post hunc regnavit pro Eliachim patre suo Ioachim filius eius annos III: fiunt simul anni IIII milia octingenti LXXXI.

Et hunc iterum adduxit Nabugodonosor rex Babyllonis ad se ligatum catenis et multitudinem populi filiorum Israhel, in quibus et Danihelem et qui cum eo erant Annaniam et Hiezechielem, captiuos duxit in Babylonia.

Et ordinavit Nabuchodonosor in loco Ioachim Sedechiam quem et Iechoniam, fratrem Ioachim iuvenem. Regnavit autem Sedechias qui et Iechonias in Israhel annos XI: fiunt simul omnes anni IIII milia octingenti XCII.

In duodecimo[174] autem anno duxit et istum in Babylonia Nabuchodonosor et cecavit eum et multitudinem populi filiorum Israhel duxit in Babylonia nisi pauci qui et in Aegyptum discenderunt. Tunc et templum in Hierusolimis venundatum est permanens per annos quadringentos XXV. Prophetabant autem in ipsa depredatione[175] Hiezechiel et Naum et Danihel et Hieremias in Aegypto et Abacum in Hostracina. In quinto autem anno regni Nabuchodonosor in Babylonia initiaverunt prophetare Hiezechiel et Naum et Malachias iuvenis et tunc Aggeus et Zacharias.[176]

Usque Sedechiam et Iechoniam tenuit regnum Iudeorum, et ultra rex in Israhel non est factus usque in hodiernum diem. Fiunt vero anni IIII milia octingenti XCII.[177]

into Media and Babylon,[222] and he bound Eliakim the king in brazen bonds[223] and brought him to Babylon. Jeremiah and Baruch and Urijah prophesied.

After him Jehoiachin his son reigned in the place of Eliakim his father for three years: altogether this makes 4,881 years.

6

And again Nebuchadnezzar the king of Babylon had him brought to him bound in chains and he led captive to Babylon the multitude of the people of the sons of Israel, among whom were Daniel and those who were with him, Hananiah and Ezekiel.

And Nebuchadnezzar appointed Zedekiah, who is also called Jechonias, the younger brother of Jehoiachin, [to rule] in the place of Jehoiachin. Zedekiah, who is also called Jechonias, reigned in Israel for 11 years: altogether these make 4,892 years in all.

In the 12th year Nebuchadnezzar led him also off to Babylon and blinded him and led the multitude of the people of the sons of Israel off to Babylon except for a few who went down to Egypt. And at that time the temple in Jerusalem was sold[224] and remained so throughout 425 years. Ezekiel and Nahum and Daniel and Jeremiah in Egypt and Habakkuk in Ostracina[225] were prophesying during this same sack of the city. In the fifth year of the reign of Nebuchadnezzar in Babylon Ezekiel and Nahum and Malachi began to prophesy, and then Haggai and Zechariah.

Up to Zedekiah, or Jechonias, the kingdom of the Jews endured, and since that time a king has not come to be in Israel up to the present day. This makes 4,892 years.

Caput VIII

Illi[178] vero reges qui in Israhel et in Iudea et in Samaria finierunt, et tunc tradedit dominus deus regnum terrae in manus Assyriorum et Chaldeorum et Persarum et Midorum, et tributaria facta est eis omnis terra.

Vixit vero Nabuchodonosor iudicans omnem terram a Caspianas portas usque in Eracliae finibus et Aegyptum et omnem Iudeam, subiectos sibi faciens Pontum et totam Asiam et omnem terram Romanorum annos XVIIII. Fiunt simul ab Adam anni IIII milia noningenti XI.[179]

Post istum autem regnavit Baltasar filius eius menses VIIII et dimidium: fiunt simul anni IIII milia noningenti XII. Prophetabant autem in his diebus Hiezechiel et Danihel et Baruch in Babyllonia.

Post hunc autem regnavit in Babyllonia Darius ille primus annos VIIII: fiunt simul anni IIII milia noningenti XXI.

In quinto autem anno Darii regis vidit Danihel visionem de illas ebdomadas et prophetauit dicens: Aedificabitur Hierusalem lata et magna.

Sexto autem anno Dario filio Asueri, quo regnavit in regno Chaldeorum, Zorobabel Ebreorum primus ascendit in Hierusolima et coepit aedificare Hierusalem.

Post istum autem regnavit Cyrus Persus annos XXX: fiunt simul anni IIII milia noningenti LI.

In secundo autem anno Cyrus regnans iussit populo filiorum Israhel ut ascenderet in Hierusolima. Tunc templum

Chapter 8

These kings who were in Israel and Judea and Samaria came to an end, and then the Lord God delivered the kingdom of the earth into the hands of the Assyrians and Chaldeans and Persians and Medes, and the whole earth was made tributary to them.

While Nebuchadnezzar lived he judged the whole earth from the Caspian Gates up to the Pillars of Hercules and Egypt and all of Judea, and made subject to himself Pontus and the whole of Asia and all the land of the Romans for 19 years. Altogether this makes 4,911 years from Adam.

After him Belshazzar his son reigned for nine and a half months: altogether this makes 4,912 years. In these days Ezekiel and Daniel and Baruch were prophesying in Babylon.

After him Darius the First reigned in Babylon for nine years: altogether this makes 4,921 years.

In the fifth year of Darius the king Daniel saw his vision concerning the weeks and prophesied, saying, "Jerusalem will be built, broad and great."[226]

In the sixth year of Darius the son of Ahasuerus, who ruled in the kingdom of the Chaldeans, Zerubbabel was the first of the Hebrews to go up to Jerusalem and begin to build Jerusalem.

After him Cyrus the Persian reigned for 30 years: altogether this makes 4,951 years.

In the second year while Cyrus was reigning he commanded the people of the sons of Israel that they should go up to Jerusalem. Then the temple was built in the time of

aedificatur sub quinquagesima quinta olympiada Cyro rege regnante. Simul Zorobabel <et> Ebrei ascendentes de Babilonia in Iudea edificare coeperunt templum. Prophetaverunt autem sub Cyro rege Hiezechiel et Danihel et Aggeus et Abacum et Zacharias Baruchei.[180] In ipsis autem temporibus Pythagoras et princeps agoras[181] famosi filosofi cognoscebantur.

In ipsis autem temporibus Cyrus interfecit Crysum regem Lydiae, et Lydiorum regnum dissipatum est sub quinquagesima quinta olympiada.

2 Post[182] Cyrum autem regnavit filius eius Cambysus annos VIII: fiunt simul anni IIII milia noningenti LVIIII. Et <sub>[183] istum iterum prophetaverunt Danihel et Aggeus et Zacharias et Abacum.

Post Cambysum autem regnavit Darius Stultus frater Cyri annos XXXIII: fiunt anni IIII milia noningenti XCII. Et sub istum iterum prophetaverunt Danihel et Aggeus et Zacharias et Abacum. Sub istum autem missus est Danihel in lacum leonum.

Post Darium autem Stultum regnavit Xerxes Persus annos XI: fiunt[184] simul anni V milia III. Iste est Xerxes qui expugnavit universa. Et in Athinas veniens conbusit eas et suspiriosus factus in Babylonia reversus est.

Post Xerxem autem regnavit Artaxerxes filius eius annos XXXIII: fiunt simul anni V milia XXXVI. Sub istum Neemias filius Achillei de genere David qui factus est et pincerna Artaxerxis regis vicesimo quarto anno regni eius petiit regi Artaxerxi, et iussus ab eo edificavit Hierusalem. Et ascendens in Iudea edificabat Hierusalem et finem dedit edificationis templi.

the 55th Olympiad while Cyrus the king was reigning.[227] At that same time Zerubbabel and the Hebrews who went up from Babylon to Judea began to build the temple. Ezekiel and Daniel and Haggai and Habakkuk and Zechariah the son of Berechiah prophesied in the time of King Cyrus. In these same times the famous philosophers Pythagoras and the Chief of the Marketplace (i.e., Anaxagoras) were renowned.

In these same times Cyrus killed Croesus the king of Lydia,[228] and the kingdom of the Lydians was destroyed in the time of the 55th Olympiad.

After Cyrus his son Cambyses reigned for eight years: altogether this makes 4,959 years. And again in his time Daniel and Haggai and Zechariah and Habakkuk prophesied.

2

After Cambyses Darius the Fool,[229] the brother of Cyrus, reigned for 33 years: altogether this makes 4,992 years. And again in his time Daniel and Haggai and Zechariah and Habakkuk prophesied. In his time Daniel was sent into the lions' den.

After Darius the Fool Xerxes the Persian reigned for 11 years: altogether this makes 5,003 years. This was the Xerxes who made war on the whole world. And he came to Athens and burned it and he became short of breath[230] and returned to Babylon.

After Xerxes his son Artaxerxes reigned for 33 years: altogether this makes 5,036 years. In his time Nehemiah the son of Hachaliah, who became the cupbearer of Artaxerxes the king, in the 24th year of his kingship petitioned Artaxerxes the king, and under orders from him he built Jerusalem. And going up to Judea he built Jerusalem and made an end of the building of the temple.

Mura autem civitatis erexit et plateas in ipsa conposuit secundum Danihelis prophetiam qui dicit sic: Et edificabitur Hierusalem et circummurabitur. Sub istum et illa adversus Mardocheum et Hesther; Aman autem suspensus est. Eo temporae Hesdras ascendens in Hierusalem legem docebat. Princeps autem sacerdotum erat Hiesus filius Iosedec.[185]

Post haec et Africanus dinumerans ipsam prophetiam septem ebdomadarum et septuagesimum numerum extendens ad Christi adventum.

3   Post Artaxerxem autem regnavit Xerxes filius eius menses V, et occisus est. Et post hunc regnavit Ogdianus menses VII: fiunt simul anni V milia XXXVII.

Post istos regnavit Darius iuvenis qui vocatur Memoratus annos XVIIII: fiunt anni V milia LVI.

Fuit autem sub istos in Hierusalem princeps sacerdotum Ioachim, filosofi autem cognoscebantur illi circa Agoram.[186]

Post Darium autem regnavit filius eius Artaxerxis secundus qui vocatur Memoratus annos XLII: fiunt simul anni V milia XCVIII. Fuit autem sub istum princeps sacerdotum in Hierusalem Heliasibus. Filosofi autem cognoscebantur temporibus Artaxerxis Sofoclus, et Traclitus, et Anaxagoras, et Hirodotus, et Melissus, et Euripidus cantoconpositor, et Protagorus, et Socrator ritor, et Fideas statuas conpositor, et Theetitus artifex, et Dimocritus Abderitus, et Ippcratis medicus,[187] et Thucudidus ritor, et Empedoclus, et Gorgias, et Zinon, et Parmenidus, et Socratus Athineus, et Periclus, et Eupolus, et Aristofanus architector.[188] Hii omnes cognos-

He raised up the walls of the city and laid out the streets in it according to the prophecy of Daniel who spoke thus, "And Jerusalem will be built and walled about."[231] In his time were also those things against Mordecai and Esther, but Haman was hanged.

In that time Ezra went up to Jerusalem and was teaching the law. Joshua the son of Josedech was the high priest.

After these things Africanus calculated [from] this prophecy the number of seven and seventy weeks stretching out to the advent of Christ.[232]

After Artaxerxes his son Xerxes reigned for five months, and was slain. And after him Sogdianus reigned for seven months:[233] altogether this makes 5,037 years. 3

After them the younger Darius who is called "the Mindful" (i.e., Mnemon)[234] reigned for 19 years: this makes 5,056 years.

In their time Joiakim was the high priest in Jerusalem, and the philosophers in the circle of Agoras[235] were renowned.

After Darius his son Artaxerxes the second, who was called "the Mindful" (i.e., Mnemon),[236] reigned for 42 years: altogether this makes 5,098 years. In his time the high priest in Jerusalem was Eliashib. The philosophers who were renowned in the days of Artaxerxes were Sophocles and Heraclitus and Anaxagoras and Herodotus and Melissus and Euripides the composer of verses and Protagoras and Isocrates the rhetorician and Phidias the sculptor of statues and Theaetetus the artificer and Democritus of Abdera and Hippocrates the physician and Thucydides the rhetorician and Empedocles and Gorgias and Zeno and Parmenides and Socrates the Athenian and Pericles and Eupolis and Aris-

cebantur: unde et Africanus sub Artaxerxe rege dinumerat filosofos.

Post Artaxerxem autem Memoratum regnavit filius eius Ochus in Babylonia annos XXI: fiunt simul anni V milia CXVIIII. Fuit autem in Hierusalem princeps sacerdotum Iodae, in Asia autem regnavit Filippus ille Alexandri.

4   In his[189] temporibus Ochus rex Persarum et Midorum proeliavit in Egyptum. <. . . Nectabo>[190] novissumus Farao regni Egypti, et cognoscens quia cessavit fortitudo Egyptiorum, capud suum radens et mutans vestimenta sua alio specie fugiit per Piluseum, et relinquens proprium regnum in Macedonia moratus ibidem astrologica arte didicebatur.[191]

Filosofi autem in Athinas Fideas statuasconpositor, et Theetitus magister ludum, et Euripidus poeta, et Dicritus Abdirus, et Ippocratis medicus, et Dimosthenus ritor cognoscebantur, ceteri autem mortui sunt.

Post hunc autem regnavit in Babyloniam Alsus Ochi filius annos IIII: fiunt anni V milia CXXIII. Fuit autem in Hierusalem princeps sacerdotum Iodae.

Post hunc autem regnavit in Babyloniam Darius Midus ille Alsami annos VI: fiunt simul anni V milia CXXVIIII. Istum deposuit Alexander Macedo et conditor. Fuit autem princeps sacerdotum Iaddus.

Tunc Alexander Macedo et conditor, postquam legem poneret in Ellada et omnem Romanorum terram Syriam quoque et Egyptum et partes Lybiae, tunc venit in partes orientales et expugnans omnes civitates et oppida gentium obsedit regem Persarum Darium. Et tradidit dominus deus

tophanes the architect.[237] All of these were renowned, for which reason Africanus numbered the philosophers in the time of Artaxerxes.

After Artaxerxes the Mindful his son Ochus reigned in Babylon for 21 years: altogether this makes 5,099 years. The high priest in Jerusalem was Jehoiada, and Philip the son of Alexander reigned in Asia.[238]

In these times Ochus the king of the Persians and Medes 4 made war on Egypt. <. . . Nectanebo>, the last pharaoh of the kingdom of Egypt, and recognizing that the strength of the Egyptians had failed, he shaved his head and changed his clothes and fled in disguise through Pelusium, and abandoning his own kingdom and dwelled in Macedonia where he taught the art of astrology.

The philosophers renowned in Athens were Phidias the sculptor of statues and Theaetetus the schoolmaster and Euripides the poet and Democritus of Abdera and Hippocrates the physician and Demosthenes the rhetorician; the rest had died.

After him Arses the son of Ochus reigned in Babylon for four years: this makes 5,123 years. The high priest in Jerusalem was Jehoiada.[239]

After him Darius the Mede, the son of Arsames, reigned in Babylon for six years: altogether this makes 5,129 years. Alexander the Macedonian, the Founder,[240] brought him down. The high priest was Jaddua.

Then Alexander the Macedonian, the Founder, after he bestowed law upon Greece and all the land of the Romans and Syria as well and Egypt and parts of Libya, then he went into the eastern regions and storming all the cities and towns of the nations he besieged Darius, the king of the Persians.

in manus eius Darium et omnem fortitudinem eius disperdit et omnem domum eius scrutavit.

Et dominavit Alexander Macedo et conditor omnem terram Chaldeorum et introivit in omnem fortitudinem Darii et legem posuit in omnes civitates eius, et tributarii facti sunt ei sicut proprio regi.

Ut enim condidit Alexander Alexandriam contra Egyptum, veniens in Hierusolima domino deo adoravit dicens: Gloria tibi, deus solus omnia tenens, qui vivis in saecula. Fuit autem tunc in Hierusalem princeps sacerdotum Iaddus.

Filosofi autem in Athinas sub Alexandro conditore Dimosthenus ritor, et Aristotelis, et Eschinus, et Dimas, et Plato, et Lysias, et Dimocritus alius cognoscebantur.

Regnauit[192] autem Alexander Macedo et conditor post Darium Midorum[193] Alsami filium annos VIII: fiunt simul ab Adam usque ad finem Alexandri conditori anni V milia CXXXVII, et tunc Ptolemei.

5   In diebus vero quibus regnavit Alexander Macedo et conditor, postquam superavit Darium regem Persarum, et Porum regem Indorum et omnes gentes subiugavit a Caspiacas portas quae sunt in ortu solis usque in exteriores terminos Eraclii qui iacent in exteriores occidentis partibus contra Garirum.

Veniens ad mortem Alexander testamentum scripsit, ut unusquisque principum Alexandri regnarent singuli in proprias eorum provintias, sicut imperavit eis Alexander, sic.

Macedonia[194] quidem Arideum quem et Filippum praecepit regnare.

Ponton autem Leona dixit regnare.

And the Lord God delivered Darius into his hands and wrecked all his strength and searched out his whole house.

And Alexander the Macedonian, the Founder, dominated all the land of the Chaldeans and entered into the whole strength of Darius and imposed law on all his cities, and they became tributary to him as to their rightful king.

For when Alexander founded Alexandria by Egypt he came to Jerusalem and worshipped the Lord God, saying, "Glory to you, Only God, grasping all things, Who liveth unto the ages." The high priest in Jerusalem was Jaddua.[241]

The philosophers in Athens renowned in the time of Alexander the Founder were Demosthenes the rhetorician and Aristotle and Aeschines and Demades and Plato and Lysias and the other Democritus.

Alexander the Macedonian, the Founder, reigned after Darius the Mede, the son of Arsames, for eight years: altogether this makes from Adam up to the end of Alexander the Founder 5,137 years, and then there were the Ptolemies.

In the days when Alexander the Macedonian, the 5 Founder, reigned, after he defeated Darius the king of the Persians he conquered Porus the king of the Indians and all the peoples from the Caspian Gates which are at the rising of the sun all the way to the outer Pillars of Hercules which are in the outer regions of the west opposite Gadeira.

As he was approaching death Alexander wrote his will, so that every one of the captains of Alexander should rule, each in his own separate province, just as Alexander commanded them, thus:[242]

He ordered Arrhidaeus, who is also called Philip, to rule Macedonia.

He told Leon (i.e., Leonnatus) to rule Pontus.

Paflagonia autem et Cappadocia Eumenium scriba memoratum praeordinavit regnare.

Insulanos autem dimisit liberos, et procuratores ac dispensatores eorum esse Rodios.

Pamphilia et Lucya Antigonum ordinavit regnare.

Frigiam autem et illam magnam Caesariam Deasandro tradidit.

Cilicia autem et Isauria et omnia circuita eius Filone ordinavit.

Syriam autem usque Mesopotamiam dedit Tapithone ut regnaret.

Syriam vero Cylem vocatam, Fynicem autem interpraetatam, Meleagrom ordinavit dominare.

Babylonia autem Seleucum praecepit regnare.

Egyptum autem et quae circa eum usque superiore Lybia Filippo qui vocabatur Ptolomeus donavit.

Quae autem de superiore Babylone usque Caspiacas portas, principes quidem in ea et satrapes, archistratigum autem eorum Perdicum ordinavit.

6   India autem qui extendit circa Ydastem fluvium Taxio dedit regnare.

India autem qui dicitur sub Indo et usque Ydastem fluvium extendens Pythonae dominare praecepit.

Super Parapannisodum autem Oxydarcum ordinavit regnare.

Arachusia autem et Cedrusia Sybartum ordinavit regnare.

Arabiam autem totam Stasanoro donavit.

Et Ogdianiam Filippo minori dedit dominare.

Illam autem qui circuit contra aquilonis partes et illam qui habet Yrcaniam Antigono donavit regnare.

He arranged beforehand for Eumenes, the famous scribe [or his secretary],[243] to rule Paphlagonia and Cappadocia.

He let the islanders go as free men, and [ordered] the Rhodians to be their managers and stewards.

He appointed Antigonus to rule Pamphylia and Lycia.

He handed Phrygia and Great Caesarea [Caria] over to Asander.

He assigned Cilicia and Isauria and all the surrounding territory to Philo.

Syria as far as Mesopotamia he gave to Pithon, that he might rule it.

He appointed Meleager to be lord of Syria which is called Coele (i.e., "Hollow"), which is interpreted as Phoenicia.

He ordered Seleucus to rule Babylon.

Egypt and the surrounding regions as far as upper Libya he gave to Philip who was called Ptolemy.

In regard to the regions from upper Babylon as far as the Caspian Gates, the chief men in them and the satraps, he appointed Perdiccas their general.

He gave India which stretches to the River Hydaspes to 6 Taxiles to rule.

He ordered Pytho[244] to be lord of India which is called "under the Indus" and stretches as far as the River Hydaspes.

He commanded Oxydraces[245] to rule over Paropanisadae.

He commanded Sibyrtius to rule Arachosia and Cedrosia.

He gave the whole of Arabia to Stasanor.

And he gave Sogdiana to Philip the Lesser to govern.

The region which lies around the parts facing the north and the region which contains Hyrcania he granted to Antigonus to rule.

Germaniam autem totam Tripolemo donavit. Persidam autem totam Perco donavit. Spaniam autem usque Alyo fluvio et Eracleoticum terminum Antipalum ordinavit regnare.

Sic uero statuit et donavit Alexander suis principibus, et unusquisque eorum sic regnaverunt, sicut ipse disposuerat. Vixit autem Alexander annos XXXVI. Regnavit quidem annos XVII sic: pugnavit enim annos VIIII usque dum factus est annorum XXVIII, illos autem alios octo annos vixit in pace et securitate. Subiugavit autem gentes barbaras XXII et Grecorum tribus XIII. Condidit autem Alexander civitates XII, qui usque nunc inhabitantur:

Alexandriam qui in Pentapolim, Alexandriam qui in Aegyptum, Alexandriam qui ad Arpam, Alexandriam qui Cabosium, Alexandriam Scythiam in Egeis, Alexandriam qui in Poro, Alexandriam qui super Cypridum fluvium, Alexandriam qui in Troada, Alexandriam qui in Babylonia, Alexandriam qui in Mesasgyges,[195] Alexandriam qui in Persida, Alexandriam fortissimam, et mortuus est.[196]

Fiunt vero ab Adam usque ad finem Alexandri conditoris simul anni V milia CXXXVII, et ab[197] obito Alexandri usque ad Cleopatram illam Egyptiam anni ducenti XCIIII sic.

Caput VIIII

Post autem mortem Alexandri, ut dictum est, regnavit in Egypto Philippus Ptolomeus, qui fuit consiliarius Alexandri, annos VII. Fiunt simul anni V milia CXLIIII. Fuit autem princeps sacerdotum Ianneus.

He gave the whole of Germany to Tlepolemus.[246]

He gave the whole of Persia to Percus (i.e., Peucestas).

He ordered Antipater to rule Spain as far as the River Halys[247] and the boundary of Hercules.[248]

Thus indeed did Alexander decide and grant gifts to his captains, and each of them ruled just as he had arranged.

Alexander lived for 36 years. He ruled for 17 years in this way: he fought for 9 years until he came to the age of 28 years, and he lived the other 8 years in peace and security. He subdued 22 barbarian peoples and 13 tribes of the Greeks. Alexander founded 12 cities which are inhabited up to the present:

Alexandria in Pentapolis, Alexandria by Egypt, Alexandria near Harpas, Alexandria Cabiosa, Scythian Alexandria among the Aegaeans, Alexandria in Porus, Alexandria on the River Cypris, Alexandria in the Troad, Alexandria in Babylonia, Alexandria among the Messagetae, Alexandria in Persia, Alexandria the Strongest, and he died.[249]

This makes from Adam up to the end of Alexander the Founder altogether 5,137 years, and from the death of Alexander up to Cleopatra the Egyptian 294 years, thus:

Chapter 9

After the death of Alexander, as has been said, Ptolemy Philip, who was Alexander's counselor, reigned in Egypt for seven years. Altogether this makes 5,144 years. The high priest was Janneus.[250]

In his temporibus Menander aedificator videbatur.

Post Philippum autem regnavit Alexander Ptolemeus quem[198] et ipse consiliaris Alexandri annos XII. Fiunt simul anni V milia CLVI. Princeps sacerdotum autem fuit in Hierusalem ipse Ianneus.

Isdem temporibus illi septuaginta Ebrei sapientes illam legem interpraetaverunt Greco sermone.[199] Post hunc regnavit in Egypto Lagaus Ptolomeus annos XX. Fiunt simul anni V milia CLXXVI. Fuit autem in Hierusalem princeps sacerdotum Iaddus.

Temporibus istis Hiesus filius Sirach cognoscebatur, qui illam a deo spiratam sapientiam Aebreis edocuit.

Post hunc autem regnavit in Aegypto Filadelphus Ptolemeus annos XXXVIII. Fiunt simul anni V milia CCXIIII. Fuit autem princeps sacerdotum Onias.

Post Filadephum autem regnavit in Aegypto Eugergetus Ptolemeus annos XXV. Fiunt simul anni V milia CCXXXVIIII. Fuit autem in Hierusalem princeps sacerdotum Simon et post hunc Onias alius.

2   Post Eugergetum autem regnavit in Aegypto filius eius Filopator Ptolemeus annos XVII. Fiunt simul anni V milia CCLVI. Fuit autem in Hierusalem princeps sacerdotum Eleazarus.

Post Filopatorem autem regnavit filius eius Epifanius Ptolemeus annos XXIIII. Fiunt simul anni V milia CCLXXX. Fuit autem in Hierusalem princeps sacerdotum Manasses.

Post Epifanium autem Ptolemeum regnavit filius eius in Aegypto Filomitor Ptolemeus annos XXXV. Fiunt simul anni V milia CCCXV. Fuit autem in Hierusalem princeps sacerdotum Simon.

In these times Menander the architect appeared.[251]

After Philip Ptolemy Alexander, who was also himself a counselor of Alexander, reigned for 12 years. Altogether this makes 5,156 years. The high priest in Jerusalem was the same Janneus.

In these same times the 70 Hebrew sages translated the law into the Greek language.

After him Ptolemy Lagus reigned in Egypt for 20 years. Altogether this makes 5,176 years. The high priest in Jerusalem was Jaddua.

In these times Jesus the son of Sirach, who taught the God-breathed wisdom to the Hebrews, was renowned.

After him Ptolemy Philadelphus reigned in Egypt for 38 years. Altogether this makes 5,214 years. The high priest was Onias.

After Philadelphus Ptolemy Euergetes reigned in Egypt for 25 years. Altogether this makes 5,239 years. The high priest in Jerusalem was Simon and after him another Onias.

After Euergetes his son Ptolemy Philopator reigned in Egypt for 17 years. Altogether this makes 5,256 years. The high priest in Jerusalem was Eleazar.

After Philopator his son Ptolemy Epiphanes reigned for 24 years. Altogether this makes 5,280 years. The high priest in Jerusalem was Manasseh.

After Ptolemy Epiphanes his son Ptolemy Philometor reigned in Egypt for 35 years. Altogether this makes 5,315 years. The high priest in Jerusalem was Simon.

Hisdem temporibus illa in Maccabeis finiebantur in Hierusalem sub Antiocho regem Syriae.

Post[200] Filomitorem autem Ptolemeum regnavit filius eius Eugergetus alius in Egypto annos XXVIIII. Fiunt simul anni V milia CCCXLIIII. Fuit autem in Hierusalem princeps sacerdotum Onias alius.

3   Post hunc autem regnavit in Aegypto Soter vocatus Ptolemeus annos XXXVI. Fiunt simul anni V milia CCCLXXX. Princeps autem sacerdotum fuit in Hierusalem Hiesus annos VI et Onias alius annos VII et Ianneus annos XV.

Post hunc autem regnavit in Aegypto novus Dionisus annos XXVIIII. Fiunt simul anni V milia CCCCVIIII. Fuit autem in Hierusalem princeps sacerdotum Simon annos VIII et Iohannis annos XX.

Hisdem temporibus Sosates cognoscebatur ille Ebraicus Omirus in Alexandria.

Post autem novum Dionisum novissimum illum et novissimorum Ptolomeorum regnavit in Aegypto Beronice Cleopatra annos XXII. Fiunt simul anni V milia quadringenti XXXI.

Quod sunt omnes anni Ptolemeorum regna a morte Alexandri usque ad mortem Cleopatre, qui et in Alexandriam Farum condidit, simul anni ducenti XCIIII.

Fiunt simul ab Adam usque ad mortem Cleopatrae anni V milia quadringenti XXXI. Et deinceps tradidit dominus deus regnum Aegyptiorum in manus Romanorum usque hodie. Et ultra rex non est in Aegypto factus usque in hodiernum diem.[201]

In these same times those things concerning the Maccabees were completed in Jerusalem in the time of Antiochus
the king of Syria.

After Ptolemy Philometor his son, another Euergetes,
reigned in Egypt for 29 years. Altogether this makes 5,344
years. The high priest in Jerusalem was another Onias.

After him Ptolemy called Soter reigned in Egypt for 36   3
years. Altogether this makes 5,380 years. The high priest in
Jerusalem was Joshua for 6 years and another Onias for 7
years and Janneus for 15 years.

After him the New Dionysus[252] reigned in Egypt for 29
years. Altogether this makes 5,409 years. The high priest in
Jerusalem was Simon for 8 years and John for 20 years.

In these times Sosates, the Hebrew Homer, was renowned in Alexandria.[253]

After the New Dionysus the last of the last Ptolemies,
Cleopatra Berenice, reigned in Egypt for 22 years. Altogether this makes 5,431 years.

All the years of the kingdom of the Ptolemies from the
death of Alexander up to the death of Cleopatra, who built
the Pharos in Alexandria,[254] are altogether 294.

Altogether this makes from Adam to the death of Cleopatra 5,431 years. And then the Lord God delivered the kingdom of the Egyptians into the hands of the Romans until
the present. And since then a king has not come to be in
Egypt up to the present day.

LIBER II

Caput I

Et quia[202] minus sunt in Christianorum et Ebreorum libris istos qui foris sunt gentium scripta temporum, necessitate conpulsus praevidi exquaerere et coniungere, qui apud nos sunt et quos in chronica deos et iroes vocatos reges, et quae ab eis historialiter acta sunt tradere, his in divino verbo incipiens a diebus protopatoris Abraham et Isaac et Iacob patriarcharum et Moyse, et qui post eos iudices facti sunt in Israhel et prophetarum singillatim regna recensare cunctatim, ut nobis per omnium scribturarum eorum unitum sit regnum.[203]

2   Assiriorum regna et tempora.

Assiriorum primum regem scribunt Bilum, quem et ab Assyriis et Fynices et Persi deum vocaverunt. Hunc Dium Greco nomine interpraetaverunt.

Bilus vero primus in Assyrios regnavit et partem Asiae annos LXII.

Post haec regnavit Ninus annos LII. Iste condidit Ninevem civitatem Assyriorum, et veniens in Asia vocatus est Picus.

Post quem Semiramis uxor eius annos XLII. Hanc Ream vocaverunt propter eius multam atrocitatem.

Post hanc Zinas regnavit annos XXXVIII.

BOOK 2

Chapter 1

And because there is less written in the books of Christians and Hebrews than there is in pagan works of chronology, forced by necessity I had the foresight to seek out and join together [an account of those] who among us are kings and which are the kings who are called gods and heroes in the chronicles, and to pass along what was in fact done by them, beginning from these days in Holy Writ, those of the forefather Abraham to recount one by one the reigns of Isaac and Jacob, the patriarchs, and of Moses and of those who after them were made judges in Israel and of the prophets each in turn, so that their dominion,[255] [found] throughout all scripture, might be united for us.

The reigns and the chronology of the Assyrians   2

They write that the first king of the Assyrians was Belus, who is called a god by the Assyrians and Phoenicians and Persians.[256] His name is translated as Zeus in Greek.

Belus was indeed the first to reign over the Assyrians and a part of Asia for 62 years.

After these things Ninus reigned for 52 years. He founded Nineveh, the city of the Assyrians, and coming to Asia[257] he was called Picus.

After him Semiramis his wife for 42 years. They called her Rhea because of her great outrages.[258]

After her Zamis reigned for 38 years.

v. Post hunc Arius ann. XXX.

vi. Post hunc Aranus ann. XL.

vii. Post hunc Xerses qui et Balleus ann. XXX.

viii. Post hunc Armamithrus ann. XXXVIII.

viiii. Post hunc Bilochus ann. XXXV.

x. Post hunc Balleus ann. LII.

xi. Post hunc Altallus ann. XXXV.

xii. Post hunc Mamithus ann. XXX.

xiii. Post hunc Magchaleus ann. XXX.

xiiii. Itas Ferus ann. XX.

xv. Mamithus ann. XXXV.

xvi. Spareus ann. XL.

xvii. Ascatagus ann. XL.

xviii. Amintus ann. L.

3 xviiii. Attosai et Semiramis femina ann. XXIII.

xx. Bilochus ann. XXV.

xxi. Belleroparus ann. XXXIIII.

xxii. Lampridus ann. XXXII.

xxiii. Sosarus ann. XX.

xxiiii. Lamparus ann. XXX.

xxv. Pannius et Zeus ann. XLV.

xxvi. Sosarmus ann. XX.

xxvii. Mithreus ann. XXXV.

xxviii. Tautalus ann. XXXII.

xxviiii. Euteus ann. XL.

Anno isto tricensimo secundo confixus est sol ab Acheis.

xxx. Thineus ann. XXX.

xxxi. Cercillus ann. XL.

xxxii. Eupalus ann. XXXVIII.

xxxiii. Laustenus ann. XLV.

5. After him Arius, 30 years.

6. After him Aralius, 40 years.

7. After him Xerxes who is also called Baleus, 30 years.

8. After him Armamithres, 38 years.

9. After him Belochus, 35 years.

10. After him Baleus, 52 years.

11. After him Altadas, 35 years.

12. After him Mamythus, 30 years.

13. After him Magchaleus, 30 years.

14. Itas Ferus,[259] 20 years.

15. Mamylus, 35 years.

16. Spartheus, 40 years.

17. Ascatades, 40 years.

18. Amyntes, 50 years.

19. Atossa, also called Semiramis, a woman, 23 years.   3

20. Belochus, 25 years.

21. Bellepares,[260] 34 years.

22. Lamprides, 32 years.

23. Sosares, 20 years.

24. Lampares, 30 years.

25. Pannias, also called Zeus, 45 years.

26. Sosarmus, 20 years.

27. Mithreus, 35 years.

28. Tautanes, 32 years.

29. Teutaeus, 40 years.

In his 32nd year Sun City (i.e., Ilium) was razed by the Achaeans.

30. Theneus, 30 years.

31. Dercylus, 40 years.

32. Eupales,[261] 38 years.

33. Laosthenes, 45 years.

xxxiiii. Peritiadus ann. XXX.

xxxv. Ofrateus ann. XX.

xxxvi. Ofratanus ann. L.

xxxvii. Acrapazus ann. XL.

xxxviii.[204] Thonos Concelerus[205] qui vocatur Grece Sardanapallus ann. XXX.

xxxviiii. Ninus ann. XVIIII.

Simul reges XXXVIIII antiqui Assyriorum perseverantes annos mille quadringentos XXX. Ab istis autem in prima olimpiada anni LXVII. Assyriorum regnum.

Caput II

Egyptiorum regnum invenimus vetustissimum omnium regnorum. Cuius initium sub Manethono[206] dicitur memoramus scribere.

Primum[207] deorum qui ab ipsis scribuntur faciam regna sic.

i. Ifestum dicunt quidam deum regnare in Aegypto annos sexcentos LXXX.

ii. Post hunc Solem Ifesti ann. LXXVII.

iii. Post istum Sosinosirim ann. CCCXX.

iiii. Post hunc Oron ptoliarchum ann. XXVIII.

v. Post hunc Tyfona ann. XLV.

Colliguntur deorum regna anni mille DL.

Deinceps Mitheorum regni sic.

i. Prota Anubes Amusim[208] qui etiam Aegyptiorum scripturas conposuit ann. LXXXIII.

34. Peritiades, 30 years.

35. Ophrataeus, 20 years.

36. Ophratanes, 50 years.

37. Aerapazes, 40 years.

38. Thonus Concolerus, who in Greek is called Sardana-pallus, 30 years.

39. Ninus, 19 years.[262]

Altogether 39 ancient kings of the Assyrians continued for 1,430 years. From them to the first Olympiad there are 67 years. The kingdom of the Assyrians.[263]

Chapter 2

We find the Egyptian kingdom to be the oldest of all the kingdoms. We recount in writing its beginning as described by Manetho.

First I will treat[264] the reigns of the gods, who are written of by them, thus:

1. Some say that the god Hephaestus ruled in Egypt for 680 years.

2. After him Helios, son of Hephaestus, 77 years.

3. After him Sosinosiris,[265] 320 years.

4. After him Horus, the ptoliarch,[266] 28 years.

5. After him Typhon, 45 years.

The reigns of the gods are added together as 1,550 years.

Then the reigns of the demigods,[267] thus:

1. First Anubis Amusim, who also wrote the scriptures of the Egyptians, 83 years.

II. Post hunc Apiona grammaticus qui secundum Inachum interpraetatur quem sub Argios initio regnaverunt ann. LXVII.

2   I. Post hec Ecyniorum reges interpraetavit Imitheus vocans et ipsos <...>[209] fortissimos vocans annos duo milia C.

II. Mineus et pronepotes ipsius VII regnaverunt ann. CCLIII.

III. Bochus et aliorum octo ann. CCCII.

IIII. Necherocheus et aliorum VII ann. CCXIIII.

V. Similiter aliorum XVII ann. CCLXXVII.

VI. Similiter aliorum XXI ann. CCLVIII.

VII. Othoi et aliorum VII ann. CCIII.

VIII. Similiter et aliorum XIIII ann. CXL.

VIIII. Similiter et aliorum XX ann. CCCCVIIII.

X. Similiter et aliorum VII ann. CCIIII.

Hec finis de primo tomo Manethoni habens tempora annorum duo milia C.[210]

XI. Potestas Diopolitanorum ann. LX.

XII. Potestas Bubastanorum ann. CLIII.

XIII. Potestas Tanitorum ann. CLXXXIIII.

XIIII. Potestas Sebennitorum ann. CCXXIIII.

XV. Potestas Memfitorum ann. CCCXVIII.

XVI. Potestas Iliopolitorum ann. CCXXI.

XVII. Potestas Ermupolitorum ann. CCLX.

Usque ad septimam decimam potestatem secundum scribitur tomum,[211] ut docet numerum, habentem annos mille quingentos XX.

Haec sunt potestates Aegyptiorum.

3   De regna autem, que in ceteris gentibus facta sunt et paulatim creverunt, proferamus temporibus regni Argiuorum.

2. After him Apion the grammarian who is understood according to Inachus as the one whom they ruled at the beginning in the time of the Argives, 67 years.[268]

1. After these things he (i.e., Manetho) explained the 2 kings of the Ecynians,[269] calling them demigods and the same <...>[270] calling them the strongest, for 2,100 years.

2. Meneus and his seven descendants reigned for 253 years.

3. Bochus and another eight, 302 years.

4. Necherochis and another seven, 214 years.

5. Likewise another seventeen, 277 years.

6. Likewise another twenty-one, 258 years.

7. Othoës and another seven, 203 years.

8. Likewise also another 14, 140 years.

9. Likewise also another 20, 409 years.

10. Likewise also another seven, 204 years.

This is the end of the first book of Manetho, containing periods of time totaling 2,100 years.

11. The dynasty of the Diospolitans, 60 years.

12. The dynasty of the Bubastites, 153 years.

13. The dynasty of the Tanites, 184 years.

14. The dynasty of the Sebennytes, 224 years.

15. The dynasty of the Memphites, 318 years.

16. The dynasty of the Heliopolites, 221 years.

17. The dynasty of the Hermoupolites, 260 years.

The second book was written up to the 17th dynasty, as the number shows, and contains 1,520 years.

These are the dynasties of the Egyptians.

Concerning the kingdoms which came into being and 3 gradually arose among other peoples, we shall mention them in the chronology of the kingdom of the Argives.

ı. Primus isargus[212] Inachus regnavit ann. L. Quo tempore Moyses natus est.

ıı. Post hunc Foroneus regnavit ann. LX. Quo anno quinquagesimo quinto ex Aegypto egressio Iudeorum per Moysen facta est.

ııı. Post hunc Apius regnavit ann. XXXV.

ıııı. Post hunc Argius regnavit ann. LXX.

v. Post hunc Criassus regnavit ann. LVI.

vı. Post hunc Forbas regnavit ann. XXXV.

vıı. Post hunc Triopas regnavit ann. LXVI.

vııı. Post hunc Crotopus regnavit ann. XXI.[213]

vıııı. Post hunc Sthenelus regnavit ann. XI.

x. Post hunc Danaus regnavit qui illas filias L ann. . . . . .

xı. Post hunc Lyggeus Aegyptius XLI.

A quo[214] Cadamus Aginorus ascendit Biotia Europissa ad exquirendum.

xıı. Post hunc Abas regnavit ann. XXIII.

Post[215] hunc Prytus regnavit ann. XXVII.

Post hunc Acrisius regnavit ann. XXXI.

Post hunc Pelops regnavit cum Nomaum ann. XXXVIII. A quo Peloponissus vocatur.

Post hunc Atreus et Thyestus[216] ann. XLV.

Post hos Agamemnus Atreus ann. XXXIII.

Colliguntur nunc[217] ab Ichano rege usque ad desolationem solis quod est octavodecimo Agamemnonis anni septingenti XVIII.

A solis devastatione usque ad primam olympiadam anni CCCCVII et Porfyrius autem in historia philosofiae sic dixit. Post autem solis devastationem Agamemnonus reliquos annos XV.

1. *Isargus* Inachus was the first to reign[271] for 50 years. In this time Moses was born.

2. After him Phoroneus reigned for 60 years. In the 55th year the departure out of Egypt of the Jews under Moses took place.

3. After him Apis reigned for 35 years.

4. After him Argos reigned for 70 years.

5. After him Criasus reigned for 56 years,

6. After him Phorbas reigned for 35 years.

7. After him Triopas reigned for 66 years.

8. After him Crotopus reigned for 21 years.

9. After him Sthenelaus reigned for 11 years.

10. After him Danaus, who had those 50 daughters, reigned for . . . years.

11. After him Lynceus the Egyptian[272] reigned for 41 years.

In his time Cadmus the son of Agenor went up to Boeotia to look for Europa.

12. After him Abas reigned for 23 years.

After him Proetus reigned for 27 years.

After him Acrisius reigned for 31 years.

After him Pelops reigned with Oenomaus for 38 years. The Peloponnese is named after him.

After him Atreus and Thyestes, 45 years.

After them Agamemnon the son of Atreus, 33 years.

Now 718 years are added together from King Inachus up to the ruin of Sun City (i.e., Ilium), which was in the 18th year of Agamemnon.

From the destruction of Sun City (i.e., Ilium) up to the first Olympiad there are 407 years: Porphyry says so in his *History of Philosophy*.[273] After the destruction of Sun City (i.e., Ilium) Agamemnon [reigned] for another 15 years.[274]

4

Post hunc Egesthus regnavit ann. VII.
Post hunc Oresthus regnavit ann. XXVIII.
Post hunc Penthilus regnavit ann. XXII.
Et Argiorum regnum dissipatum est. Colliguntur uero Argiorum regna simul anni septingenti XC.[218]

Caput III

Siciniorum qui nunc Elladicorum vocantur
reges et tempora.[219]
Proferamus iterum et Syciniorum qui nunc Elladici vocantur.

Disponamus regna a quibus initiata sunt temporibus, et in quibus diffinierunt manifestemus.

Africanus quidem dixit sic tenere eis omnes annos mille VII: a minuetate autem eorum in primam olympiadam anni CCCXXVIIII, sicut numeratur ab initio Sicyoniorum regna in primam olympiadam omnes anni mille CCCXXXVI.

Vicesimo nono autem anno patriarchae Iacob illum Syciniorum initiavit regnum sic:

i. Egialeus ann. LII. anni autem Iacob XXVIIII,

ii. Europs ann. XLV. anni Isaac LXXXVIIII,

iii. Telchus ann. XX.
iiii. Amfus ann. XXV. anni Abraham CXIIII Ellada[220] initiaverunt regna.

After him Aegisthus reigned for seven years.
After him Orestes reigned for 28 years.
After him Penthilus reigned for 22 years.
And the kingdom of the Argives was overthrown. Added together the reigns of the Argives total 790 years.

Chapter 3

The kings and the chronology of the Sicyonians
who are now called Helladics.

We shall set out the reigns of the Sicyonians who are now called Helladics.

We shall draw up the reigns from the times in which they were started, and show those times in which they came to an end.

Africanus[275] says that they lasted for in all 1,007 years: from their end[276] to the first Olympiad there are 329 years, just as in all 1,336 years are counted from the beginning of the kingdom of the Sicyonians to the first Olympiad.

The kingdom of the Sicyonians began in the 29th year of the patriarch Jacob, thus:

1. Aegialeus, 52 years.	In the 29th year of Jacob,
2. Europs, 45 years.	the 89th year of Isaac,
3. Telchin, 20 years.	the 114th year of Abaraham
4. Apis, 25 years.	the Helladic reigns began.

v. Thelxius ann. LII.
vi. Egydrus ann. XXXIIII.
vii. Turimachus ann. XLV   Anno quadragesimo
viii. Leucippus ann. LIII.   tertio Leucippi
viiii. Mesapfus ann. XLVII.   egressio Iudeorum
x. Eratus ann. XLVI.   ex Aegypto.[221]
xi. Plammeus ann. XLVIIII.
xii. Ortopolus ann. LXV.
xiii. Marathus ann. XXX.
2 xiiii. Maratheus ann. XX.
xv. Echyrus ann. LV.
xvi. Corax ann. XX.
xvii. Epopeus ann. XXXV.
xviii. Laomedus ann. XLIII.
xviiii. Inachus annos XLV.
xx. Festus annos L.
xxi. Adrastus annos IIII.
xxii. Polifidus annos XXXI.
xxiii. Pelastus annos XX.
xxiiii. Zeuxippus annos XXXV.
xxv. Polybus annos XLV.

Usque Zeuxippum tenuit Sicyoniorum regnum permanens annos quingentos LXXXI.[222] Post Zeuxippum autem reges quidem non fuerunt, sed praeibant eis sacerdotes Carnii annos XXVII.

Quem[223] primus sacerdos Archelaus annum I.
Post hunc Automidus annum I.
Post hunc Methudutus annum I.
Post hunc Euneus annos IIII.
Post hunc Theonomus annum I.
Post hunc Amficyus annos VIIII.

5. Thelxion, 52 years.

6. Aegydrus, 34 years.

7. Thourimachus, 45 years.

8. Leucippus, 53 years.

9. Messapus, 47 years.

10. Erastus, 46 years.

11. Plemmeus, 49 years.

12. Orthopolis, 65 years.

13. Marathus, 30 years.

14. Marathius, 20 years.

15. Echyreus, 55 years.

16. Corax, 20 years.

17. Epopeus, 35 years.

18. Laomedon, 43 years.

19. Inachus, 45 years.

20. Phaestus, 50 years.

21. Adrastus, 4 years.

22. Polypheides, 31 years.

23. Pelasgus, 20 years.

24. Zeuxippus, 35 years.

25. Polybus, 45 years.

In the 43rd
year of Leucippus
the exodus of the Jews
from Egypt [took place].

2

The kingdom of the Sicyonians lasted up to Zeuxippus, enduring for 581[277] years. After Zeuxippus there were no kings, but the priests of [Apollo] Carneius[278] led them for 28 years.

The first priest was Archelaus for one year.

After him Automedon for one year.

After him Methudutus for one year.

After him Euneus for four years.

After him Theonomus for one year.

After him Amphigyes for nine years.

Post hunc Charidus annum I.

Osuch sustinens cibaria fugiit. A quo in prima olimpiada ut fertur scriptura anni CCCXXVIIII.[224]

Fiunt uero omnes Sicioniorum regna ab Egialeo usque in prima olympiada anni mille CCCXXXVI.[225]

3   Athineorum reges.[226]

Nondum multo transacto tempore Aethineorum regnum ab Aegypto populi egressio. Anno enim ducentesimo octavo egressionis primus in Athinas regnavit Cecrops procerus et qui post eum, sicut manifestantur, sic.

i. Cecrops procerus ann. L.

Anno trecesimo quinto Cecropus Promitheus et Epimetheus et Atlas scribuntur, qui et Diu scribuntur.

ii. Amfictryus ann. XL.

iii. Ericthonius ann. X.

iiii. Pandius ann. L.

v. Erectheus ann. XL.

vi. Cecrops Erectheus ann. LIII.

vii. Pandius Cecropus ann. XLIII.

viii. Temporibus Pandii Cecropi Cadmus Aginori litterarum versos primus duxit ad Grecos.

viiii. Egeus Pandionus annos XLVIII.

x. Thiseus Egei ann. XXXI.

xi. Menestheus ann. XVIIII.

xii. Dimofus ann. XXXV.

xiii. Oxyntus ann. XIIII.

xiiii. Afydus ann. I.

After him Charidemus for one year.

Osuch [*Who not*] maintaining the food fled.²⁷⁹ From him to the first Olympiad, as the writing bears out, there are 329 years.

All of the reigns of the Sicyonians from Aegialeus up to the first Olympiad make 1,336 years.

The kings of the Athenians   3

A great deal of time had not yet passed since the exodus of the people from Egypt when the kingdom of the Athenians came into being. For in the 208th year since the exodus Cecrops the Tall²⁸⁰ was the first to rule in Athens, and those who came after him, just as they are made clear, thus:

1. Cecrops the Tall, 50 years.

In the 35th year of Cecrops Prometheus and Epimetheus and Atlas are recorded, and those descended from Zeus are recorded.

2. Amphictyon, 40 years.²⁸¹

3. Erichthonius, 10 years.

4. Pandion, 50 years.

5. Erechtheus, 40 years.

6. Cecrops the son of Erechtheus, 53 years.

7. Pandion the son of Cecrops, 43 years.

8. In the time of Pandion, the son of Cecrops, Cadmus the son of Agenor first brought verses [*or rather* the figures]²⁸² of letters to the Greeks.

9. Aegeus the son of Pandion, 48 years.

10. Theseus the son of Aegeus, 31 years.

11. Menestheus, 19 years.

12. Demophon, 35 years.

13. Oxyntes, 9 years.

14. Apheidas, 1 year.

xv. Thymytus ann. VIIII.

xvi. Melanthus ann. XXXVII.

xvii. Codrus ann. XXI.

A Cecropo procero usque Codrum anni quadringenti XCII. Post Codrum autem fuerunt sicut[227] vixerunt principes. Difyis autem vocatus est Cecrops, quoniam procer staturae fuit prae omnibus.

4   Principes diabii.[228]

Post Codrum autem primus filius eius diabius factus est princeps Athineorum.

i. Medrus Codri ann. XX.

ii. Acastus ann. XXXVIIII.

iii. Archippus ann. XL.

iiii. Forbus ann. XXXIII.

v. Megaclus ann. XXVIII.

vi. Diognitus ann. XXVIII.

vii. Fereclus ann. XV.

viii. Arifrus ann. XXX.

viiii. Thispeus ann. XL.

x. Agamistor ann. XXVI.

xi. Thersippus ann. XXIII.

xii. Eschylus ann. . . . .

5   Eschylo anno secundo prima olympiada adducta est a Grecis.

Colliguntur vero ab initio regni Cecropi in prima olympiada anni octingenti XIIII. Post Eschylum autem illi:[229]

xiii. Almeus ann. X.

xiiii. Corops ann. X.

xv. Esimidus ann. X.

xvi. Celdicus ann. X.

15. Thymoites, 9 years.

16. Melanthus, 37 years.

17. Codrus, 21 years.

From Cecrops the Tall to Codrus there are 492 years. After Codrus there were princes [i.e., archons] as long as they lived. Cecrops was called *Diphyes* ["Double-form"] because he was tall of stature beyond all men.

The princes [archons] for life. 4

After Codrus his son became the first archon for life of the Athenians.

1. Medon the son of Codrus, 20 years.

2. Acastus, 39 years.

3. Archippus, 40 years.

4. Phorbas, 33 years.

5. Megacles, 28 years.

6. Diognetus, 28 years.

7. Pherecles, 15 years.

8. Ariphron, 30 years.

9. Thespieus, 40 years.

10. Agamestor, 26 years.

11. Thersippus, 23 years.

12. Aeschylus, . . . years.

In the second year of Aeschylus the first Olympiad was 5 held by the Greeks.

From the beginning of the reign of Cecrops to the first Olympiad 814 years are added together. After Aeschylus there were these:

13. Alcmaeon, 10[283] years.

14. Carops, 10 years.

15. Aesimides, 10 years.

16. Cleidicus, 10 years.

xvii. Ippomenus ann. X.

xviii. Leocratis ann. X.

xviiii. Apsandrus ann. X.

xx. Erygius ann. X.

Et cessavit regnum Athineorum in olympiada vicesima quarta. Fiunt vero omnem Athineorum fortitudinem a Cecropo usque Oxyrium ann. noningenti septem.

Caput IIII

Latinorum qui et Romanorum reges.[230]
Latinorum autem qui et Romanorum regnum fortiorem Assyriorum et Aegyptiorum et Argiorum seu et Sicyoniorum quem[231] et Grecorum et Athineorum in historia invenimus memorantem. Et nos quidem sequi pedes Romanorum quem et Latinorum tempora disponimus.

Latinorum autem regnum ab Eraclio quidem et Telefo, qui et Latinus vocatur, conamur in quibus prescripsimus[232] dicendo, cum quibus regnavit Eneas ille Frygius, Agchissi et Afroditis filius, nono et decimo post vastationem solis, in diebus Heli sacerdotis et Samuhelis prophetae secundum Ebraicam historiam.

Optinuit autem Romanorum imperium usque annos sexcentos LIII sic.

i. Eneas Silvius annos XXXVIII.

ii. Ascanius Silvius annos XXXV.

17. Hippomenes, 10 years.

18. Leocrates, 10 years.

19. Apsandrus, 10 years.

20. Eryxias, 10 years.

And the kingdom of the Athenians came to an end in the 24th Olympiad. This makes 907 years of the sovereignty of the Athenians from Cecrops to Eryxias.

Chapter 4

The kings of the Latins, also known as the Romans.

We find the kingdom of the Latins, who are also known as the Romans, remembered in history as stronger than that of the Assyrians or the Egyptians or the Sicyonians, who are also known as the Greeks,[284] or the Athenians. And we will follow the footsteps of the Romans, who are also the Latins, as we set out the chronology.

The kingdom of the Latins [takes its beginning] from Heracles and Telephus, who is also called Latinus, [of whom] we attempted to speak in what we have written above,[285] with whom Aeneas the Phrygian, the son of Anchises and Aphrodite, reigned, in the 19th year after the destruction of Sun City [Ilium], in the days of Eli the priest and Samuel the prophet according to Hebrew history.

The empire[286] of the Romans continued for 653 years, thus:

1. Aeneas Silvius, 38 years.

2. Ascanius Silvius, 35 years.

III. Albas Silvius annos XXXVI.
IIII. Tittus Silvius annos XXXVIII.
v. Francus Silvius annos LIII.
VI. Latinus Silvius annos LVI.
VII. Procnax Silvius annos XLVI.
VIII. Tarcinius Silvius annos XVIII.
VIIII. Cidensus Silvius annos XXXII.
x. Abintinus Silvius annos XXI.
XI. Rimus Silvius annos XXVIIII.

Usque Rimum Sylvium Latinorum regnum diffamabatur, permanens usque ad annos CCCCII.[233]

2 Post hunc autem regnavit Romulus qui et condidit Romam, a quo Romani vocati sunt.

Romulus regnavit ann. XXXVIII.
Nummus Pompiius ann. XLI.
Tullius Servilius ann. XXXII.
Lucius Tarcinius ann. XXIII.
Tittus Superbus ann. XXXVIII.
Tulius Servius ann. XLIIII.[234]
Cyintus Tarcinius ann. XXXV.

Colliguntur autem et a Romulo anni ducenti LI. Fiunt uero simul Latinorum qui et Romanorum anni sexcenti LIII. Defexit autem regnum in olympiada sexagesima sexta. Et tunc princepes ordinati sunt, usque dum regnaret Gaius Iulius Caesar.

3   Tempora regni Lacedemoniorum.

Regnaverunt et Lacedemonii per annos CCCXXV et defecerunt in prima olympiada quae facta est sub Achaz regem Iudae in diebus Esaiae prophetae, sicut scirent eorum initium ab Erystheum initiatum.

3. Albas Silvius, 36 years.
4. Titus Silvius, 38 years.
5. Francus Silvius, 53 years.
6. Latinus Silvius, 56 years.
7. Procnax Silvius, 46 years.
8. Tarquinius Silvius, 18 years.
9. Cidensus Silvius, 32 years.
10. Abintinus Silvius, 21 years.
11. Remus Silvius, 29 years.

Up to Remus Silvius the kingdom of the Latins was widely famed,[287] enduring for 402 years.

After him Romulus ruled, who also founded Rome and 2 from whom they are called Romans.

Romulus ruled for 38 years.
Numa Pompilius, 41 years.
Tullius Servilius, 32 years.
Lucius Tarquinius, 23 years.
Titus Superbus, 38 years.
Tullius Servius, 44 years.
Quintus Tarquinius, 35 years.

Two hundred fifty-one years are added together from Romulus. Altogether this makes 653 years of the Latins, who are also known as Romans. The kingdom ceased in the 66th Olympiad. And then the princes [i.e., consuls] succeeded until Gaius Julius Caesar reigned.

The chronology of the kingdom of the 3 Lacedaemonians.

The Lacedaemonians also reigned, through 325 years and failed in the first Olympiad which took place in the time of Ahaz the king of Judah, in the days of Isaiah the prophet, as they might know who trace their start[288] from its beginning under Eurystheus.

Anno vicesimo Sahul initiaverunt Lacedemoniorum reges, et defecerunt in anno primo Achaz regi Iude, in quo tempore prima olympiada a Grecis adducta est.

I. Illa autem singillatim regnorum haec.

II. Erystheus ann. XLII.

III. Egeus ann. II.

IIII. Echestratus ann. XXXIIII.

Labotus ann. XXXVII.

V. Dorystheus ann. XXVIIII.

VI. Agisilaus ann. XXX.

VII. Cemenelaus ann. XLIIII.

VIII. Archelaus ann. LX.

VIIII. Celeclus ann. XL.

X. Alcamanus ann. XXVII.

XI. Automedus ann. XXV.

Simul reges Lacedemioniorum permanserunt in regno annos CCCL. Et Lacedemoniorum regnum dissipatum est.

4   Corinthinorum reges et tempora.

Corinthinorum regnum stabilitum est secundo anno Erysthei regi Lacedemoniorum. Permansit autem per annos CCCXXIII. Eodem vero temporae Lacedemonii congregantes conmutaverunt illos tricentos XXIII annos, quos obtinuerunt Corinthinorum reges. Erystheo regnante Lacedemoniorum anno secundo regnavit autem Corinthinorum primus Alitus, et qui sequuntur post haec sic regnaverunt.

I. Alitus ann. XXXV.

II. Exius ann. XXXVII.

III. Agelaus ann. XXXIII.

In the 20th year of Saul the kings of the Lacedaemonians had their beginning, and they failed in the first year of Ahaz the king of Judah, at the time when the first Olympiad was held by the Greeks.

1. These are their reigns one by one:[289]
2. Eurystheus, 42 years.
3. Aegis, 2 years.
4. Echestratus, 34 years.
Labotes, 37 years.
5. Dorysthus, 29 years.
6. Agesilaus, 30 years.
7. Cemenelaus,[290] 44 years.
8. Archelaus, 60 years.
9. Telechus, 40 years.
10. Alcamenes, 27 years.
11. Automedon, 25 years.[291]

Altogether the kings of the Lacedaemonians remained in their kingdom for 350 years. And the kingdom of the Lacedaemonians was overthrown.

The kings and chronology of the Corinthians. 4

The kingdom of the Corinthians was established in the second year of Eurystheus the king of the Lacedaemonians. It endured through 323 years. At the same time the Lacedaemonians, being contemporary, shared those 323 years, which the kings of the Corinthians occupied. While Eurystheus was ruling the Lacedaemonians, in his second year, Aletes was the first to reign over the Corinthians, and those who followed after these things reigned thus:

1. Aletes, 35 years.
2. Ixion, 37 years.
3. Agelaus, 33 years.

IIII. Prymnus ann. XXXV.
v. Bacchus ann. XXXV.
vi. Agelas ann. XXXIIII.
vii. Eumidus ann. XXV.
viii. Aristomidus ann. XXXV.
viiii. Igemonius ann. XVI.
x. Alexander ann. XXV.
xi. Telestus ann. VIIII.
xii. Automenus ann. IIII.

Hii Corinthinorum reges sub anno tricesimo[235] primo Sahulis regi Iudae initiaverunt, et defecerunt anno quinto[236] decimo regni Ioatham fili Oziae, patri autem Achaz regis Iudae.

Caput V

Macedoniorum reges et tempora.

Macedoniorum autem regnum non silendum est. Et enim Romeis obtinentibus fortitudinem nondum longinquo tempore sub Ozia regem Iudeorum anno tricensimo tertio novimus eam sustentare. Et regnavit per annos DCXLVII, cessavit autem annos unusquisque in quinquagesima tertia olympiada. Regnavit autem Ozias in Hierusalem et in Iuda annos LII.

Sub tricensimo tertio autem anno Oziae Macedonorum regnum ordinatum est, Cranaus primus in Macedonia regnans, sicut numerus manifestat, sic.

i. Cranaus ann. XXVIII.
ii. Cynus ann. XII.

4. Prymnis, 35 years.
5. Bacchis, 35 years.
6. Agelas, 34 years.
7. Eudemus, 25 years.
8. Aristomedes, 35 years.
9. Agemon, 16 years.
10. Alexander, 25 years.
11. Telestes, 9 years.
12. Automenes, 4 years.

These kings of the Corinthians started in the 31st[292] year of Saul the king of Judah, and ceased in the 15th[293] year of the reign of Jotham, the son of Uzziah, the father of Ahaz, the king of Judah.

Chapter 5

The kings and chronology of the Macedonians.

The kingdom of the Macedonians ought not to be passed over in silence. For we acknowledge that even the Romans when they held power did not sustain it as far back as the time of the 33rd year of Uzziah the king of the Jews. And there was kingship through 667 years, and [its] years ceased altogether in the 53rd Olympiad.[294] Uzziah reigned in Jerusalem and in Judah for 52 years.

In the 33rd year of Uzziah the kingdom of the Macedonians was set up, and Cranaus was the first to rule in Macedonia, just as the reckoning shows, thus:

1. Cranaus, 28 years.
2. Coenus, 12 years.

III. Tyrimmus ann. XXXVIII.

IIII. Perdicus ann. LI.

v. Argeus ann. XXXVIII.

vI. Filippus ann. XXVI.

vII. Aeropus ann. XXXVIII.

vIII. Alcetus ann. XXVIIII.

vIIII. Amyntus ann. L.

x. Alexander ann. XLIII.

xI. Perdicus ann. XXVIII.

xII. Arcelaus ann. XXIIII.

2   xIII. Orestus ann. III.

xIIII. Arcelaus alius ann. unum et dimidium.

xv. Amyntus ann. III.

xvI. Pausanias ann. I et dimidium

xvII. Argeus ann. III.[237]

xvIII. Amyntus alius ann. XVIII.

xvIIII. Alexander alius ann. II.

xx. Ptolemaus ann. III.

xxI. Perdicus alius ann. VI.

xxII.[238] Filippus ann. XXVI.

xxIII.[239] Amyntus alius ann. VI.

xxIIII. Alexander alius ann. XIII.[240]

Alexander omnia regna tenens Macedonorum regno coniunxit.

Post Alexandrum autem conditorem in principes eius rebus venerunt.

3   Et Macedonorum principato successit Filippus frater
Alexandri, et sic secundum ordinem.

xxv. Filippus frater ann. VII.

xxvI. Casandrus ann. XVIIII.

3. Tyrimmas, 38 years.
4. Perdiccas, 51 years.
5. Argaius, 38 years.
6. Philip, 26 years.
7. Aeropus, 38 years.
8. Alcetas, 29 years.
9. Amyntas, 50 years.
10. Alexander, 43 years.
11. Perdiccas, 28 years.
12. Archelaus, 24 years.
13. Orestes, 3 years.   2
14. Another Archelaus, one and a half years.
15. Amyntas, 3 years.
16. Pausanias, one and a half years.
17. Argaius, 3^{295} years.
18. Another Amyntas,^{296} 18 years.
19. Another Alexander, 2 years.
20. Ptolemy, 3 years.
21. Another Perdiccas, 6 years.
22. Philip, 26 years.
23. Another Amyntas, 6 years.^{297}
24. Another Alexander, 13^{298} years.

Alexander held all kingdoms in his power and joined them to the kingdom of the Macedonians.

After Alexander the Founder his affairs devolved to his captains.

And Philip the brother of Alexander succeeded to the   3
sovereignty of the Macedonians, and then the following in order:

25. Philip the brother, 7 years.
26. Casander, 19 years.

xxvii. Pedes Casandrus ann. IIII.

xxviii. Dimitrius ann. V.

xxviiii. Pyrrus mens. XI.

xxx. Lysimachus ann. V.

xxxi. Ptolomeus Ceraunus ann. II.

xxxii. Meleagrus mens. VII.

xxxiii. Antipatrus mens. II.

xxxiiii. Sosthenus ann. II.

xxxv. Antigonus Gonata ann. XXXV.

xxxvi. Dimitrius ann. X.

xxxvii. Antigonus alius ann. XV.

xxxviii. Filippus alius ann. XLV.[241]

xxxviiii. Perseus ann. X.

Haec Macedonorum regna regnantes ab anno Oziae regis Iudae tricensimo tertio obtinuerunt per annos DCXLVII et cessaverunt in olympiada centesima LIII.

4 Lydiorum regna et tempora.

Et Lydiorum regnum tenuit per annos CCXXXII. Incipiens ab Ardio primum regem Lydiorum sub Cryssum illum a Cyro Persarum dissipatum finiit in olympiada quinquagensima octava.

Initium vero primae olympiadae invenitur exordium regni Lydiorum in anno primo Achaz. Regnavit quidem et Lydiorum principatus per annos CCXXXII sic.

i. Ardirus ann. XXXVI.

ii. Alyatus ann. XIIII.

iii. Midus ann. XII.

iiii. Caudalus ann. XVII.

v. Gygus ann. XXXVI.

27. The children of Casander, 4 years.

28. Demetrius, 5 years.

29. Pyrrhus, 11 months.

30. Lysimachus, 5 years.

31. Ptolemy Ceraunus, 2 years.

32. Meleager, 7 months.

33. Antipater, 2 months.

34. Sosthenes, 2 years.

35. Antigonus Gonatas, 35 years.

36. Demetrius, 10 years.

37. Another Antigonus, 15 years.

38. Another Philip, 45[299] years.

39. Perseus, 10 years.

These are the reigns of the rulers of the Macedonians from the 33rd year of Uzziah king of Judah, which lasted through 647 years and ended in the 153rd Olympiad.

The reigns and chronology of the Lydians. 4

And the kingdom of the Lydians lasted for 232 years. It began with Ardysus, the first king of the Lydians, was overthrown by Cyrus of the Persians in the time of Croesus, and came to an end in the 58th Olympiad.

The start of the first Olympiad is found to be the beginning of the kingdom of the Lydians, in the first year of Ahaz. And the sovereignty of the Lydians reigned for 232 years, thus:

1. Ardysus, 36 years.

2. Alyattes, 14 years.

3. Midas,[300] 12 years.

4. Candaules, 17 years.

5. Gyges, 36 years.

vi. Ardyssus ann. XXXVIII.

vii. Salyatus ann. XV.

viii. Aliatus alius ann. XLVIIII.

viiii. Cryssus ann. XV.

Haec Lydiorum regnum, incipiens a principio primae olympiadae in primo anno Achaz, regis Iudae. Et cessavit in olympiada quinquagensima octava. Fiunt anni CCXXXII.

5   Midorum regna et tempora.

Midorum autem regnum obtinuit per annos CCLXVIIII. Et haec Cyrus Persus destruens regnum eorum in Persida duxit in principio quinquagensimae quintae olympiadae. In ipsa nunc²⁴² quinquagensima quarta olympiada fiunt CCXVI, sicut pridem²⁴³ trium²⁴⁴ annorum primae olympiade Midorum initium invenimus esse regnum, quod est quinto decimo anno Oziae regis Iudae.

Quod vero CCLXVIIII annorum Midorum obtinuerunt tempora sic a principio Abbaci, qui primus regnavit in Midia, usque Artyagum, quem Cirus exterminans in Persida regnum migravit.

    i. Arbacus ann. XXVIII.

    ii. Sosarmus ann. IIII.

    iii. Mamythus ann. XL.

    iiii. Cardyceus ann. XXIII.

    v. Diycus ann. LIIII.

    vi. Fraortus ann. XXIIII.

    vii. Cyaxarus ann. XXXII.

    viii. Astyagus ann. XXXVIII.

Haec Midorum regna permanserunt per annos CCLXVIIII, a quinto decimo anno Oziae regis Iuda, hoc est LIII annorum primae²⁴⁵ olympiadae. Finiit autem quin-

6. Ardysus, 38 years.

7. Sadyattes, 15 years.

8. Another Alyattes, 49 years.

9. Croesus, 15 years.

These are the reigns of the Lydians which began at the start of the first Olympiad in the first year of Ahaz the king of Judah and ended in the 58th Olympiad. This makes 232 years.

The reigns and chronology of the Medes.   5

The kingdom of the Medes lasted for 269 years. And Cyrus the Persian toppled their kingdom and brought it to Persia at the start of the 55th Olympiad. Now 216 [years] had elapsed in the 54th Olympiad, so we find that the kingdom of the Medes began three[301] years before the first Olympiad, that is in the 15th year of Uzziah the king of Judah.

The kingdom and the chronology of the Medes lasted 269 years from its beginning under Arbaces, who was the first to reign in Media, up to Astyages, whom Cyrus deposed and transferred the kingdom to Persia.

1. Arbaces, 28 years.

2. Sosarmus, 4 years.[302]

3. Mamythus,[303] 40 years.

4. Cardyceas, 23 years.

5. Deioces, 54 years.

6. Phraortes, 24 years.

7. Cyaxares, 32 years.

8. Astyages, 38 years.

These reigns of the Medes endured for 269 years, from the 15th year of Uzziah king of Judah, this is 53 years before the first Olympiad. It ended in the 54th Olympiad, in the

quagensima quarta olympiada, anno tricensimo octavo regnante Astuago, quem exterminavit Cyrus Persus in quinquagensima quarta olympiada.

Et Lydorum et Midorum regna dissipata sunt sub Cyro Persarum.

6 Tempora regni Persarum.[246]
Cyrus Persarum rex dissipans regna Lydorum et Midorum regnavit olympiadas VII et dimidiam. In anno autem primo regni ipsius, in quo contigit consumari septuaginta annos depredicationi genti Iudeorum, relaxavit multitudinem filiorum Israhel remeare ad propriam habitationem. In quo anno fuit initium quinquagensimae quintae olympiade. Tenuit autem Persarum regnum usque Darium, quem occidit Alexander Macedo et conditor, annos CCXXX sic.

i. Cirus Persus ann. XXX.

ii. Cambysus ann. VIIII.

iii. Serdius . . . VII.[247]

iiii. Darius iuvenis ann. <. . .>VI.[248]

v. Xerxes maior ann. XX.

vi. Artabanus . . . VII.[249]

vii. Artaxerxes minor ann. XL.

viii. Xerxes iunior mens. II.

x. Sogdianus mens. VII.

xi. Darius Stultus ann. <. . .> VIIII.[250]

xii. Artaxerxes Memoratus ann. XLII.

xiii. Ochus filius Artaxerxi ann. XXII.

xiiii. Alsus filius Ochi ann. IIII.

Alexander Macedo et conditor exterminans Persarum regnum traduxit in Macedonia regnum permanentem annos CCXXX, sub olympiada centesima duodecima.

38th year of the reign of Astyages, whom Cyrus the Persian deposed in the 54th Olympiad.

And the kingdoms of the Lydians and the Medes were overthrown in the time of Cyrus of the Persians.

The chronology of the kingdom of the Persians.   6

Cyrus the king of the Persians scattered the kingdoms of the Lydians and the Medes and reigned for seven and a half Olympiads. In the first year of his reign, in which it came to pass that the 70 years of the despoiling of the people of the Jews was completed, he released the multitude of the sons of Israel to return to their proper dwelling place. In this year was the beginning of the 55th Olympiad. The kingdom of the Persians lasted up to Darius, whom Alexander the Macedonian, the Founder, slew, for 230 years, thus:

1. Cyrus the Persian, 30 years.
2. Cambyses, 9 years.
3. Smerdis, 7 <months>.
4. Darius, the Youth, <3>6 years.
5. Xerxes the Elder,[304] 20 years.
6. Artabanus, 7 <months>.
7. Artaxerxes the Less, 40 years.
8. Xerxes the Younger, 2 months.
10. Sogdianus, 7 months.
11. Darius the Fool (i.e., *Nothos*), <1>9 years.
12. Artaxerxes the Mindful [*Mnemon*],[305] 42 years.
13. Ochus the son of Artaxerxes, 22 years.
14. Arses the son of Ochus, 4 years.[306]

Alexander the Macedonian, the Founder, brought the kingdom of the Persians, which had lasted for 230 years, to an end and transferred the kingdom to Macedonia in the time of the 112th Olympiad.

Caput VI

Macedonorum regna et Syrie et tempora ab
Alexandro conditore[251]

Alexander Filippi coepit regnare Macedonorum in olympiada centesima undecima, omnia simul regna conprehendens et sub Macedonorum iure redigens,[252] per annos duodecim et dimidium. Obiit in anno . . . relinquens post se principes IIII.

Filippum fratrem suum Macedoniae regnum, Antigonum autem Asiae reliquid[253] regnare, Filippum vocatum Ptolomeum omnem Aegyptum precepit regnare, Seleucum autem quem et Nicanorem Syriam omnem iussit regnare.

Qui autem regnaverunt in Syria per tempora sunt ita.

i. Seleucus qui et Nicanor ann. XXXII.

ii. Antiochus Soter ann. XVIIII.

iii. Antiochus Theoidus ann. XV.

iiii. Seleucus Callinicus ann. XXI.

v. Seleucus Ceraunus ann. III.

vi. Antiochus Megaclus ann. XXXVI.

vii. Antiochus Filomitor ann. XII.

<viii.> Antiochus[254] Epifanius ann. XI.

Iste est, qui in Iudeis iniquitatem inposuit, cuius historia in Maccabeis.

2   viiii. Aniochus Eupator ann. II.

x. Dimitrius Soter ann. XII.

xi. Alexander Grypus ann. X.

xii. Dimitrius Grypus ann. III.

xiii. Antiochus Situs ann. VIIII.

xiiii. Dimitrius iuvenis ann. IIII.

Chapter 6

The reigns of the Macedonians and of Syria and
the chronology from Alexander.

Alexander the son of Philip began to reign over the Macedonians in the 111th Olympiad; he seized control of all the kingdoms together and brought them under the law of the Macedonians in the course of twelve and a half years. He died in the . . . year, leaving four princes behind him.

He ordered his brother Philip to rule the kingdom of Macedonia, Antigonus to rule the rest of Asia, Philip called Ptolemy to rule all of Egypt, and he commanded Seleucus who is also known as Nicanor to rule all of Syria.

Those who reigned in Syria over time are as follows:

1. Seleucus who is also known as Nicanor,[307] 32 years.
2. Antiochus Soter, 19 years.
3. Antiochus Theoeides, 15 years.
4. Seleucus Callinicus, 21 years.
5. Seleucus Ceraunus, 3 years.
6. Antiochus Megas, 36 years.
7. Antiochus Philometor, 12 years.
<8.> Antiochus Epiphanes, 11 years.

This is he who imposed iniquity upon the Jews, whose story is told in Maccabees.

9. Antiochus Eupator, 2 years.
10. Demetrius Soter, 12 years.
11. Alexander Grypus, 10 years.
12. Demetrius Grypus, 3 years.
13. Antiochus Sidetes, 9 years.
14. Demetrius the Younger, 4 years.

2

xv. Antiochus ille Grypi ann. XII.

xvi. Antiochus Cizicinus ann. XVIII.

xvii. Filippus ... II.

Sub Filippo novissimo Syriorum regnum dissipatum est. Macedonorum principatum venit in Romanos, Gaio Iulio Romanorum Caesare migrans eam. Et permanens per annos CCXXI et Siriorum principatum dissipatum est.

3   Egyptiorum regna et tempora.

Egypti autem reges, qui et Ptolemei nuncupati sunt, regnaverunt post Alexandri discessum annos CCXCIIII sic.

i. Filippus Ptolemeus ann. VII.

ii. Filadelfus Alexander ann. XII.

iii. Lagous Ptolemeus ann. XX.

iiii. Eugergetus Ptolemeus ann. XXXVIII.

v. Filopator Ptolemeus ann. XVII.

vi. Epifanius Ptolemeus ann. XXIIII.[255]

vii. Filomitor Ptolemeus ann. XXXV.

viii. Eugergetus Fauscus Ptol. ann. XXVIIII.

viiii. Soter Ptolemeus ann. XXXVI.

x. Filadelfus Soter Ptol. ann. XXV.

xi. Novus Dionysus Ptol. ann. XXVIIII.

xii. Cleopatra ann. XXII.[256]

Dissipatum est Ptolemeorum principatum sub Octaviano Agusto Romanorum imperatorem, sub imperium eius anno XIIII, permanens annos CCXCIIII.

4   i. Primus factus est princeps sacerdotum Hiesus filius Iosedec simul Zorobabel.

ii. Post hunc Iacimus filius Hiesu.

iii. Post hunc Eliasibus filius Iacimi.

15. Antiochus the son of Grypus, 12 years.

16. Antiochus Cyzicenus, 18 years.

17. Philip, 2 <years>.

In the time of Philip, the last [of his line], the kingdom of the Syrians was overthrown. The dominion of the Macedonians came to the Romans; Gaius Julius the Caesar of the Romans transferred it.[308] And after lasting for 221 years the dominion of the Syrians was overthrown.

The reigns and chronology of the Egyptians. 3

The kings of Egypt, who were also named the Ptolemies, reigned after the departure[309] of Alexander for 294 years, thus:

1. Ptolemy Philip, 7 years.

2. Alexander Philadelphus, 12 years.

3. Ptolemy Lagus, 20 years.

4. Ptolemy Euergetes, 38 years.

5. Ptolemy Philopator, 17 years.

6. Ptolemy Epiphanes, 24 years.

7. Ptolemy Philometor, 35 years.

8. Ptolemy Euergetes Physkon, 29 years.

9. Ptolemy Soter, 36 years.

10. Ptolemy Philadelphus Soter, 25 years.

11. Ptolemy the New Dionysus, 29 years.

12. Cleopatra, 22 years.

The dominion of the Ptolemies was overthrown in the time of Octavian Augustus the emperor of the Romans, in the 14th year of his rule, after lasting for 294 years.

1. Joshua the son of Josedech became the first high priest 4 at the time of Zerubbabel.

2. After him Joiakim the son of Joshua.

3. After him Eliashib the son of Joiakim.

IIII. Post hunc Iodae filius Eliasibi.

v. Post hunc Iohannes filius Iodae.

vi. Post hunc Iaddus filius Iohanni.

Quo tempore Alexander Macedo et conditor Alexandriam condidit. Et veniens in Hierusalem domino deo adoravit dicens: Gloria tibi, deus, qui vivis in secula, solus princeps.

vii. Post hunc Onias filius Iaddi.

viii. Post hunc Eleazarus filius Oniae.

Quo tempore illi septuaginta Ebreorum sapientes in Alexandria legem interpretaverunt Greco eloquio.

viiii. Post hunc Onias filius Simoni frater Eleazari.

x. Post hunc Simon filius Iaddi.

Quo tempore Hiesus filius Sirach, qui et magnam Ebreis scripsit sapientiam, agnoscebatur.

xi. Post hunc Onias filius Simoni.

Quo tempore Antiochus Syrorum rex Iudeos expugnans Greca loquutione coegebat.

5   xii. Post hunc Iudas Maccabeus filius Oniae.

xiii. Post hunc Ionathas frater Iudae.

xiiii. Post hunc Simon frater Ionathae.

xv. Post hunc Iohannis filius Ionathae, qui dicebatur Yrcanus.

xvi. Post hunc Aristobolus filius Iohannis.

Qui primus inposuit deadema regni principatum sacerdotii.

xvii. Post hunc Ianneus qui et Alexander, rex simul et princeps sacerdotum.

Usque ad istum illi qui a Cyro uncti praefuerunt perma-

4. After him Jehoiada the son of Eliashib.

5. After him John the son of Jehoiada.

6. After him Jaddua the son of John,

In which time Alexander the Macedonian and the Founder, founded Alexandria. And he came to Jerusalem and worshipped the Lord God, saying, "Glory to You, God, Who liveth unto the ages, Only Prince."[310]

7. After him Onias the son of Jaddua.

8. After him Eleazar the son of Onias,

In which time the seventy sages of the Hebrews in Alexandria translated the law into the Greek language.

9. After him Onias the son of Simon, the brother of Eleazar.

10. After him Simon the son of Jaddua,

In which time Jesus the son of Sirach, who wrote the lofty wisdom for the Hebrews, was renowned.

11. After him Onias the son of Simon,

In which time Antiochus the king of the Syrians overcame the Jews and compelled them to employ Greek speech.[311]

12. After him Judas Maccabeus the son of Onias.   5

13. After him Jonathan the brother of Judas.

14. After him Simon the brother of Jonathan.

15. After him John the son of Jonathan, who was called Hyrcanus.

16. After him Aristobolus the son of John,

Who was the first of the high priests to assume the diadem of kingship.

17. After him Janneus, also known as Alexander, was simultaneously king and high priest.

Up to him those who were anointed by Cyrus were in

nentes per annos quadrintis LXXXIII, quae sunt ebdomadas annorum LXVIIII, quae et a Danihele quemadmodum diffinierunt.

Post Ianneum autem quem et Alexandrum principem sacerdotum et regem, in quo finierunt, qui secundum ritum principes sacerdotum uncti nominabantur <...>. XVIII. Post hos regnavit Salinai et Alexandra uxor eius. XVIIII. Post hunc tumultum inter se eius pueri facientes Pompiius Romanorum archistratigus expugnavit Hierusalem tenens usque ad progressionem templi apertionis.[257] Tunc gens illa Iudeorum tributaria facta est Romanis. Principatum quidem sacerdotii Yrcano tradidit, Antipatrum autem Ascalona Palestine procuratorem faciens.

Quo tempore Romanorum primus monarchus Gaius Iulius Caesar. Regnavit autem annos XVIII. Post hunc Augustus regnavit annos LVI et qui post eos sequentes.[258]

Caput VII

Tempora regni Romanorum.[259]

Romanorum autem[260] regnavit monarchus primus Gaius Iulius Caesar[261] in olympiada centesima octuagesima tertia. Iste est Gaius Iulius Caesar, qui bisextum et solis cursum adinvenit.[262]

Post istum regnavit Octauianus qui et Augustus et qui sequuntur sic.

266

charge and remained so for 483 years, which are 69 weeks of years, which came to an end just as [was predicted] by Daniel.[312]

After Janneus, also known as Alexander, the high priest and king, in whose time those who were anointed high priests and nominated according to the rite came to an end <. . .>.

18. After them Salina reigned, and his wife Alexandra.[313]

19. After him, because his sons were causing a disturbance among themselves, Pompey the general of the Romans took Jerusalem by storm and held it until he went to the entrance of the temple. Then the people of the Jews were made tributary to the Romans. He handed over the high priesthood to Hyrcanus and made Antipater of Ascalon the procurator of Palestine.

In this time Gaius Julius Caesar was the first monarch of the Romans. He reigned for 18 years. After him Augustus reigned for 56 years, and those who followed after them.

Chapter 7

The chronology of the kingdom of the Romans.

Gaius Julius Caesar was the first monarch to rule the Romans, in the 183rd Olympiad. This is the Gaius Julius Caesar who discovered the intercalary day and the course of the sun.

After him Octavian, also known as Augustus, reigned, and those who followed him, thus:

Consules.

I. Augustus regnavit ann. LVI. Dedit consulatus XIII.

II. Tiberius regnavit ann. XXIII. Consules V.

III. Gaius regnavit ann. X. Consules IIII.

IIII. Claudius regnavit ann. XV. Consules V.

V. Nero regnavit ann. XIIII. Consules IIII.

Galbas, Stultus, Bitellio ann. I et dimidium.

VI. Titus regnavit ann. III. Consules VIII.

VII. Dometianus regnavit ann. XVI. Consules VII.

VIII. Nerva regnavit ann. II. Consules IIII.

VIIII. Traianus regnavit ann. XX. Consules VI.

X. Hadrianus regnavit ann. XII. Consules III.

XI. Antoninus regnavit ann. XIII. Consules IIII.

XII. Marcus Byrrus regnavit ann. XX. Consules XXIIII.

XIII. Commodus regnavit ann. XIII. Consules VII.

XIIII. Vespasianus regnavit ann. VIIII. Consules X.

XV. Pertinax, Didius ann. <....> Consules IIII.

XVI. Severus regnavit menses III. Consules. <...>

XVII. Gitas, Caracallus regnavit ann. <...> Consules XXV.

XVIII. Macrinus, Iliogabalus regnavit ann. V. Consulem I.

XVIIII. Alexander Mameas regnavit ann. XIII. Consules III.

Maximus regnavit ann. III. Consules II.

2   XX. Balbinus et Publianus et Cordus annum I.

XXI. Gordianus regnavit ann. VI. Consules II.

XXII.[263] Filippus regnavit ann. VI. Consules III.

XXIII. Decius regnavit annos II. Consulem I.

XXIIII. Gallus et Volusianus, hii duo regnaverunt ann. III. Dederunt consulatos VII.

Consuls

1. Augustus reigned for 56 years. He served 13 consulships.

2. Tiberius reigned 23 years. Consul 5 times.

3. Gaius reigned 10 years. Consul 4 times.

4. Claudius reigned 15 years. Consul 5 times.

5. Nero reigned 14 years. Consul 4 times.
Galba, the Fool [*Otho*],[314] Vitellius, one and a half years.[315]

6. Titus reigned 3 years. Consul 8 times.

7. Domitian reigned 16 years. Consul 7 times.

8. Nerva reigned 2 years. Consul 4 times.

9. Trajan reigned 20 years. Consul 6 times.

10. Hadrian reigned 12 years. Consul 3 times.

11. Antoninus reigned 13 years. Consul 4 times.

12. Marcus Verus reigned 20 years. Consul 24 times.

13. Commodus reigned 13 years. Consul 7 times.

14. Vespasian reigned 9 years. Consul 10 times.[316]

15. Pertinax, Didius, <. . .> years. Consul 4 times.

16. Severus reigned 3 months. Consul <. . .> times.

17. Geta, Caracalla reigned <. . .> years. Consul 25 times.

18. Macrinus, Heliogabalus reigned 5 years. Consul once.

19. Alexander the son of Mamaea reigned 13 years. Consul 3 times.
Maximus [Maximinus] reigned 3 years. Consul twice.

20. Balbinus and Publianus [Pupienus] and Cordus [Gordianus], 1 year. 2

21. Gordianus reigned 6 years. Consul twice.

22. Philip reigned 6 years. Consul 3 times.

23. Decius reigned 2 years. Consul once.

24. Gallus and Volusianus, these two reigned for 3 years. They served 7 consulships.

xxv. Emilianus et Valerianus et Calerianus, hii tres simul ann. XV. Consules VII.

xxvi. Gallianus cum Claudio ann. II. Consulem I.

xxvii. Cyintillus et Aurilianus regnaverunt ann. VI. Dederunt consulatos III.

xxviii.²⁶⁴ Tacitus et Florianus ann. I. Consulem I.

xxviiii. Probus regnavit annos VI. Consules V.

xxx. Carus et Carinus et Numerianus, simul hii tres ann. II et dimidium. Dederunt consulatos unusquisque II.

xxxi. Dioclitianus et Maximianus regnaverunt ann. XXI, regnaverunt et Constantius et Maximus cum eis annos XII.

xxxii. Constantius et Constantinus magnus cum Constantino filio eius ann. XXXI.

xxxiii. Constantinus et Costa et Constantinus iunior simul ann. XXIIII.

xxxiiii. Iulianus regnavit ann. II. Consules II.

xxxv. Iobianus regnavit menses VIII.

xxxvi. Valentinianus et Valens et filii eorum Gratianus et Valentinianus annos XXII.

3   xxxvii. Theodosius magnus cum Arcadio et Honorio filios eius simul annos XXXVI.

xxxviii. Theodosius cum Valentiniano ann. LI.

xxxviiii. Valentinus cum Marciano ann. V.

xl. Marcianus solus ann. VII.

xli. Leo cum Anthimo ann. XVIIII.

xlii. Leo iunior cum Zinone ann. II.

xliii. Basiliscus et Marcus mens. XX.

xliiii. Zino solus ann. <. . .>

xlv. Anastasius solus ann. <. . .>

25. Aemilianus and Valerian and Gallienus,[317] these three together, 15 years. Consuls 7 times.

26. Gallienus with Claudius, 2 years. Consul once.

27. Quintillus and Aurelian reigned 6 years. They served 3 consulships.

28. Tacitus and Florianus, 1 year. Consul once.

29. Probus reigned 6 years. Consul 5 times.

30. Carus and Carinus and Numerianus, these three together, two and a half years. They served 2 consulships each.

31. Diocletian and Maximianus reigned for 21 years, and Constantius and Maximus reigned with them for 12 years.

32. Constantius and Constantine the Great with Constantine his son, 31 years.

33. Constantius and Constans and Constantine the younger together, 24 years.

34. Julian reigned for 2 years. Consul twice.

35. Jovian reigned for 8 months.

36. Valentinian and Valens and their sons Gratian and Valentinian, 22 years.

37. Theodosius the Great together with Arcadius and 3 Honorius his sons, 36 years.

38. Theodosius and Valentinian, 51 years.

39. Valentinian and Marcian, 5 years.

40. Marcian alone, 7 years.

41. Leo with Anthemius, 19 years.

42. Leo the younger with Zeno, 2 years.

43. Basiliscus and Marcus, 20 months.

44. Zeno alone, <. . .> years.

45. Anastasius alone, <. . .> years.

Ecce quidem manifestauimus veraciter omnium potestatem regum. Volumus praecurrere quod[265] ad Romanorum pertinet imperium.

Usque Cleopatra enim facta est omnis Egyptiorum Ptolemeorum potestas permanens annos CCXCIIII, et post Cleopatra ultra non regnaverunt in Egypto usque in hodiernum diem.

Caput VIII

In diebus, quibus regnaverunt Ptolomei in Egypto et fecerunt Romani proelium cum Spanis, et superaverunt Romani Spanos et levauerunt imperatorem Iulium quem et Caesarem uocaverunt. Iste est Gaius[266] Iulius Caesar, qui et bissextum[267] et solis cursum adinvenit. Hic est consolatum unumquemque annum fieri constituit.

Regnauit autem Gaius Iulius Caesar annos XVIII, et post hunc Octauianus qui et Augustus.

i. Gaio Iulio Caesare secundo, Marco clarissimo.

ii. Gratiano et Antonino clarissimorum.

iii. Gaio Iulio Caesare secundo et Flauio.

Marco clarissimo.[268]

Iurto[269] et Paneo uirorum inlustrium.

Burto et Cortilano clarissimorum.

Gaio Iulio Caesare tertio et Lepido inlustrium.

Munatio et Plachano inlustrium.

So you see we have indicated truly the dynasty of all the kings. [For] we wish to go over what pertains to the empire of the Romans.

For up to Cleopatra the whole dynasty of the Egyptian Ptolemies came to last for 294 years, and after Cleopatra they have no longer reigned in Egypt up to the present day.

Chapter 8

In the days in which the Ptolemies reigned in Egypt the Romans made war upon the Spaniards, and the Romans conquered the Spaniards and raised up the emperor Julius, whom they also called Caesar. This is Gaius Julius Caesar who discovered the intercalary day and the course of the sun. He was also the one who decided that each consulship should be for a single year.[318]

Gaius Julius Caesar reigned for 18 years, and after him Octavian, who is also known as Augustus.[319]

1. Gaius Julius Caesar for the second time, the most distinguished[320] Marcus. [44 BCE]

2. The most distinguished Gratian and Antoninus.

3. Gaius Julius Caesar for the second time and Flavius [Fabius]. [45][321]

The most distinguished Marcus.

The illustrious men Hirtius and Pansa. [43]

The most distinguished Brutus and Collatinus. [509][322]

The illustrious Gaius Julius Caesar for the third time and Lepidus. [46]

The illustrious Munatius and Plancus.[323] [42]

Emelio et Caesario inlustrium.

Antonino et Seruiliano clarissimorum.

Chryssaorico et Crispo clarissimorum.

Octavio et Polione clarissimorum.

Consorio et Savino clarissimorum.

Pulco et Enobaudo clarissimorum.

Gallo et Agrippino clarissimorum.

Octaviano et Neru filio[270] clarissimorum.

Pompiio et Cornilio clarissimorum.

Libono et Antonino clarissimorum.

Cicerone et Publicollatonem inlustrium.[271]

Hisdem consulibus Iulius Caesar occisus est. Et sumpsit imperium Octavianus qui et Augustus ann. LVI, et dedit consulatos XIII. Fiunt vero ab Adam usque initium imperii Augusti anni V milia CCCCLXVII.

2   I. Augusto primo et Tollio.

II. Augusto secundo et Socio.

III. Augusto tertio et Crasso.

IIII. Augusto quarto et Messalo.

V. Thenebaudo quinto et Scipione.

VI. Augusto sexto et Apulia.

VII. Augusto septimo et Agrippa.[272]

Hisdem consulibus Chartagina renovata est idos Iulias, Epifi XVIII.

The illustrious Aemilius and Caesar. [46]

The most distinguished Antoninus [Antony] and Servilius. [41]

The most distinguished Chryssaoricus [Isauricus] and Crispus. [41 BCE, 44 CE]

The most distinguished Octavian and Pollio. [43, 40]

The most distinguished Censorinus and Sabinus. [39]

The most distinguished Pulcher and Ahenobarbus. [38, 32]

The most distinguished Gallus and Agrippinus [Agrippa]. [37]

The most distinguished Octavian and Nerva the son [*Cocceius*].[324] [43, 36]

The most distinguished Pompey and Cornelius [Cornificius]. [35]

The most distinguished Libo and Antoninus [Antony]. [34]

The illustrious Cicero and Publicollato [Poplicola]. [30, 36]

When these men were consuls Julius Caesar was killed. And Octavian who is also known as Augustus took up the sovereignty for 56 years, and served 13 consulships. This makes from Adam up to the beginning of the sovereignty of Augustus 5,467 years.

1. Augustus for the first time and Tullus. [33]

2. Augustus for the second time and Sosius. [32]

3. Augustus for the third time and Crassus. [30]

4. Augustus for the fourth time and Messala. [31]

5. Ahenobarbus for the fifth time and Scipio. [32, 35]

6. Augustus for the sixth time and Appuleius. [29]

7. Augustus for the seventh time and Agrippa. [28]

When these men were consuls Carthage[325] was restored on the ides of July, the 18th of Epeiph [July 15].

VIII. Augusto ocatavo et Silvano.

VIIII. Augusto nono et Tauro.

X. Augusto decimo et Sullio.

XI. Augusto undecimo et Pisone.

In his temporibus, sub consulato Lentuli et Silvani, vidit Zacharias visionem angeli in templo domini.

XII. Aruntio et Marcellio.

XIII. Celso et Tiberio.

XIIII. Tullio et Emellio.[273]

XV. Asperio et Severio.

XVI. Saturnino et Cinno.

Lentulo et Silvano.

In his temporibus adnuntiat Elisabeth angelus de Io-hanne, in eodem consulatum Lentuli et Silvani, VIII kl. Aprilis.

3   XVIII. Savino et Antonino.

XVIIII. Lentulo secundo et Lepido.

XX. Rufino et Pisone.

XXI. Mesallo et Seriniano.

XXII. Maximo et Tuberone.

XXIII. Africano et Maximo.

XXV. Aruntio et Prisco.

XXVI. Censorino et Gallione.

XXVII. Neronte et Placido.

XXVIII. Balbino et Bereto.

Eodem tempore missus est angelus Gabrihel ad Mariam virginem, sub Augusto tertio decimo, octavarum kalenda-rum Aprilium.

XXVIIII. Felecio et Suilio.

XXX. Lentulo et Auxonio.

8. Augustus for the eighth time and Silvanus [Silanus]. [25]

9. Augustus for the ninth time and Taurus. [26]

10. Augustus for the tenth time and Sullius [Silanus]. [25]

11. Augustus for the eleventh time and Piso. [23]

In these times, in the consulate of Lentulus and Silvanus [3, 2], Zacharias saw a vision of an angel in the temple of the Lord.[326]

12. Arruntius and Marcellus. [22]

13. Celsus and Tiberius. [?]

14. Tullius [Lollius] and Aemilius. [21]

15. Asperius [Appuleius] and Severius [Silius]. [20]

16. Saturninus and Cinna. [4 CE, 5 CE]

Lentulus and Silvanus. [18 or 3, 2]

In these times the angel told Elizabeth about John, in the same consulate of Lentulus and Silvanus, on the eighth of the calends of April [March 25].[327]

18. Sabinus and Antony. [4, 10]

19. Lentulus for the second time and Lepidus. [14, 21]

20. Rufinus [Rufus] and Piso. [16, 15]

21. Messalla and Serinianus [Quirinius]. [12]

22. Maximus and Tubero. [11]

23. Africanus and Maximus. [10]

25. Arruntius and Priscus [Crispinus]. [9]

26. Censorinus and Gallio [Gallus]. [8]

27. Nero and Placidus [Piso]. [7]

28. Balbinus [Balbus] and Veretus [Vetus]. [6]

In this same time the angel Gabriel was sent to the virgin Mary, in the 13th year of Augustus, on the 8th of the calends of April [March 25].[328]

29. Felecius and Sulla. [5]

30. Lentulus and Auxonius. [3]

3

XXXI. Caesario et Austorino.

XXXII. Silvano et Paulino.

In sexto autem mense abiit Maria ad cognatam suam Elisabeth.

Et salutavit eam, et dixit ei Elisabeth: Unde hoc mihi, ut mater domini mei veniat ad me. Ecce enim quod est in me exultavit infans et benedixit te.

XXXIII. Prisco et Romano.

XXXIIII. Iuctore et Protarcho.

XXXV. Senecione et Bardone.

XXXVI. Timageno et Nigriano.

XXXVII. Syriano et Peregrino.

XXXVIII. Xifidio et Marcello.

In his temporibus, sub Augusto, natus est Iohannis praecursor, Zachariae filius, VIII kl. Iulias.

4   XXXVIIII. Fruro et Autorino.

XL. Augusto et Sacerdo.

XLI. Pompiiano et Plutone.

XLII. Augusto et Silvano.

XLIII. Antulo et Iulio.

XLIIII. Augusto et Silvano.

Hisdem consulibus dominus noster Iesus Christus[274] natus est, sub Augusto, VIII kl. Ianuar.: in deserto natus est cuiusdam nomine Fuusdu, quod est Eusebii. In ipsa enim die, in qua natus est, pastores viderunt stellam, Chuac XXVIII.

Fiunt vero ab Adam usque ad nativitatem domini nostri Iesu Christi[275] anni V milia quingenti.

31. Caesar and Austorinus. [1 CE]

32. Silvanus and Paullus. [2 BCE, 1 CE]

In the sixth month Mary left [to go] to her cousin Elizabeth.

And she saluted her, and Elizabeth said to her, "Whence is this to me, that the mother of my Lord should come to me? For lo the babe which is in me leaped for joy and blessed you."³²⁹

33. Priscus and Romanus. [?]

34. Juctos and Protarchus. [?]

35. Senecio and Bardo. [?]

36. Timagenes and Nigrianus. [?]

37. Syrianus and Peregrinus. [?]

38. Xiphidius and Marcellus. [?]

In these times, under Augustus, John the Forerunner, the son of Zacharias, was born on the eighth of the calends of July [June 24].

39. Frurus and Autorinus. [?]   4

40. Augustus and Sacerdus. [?]

41. Pompeianus and Pluto. [?]

42. Augustus and Silvanus. [2 BCE]

43. Antulus and Julius. [?]

44. Augustus and Silvanus. [2 BCE]

When these men were consuls Our Lord Jesus Christ was born, in the time of Augustus, on the eighth of the calends of January [December 25].³³⁰ In the desert a certain man was born by the name of Fuusdu, which is of Eusebius.³³¹ For on the very day on which he was born the shepherds saw the star, on the 28th of Choiak [December 24/25].

This makes from Adam up to the nativity of Our Lord Jesus Christ 5,500 years.³³²

XLV. Bincio et Birro.

XLVI. Caesario et Serbilio.

XLVII. Macrino et Saturnino.

XLVIII. Sacerdo et Bolenso.

XLVIIII. Lepido et Arruntio.

In his diebus, sub Augusto, kalendas Ianuarias, Magi obtulerunt ei munera et adoraverunt eum. Magi autem vocabantur Bithisarea, Melchior, Gathaspa. Audiens autem Herodes a Magis, quoniam rex natus esset, conturbatus est, et omnes Hierusolima cum eo. Et videns, quia inlusus esset a Magis, misit homicidas suos dicens eis: Interficite omnes pueros a bimatu et infra.[276]

Herodes autem querebat Iohannem et misit ministros ante altarem[277] ad Zachariam dicens illi: Ubi abscondisti filium tuum? An ignoras quia potestatem te habeo occidendi et sangui tuus in manibus meis est? Et dixit Zaxarias: Ego testes sum dei viuentis.[278] Tu effundis sanguinem meum, spiritum autem meum dominus recipiet. Et sub aurora occisus est Zacharias.

Caput VIIII

L. Critico et Nerva.

LI. Camerino et Birillo.

LII. Dolomallo et Sofiano.

LIII. Cyntilliano et Babilio.

45. Vinicius and Varus. [2 CE]
46. Caesar and Servilius. [1 CE, 3 CE][333]
47. Macrinus and Saturninus. [5, 4]
48. Sacerdo and Volesus. [5]
49. Lepidus and Arruntius. [6]

In these days, in the time of Augustus, on the calends of January [January 1], the Magi brought gifts to him and worshipped him. The Magi were called Balthazar, Melchior, and Gaspar.[334]

When Herod heard from the Magi that a king was born he was troubled and all Jerusalem with him. And when he saw that he was tricked by the Magi he sent his murderers telling them, "Kill all the boys from two years old and under."[335]

Herod sought out John and sent his servants before the altar to Zacharias, saying to him, "Where have you hidden your son? Or do you not know that I have the power to kill you and your life [lit., blood] is in my hands?" And Zacharias said, "I am the witness of the Living God. [If] you shed my blood, the Lord will receive my spirit." And just before dawn Zacharias was killed.[336]

Chapter 9

50. Creticus and Nerva. [7]
51. Camerinus and Virillus. [9]
52. Dolabella and Sofianus [Silanus]. [10]
53. Quinctilianus and Barbilius. [8]

Elisabeth autem cognoscens quia querebatur Iohannes, adprehendens eum ascendit in montana et aspiciebat, ubi eum absconderet, et non erat locus abscondendi. Tunc suspirans Elisabeth exclamavit dicens: Mons dei, suscipe me matrem cum filio. Et statim scissus est mons et recepit eos.

LIIII. Germanico et Carpo.

LV. Austorio[279] et Silvano.

LVI. Plachno et Auito.

LVII. Pompiiano et Flacco.

His consulibus Augustus obiit. Et regnavit Tiberius ann. XXII. Dedit consulatus VII.

LVIII. Tiberio Augusto et Germano.

LVIIII. Flaubio et Rufino.

LX. Drusullo et Sorano.

In his diebus planxerunt Zachariam et fleverunt eum tribus diebus et tribus noctibus. Et suscitavit eis dominus deus in loco Zachariae Symeonem.

Iste acceperat responsum ab angelo non visurum se mortem, nisi videret Christum domini in carne. Et videns eum dixit: Nunc dimittis servum tuum, domine, in pace, quia viderunt oculi mei salutarem tuum, quod parasti ante faciem omnium populorum, lumen ad revelationem gentium et gloria plebis tuae Israhel.

2 LXI. Tauro et Libone.

LXII. Silvano et Gerontio.

LXIII. Mesaulico et Balbino.

LXIIII. Tiberio Aūg. secundo et Colta.

LXV. Agrippa et Druso.

When Elizabeth learned that John was being sought she seized him and went up into the mountains and looked for a place where she might hide him, and there was no place for hiding. Then Elizabeth heaved a sigh and cried out, saying, "Mountain of God, take me up, a mother with her son." And at once the mountain was split and received them.[337]

54. Germanicus and Carpus [Capito]. [12]

55. Austorius and Silvanus [Silanus]. [10]

56. Plancus and Avitus. [13]

57. Pompeianus [Pompey] and Flaccus. [14, 15]

When these men were consuls Augustus died. And Tiberius reigned for 22 years. He served seven consulships.

58. Tiberius Augustus and Germanicus. [18]

59. Flavius [Flaccus] and Rufinus [Rufus]. [17]

60. Druollus [Drusus] and Soranus [Nortanus]. [15]

In these days they lamented Zacharias and wept over him for three days and three nights. And the Lord God raised up for them Simeon in the place of Zacharias.[338]

It was revealed unto this man by an angel, that he should not see death, unless he saw the Lord's Christ in the flesh. And when he saw him he said, "Lord now lettest thou thy servant depart in peace, for mine eyes have seen thy salvation, which thou has prepared before the face of all peoples, a light to lighten the Gentiles and the glory of thy people Israel."[339]

61. Taurus and Libo. [16]

62. Silvanus [Silanus] and Gerontius. [19]

63. Mesaulicus [Messala] and Balbinus [Balbus]. [20, 19]

64. Tiberius Augustus for the second time and Cotta. [21, 20]

65. Agrippa and Drusus. [22, 21]

Tunc responsum accepit Ioseph, et accipiens Iesum et Mariam fugiit in Egyptum et fuit ibi menses XII, de quo nunc sileam.

LXVI.[280] Nerone et Lentulo.

LXVII.[281] Celetho et Pisone.

LXVIII.[282] Getulo et Barro.

Et veniens Iesus faciebat mirabilia sub consulato Asiatici et Silvani, in quibus ex aqua uinum fecit VI kl. Noū.[283] Crasso Tiberio.

Seriniano Secundo.

Baptizatus est autem ab Iohanne sub consolato Meura, VIII kl. Ianuarias.

LXVIIII. Tiberio quarto et Antonino.

Transfiguratus est autem in monte sub consolato Rubellionis, XIIII kalendas Aprelis. Quando autem mysterium agebat cum discipulis suis, sub consolato Rubellionis, VIIII kal. Aprilis.

LXX. Tiberio quinto et Prisco.

LXXI. Bicino et Arruntio.

Eodem tempore natalicium factum est Herodis. Saltavit filia Herodiadis in medio et petiit capud Iohannis. Et adductum est capud Iohannis in disco VI kl. Iunias, Pauni II.[284]

3   Traditus est autem dominus noster Iesus Christus a Iuda sub consolato Rubellionis, VIII kl. Aprilis.

Videns autem hostiaria[285] Petrum agnovit eum et ait illi:

Then Joseph received an answer and took Jesus and Mary and fled to Egypt and was there for 12 months, concerning which I shall now be silent.

66. Nero and Lentulus. [7 BCE, 25]

67. Celethus [Cethegus] and Piso. [24, 27]

68. Getulus [Gaeulicus] and Varro. [26, 24]

And Jesus came performing miracles in the consulate of Asiaticus and Silvanus [Silanus] [46 CE],[340] during which he made wine out of water on the sixth of the calends of November [October 27].

Crassus, Tiberius. [27, 31]

Serinianus, Secundus. [?]

He was baptized by John in the consulate of Nerva [28 CE], on the eighth of the calends of January [December 25].

69. Tiberius for the fourth time and Antoninus. [21, 53]

He was transfigured on the mountain in the consulate of Rubellius [29 CE], on the 14th of the calends of April [March 19], at which time he performed the mystery with his disciples,[341] in the consulate of Rubellius, on the ninth of the calends of April [March 24].

70. Tiberius for the fifth time and Priscus. [31, 78]

71. Vicinus [Vinicius] and Arruntius. [30, 32]

At the same time the birthday of Herod came around. The daughter of Herodias danced in their midst and asked for the head of John. And the head of John was brought on a charger, on the sixth of the calends of June [May 27], the second of Pauni.

Our Lord Jesus Christ was betrayed by Judas in the consulate of Rubellius, on the eighth of the calends of April [25 March].[342] 3

When the portress saw Peter she recognized him and said

Vere et tu ex illis es, nam et loquilla tua manifestum te fecit. Et ille negavit dicens: Non sum. Et confestim gallus cantavit. Nomen autem hostiariae Ballia dicebatur, quod interpraetatur querens. LXXII.[286] Tiberio Augusto sexto et Silio.

Eodem anno dominus noster Iesus Christus crucifixus est sub consolato Rubellionis, VIII kl. Aprilis, quod est Famenoth XXVIIII.[287] Milex autem vocabatur Hieremias, id est Adlas crucem custodiens. Centurio vocabatur Apronianus.[288]

Illi autem duo angeli qui in sepulchro vocabantur unus Azahel, quod est iustus deo, alius autem Caldu, quod est fortis. Iudas autem abiens suspendit se in arbore nomine tramarice.

Surrexit autem dominus noster Iesus Christus sub consolato Rubellionis, VI kl. Aprilis. Ascendit autem dominus noster III nō. Maias.[289]

Missus est autem Spiritus Sanctus idos Maias. Paulus autem apostolus post ascensionem domini et post passionem Stephani dierum in apostulatum ordinatur VI idos Ianuarias, sub consolato Rubellionis, post ascensionem Salvatoris nostri menses VIII, post dies XI passionis Stephani, pridie Epiphaniae.

4   LXXII. Sipio et Sulano.

LXXIII. Persico et Bitellio.

LXXIIII. Tiberio Augusto et Druso.

Hisdem consulibus Tiberius obiit. Et regnavit pro eo Gaius ille Gallus annos IIII. Dedit consulatos IIII.

to him, "Surely thou also art one of them, for thy speech be-wrayeth thee." And he denied saying, "I am not." And im-mediately a cock crowed.[343] The name of the portress was said to be Ballia, which is translated as "asking."[344]

72. Tiberius Augustus for the sixth time[345] and Silius. [31, 28]

In the same year Our Lord Jesus Christ was crucified in the consulate of Rubellius, on the eighth of the calends of April [March 25], which is the 29th of Phamenoth.

The soldier guarding the cross was called Jeremiah, that is Adlas. The centurion was called Apronianus.

The two angels who were in the tomb were called the one Azahel, which is "righteous in God," and the other Caldu, which is "strong." Judas went away and hanged himself from a tree called the tamarisk.[346]

Our Lord Jesus Christ rose in the consulate of Rubellius, on the sixth of the calends of April [March 27]. Our Lord ascended on the third of the nones of May [May 5].

The Holy Spirit was sent on the ides of May [May 15]. In the days after the ascension of the Lord and after the pas-sion of Stephen the apostle Paul was numbered among the apostles on the sixth of the ides of January [January 8], in the consulate of Rubellius, eight months after the ascension of Our Savior, eleven days after the passion of Stephen, on the day before Epiphany.[347]

72. Sipius [Sulpicius] and Sulanus [Sulla]. [33]   4

73. Persicus and Vitellius. [34]

74. Tiberius Augustus and Drusus. [21]

When these men were consuls Tiberius died. And Gaius Gallus (or the Gaul) reigned in his stead for four years. He served four consulships.

LXXV. Gaio Gallo Agusto tertio et Sulla.

LXXVI. Gaio Agusto quarto et Apollione.

LXXVII. Venusto et Saturnino.

Scurdo et Clemente.

His consulibus Gaius Gallus obiit. Et regnavit pro eo
Claudius ann. IIII. Dedit consulatos V.

LXXVIII. Claudio et Tauro.

LXXVIIII. Crispino et Cornilio.

LXXX. Asiatico et Silvano.

LXXXI. Bincomallo et Bereto.

LXXXII. Claudio secundo et Publio.

LXXXIII. Bitello et Gallione.

LXXXIIII. Cladio tertio et Antonino.

LXXXV. Bereto et Siluio.

LXXXVI. Cladio quarto et Orfito.

LXXXVII. Silvano et Crispino.

LXXXVIII. Marcellino et Agiolao.

LXXXVIIII. Nerone filio Claudio et Bereto.

XC.²⁹⁰ Claudio Augusto quinto et Nerva.

XCI.²⁹¹ Saturnino et Scipione.

Hisdem consulibus Claudius obiit. Et imperium sumpsit
filius eius Nero annos IIII. Dedit consulatos XIIII.

5   XCII.²⁹² Nerone Augusto secundo et Rufo.

XCIII.²⁹³ Saturnino et Puplio.

75. Gaius Gallus Augustus for the third time and Sulla. [40, 33]

76. Gaius Augustus for the fourth time and Apollio [Apronius—?]. [41, 39]

77. Venustus and Saturninus. [?, 41]

Scurdus and Clement. [?]

When these men were consuls Gaius Gallus died. And Claudius reigned in his stead for four years.[348] He served five consulships.

78. Claudius and Taurus. [43, 44]

79. Crispinus [Crispus] and Cornelius [Corvinus]. [44, 45]

80. Asiaticus and Silvanus [Silanus]. [46]

81. Vincomallus [Vinicius] and Veretus. [45, ?]

82. Claudius for the second time and Publius [Publicola]. [47, 48]

83. Vitellius and Gallio [Gallus]. [48, 49]

84. Claudius for the third time and Antoninus. [51, 53]

85. Veretus and Silvius [Suilltus]. [?, 50]

86. Claudius for the fourth time and Orfitus. [51]

87. Silvanus [Silanus] and Crispinus [Crispus]. [46, 44]

88. Marcellinus [Marcellus] and Aviola. [54]

89. Nero the son of Claudius and Veretus. [55, ?]

90. Claudius Augustus for the fifth time and Nerva. [51, 65]

91. Saturninus and Scipio. [56]

When these men were consuls Claudius died. And his son Nero took up the imperial power for four years.[349] He served 14 consulships.

92. Nero Augustus for the second time and Rufus. [57, 63]   5

93. Saturninus and Publius. [56]

XCIIII. Nerone Augusto[294] tertio et Posone.

Hisdem consulibus passus est beatus Petrus apostolus, crucifixus in Roma capite deorsum, sub Nerone, similiter et Sanctus Paulus apostolus capite truncatus. Martyrizaverunt III kl. Iulias, quod est Epifi V.

XCV. Marcellino et Galliano.

XCVI. Nerone et Cornifilo.

XCVII. Rigolo et Bassiano.

XCVIII. Silvano et Crispino.

XCVIIII. Celestino et Salustio.

C. Capitone et Flavio.

CI. Romillo et Lucio.

CII. Secundo et Maronio.

CIII. Longino et Apulio.

CIIII. Iulio et Paulino.

Hisdem consulibus Nero de imperio labefactus est. Et imperium eius Galba suscepit[295] menses IIII et occisus est. Et regnavit Otho menses VII et occisus est. Et regnavit Bitelleo menses V et occisus est. Et imperium sumpsit Vespasianus annos X. Dedit consulatos VIIII.

6   Post consulatum Galbe Italico.

CV. Vespasiano Augusto et Tito filio eius Caesare primo.

CVI. Vespasiano Augusto secundo et Tito Caesare.

CVII.[296] Vespasiano tertio et Tito Caesare.

CVIII.[297] Vespasiano quarto et Tito quinto.

94. Nero Augustus for the third time and Piso. [58, 57]

When these men were consuls the blessed apostle Peter suffered; he was crucified in Rome with his head downward, under Nero, and likewise Saint Paul the apostle was beheaded. They were martyred on the third of the calends of July [June 29], which is the fifth of Epeiph.

95. Marcellinus [Marcus] and Gallienus [Gallus]. [62]

96. Nero and Cornelius. [60]

97. Regulus and Bassianus [Bassus]. [63, 64]

98. Silvanus [Silianus] and Crispinus [Crispus]. [65, 44]

99. Celestine [Telesinus] and Salustius. [66, ?]

100. Capito and Flavius. [67, 70]

101. Romillus and Lucius. [?]

102. Secundus and Maronius. [?]

103. Longinus and Apulius. [?]

104. Julius and Paullinus. [67, 66]

When these men were consuls Nero was toppled from power. And Galba took up his imperial power for four months and was killed. And Otho reigned for seven months and was killed. And Vitellius reigned for five months and was killed. And Vespasian took up the imperial power for 10 years. He served nine consulships.

After the consulate of Galba [69], Italicus [68].   6

105. Vespasian Augustus and Titus, his son, the Caesar, for the first time. [70]

106. Vespasian Augustus for the second time and Titus Caesar. [70]

107. Vespasian for the third time and Titus Caesar. [71, 70]

108. Vespasian for the fourth time and Titus for the fifth time. [72, 72/76]

Hisdem consulibus victi sunt Iudei sub Vespasiano et Tito imperatoribus et Iudea depopulata est.[298]
CVIIII. Vespasiano et Tito sexto.
CX. Vespasiano septimo et Nerva.
CXI. Vespasiano octavo et Commoda.
CXII. Vespasiano nono et Tito.
Hisdem consulibus Vespasianus[299] obiit. Et imperium Titus invasit annos II. Dedit consulatos II.
CXIII. Tito Augusto octavo et Birro.
CXIV. Silvano et Commodo.
Hisdem consulibus Titus obiit. Et imperium eius sumpsit Dometianus annos. . . . Dedit consulatos VIIII.
CXV. Dometiano Augusto primo et Messalino et Rufo.
CXVI. Dometiano secundo et Sabiniano.
CXVII. Dometiano tertio et Cerilao.
CXVIII. Dometiano quarto et Dolomallo.
CXVIIII. Dometiano quinto et Savino.
CXX. Flavio et Crispo inlustrium.
CXXI. Glabrione et Nerva.
CXXII. Dometione sexto et Rufino.
CXXIII. Dometiano septimo et Nigriano.
CXXIV. Asperiato et Papisco.
CXXV. Sinatore et Longino.
CXXVI. Modesto et Bustro.

When these men were consuls the Jews were defeated under the emperors Vespasian and Titus and Judea was laid waste.

109. Vespasian and Titus for the sixth time. [75, 75/77]

110. Vespasian for the seventh time and Nerva. [76, 71]

111. Vespasian for the eighth time and Commodus. [77, 78]

112. Vespasian for the ninth time and Titus. [79]

When these men were consuls Vespasian died. And Titus entered into the imperial power for two years. He served two consulships.

113. Titus Augustus for the eighth time and Verus. [80, 81]

114. Silvanus (i.e., Silva) and Commodus. [81, 78]

When these men were consuls Titus died. And Domitian took up his power for . . . years. He served nine consulships.

115. Domitian Augustus for the first time and Messallinus and Rufus. [73, 73, 83]

116. Domitian for the second time and Sabinus. [82]

117. Domitian for the third time and Ccrilaus [Aurelius]. [85]

118. Domitian for the fourth time and Dolabella. [86]

119. Domitian for the fifth time and Savinus [Saturninus/Sabinus]. [87, 87/84]

120. The illustrious Flavius and Crispus. [?]

121. Glabrio and Nerva. [91, 90]

122. Domitian for the sixth time and Rufinus [Rufus]. [88]

123. Domitian for the seventh time and Nigrianus. [90, ?]

124. Asperiatus [Asprenas] and Papiscus. [94, ?]

125. Sinator and Longinus. [?]

126. Modestus and Bustrus. [?]

CXXVII. Dometiano et Prisco.

CXXVIII. Senetione et Palmato.

CXXVIIII. Crispo et Sorano.[300]

· · ·

Caput X

XII. Diocletiano Augusto quinto et Maximino Caesare secundo.

XIII. Maximino Caesare quinto et Maximino Caesare quinto.

Fausto et Tatiano clarissimorum.

Constantino et Maximiano clarissimorum.

Dioclitiano et Maximiano clarissimorum.

Tatiano et Nepotiano clarissimorum.

Constantino et Maximo novorum Caesarum quarto.

Hisdem consulibus venit Dioclitianus in Alexandria et ecclesias exterminavit. Et multi martyrizaverunt, in quibus et beatus Petrus episcopus Alexandrinus capite truncatus est. Martyrizavit VII kl. Decem̄.[301]

In eodem anno castrisius in Alexandria donatus est et Dioclitiano balneum edificatum est.

Dioclitiano et Maximo nobilium Augustorum septimo.

Dioclitiano et Maximo octavo.

127. Domitian and Priscus [Priscinus]. [92, 93]
128. Senecio and Palma. [99]
129. Crispus and Soranus. [?]
...[350]

Chapter 10

12. Diocletian Augustus for the fifth time and Maximian Caesar for the second time. [293]

13. Maximian Caesar for the fifth time and Maximian Caesar for the fifth time. [297]

The most distinguished Faustus and Titianus. [298, 301]

The most distinguished *Constantine* [Constantius][351] and Maximian. [300]

The most distinguished Diocletian and Maximian. [299]

The most distinguished Titianus and Nepotianus. [301]

Constantine [Constantius] and Maximian the new Caesars for the fourth time. [302]

When these men were consuls Diocletian came to Alexandria and abolished the churches. And many were martyred, among whom also the blessed Peter, the Alexandrian bishop, was beheaded.[352] He was martyred on the seventh of the calends of December [November 25].

In the same year a *castrisius* [?][353] was granted to Alexandria and a bath was built by Diocletian.

Diocletian and Maximian the noble Augusti for the seventh time. [303]

Diocletian and Maximian for the eighth time. [304]

Hisdem consulibus persecutio Christianorum facta est in occiduum. Et multi martyrizaverunt, in quibus et Timotheus episcopus in Chartaginae gloriosae martyrizavit.[302] Dioclitiano nono et Constantio quinto nobilium Augustorum.

Dioclitiano decimo et Maximiano octavo invictissimorum.

Constantino Caesare et Maximiano nobili[303] quinto.

Hisdem consulibus Dioclitianus a regno recessit, et Constantius abiens sedit in Bizantio.

2   Licinio et Constantino primo, novorum Augustorum.

Licinio et Constantio secundo.

Hisdem consulibus filius Dioclitiani Maximus obiit. Et imperium tenuit Constantius cum filios suos.

Constantino et Constantio clarissimorum.

Rufo et Savino clarissimorum.

Constantio Augusto quarto et Licinio Caesare tercio.

Volusiano et Annania clarissimorum.

Gallicano[304] et Basso clarissimorum.

Licinio et Crispo Caesaris.

Hisdem consulibus Constantius obiit. Et imperium obtinuit Constantinus cum quinque filios suos, <...>[305] Constantio et Licinio et Crispo et Constantino, et condidit Constantinopolim.

When these men were consuls a persecution of the Christians occurred in the west. And many were martyred, among whom Timothy the bishop was gloriously martyred in Carthage.

The noble Augusti Diocletian for the ninth time and Constantius for the fifth time. [304, 305]

The most unconquered Diocletian for the tenth time and Maximian for the eighth time. [?, 304]

Constantine [Constantius] Caesar and the noble Maximian for the fifth time. [305]

When these men were consuls Diocletian withdrew from the kingship, and Constantius went away and settled in Byzantium.[354]

Licinius and Constantine for the first time, the new Augusti. [312]   2

Licinius and *Constantius* [Constantine] for the second time. [313]

When these men were consuls Maximian the son of Diocletian died.[355] And Constantius [Constantine?] held the imperial power with his sons.[356]

The most distinguished Constantine and Constantius. [?]

The most distinguished Rufus (Rufinus) and Sabinus. [316]

Constantius [Constantine] Augustus for the fourth time and Licinius Caesar for the third time. [315]

The most distinguished Volusianus and Annianus. [314]

The most distinguished Gallicanus and Bassus. [317]

The Caesars Licinius and Crispus. [318]

When these men were consuls Constantius died. And Constantine came to possess the imperial power with his five sons, <. . .> Constantius and Licinius and Crispus and Constantinus,[357] and he founded Constantinople.

Constantino Augusto quinto et Constantio novo Caesare.

Constantio Augusto sexto et Licinio minimo primo.

Eodem anno manifestatum est honorabile lignum, crux domini et Salvatoris nostri Iesu Christi, in Hierusolima per beatam Helenam imperatrissam et matrem Constantini, VIII kl. Decembris, quod est Thoth XVII.

Crispo et Constantio nobilissimos Caesares, filios Augusti, secundo.

Seuero et Rufino clarissimorum.

Crispo et Constantio secundo Caesare.

Probino et Iuliano clarissimorum.

Eodem anno congregata est synodus in Nicea tricentorum decem et octo episcoporum sub Alexandro archiepiscopo Alexandriae, in qua et symbolum sanctae trinitatis manifestatum est et Arrii ferrocitas atque haeresis diminuta est.[306]

3   Constantino[307] Augusto quarto et Constante Augusto tercio.

Constantino Augusto quinto et Constante secundo, inuictissimorum Augustorum.

Licinio et Crispino novorum Caesarum.

Eodem anno in Alexandria episcopus Alexander obiit Farmuthi XXII, et successit ei in sacerdotio Athanasius annos XLVI.

Constantio Augusto septimo et Constantio sexto.

Crispinio et Licinio secundo.

Constante septimo et Constante tercio Augustorum.

Constantine Augustus for the fifth time and *Constantius* [Constantine], the new Caesar. [319, 320]

Constantius [Constantine] Augustus for the sixth time and Licinius the Younger[358] for the first time. [320, 319]

In the same year the worshipful timber, the cross of Our Lord and Savior Jesus Christ, was revealed in Jerusalem through the blessed Helena, the empress and mother of Constantine, on the eighth of the calends of December [November 24], which is the 17th of Thoth.[359]

Crispus and *Constantius* [Constantine], the most noble Caesars, the sons of the Augustus, for the second time. [321]

The most distinguished Severus and Rufinus. [323]

Crispus and *Constantius* [Constantine] the second, the Caesar. [324]

Probianus and Julianus. [322]

In the same year a synod was convened in Nicaea of 318 bishops under Alexander the archbishop of Alexandria, at which the creed[360] of the Holy Trinity was revealed and the savagery of Arius and his heresy was broken.

Constantine Augustus for the fourth time and Constans   3 Augustus for the third time. [315, ?]

Constantine Augustus for the fifth time and Constans for the second time, the most unconquered Augusti. [319, ?]

Licinius and Crispus, the new Caesars. [318]

In the same year Bishop Alexander died in Alexandria on the 22nd of Pharmouthi [April 17], and Athanasius succeeded him in the priesthood for 46 years.[361]

Constantius [Constantine] Augustus for the seventh time and Constantius for the sixth time. [326]

Crispus and Licinius for the second time. [318]

The Augusti *Constans* [Constantine] for the seventh time and *Constans* [Constantius] for the third time. [326]

Lolliano et Iusto clarissimorum.

Constantino magno octavo et Constante Augustorum quarto.

Gallicano[308] et Simmacho clarissimorum.

Basso et Albino clarissimorum.

Pacatiano et Hilariano clarissimorum.

Dermatio et Zinolfo clarissimorum.

Optato et Paulino clarissimorum.

Constantino novo Augusto primo et Sauino.

Nepotiano et Facundo clarissimorum.

Hisdem consulibus translati sunt in Constantinopolim Sanctus Andreas apostolus et Lucas evangelista X kl. Iulias.

Feliciano et Taciano clarissimorum.

Urso et Polemio clarissimorum.

Constantio Augusto[309] secundo et Constante novo Caesare primo.

4   Acindyno et Proclo clarissimorum.

Constantio tertio et Costante secundo Augustorum nobilium.

Marcellino et Probino clarissimorum.

Placidiano et Romulo clarissimorum.

Leontio et Salustio clarissimorum.

Amantio et Saviniano clarissimorum.

Eodem anno Constantinus maior imperator obiit, VI kl. Decembris. Et susceperunt imperium V filii eius.

The most distinguished Lollianus and Justus. [?, 328]

The Augusti Constantine the Great for the eighth time and *Constans* [Constantine] for the fourth time. [329]

The most distinguished Gallicanus and Symmachus. [330]

The most distinguished Bassus and Albinus [Ablabius]. [331]

The most distinguished Pacatianus and Hilarianus. [332]

The most distinguished Delmatius and Zenofilus. [333]

The most distinguished Optatus and Paulinus. [334]

Constantine [Constantius] the new Augustus for the first time and Sabinus [Albinus]. [335]

The most distinguished Nepotianus and Facundus. [336]

When these men were consuls Saint Andrew the Apostle and Luke the Evangelist were conveyed to Constantinople, on the 10th of the calends of July [June 22].[362]

The most distinguished Felicianus and Titianus. [337]

The most distinguished Ursus and Polemius. [338]

Constantius Augustus for the second time and Constans the new Caesar for the first time. [339]

The most distinguished Acyndinus and Proclus [Proculus]. [340]

The noble Augusti Constantius for the third time and Constans for the second time. [342]

The most distinguished Marcellinus and Probinus. [341]

The most distinguished Placidianus [Placidus] and Romulus. [343]

The most distinguished Leontius and Sallustius. [344]

The most distinguished Amantius and Sabinianus. [345]

In the same year the emperor Constantine the Elder died, on the sixth of the calends of December [November 26]. And his five sons took up the imperial power.[363]

Constantino quarto et Constante tercio.

Constantino quinto et Constante quarto, invictissimorum Augustorum.

Rufino et Eusebio clarissimorum.

Limenio et Tolino clarissimorum.

Sergio et Nigriano clarissimorum.

Constantio sexto et Constantino, novorum Augustorum.

Hisdem consulibus Arriani invaserunt ecclesias, et expulsus est beatus episcopus Alexandriae Athanasius.[310]

Constantio septimo et Constantino novo secundo Augustorum.

Arbethione et Iuliano clarissimorum.

Constantio octavo et Constantino tercio Augustorum.

Constantio nono et Lolliano.

Datiano et Cerilao clarissimorum.

5   Constantino Augusto decimo et Iuliano Caesare secundo.

Eusebio et Ypatio clarissimorum.

Constantio Augusto undecimo et Iuliano Caesare tercio.

Hisdem consulibus Constantinus imperator obiit. Et regnauit pro eo Iulianus annos V et dimidium.[311]

Eodem anno conpleti sunt X cycli saeculares, ab anno quingentesimo trecensimo secundo. Fiunt vero ab Adam usque ad consulatum huius[312] anni omnes anni V milia octingenti LIIII.[313]

Constantine [Constantius] for the fourth time and Constans for the third time. [346]

The most unconquered Augusti *Constantine* [Constantius] for the fifth time and Constans for the fourth time. [352, ?]

The most distinguished Rufinus and Eusebius. [347]

The most distinguished Limenius and Tolinus [349, ?]

The most distinguished Sergius and Nigrianus [Nigrinianus]. [350]

Constantius for the sixth time and Constantine,[364] the new Augusti. [353]

When these men were consuls the Arians invaded the churches, and Athanasius, the blessed bishop of Alexandria, was expelled.

The Augusti Constantius for the seventh time and the new Constantine for the second time. [354]

The most distinguished Arbitio and Julian. [355, 356]

The Augusti Constantius for the eighth time and Constantine for the third time. [356, 354]

Constantius for the ninth time and Lollianus. [357, 355]

The most distinguished Datianus and Cerialis. [358]

Constantine [Constantius] Augustus for the 10th time and 5 the Caesar Julian for the second time. [357]

The most distinguished Eusebius and Hypatius. [359]

Constantius Augustus for the 11th time and the Caesar Julian for the third time. [360]

When these men were consuls the emperor *Constantine* [Constantius] died. And Julian reigned in his stead for five and a half years.

In the same year 10 saecular cycles were completed, from the 532nd year.[365] This makes from Adam up to the consulate of this year in all 5,854 years.

Iuliano Augusto quarto et Sallustio clarissimo.

Eo anno maris ascendit et iterum recessit, X kl. Augustas, Epifi XXVII.[314]

Barroniano et Iuliano et Iobiniano clarissimorum.

Eodem anno Iulianus imperator obiit, VI kl. Maias. Et regnavit Iobinianus menses VII et occisus est. Et regnaverunt pro eo duo fratres, Valentinianus annos XI et dimidium, similiter et Valens frater eius annos XIII. Dedit autem Valentinianus consulatos IIII et Valens consulatos VI.[315]

Valentiniano et Valente Augustorum.

Paulo et Frorentio clarissimorum.

Valentiniano et Valente Augustorum.

Gratiano filio Valentiniani Caesare et Dagalaifo.[316]

Luppiciano et Iobino clarissimorum.

Caput XI

Eo anno introivit Tatianus in Alexandria primus Augustalius,[317] VI kl. Februarias.

Valentiniano et Valente Augustorum tercio, sub Tatiano Augustalio.

Julian Augustus for the fourth time and the most distin-guished Sallustius. [363]

In this year the sea rose and receded again,[366] on the tenth of the calends of August [July 23], the 27th of Epeiph.[367]

The most distinguished Varronianus and Julian and Jo-vian. [364, 363, 364]

In the same year the emperor Julian died, on the sixth of the calends of May [April 26]. And Jovian reigned for seven months and was killed. And two brothers reigned in his stead, Valentinian for 11 and a half years, and likewise Valens his brother for 13 years. Valentinian served four consulships and Valens six consulships.

The Augusti Valentinian and Valens. [365]

The most distinguished Paulus [Taurus] and Florentius. [361]

The Augusti Valentinian and Valens. [368]

Gratian, the son of Valentinian, the Caesar and Dagalai-phus. [366]

The most distinguished Lupicinus and Jovinus. [367]

Chapter 11

In this year Tatian entered Alexandria as the first Au-gustal,[368] on the sixth of the calends of February [January 27].

The Augusti Valentinian and Valens for the third time, in the time of Tatian the Augustal. [370]

Valentiniano et Valente Augustorum quarto, sub eodem Tatiano Augustalio.

Gratiano[318] secundo <et . . .> clarissimo, sub eodem Tatiano Augustalio.[319]

Eo anno martyrizavit beatus Dorotheus in Alexandria, VII idos Octobris, quod est Faofi duodecimo. Ferarum esca traditus est sub Tatiano praeside, pro quo tunc erant heretici.

Modesto et Arintheo clarissimorum, sub Publio Augustalio.

Valentiniano et Valente quinto, sub eodem Publio Augustalio.

Hisdem consulibus Sarmati[320] omnem Campaniam desolaverunt,[321] et eo anno Valentinianus in bello mortuus est, VII idos Octobris.

Gratiano Augusto tertio et Equitio clarissimo, sub Tatiano praeside.[322]

Gratiano Augusto quarto et Merobaudo, sub eodem Tatiano Augustalio secundo.

Hic condidit in Alexandria fluvium, qui vocatur Tatianus, et portas fecit auro perfusas, quae nunc dicuntur Petrinas.[323]

2   Valentiniano Augusto quinto et Valente filio eius Augustorum, sub eodem Tatiano Augustalio.

Eo anno Athanasius episcopus obiit in Alexandria,[324] Pachon VII, et sedit pro eo Petrus archipresbiter annos VII.

The Augusti Valentinian and Valens for the fourth time, in the time of the same Tatian the Augustal. [373]

Gratian for the second time <and> the most distinguished <. . .>, in the time of the same Tatian the Augustal. [371]

In this year the blessed Dorotheus was martyred in Alexandria, on the seventh of the ides of October [October 9], which is the 12th of Phaophi. He was handed over as food for the beasts in the time of Tatian the Prefect,[369] for whose sake they were then heretics.[370]

The most distinguished Modestus and Arintheus, in the time of Publius the Augustal. [372]

Valentinian and Valens for the fifth time, in the time of the same Publius the Augustal. [376]

When these men were consuls the Sarmatians laid waste all of Campania, and in this year Valentinian died in war, on the seventh of the ides of October [October 9].[371]

Gratian Augustus for the third time and the most distinguished Equitius, in the time of Tatian the Prefect. [374]

Gratian Augustus for the fourth time and Merobaudes, in the time of the same Tatian the Augustal for the second time. [377]

This man established a river course in Alexandria, which is called the Tatian, and he made doors covered with gold, which are now called the Petrine doors.[372]

The Augusti Valentinian Augustus for the fifth time and 2 Valens his son, in the time of the same Tatian the Augustal.[373] [376]

In this year Athanasius the bishop died in Alexandria, on the seventh of Pachon [May 2],[374] and the archpresbyter Peter sat in his place for seven years.

Valentiniano novo Augusto quinto et Merobaudo clarissimo, sub Palladio Augustalio.

Valente sexto et Valentiniano Augustorum, sub Tatiano Augustalio praesidae.[325]

Hisdem consulibus Valens obiit. Et imperium obtinuerunt Gratianus et Valentinianus novus.

Ausonio et Olybrio clarissimorum, sub Hadriano[326] Augustalio.

Eusebio et Olybrio clarissimorum, sub Hadriano[327] Augustalio.[328]

Gratiano quarto et Dagalaifo[329] clarissimorum.

Luppiciano et Eutropio clarissimorum.

Antonino et Eutropio clarissimorum, sub Paulino Augustalio.

Eo anno Petrus episcopus Alexandrinus obiit in Alexandria, Mechir vicensimo,[330] et sedit pro eo Timotheus frater eius annos V.

3   Ausonio et Olybrio secundo clarissimorum, sub Bassiano praeside.

Eo anno Theodosius elevatus est in imperio sub Gratiano imperatore, in Sirmio, XIIII kl. Febroār.[331]

Et regnavit annos XVI. Dedit consulatos III.

Gratiano quinto et Theodosio primo nobilium Augustorum, sub Ypatio Augustalio.

Valentinian the new Augustus for the fifth time and the most distinguished Merobaudes, in the time of Palladius the Augustal. [376, 377]

The Augusti Valens for the sixth time and Valentinian, in the time of Tatian the Augustal Prefect. [378]

When these men were consuls Valens died. And Gratian and the new Valentinian came into possession of the imperial power.

The most distinguished Ausonius and Olybrius, in the time of Hadrian the Augustal. [379]

The most distinguished Eusebius and Olybrius, in the time of Hadrian the Augustal. [359, 379]

The most distinguished Gratian for the fourth time and Dagalaiphus. [377, 366]

The most distinguished Luppicianus (i.e., Lupicinus) and Eutropius. [367, 387]

The most distinguished Antoninus (i.e., Antonius) and Eutropius, in the time of Paulinus the Augustal. [382, 387]

In this year Peter the Alexandrine bishop died in Alexandria, on the 20th of Mecheir [February 14], and Timothy his brother sat in his place for five years.

The most distinguished Ausonius and Olybrius for the second time, in the time of Bassianus the Prefect. [379] 3

In this year Theodosius was raised to the imperial power under[375] Gratian, at Sirmium, on the 14th of the calends of February [January 19].

And he reigned for 16 years. He served three consulships.

The noble Augusti Gratian for the fifth time and Theodosius for the first time, in the time of Hypatius the Augustal. [380]

Suagrio et Eucerio clarissimorum, sub Antonino Augustalio.

Eo anno occisus est Gratianus imperator sub Maximo tyranno in Leuduna, VIII kl. Septembris, et eodem anno coronatus est in imperio Arcadius in Constantinopolim, V idus Septembris.[332]

Richomedo et Chlearco clarissimorum, sub eodem Antonino.

Eo anno Timotheus episcopus Alexandrinus obiit, Epifi XXVI, et sedit pro eo Theofilus archidiaconus annos XXVIII et illos sacrilegos exterminavit.

Arcadio Augusto filio Theodosii et Baudone clarissimo, sub Frorentio Augustalio.

Eo anno natus est Honorius in Constantinopolim, V idus Sep.

Valentiniano Augusto III et Eutropio clarissimo.[333]

The most distinguished Syagrius and Eucherius, in the time of Antoninus the Augustal. [381]

In this year the emperor Gratian was killed under[376] the tyrant Maximus at Lugdunum [Lyons], on the eighth of the calends of September [August 25], and in the same year Arcadius was crowned with the imperial power at Constantinople, on the fifth of the ides of September [September 9].

The most distinguished Richomedus (i.e., Ricimer) and Clearchus, in the time of the same Antoninus. [384]

In this year Timothy the Alexandrine bishop died, on the 26th of Epeiph [July 20],[377] and Theophilus the archdeacon sat in his place for 28 years and he drove out the sacrilegous.[378]

Arcadius Augustus the son of Theodosius and the most distinguished Bauto, in the time of Florentius the Augustal. [385]

In this year Honorius was born in Constantinople, on the fifth of the ides of September [September 9].

Valentinian Augustus for the third time and the most distinguished Eutropius. [387]

Note on the Texts

APOCALYPSE OF PSEUDO-METHODIUS

The evidence for the Greek text of Pseudo-Methodius rests primarily on the following manuscripts:

B = Bodleian, Laud. Gr. 27, fols. 8–24, s. XV
D = Vienna, Vindob. Cod. med. 23, fols. 81r–95v, s. XVI
G = Vaticanus Gr. 1700, fols. 117r–57, ann. 1332/3
R = Pii II Gr. 11, fols. 257v–58, 244–51, 259–63, s. XV

The earliest recension of the Latin text is represented by some particularly early manuscripts. They are identified as follows:

P = Paris, Bibliothèque Nationale, lat. 13348, fols. 93v–110v, s. VIII
B = Bern, Burgerbibliothek, 611, fols. 101–13, s. VIII (727 CE)
G = Sankt Gallen, Stiftsbibliothek, ms. 225, pp. 384–439, s. VIII^{EX}
V = Città del Vaticano, Barb. Lat. 671, fols. 171r–74v, s. VIII^{MED} (a fragment from 1.1 to 5.9)

The *praefaciuncula* of Peter the Monk has been edited by J. Pitra, *Analecta sacra Spicilegio Solesmensi parata* (Paris: A. Jouby et Roger, 1883), vol. III, p. 627, and Sackur (see the

Bibliography). It comes down to us in a longer form, comprising the entire preface as presented here, and a shorter form, consisting of only the third paragraph. The longer form is found in:

P = Paris, Bibliothèque Nationale, lat. 13348, fol. 93v, s. VIII

P² = Paris, S. Genevieve nr. 80, fol. 105r, s. XIII

B = Bern, Burgerbibliothek, 611, fols. 106v–7r, s. VIII (727 CE) (a fragment from *tramite* to *viciis que*)

K = Karlsruhe, Badische Landesbibliothek, Aug. perg. CXCVI, fols. 29v–30r, s. IX (without the text of the *Apocalypse* itself)

Pº = Poitiers, M. B. 121, fol. 98r, s. XI^{EX}–XII^{IN}

The shorter form is found in:

M = Montpellier, École de Médicine 374, fols. 59v–60r, x. XI

P³ = Paris, B. N. 3796, fol. 8r, s. XII

AN ALEXANDRIAN WORLD CHRONICLE

The text of the *Excerpta Latina Barbari* is based entirely on the sole surviving manuscript:

Paris, Bibliothèque Nationale, lat. 4884, s. VIII,

referred to as the codex in the notes.

Notes to the Texts

Abbreviations

Chron. Pasch. = *Chronicon Paschale,* ed. L. A. Dindorf (Bonn: Weber, 1832)

Lib. Gen. = *Liber Generationis. Chronica Minora,* ed. C. Frick (Leipzig: Teubner, 1892), I: 1–76

Syncellus = Georgius Syncellus, *Ecloga Chronographica,* ed. A. A. Mosshammer (Leipzig: Teubner, 1984)

The *Apocalypse* Attributed to Saint Methodius (Greek)

1 Ἀδὰμ ... συλλαβοῦσα: There appears to be a lacuna in the text which Aerts has supplied from Genesis 4:1.

2 τέτοκεν B: τέτοκαν DR

3 τὴν ἀδελφὴν DR: τὸν ἀδελφὸν B

4 ὅ DB: ἥ R

5 ὀκτακοσιοστῷ R: ἑπτακοσιοστῷ DB

6 τὸ μύσος D: τὸ μῖσος B, τὸ μῖσος R

7 πλήρεις Aerts: πλήρης DBGR

8 μουσικῶν DGR: μουσικὸν B

9 τῇ ἀθέσμῳ πορνείᾳ G: τῇ ἀθέσμῳ πονηρίᾳ B, τῆς ἀθέσμου πορνείας D, ταῖς ἀθεμίτοις πορνείαις R

10 τὸ θῆλυ, ἐπὶ δὲ θῆλυ τὸ ἄρρεν DB: τὸ θῆλυ γένος. Ὁμοίως δὲ (om. R) καὶ οἱ (om. G) ἐκ τῆς τοῦ Κάϊν συγγενείας τοῖς αὐτοῖς μυσαροῖς καὶ ἐναγέσιν ἐκέχρηντο πράγμασιν GR

11 ἐν χρόνῳ δωδεκάτῳ conjectured by Aerts on the basis of the Syriac text: ἐν χρόνῳ δεκάτῳ R, om. DBG

12 τῶν ἡρώων ἐτύγχανεν D: ἀδελφὸς τῶν ἡρώων ἐτύγχανε R, τῶν ἱερέων ἐτύγχανε B, ἐτύγχανεν τῶν ὁρίων G

13 τῆς θαλάσσης added by Aerts from the Syriac and Latin texts: DBR om

14 Ὀβοίας D: Οὐρανίας B, Ὀρβανίας R, Ἀλβανίας G

15 ἀνίκητον supplied by Aerts from the Syriac and Latin texts

16 Ἀρράβων G: Ἀράβων R, Ἀβάρων D, Ἀβάρον B

17 γενόμενα G: τελούμενα R

18 εὐθὺς B: αὖθις DGR

19 παρακαλέσας DB: ἐλιπάρησε GR

20 ὑπαντῶν conj. Aerts: ὑπ᾽ αὐτῶν R, ἀπαντῶν G, ἀντῶν B, ὑπ᾽ αὐτοῦ D

21 κατάκλασιν conj. Aerts: κατάκλησιν DB, κατάκλυσιν R, κατάβασιν G

22 τοῦ πρώτου βασιλέως conjectured by Aerts on the basis of the Syriac and Latin texts: τοῦ πρώτου ἐν βασιλεῦσιν G, τοῦ βασιλέως DB, om. R

23 Ἑλλήνων added by Aerts on the basis of the Syriac and Latin texts

24 εἰδῶν Αἰθιοπίας conjectured by Aerts on the basis of the Syriac and Latin texts: Ἰνδῶν Αἰθιοπίας DG, Ἰνδῶν καὶ Αἰθιοπίας R

25 πέραν added by Aerts on the basis of comparison with the Latin translation 'trans'.

26 δωρήματα conjectured by Aerts on the basis of the Syriac and Latin texts: δώματα DR, δόματα G

27 τήν τε D: τῆς τε R, τήν τε ... Αἰθιοπίας om. G

28 Αἰθιοπίσσης conjectured by Aerts on the basis of the Latin text: Αἰθιοπίσης D, τῆς Αἰθιοπίας GR

29 οὗ ... ἡμῶν D, deleted by Aerts, the sentence is not in G, R, or the Syriac or Latin texts

30 ἕως added by Aerts on the basis of the Syriac text

31 ὑμῶν DGR: ἡμῶν B

32 ἀνομίας DB: ἁμαρτίας R

33 ἐπὶ DR: ὑπὲρ B, καὶ ὑπὲρ G

34 ἐκτίλαντα conj. Aerts: ἐκτίλλαντα G, ἐκτείλαντα DB,R(?), ἐκστείλαντα R(?)

35 Ἐλώμ added by Aerts from R

36 ἠροτρίασεν scripsit Aerts: ἠρωτρίασεν DBG, ἠρωτρίασε R

37 ἐκόπησαν conjectured by Aerts on the basis of the Syriac text: ἐκκοπήσονται DGR, ἐκκοπῇ ἐκκοπήσονται B

38 Τοῦρκοι καὶ Ἄβαρεις D (-ις), R: Τούρκους καὶ Ἄραβες B, Τοῦρκοι καὶ Ἄβαροι G

39 καὶ added by Aerts

40 Ἐθρίβου conj. Aerts: Αἰθρίβου B, Αἰθρήβου G, Ἐθρὶ D, Ἐθρίβων R

41 ὄναγρος DBR: ὄνος ἄγριος G

42 ἀνίλεως: ἀνήλεως DGR, ἀνήλεος B

43 παραδοθήσονται DBR: πεσοῦνται G

44 Κιλικία DG: καὶ ἡ Λιβία B

45 καὶ εἰς σφαγὴν ἔσται added by Aerts on the basis of the Syriac and Latin texts

46 οἱ κοικοῦντες ἐν αὐτῇ added by Aerts on the basis of the Syriac text

47 εἰς added by Aerts on the basis of the Latin text

48 ἑπταπλασίονι conj. Aerts: ἑπταπλασίων DB, ἑπταπλασίονα GR

49 καὶ δυσμῶν DBG: ἕως δυσμῶν R

50 αἱ χηρωθεῖσαι conj. Aerts: αἱ χωροθῆσαι D, αἳ χηρευθήσονται G, αἳ ἐθηρεύθησαν R, αἳ ὀχυροθήσονται B

51 ὑπεραρθήσεται DB: ὑψωθήσεται G, ὑπερυψωθήσεται R

52 καὶ ἔμφοβοι added by Aerts on the basis of the Syriac and Latin texts

53 ἐπιμέμψασθαι conj. Aerts: ἐπιπέμψασθαι D, ἀποπέμψασθαι G, ἀντιμέμψασθαι R

54 ἀτιθάσων τε καὶ ἡμέρων conjectured by Aerts on the basis of the Latin text: ἀτίθασόν τε καὶ ἥμερον R, ἀτίθασόν τε καὶ ἀνήμερον D, τιθασσοῦται καὶ ἡμεροῦται G

55 ἀληθῆ DB: ἀληθινὴν GR

56 καὶ DB: ἢ GR

57 After αὐτός G adds φησιν

58 ἄχρηστοι DB: ἀχάριστοι GR

59 ἀφορίσουσι GR: ἀφορίσωσι DB

60 ὁ καιρὸς προσκαλεῖται DB: ὁ καιρὸς προσκαλεῖ G, ὁ καιρὸς [a space of about four letters] καὶ προσκαλεῖται R

61 ἐπίλεκτοι DBG: ἔκλεκτοι R
62 ἀλλ᾽ ἀντὶ τούτων R: om. DBG
63 ἀχάριστοι GR: ἄχρηστοι DB
64 ἀτίθασοι RG: om. DB
65 ὃν τρόπον DGR: εἰς ὃν τρόπον B
66 ὑπείξει conj. Aerts: ἡμώξει DBR, οἰμώξει G
67 ‹δι᾽› ἧς conjectured by Aerts on the basis of the Latin text: ἧς DBGR
68 φλιᾶς conj. Aerts: φλυὰς B, φλοιᾶς DGR
69 ὅλκην χρυσίου ἢ ἀργυρίου conjectured by Aerts on the basis of the Latin text and B: ὁλκὴν χρυσίου καὶ ἀργυρίου G, ὁλκὴν χρυσίου (om. ἢ ἀργυρίου) D, χρυσίου ὁλκὴν R, καὶ οὐκ ἦν (οὐκ ἦν < ὁλκὴν?) χρυσίου ἢ ἀργυρίου B
70 δοσοληψία R: δωσοληψία B, δυσολυψία D, δωροληψία G
71 διώξουσι DB: διώξωσι GR
72 αἰφνίδιον conj. Aerts: ἐφνίδιον B, αἰφνήδιον D, om. G
73 συλλαβέτω D: συλλάβεται B, συλλάβωσι G
74 εἰς ἀρχὰς τρεῖς DB: εἰς τρία G
75 οὐαί σοι ... Ἰσμαὴλ om. G
76 θλῖψις καὶ στενοχωρία conjectured by Aerts on the basis of the Latin text: θλίψεις καὶ στενοχωρία D, θλίψεις καὶ στενοχωρίαι B
77 ὁ ὑπολιμπασθεὶς conj. Aerts: ὁ ὑπολειπαπὴς B, ὁ ὑπολυπασθὴς D, ὁ ἀπολιπασθεὶς R, ὁ εἰς αἰχμαλωσίαν G
78 ἐν τῇ ἐσχάτῃ ἡμέρᾳ B: ἐν ταῖς ἐσχάταις ἡμέραις GR
79 κρύψουσιν DR: κρύψωσιν BG
80 αἵματα DB: αἷμα GR
81 παράσχωνται conj. Aerts: παράσχονται D, παράσχωσι G, παράσχουσι R
82 ἅμα conj. Aerts: αὐτὴ D
83 καὶ Ἰούδας ... τοῦ Δάν: an interpolation in DB
84 οὐρανίου R: αἰωνίου DB, πολλῆς G

The *Apocalypse* Attributed to Saint Methodius (Latin)

1 effectum *codd.*: effatum *conj. Pitra*
2 ut viri P, *i.e.,* vere: vere K

3   insinuavi *conj.*: insinuari *codd.*, insinuare K

4   ut iam: utinam K

5   et PBG: est V

6   maius PBG: magis V

7   terra G: terram P

8   in eosdem: eisdem V

9   disperse BV, -i G

10   articulorum B

11   *A lacuna is supplied by Aerts and Kortekaas from the Greek.*

12   expleta BV

13   tercia B

14   Eresdem PGV: Chresdem B

15   rigem B, rege V

16   Sampsisahib P: Samsisahib B, Samsishibus G, Sampsisaibus V

17   omnia regna V

18   manubus V

19   obtenuit PB: obti- G

20   Babillonis B, -bylonie G

21   obtinuit B

22   redimit B

23   terram B

24   in coniugio B

25   Cuseth P: Chuseth B, Chuset G

26   exhorruit B

27   immundarum B

28   minans PG: manus G

29   per quod <*quis*> *corrected by Sackur*: quis per quod PBG

30   ictus P: ictu BG

31   ferientes PBG, *i.e.,* -tis

32   operatur *corrected by Aerts and Kortekaas*: operantur PBG

33   cuncte B

34   Zarmatae B

35   speciorum BG: -erum P

36   foras PB: -is G

37   Romyllus P: Romolus B, Rumillius G

38   poterit PG: possit B

39   distruetur PB: -itur G

40 clareque G: clare quod P, clare quid B
41 universus PB: -sa G
42 ipse PB: ipsi G
43 consurgent PB: -gunt G
44 novissimo enim miliario B
45 diligit PB: -lexit G
46 retribucionis mercedem B
47 omne B, *omitted in* G
48 elabitur PBG
49 obtinibunt B
50 magnificantur PB: signifi- G
51 ipsa B
52 percorrupte B
53 perfectorum PG: -turum B
54 tormenta (tur- B) PB: -to G
55 praecidens PBG: *i.e.,* praecedens
56 vinculo PB: -culis G
57 vituperacione B
58 adcuvabit P, *i.e.,* -babit: acubabit B, adcupavit G
59 exigant BG
60 barbaris PG: -es B
61 terram G
62 Auraniae BG: Ausaniae P
63 terram G
64 monumentes B, mumentis G
65 inmunda *corrected by Aerts and Kortekaas from the Greek*: -as (serpentes) PBG
66 terra BG
67 iam P
68 conpraehenderint *Aerts:* conprehenderent B, conprehenderunt G, praehenderint P
69 dimidium: dmidium P, dimedium B, demedium G
70 perditionis: experditiones P, perdiciones B, -tionis G
71 etenim P: enim BG
72 terram B
73 invicillia (*i.e.,* imbecilla) P: -cilla G, inve//cillis B

74 sanguine: sanguinem PBG
75 fervens (-bens B) PB: serpens G

An Alexandrian World Chronicle

1   *In the upper margin of the first MS page in smaller letters*: Cronica
    georgii ambionensis epi̅ vel sicut alii dicunt victoris turonensis
    epi̅

2   *After* duo *there is an empty space of twelve MS lines.*

3   CCV *corrected by Frick*: CV *codex*

4   viginti: quinquaginta *codex*

5   noningentorum XC *codex*: *rather* noningentorum X (*cf. Genesis 5:14*)
    In the lower margin of the first MS page in smaller letters: Cronica
    georgii ambione

6   nonaginta *codex*: *rather* nonaginta quinque (*cf. Genesis 5:17*)

7   translatus est: *cf. Genesis 5:24, Vulg.*: tulit eum Deus, *LXX*: μετέθηκεν
    αὐτὸν ὁ θεός; *but Vulg. Hebrews 11:5*: fide Enoch translatus est . . .
    transtulit illum Deus

8   septingentorum *codex*: *rather* septingentorum LIII

9   Et dixit dominus deus: *cf. Genesis 6:3, Vulg.*: dixitque Deus, *LXX*:
    καὶ εἶπεν κύριος ὁ θεός

10 eruntque *corrected by Frick*: erunt que *codex*

11 illeque *corrected by Frick*: ille que *codex*

12 quia *corrected by Frick*: quia quia *codex*

13 Tempus omnium rerum: *cf. Genesis 6:13, Vulg.*: finis universae carnis,
    LXX: καιρὸς παντὸς ἀνθρώπου

14 corumpam: *cf. Genesis 6:13, LXX*: καταφθείρω

15 de lignis quadratis: *cf. Genesis 6:14, Vulg.*: de lignis levigatis, *LXX*: ἐκ
    ξύλων τετραγώνων

16 Et fecit Noe: *cf. Genesis 6:22, Vulg.*: fecit ergo Noe, *LXX*: καὶ ἐποίησε
    Νῶε

17 *After* duo *there is an empty space of about twenty-six MS lines.*

18 *By comparison with Genesis 10:1 Frick suggested there was a lacuna after*
    Iafeth, *probably to be supplied with*: natique sunt eis filii.

19 diluvium *corrected by Frick*: dilu um *codex*

20 septuaginta duo: duodecim *codex*

21 et Ragau fratrem eius *bracketed by Frick*
22 Et fuit omnis terra labia et vox una omnibus: *cf. Genesis 11:1, Vulg.*:
 erat autem terra labii unius et sermonum eorundem, *LXX*: καὶ
 ἦν πᾶσα ἡ γῆ χεῖλος ἓν, καὶ φωνὴ μία πᾶσι
23 Et facta est eis ipsa latera quasi lapis, et bitumen erat illis lutus: *cf.
 Genesis 11:3b, Vulg.*: habueruntque lateres pro saxis et bitumen
 pro cemento, *LXX*: καὶ ἐγένετο αὐτοῖς ἡ πλίνθος εἰς λίθον, καὶ
 ἄσφαλτος ἦν αὐτοῖς ὁ πηλός
24 capud: *cf. Genesis 11:4, Vulg.*: culmen, *LXX*: ἡ κεφαλὴ
25 *In the margin in smaller letters*: non corporaliter intellegitur quod descendit d̄n̄s d̄s̄
26 cessaverunt aedificantes: *cf. Genesis 11:8, Vulg.*: cessaverunt aedificare, *LXX*: ἐπαύσαντο οἰκοδομοῦντες
27 *Before* terrae *there is an empty space of fourteen MS lines.*
28 *It seems reasonable to assume that the genitive* trium fratrum *is inten-
 tional, not some error for the nominative, and that a word, most likely*
 filii *or* generationes, *has fallen out of the text; cf. Genesis 10:1. The
 omission might have arisen from the name of an eponymous progenitor
 being used to refer to his descendants collectively, as often happens in the
 Bible, particularly in the story (Genesis 9:24–27) immediately preceding the Table of Nations in Genesis.*
29 septuaginta duo: septuaginta *codex*
30 in linguis: *cf. Vulg., Genesis 10:20*: in . . . linguis, *as opposed to Genesis
 10:5*: unusquisque secundam linguam, *Genesis 10:31*: secundam . . .
 linguas
31 gigans: *cf. Genesis 10:8, Vulg.*: potens, *LXX*: γίγας
32 septuaginta duo: septuaginta *codex*
33 Yoias *corrected by Frick*: y ̇ oias *codex*
34 Cittei *corrected by Frick*: cti ci *codex*
35 Ex istis dispersae sunt insulae gentium: *cf. Vulg., Genesis 10:5*: ab his
 divisae sunt insulae gentium
36 Qui habitaverunt, *as Frick indicates, ought to have been* qui transmi-
 graverunt.
37 *In classical Latin* accola *means "dweller nearby" or "neighbor," but in the*
 Excerpta *it is consistently used of a "colonist" or "settler." Frick suggested that the translator had confused* ἄποικος *and* πάροικος. *This,*

however, hardly seems necessary in light of Isidore's definition, Etym.
10.16: accola, eo quod adveniens terram colat, *which seems to presume that arrival from elsewhere before cultivation of the land was
part of the late antique sense of the word; cf. Vulg. Psalm 104:23.*

38   usque ad Speriam: *cf.* Chron. Pasch. *47.13, Syncellus (92)*: ἕως τοῦ
      ἑσπερίου

39   Challyri: *cf.* Lib. Gen. *12.16*: Chalibes, Chron. Pasch. *47.16, Syncellus
      (92)*: Χάλυβες

40   Celtei: Latini *codex*. Celtei *as in 11a below*. Latini *has been copied from
      the line above.*

41   qui utuntur: *cf.* Pasch. Chron. *48.4*: οἷς χρῶνται

42   a fluvio et fluvium: *from* ἀπὸ Ποταμίδος ποταμοῦ *as in* Chron.
      Pasch. *48.8 (cf.* Lib. Gen. *14.9*: a Potameda fluvio), *preserved cor-
      rectly in Syncellus (93)*: ἀπὸ Τανάϊδος ποταμοῦ

43   contra solem: *Frick suggested that* contra solem *resulted from a mis-
      reading of* κατὰ Ἴλιον *as* κατὰ ἥλιον, *which would be consistent
      with the regular confusion of* Ἴλιος *with* ἥλιον *throughout the Ex-
      cerpta, but Syncellus (93) preserves the reading* ἕως Μαστουσίας
      τῆς κατὰ ἥλιον. *Either would be appropriate to the promontory of
      Mastousia at the southern tip of the Thracian Chersonese.*

44   *lucidissima: that is,* Λυχνῖτις; *cf.* Chron. Pasch. *48.10, Syncellus (93)*

45   quadraginta duae: quadraginta *codex*
      After quadraginta *evenly distributed over the rest of the page in smaller
      letters*: albania amazonia armenia cappadocia paflagonia galatia
      colchus india italia bosporina meotia derris sarmatia tauriannia
      bastarnia scythia thracia macedonia dermatia molchia thettalia
      lucria byotia etolia attica achaia illyria acarnia gallia celtica tus-
      cinia lysitania messalia italia adriacia illychinitia ipeirotia spano-
      callia ibiria.

46   *After* Ionia *evenly distributed over twelve MS lines in smaller letters*: si-
      cilia eubia chius cefalinia lesbus zacynthus thaci corcyra ionia in
      asia

47   illus: *a misuse of the pronoun* ille, *either attempting to reproduce the
      Greek* τούς *which precedes these names in the LXX, or a nominative/
      accusative singular agreeing with* ex quo

48   Fygabii: *cf.* Chron. Pasch. *51.9*: Φρύγες

49 ex quo Criti, et illus Chaslomiim ex quo Licii: ex quo Licii *codex.*
Frick identified a lacuna before Licii, *and proposed that the text of
the Greek original could be supplied from* Chron. Pasch. *51.10–11*:
Πατρωσονιείμ, ἐξ οὗ <Κρῆτες. Χασλωμιείμ, ἐξ οὗ> Λύκιοι

50 Aeggeum: *cf. LXX, Genesis 10:17, Josephus,* AJ *r.139*: Εὐαῖον

51 Aruceum: *cf. LXX, Genesis 10:17, Josephus,* AJ *r.138*: τὸν Ἀρουκαῖον

52 aspiciente ad septentrionem *codex: Contrast the reading in Syncellus
(87, 89)*: τὰ πρὸς νότον

53 Gagarini: *cf. Syncellus (87)*: Γαγγινοί

54 Isabini: *cf.* Chron. Pasch. *50.3*: Ἰταβηνοί, *Syncellus (87, 89)*: Σαβῖνοι

55 Mososini: *cf.* Lib. Gen. *18.13*: Mossynoeti

56 Mososini: *cf. Syncellus (89)*: Μοσσυνοί

57 ad septentrionalem oceanum: *cf.* Chron. Pasch. *52.6*: ἕως τοῦ
νοτιαίου Ὠκεανοῦ, *Syncellus* (89): ἕως τοῦ δυτικοῦ πρὸς λίβα
καὶ νότον Ὠκεανοῦ

58 a Syria *corrected by Frick*: asyria *codex*

59 ad *corrected by Frick*: ad ad *codex*

60 usque Corcyna: *cf.* Chron. Pasch. *52.15*: μέχρι Κυρήνης

61 qui respicit et extendit: *the translator read* ἀποβλέπουσα καὶ
ἐκτείνουσα *for* ἀπὸ Λέπτεως παρεκτείνουσα *("which stretches
from Leptis") as attested in* Chron. Pasch. *52.17, Syncellus (90)*.

62 Numeda, Massyris *corrected by Frick*: numedamassyris *codex*

63 Lygdoniam: *cf.* Chron. Pasch. *52.20*: Λυγδονίαν, *but* Lib. Gen. *20.20*:
Lycaoniam, *Syncellus (90)*: Λυκαονίαν

64 Cargam: *cf.* Lib. Gen. *22.1*: Cariam, Chron. Pasch. *52.20, Syncellus
(90)*: Καρίαν

65 *After* provintias XIII *evenly distributed over twenty MS lines in
smaller letters*: cilicia pamphylia pisidia mysia ligdonia frygia camilia lycia caria lydia troada eolia bithynia

66 Gaula: *cf. Syncellus (90)*: Γαῦδον

67 Taurana: *cf.* Chron. Pasch. *53.3*: Ταυριανίς

68 Iasa: *cf.* Chron. Pasch. *53.7*: Ἴασος, *but Syncellus (90)*: Θάσον

69 *After* insulas XXV *there is an empty space of thirteen MS lines.*

70 Genealogia Sem primo genito filio Noe: *in the upper margin of the
page in smaller letters*

71 Alazonii: *perhaps a corruption of* Μαζῶνες, *descendants of Lud in* Chron. Pasch. *54.5, taking* M *for* ΑΛ

72 et Futh, unde Persi: *Frick considered this a gloss, as it is not found in the other versions of the dispersion of the nations.*

73 filius: filii *is required.*

74 qui et Hul: *mistaking* Ὡς καὶ Οὔλ *(as in the Alexandrian text of the LXX) for* ὃς καὶ Οὔλ

75 Eber autem nati sunt ei filii duo: *cf. LXX Genesis 10:25:* Καὶ τῷ Ἕβερ ἐγεννήθησαν δύο υἱοί

76 et Milii: *the translator has read* καὶ Μήλιοι *or* καὶ Μίλιοι, *but see* Chron. Pasch. *55.3:* Κάμπλιοι, Syncellus *(86):* Καμήλιοι.

   Frick identified a lacuna after Milii *and proposed that the text of the Greek original could be supplied from Syncellus* (86): Καμήλιοι [ιη΄] Δερά, αφ᾽ οὗ [*read* ὅθεν] Μῆδοι [ιθ΄] Ἰεζιά.

77 Adamosynii: *cf.* Chron. Pasch. *55.8:* Ἄραβες ἐσώτεροι, *Syncellus (86):* Ἄραβες Ἰνδῶν

78 a Bactriona: abactriona *codex*

79 usque Rinocorurum . . . Arsinoita India: *cf.* Chron. Pasch. *55.11–13, Syncellus (86):* ἕως Ῥινοκουρούρων τῆς ὁριζούσης Συρίαν καὶ Αἴγυπτον καὶ τὴν ἐρυθρὰν θάλασσαν ἀπὸ στόματος τοῦ κατὰ Ἀρσινόην τῆς Ἰνδικῆς

80 Magardi: *cf.* Lib. Gen. *24.14:* Macardi, Chron. Pasch. *55,17:* Μακαρδοί

81 ab *supplied by Frick*

82 Cordilia: *cf.* Lib. Gen. *26.5:* Cordulia, Chron. Pasch. *(P) 56.8:* Κορδυλία

83 *After* tribus LXXII *evenly distributed over twenty MS lines in smaller letters*: persida bactriana yrcania babylonia cordyna assyria mesopotamia fynicia arabia antiqua arabia famosa elymea rinocorura cedrusia commagina india

84 terras: *for* terrae. *The translator seems to have been distracted by the Greek genitive:* τῆς γῆς.

85 Salamossini: *cf.* Lib. Gen. *26.11:* Alamosenni, Chron. Pasch. *56.18:* Ἀλαμοσυνοί

86 Euri: *the translator read* Εὔροι *for* Σύροι.

325

87   Bibrani: cf. Lib. Gen. 26.15: Librani, Chron. Pasch. 57.3: Βεβρανοί
88   Lygurii corrected by Frick: Lygii codex
89   Tarantii: cf. Chron. Pasch. 57.13: Ταράμαντες for Γαράμαντες
90   Boradii: cf. Chron. Pasch. 57.13: Βοράδες
91   Celtionii: cf. Chron. Pasch. 57.14: Κελτίονες
92   Before Tinus in the upper margin in smaller letters: insulas elladicas quae vocantur cycladas
93   Nirea: cf. Lib. Gen. 28.21: Renea, Chron. Pasch. 58.17: Νηραία for Ῥήνεια
94   After Marathrum evenly distributed over eleven MS lines in smaller letters: andrus naxus curus dilus tio ceus nirea tinus cyrnus sifnus marathū
95   Tamus: cf. Lib. Gen. 30.4: Samus, Chron. Pasch. 59.2: Σάμος
96   After Samothraci evenly distributed over nine MS lines in smaller letters: eubya sicilia cous thassus limnus samothraci crita cyprus tamus rodus chius lesbus, then, but no longer in smaller letters: insulas Elladicas quae vocantur Esporadas
97   Before Est in the upper margin in smaller letters: insulae ioniae civitates habentes
98   ab Biotes corrected by Frick: abbiotes codex
99   ab Hiones corrected by Frick: abhiones codex
100   After eleuthera evenly distributed over thirteen MS lines in smaller letters: mitylyna chius erythra colofa efesus zayrna focea tamus perinthus byzantius chalcedona priinia teus pontus amissus eleuthera
101   Nebdini: cf. Lib. Gen. 30.15: Lepdeni, Chron. Pasch. 59.12: Νεβδηνοί
102   Cnithi: cf. Lib. Gen. 30.16: Cinti, Chron. Pasch. 59.12: Κνῆθοι
103   Sii: cf. Lib. Gen. 30.16: Saei, Chron. Pasch. 59.13: Σαιοί
104   Before Sardinia in the upper margin in smaller letters: insulas africae famosas et magnas
105   After Galata evenly distributed over six MS lines in smaller letters: sardinia corsica cercina girba galata
106   Paraconnisii: cf. Lib. Gen. 32.1: Terraconenses, Chron. Pasch. 59.19: Ταρρακονησίων
107   Aspores: cf. Lib. Gen. 32.2: Astures, Chron. Pasch. (V) 60.2: Ἄστορες

108 Tallorum: *cf.* Lib. Gen. *32.14*: Gallorum, Chron. Pasch. *(V) 60.3*: τ' ἄλλων

109 *Before* Et hoc *in the upper margin in smaller letters*: de ignotas gentes

110 Tainaii *corrected by Frick*: taina ii *codex; cf.* Lib. Gen. *34.1*: Taieni, Chron. Pasch. *60.13*: Ταϊανοὶ

111 Alamosyni: *cf.* Chron. Pasch. *60.14*: Ἀλαμοσσυνοὶ

112 Saccini: *cf.* Lib. Gen. *34.1*: Saraceni, Chron. Pasch. *60.15*: Σακκηνοὶ

113 ultra Taones: *cf.* Lib. Gen. *34.2*: alii ad Taienos contra Arabiam, Chron. Pasch. *60.15*: πέραν τῶν Ταϊανῶν

114 modica Madian: *cf.* Lib. Gen. *34.5*: minor autem Madian, Chron. Pasch. *(V) 60.19*: ἡ μικρὰ δὲ Μαδιὰμ

115 Birri: *cf.* Lib. Gen. *34.8*: Hiberii, Chron. Pasch. *61.4*: Ἴβηρες

116 Birrani: *cf.* Lib. Gen. *34.8*: Birrani, Chron. Pasch. *61.4*: Βέρρανοὶ

117 congregatio Apsari: *cf.* Lib. Gen. *34.10*: accessus Absarus *or* Accessus, Absarus, Chron. Pasch. *61.6*: ἡ παρεμβολὴ Ἄψαρος

118 Causolimin: *cf.* Lib. Gen. *34.12*: Yssilimen, quod est portus, Chron. Pasch. *61.7*: ὁ Ἴσσου λιμὴν

119 *Before* Montes *in the upper margin in smaller letters*: de duodecim nominatos montes

120 Aulas: *cf.* Chron. Pasch. *61.10*: Ἄτλας

121 Lycabantus in Italia et Gallia, Pinnius in Chio qui et Mimas: *cf.* Chron. Pasch. *61.13*: ι' Λυκαβηττὸς ἐν Χίῳ, ια' Πίννιον ἐν τῇ Ἰταλίᾳ

122 *After* Macedonia *evenly distributed over sixteen MS lines in smaller letters*: libanus caucasus taurus atlanticus parnasus citherus eliconius parthenius nysseus lycabantus pinnius olympius

123 *Before* Significantes *in the upper margin in smaller letters*: de flumina qui merguntur in maria

124 *Frick would add* maria *after* currentes.

125 *After* currentes XL *in a space of eleven MS lines in smaller letters*: arbor vitae fluens aquas, *then, but no longer in smaller letters*: maria et flumina convenientes in semet ipsis dant voces.

126 sexcenti tres *codex: rather* sexcenti tredecim

127 *After* quadringenti XIII *over a space of twelve MS lines in smaller letters*: uox dn̄i / abraham / altarium / isaac / arbor sabec / oblatio.

128 *After* quadringenti *there is a* quadraginta *suppressed by Frick.*

129 *After* aridam *in a space of nine MS lines in smaller letters*: mare rubrum / filii israhel transeuntes rubram mare.

130 *Before* Fecerunt *around a space of sixteen MS lines in smaller letters*: ortygo mitrac id sunt coturnices / columna nubis / columna ignis / manna / aaron / vox dn̄i / moyses / populus ebreorū

131 *There may be a lacuna between* autem *and* et, *and a subject for* fecerunt, *such as* vagationem, *should be supplied.*

132 *After* decem *below a space of twelve MS lines*: populus Ebreorum transeuntes Iordanem

133 quadragenti XLV *corrected by Gelzer*: quadragenti XXX *codex*

134 *After* Memoratur *there is an empty space of fourteen MS lines.*

135 phittonissae *corrected by Frick*: phit tonissae *codex*

136 Dena: *presumably from the Greek accusative* Δία

137 *The translator read* διψυής *for* διφυής.

138 *After* erat *there is an empty space of ten MS lines.*

139 et Zeb: *supplied from below*

140 *After* Thibeae *there is an empty space of fourteen MS lines.*

141 CCVI *corrected by Gelzer*: CCII *codex*

142 *Another hand has corrected* illos *to* illis.

143 Atrea *corrected by Scaliger*: erat rea *codex*

144 *After* scripsit *there is an empty space of nine MS lines.*

145 *Before* Et post *in the upper margin in smaller letters*: finis iudicum israhel et initium inventionibus idolorum

146 *After* constaverunt *there is an empty space of twelve MS lines.*

147 successiones *corrected by Frick*: successiores *codex*

148 sculptilia: *another hand has added the* p

149 *After* gloriabantur *there is an empty space of fourteen MS lines.*

150 Dicebat *corrected by Frick*: decipiebat *codex*

151 ec Dius *corrected by Frick*: ecdius *codex*

152 XXXII *corrected by Frick*: XXXV *codex*

153 *After* XXVIIII *there is an empty space of fifteen MS lines.*

154 *In the codex the Roman numerals* I *through* VII *appear in the margin, not in the midst of the text as here.*

155 CCLI *corrected by Frick*: CCLV *codex*

156 DCLXXI *corrected by Frick*: DCLXXX *codex*

157 CCLI *corrected by Frick*: CCL *codex*

158 *Frick indicated a lacuna at this point.*

159 XLV *codex*: XCV et dimidium *is required.*

160 septem *codex*: septendecim *is required; cf. 1 Kings 15:21, 2 Chronicles 12:13*

161 XII *corrected by Frick*: XVIII *codex*

162 et dimidium: *transposed by Frick from after* septem

163 regnavit *corrected by Frick: the codex repeats* prophetavit *from the previous line.*

164 *Before* Post *in the upper margin in smaller letters*: de prima olimpiada grecorum et in babilone transmigratio iudeorum

165 XVI *codex: rather* VI, *cf. 2 Kings 18:10*

166 *After* regnaturi *there is an empty space of five MS lines.*

167 XXV *corrected by Frick*: XXVIIII *codex*

168 octingenti XXX *corrected by Frick*: octingenti XXXI *codex. sic: bracketed by Frick; possibly a result of dittography in the Greek text,* οὕτως οὗτος *for* οὗτος.

169 XXXII *corrected by Frick*: XXXIII *codex*

170 *Before* pascha *in the upper margin in smaller lettters*: depredatio iudeorum in egypto

171 Sennachaoch: Frick suggests that this erroneous name arose from a dittography of σεν in the phrase ἔδησεν Νεχαώ.

172 *After* LXXVIII *there is an empty space of thirteen MS lines.*

173 *After* Hurias *there is an empty space of ten MS lines.*

174 *Before* In duodecimo *in the upper margin in smaller letters*: finis regum iudeorum

175 depredatione *corrected by Frick*: deprecatione *codex*

176 *After* Zacharias *there is an empty space of nine MS lines.*

177 XCII *corrected by Frick*: XLV *codex; after* XLV *there is a space of five MS lines.*

178 *Before* Illi *in the upper margin in smaller letters*: regna assyriorum et chaldaeorum et midorum et persarum

179 noningenti XI *corrected by Frick*: noningenti XII *codex*

180 *From* olympiada *to* Baruchei *the text is isolated to the left side of the page, leaving an empty space of sixteen MS lines.*

181 *The translator read* Ἀναξαγόρας *as two words* (ἄναξ ἀγορὰς) *rather than one.*

182 *Before* Post *in the upper margin in smaller letters*: de danihel propheta et qui post eum

183 sub: *supplied by Frick*

184 *From* noningenti XCII *to* fiunt *the text is isolated to the left side of the page, leaving an empty space of thirteen MS lines.*

185 *After* Iosedec *there is an empty space of eight MS lines.*

186 *The translator read* οἱ περὶ ἀγοράν *for* οἱ περὶ Διαγόραν.

187 *From* Melissus *to* medicus *the text is isolated to the left side of the page, leaving an empty space of fourteen MS lines.*

188 architector: *the translator seems to have mistaken* κωμῳδός *for* οἰκοδόμος.

189 *Before* In his *in the upper margin in smaller letters*: de nectabo nouissimo rege aegypti

190 *A lacuna before* novissumus *is indicated by Frick. The lacuna may at least partially be supplied from the caption in the upper margin of this page.*

191 Didicebatur *appears to be a compounding of the perfect forms of* dico *and* dido *used deponently in the sense of* doceo.

192 *Before* Regnauit *in the upper margin in smaller letters*: persarum reges anabuchodonosor usque da ri um, *followed by an empty space of eleven MS lines.*

193 Midorum: *the translator read* Μήδων *for* Μῆδον.

194 *Before* Macedonia *in the upper margin in smaller letters*: testamentum alexandri conditoris

195 Mesasgyges: *another hand has corrected the* i *of* mesasgiges *to a* y.

196 *After* mortuus est *there is an empty space of seventeen MS lines.*

197 *Before* et ab *in the upper margin in smaller letters*: deptolemeos egypti

198 quem: *the translator apparently read* ὄν *for* ὧν.

199 *After* Greco sermone *there is an empty space of thirteen MS lines.*

200 *Before* Post Filomitorem *there is an empty space of seventeen MS lines.*

201 *After* diem *there is an empty space of fourteen MS lines.*

202 *Before* Et quia *in the upper margin in smaller letters*: singillatim antiquorum regum qui regnaverunt eorundem tempora de primo et secundo tomo manethone

203 *After* regnum *there is a space of two MS lines.*

204 XXXVIII *corrected by Frick*: XXVIII *codex*

205 Thonos Concelerus *corrected by Frick*: Thonosconcelerus *codex*

206 *Scaliger suggested* sub Manethono *is a translation of* ὑπὸ Μανέθωνος.

207 *Before* Primum *there is an* I *in the margin.*

208 Anubes Amusim *corrected by Frick*: anube samusim *codex*

209 *Lacuna indicated by Frick.*

210 Hec . . . milia C: *this sentence is written in the lower margin in smaller letters. Frick considered it properly a part of the text.*

211 tomum *corrected by Frick on the basis of a note of Scaliger's*: totum *codex*

212 isargus: *probably the translator's reading of* εἰς Ἄργος

213 XXI: *corrected from* XXXI *in the codex*

214 A quo: *reading* ἀφ' οὖ *for* ἐφ' οὖ

215 *Before* Post *in the upper margin in smaller letters*: qui apices litterarum grecorum primus tradidit et regnavit in thibeis

216 et Thyestus *corrected by Frick*: ethyestus *codex*

217 nunc: *reading* νῦν *for* τοίνυν

218 *After* septingenti XC *there is an empty space of ten MS lines, and then in the lower margin in smaller letters*: reges argivorum ab inacho usque agamemnonum.

219 Sicinorum . . . tempora: *this sentence is writtten in the upper margin in smaller letters. Frick considered it properly a part of the text.*

220 Ellada *has been displaced to the space following the numeral indicating the regnal years of Plammeus.*

221 Aegypto *corrected by Frick*: ae gypto *codex*

222 quingentos LXXXI: *rather* noningentos LXXIX

223 Quem: *reading* ὃν *for* ὧν

224 CCCXXVIIII *corrected by Frick*: CCCXXVII *codex*

225 *After* CCCXXXVI *in smaller letters*: reges argivorum sacerdotes carnii, *followed by an empty space of eight MS lines.*

226 Athineorum reges: *in the upper margin in smaller letters*

227 sicut: *reading* ὡς *for* ἕως

228 Principes diabii: *in the upper margin in smaller letters*

229 illi: illi XIII *codex. Suspecting dittography of the beginning of the next line, Frick omitted* XIII.

230 Latinorum . . . reges: *in the upper margin in smaller letters*

231 quem: *here and below the translator has read* τὸν *for* τῶν.

232 *Before* prescripsimus *the word* regnavit *has been erased in the MS.*

233 CCCCII *corrected by Frick:* CCCII *codex*

234 XLIIII *corrected by Frick:* XLI *codex*

235 tricesimo: vicesimo *is required.*

236 quinto: sexto *is required.*

237 III: II *is required.*

238 XXII *corrected by Frick:* XII *codex*

239 XXIII *and* XXIIII: *corrected by another hand in the MS from* XIII *and* XIIII

240 XIII: XII *is required.*

241 XLV: XLII *is required.*

242 nunc: *reading* νῦν *for* τοίνυν

243 pridem: *for* πρὸ. Pridem *is marked as if the end of the sentence.*

244 trium: L trium *is required, cf. below.*

245 primae: *reading* πρώτης *for* πρὸ τῆς ά

246 Tempora regni Persarum: *in the upper margin in smaller letters*

247 *Before* VII *a word has been erased.*

248 VI: *It seems likely that this is a corruption of* λς'.

249 *Before* VII *a word has been erased.*

250 XVIIII *is required, as confirmed by other sources:* VIIII *codex*

251 Macedonorum . . . conditore: *in the upper margin in smaller letters*

252 redigens: rediens *codex*

253 *The translator seems to have created a word for himself, the neuter singular accusative substantive of* reliquus *as if it were declined like the pronoun* quis.

254 VIII. *has fallen out before* Antiochus.

255 XXIIII *corrected by Frick:* XIXIIII *codex*

256 XXII *corrected by Frick:* XII *codex*

257 apertionis: *a single letter has been erased between the* r *and the* t

258 Romanorum . . . sequentes: *these words have been crossed out in the MS*

259 Tempora regni Romanorum: *in the upper margin in smaller letters*

260 autem: *this word has been crossed out in the MS*

261 *After* Caesar *in particularly small letters* annos XVIII *has been added above the line.*

262 Iste . . . adinvenit: *these words have been crossed out in the MS*

263 XXII *corrected by Frick*: XXI *codex*

264 XXVIII *corrected by Frick*: XVIII *codex*

265 quod *corrected by Frick*: qud *codex*

266 Gaius *corrected by Frick*: cuius *codex*

267 bissextum: ss *has been erased in the MS*

268 Marco clarissimo: *perhaps repeated from three lines above*

269 *Before* Iurto *in the upper margin in smaller letters*: primus imperavit in
     Roma Gaius Iulius Cesar. ann. XVIII.

270 filio: *reading* υἱοῦ *for* Κοκίου

271 *After* inlustrium *there is an empty space of ten MS lines.*

272 Agrippa *corrected by Frick*: Agrppa *codex*

273 et Emellio *corrected by Frick*: etemellio *codex*

274 Iesus Christus: i͞h͞s x͞p͞s *codex*

275 Iesu Christi: i͞h͞u x͞p͞i *codex*

276 *After* et infra *there is an empty space of twelve MS lines.*

277 altarem: *the* m *has been erased in the codex*

278 viventis: tis *has been corrected from* tes *in the codex*

279 Austorio: *the* u *has been written above the* s

280 LXVI: LVI *codex*

281 LXVII: LVII *codex*

282 LXVIII: LVIII *codex*

283 *After* No͞v *there is a blank line.*

284 *After* Pauni II *there is an empty space of thirteen MS lines.*

285 hostiaria *for* ostiaria

286 LXXII: XXII *codex*

287 *After* XXVIIII *there is an empty space of twelve MS lines.*

288 Apronianus: Apronianus [alius] *codex. Frick assumed* alius *was the re-
     sult of dittography in the Greek text* (-ανὸς [ἄλλος]).

289 *After* Maias *there is an empty space of twelve MS lines.*

290 XC: CX *codex*

291 XCI: CXI *codex*

292 XCII: CXII *codex*

293 XCIII: CXIII *codex*

294 Augusto: Augto *codex*

295 *After* suscepit *there is an empty space of five MS lines.*

296 CVII: CVIII *codex*

297 CVIII: CVIIII *codex*

298 *After* depopulata est *there is an empty space of ten MS lines.*

299 Vespasianus: *a later hand has written* Vespasia- *(followed by* -nus *in the next line) in an erasure.*

300 *After* Sorano *in the lower margin a much later hand has written*: desiderantur plurima.

301 *After* Decem̄ *there is an empty space of twelve MS lines.*

302 *After* martyrizauit *there is an empty space of eight MS lines.*

303 nobili: *the second* i *appears to have been corrected from an* e.

304 *Before* Gallicano *the name* Licinio *has been written and erased.*

305 *Frick identified a lacuna after* suos.

306 *The words from* Eodem anno *to* diminuta est *have been moved away from the left margin, leaving an empty space, and an empty space of four MS lines appears below* diminuta est.

307 *Before* Constantino *there is an empty space of eight MS lines.*

308 Gallicano: Galliano *codex*

309 *The words from* Constantino novo *to* Constantio Augus- *have been moved away from the right margin, leaving an empty space.*

310 *After* Athanasius *there is an empty space of eleven MS lines.*

311 *After* dimidium *in the interval between the lines in later and much smaller letters*: a quo factus est caesar annos III et dimidium.

312 huius: hius *codex*

313 LIIII: LII *is required.*

The words from Caesare tercio *to* octingenti LIIII *have been moved away from the left margin, leaving an empty space.*

314 *The words from* Eo anno *to* Epifi XXVII *have been laid out in two narrow columns separating three empty spaces across the bottom of the page.*

315 *The words from* clarissimorum *to* consulatos VI *have been moved away from the left margin, leaving an empty space.*

316 Dagalaifo: Galaifo *codex*

317 primus Augustalius: *has been underlined in the codex and a much later hand has written in smaller letters in the right margin*: primus Ausgustalius.

318 *Before* Gratiano *in the upper margin in smaller letters:* initium august-
aliorum qui et praesites

319 Augustalio: *appears after* Gratiano *in the codex, transposed by Frick.*

320 Sarmati: Armati *codex*

321 desolaverunt: *added by another hand. After* desolaverunt *there is an
empty space of eleven MS lines.*

322 *The words from* et eo anno *to* Tatiano praeside *have been moved away
from the left margin, leaving an empty space.*

323 *After* Petrinas *there is an empty space of ten MS lines.*

324 Alexandria: Alexandri *codex*

325 praesidae: *the* d *has been added above the line by another hand.*

326 Hadriano: *the* h *has been added above the line by another hand.*

327 *The words from* Augustorum, sub Tatiano *to* sub Hadriano *have been
moved away from the left margin, leaving an empty space.*

328 Augustalio: *appears after* Gratiano *in the codex, transposed by Frick.*

329 Dagalaifo: Gadalaifo *codex*

330 Mechir vicensimo: *appears after* annos V *in the codex, transposed by
Frick*

331 *The words from* sub Paulino *to* XIIII kl. Febroār *have been moved
away from the left margin, leaving an empty space.*

332 *The words from* Et regnavit *to* V idus Septembris *have been moved
away from the left margin, leaving an empty space.*

333 *The words from* sub eodem Antonino *to* Eutropio clarissimo *have
been moved away from the left margin, leaving an empty space.*
Below clarissimo *a much later hand has written in smaller letters:* desunt
pluscula.

Notes to the Translations

THE *APOCALYPSE* ATTRIBUTED TO SAINT METHODIUS (GREEK)

1   This word, *theelatos,* provides the Greek translation with something of a literary flourish. It also appears in Aeschylus, *Agamemnon* 1297; Euripides, *Ion* 1392; and Christian literature at Eusebius, *Ecclesiastical History* 8.16.3.

2   According to the *Cave of Treasures* (trans. Budge 87–90, 119–20), devils lived in the musical instruments made by Jubal and Tubal-Cain, and when these instruments were played the devils sang out, increasing lust among the sons of Cain and tempting the sons of Seth to come down and join them.

3   *Temânôn* is the Syriac word for "eight."

4   The fact that Nimrod was the first to rule as king and his visit to Jonetos ("Yonton") are mentioned in the *Cave of Treasures* (trans. Budge 135, 143). In the *Cave of Treasures,* Nimrod, not Jonetos, is associated with astrology (trans. Budge 171).

5   The original Syriac text can be reconstructed to read "in the seventy-fourth year of Reu," Reu being the son of Peleg in the genealogy of the descendants of Noah (Gen 11:18–19). The Syriac words for "Reu" (*r'w*) and for "four" (*'rb'*) are sufficiently similar that it seems the two words together were taken for scribal duplication, and one excised. There are Syriac manuscripts that read "in the seventieth year of Reu" and "in the seventy-fourth year" respectively. The Greek translator apparently depended on a text similar to the latter form, and noted that the following event took place in the 74th year, although he did not know

337

whose 74th year or the 74th year of what. See Reinink, *Die syrische Apokalypse* (541) 8–9.

6   The former name of Medina.

7   The Greek text is corrupt at this point; it would seem to imply that the Ishmaelites prepared their food in dyers' vats. The Syriac and Latin texts make it clear that they are actually supposed to use vessels of flesh or skin.

8   Kaegi has identified "Gigetum" as the African port of Gigthis, opposite the island of Jerba; see W. Kaegi, "Gigthis and Olbia in the Pseudo-Methodius Apocalypse and Their Significance," *Byzantinische Forschungen* 26 (2000): 161–67; idem, "The Interrelationship of Seventh-century Muslim Raids into Anatolia with the Struggle for North Africa," *Byzantinische Forschungen* 28 (2004): 21–43; idem, "Byzantine Sardinia Threatened: Its Changing Situation in the Seventh Century," in *Forme e caratteri della presenza bizantina nel Mediterraneo occidentale: la Sardegna (secoli VI–XI)*, ed. P. Corrias (Cagliari: MT, 2013): 43–56.

9   Judges 7:25, 8:3, 5–11; Psalm 83:11.

10   The translator has literally rendered a phrase he did not understand. "Civilization" or "cultivation" is another meaning of the Syriac word for "peace," and the phrase might have been read "entrances to the civilized world or cultivated land."

11   The land of Nod, "on the east of Eden," is mentioned as the dwelling place of Cain after his exile by the Lord at Genesis 4:16.

12   A number of places were called Olbia in the ancient Mediterranean world, but Kaegi (refs. above, n. 8) has plausibly identified this Olbia as the port on Sardinia.

13   The "yoke of Ishmael" may have been something of a commonplace in Syriac literature. The *Cave of Treasures* (trans. Budge 155) says that Ishmael made "a handmill, a mill of slavery" in the desert, suggesting that the Ishmaelite way of life necessitated the subjugation of other nations.

14   Literally, "number."

15   The "invincible weapon" would seem to be the True Cross; see 9.8–9 below.

16   Isaiah 37.38.

17   Daniel 7:2.

18   There is no early attestation of the Greek word used here for "cats," and in this passage the cats may be a later addition to the list of unclean animals.

19   That is, presumably, they eat fetuses of any age.

20   This fantastic material seems to be an invention of Pseudo-Methodius. Its name has often been taken to be related to *asynchutos,* the Greek word for "unalloyed," but Aerts suggests that it is actually either a made-up word or a Syriac word *(tâsaqtîs)* derived from the Persian stem *(s-kh-t),* also found in Arabic, for "hard, solid, or tough." See Aerts, "Alexander's Wondercoating."

21   See Ezekiel 38:14–16, 18; Apocalypse 20:8–9.

22   Most of the peoples listed here cannot be identified with any real or imaginary people known to antiquity. Ashkenaz and the Alans, however, suffice to situate the enclosed nations in the northeast beyond the Caucasus.

23   *Paides,* the Greek word here translated "servants," could mean either "children" or "servants." The Syriac text makes it clear that "servants" was originally intended, since it is noted that Alexander never married and had no sons. P. J. Alexander (1985, 57–58) assumes that the Greek translator changed the sense by removing the phrase "he had no sons" and intended that Alexander was succeeded by his sons, but the idea that he had no heirs is certainly implied by the clause that is retained in the Greek translation, saying that he never married. *Pais* is, moreover, an odd term for sons in a position to inherit. Perhaps the translator used the word for servants or slaves because he imagined a similar situation pertained as in the Old Testament when Abraham asserted that without a son his heir would be his servant Eliezer (Genesis 15:2).

24   Or "gathered together from all of the sorts of Ethiopia." Εἰδῶν ("of kinds, sorts, appearances") is an emendation of Ἰνδῶν ("of Indians"), which appears in the Greek text. It is possible that the manuscript tradition requires no emendation, since the people of Ethiopia were regularly identified as Indians in late antiquity.

25   See Psalm 68:31.

26   2 Thessalonians 2:1–4, 7–8. Deviations from the received lectionary text are indicated in italics.

27   "Kingdom" is a feminine noun in Greek; nevertheless, the corresponding pronoun should be the neuter "it" (as in 5.9). The degree of personification in this passage, however, and the implicit identification of the Roman kingdom with the Church, the Bride of Christ—easily and almost imperceptibly accomplished with the gendered grammar of Greek nouns—makes the feminine pronoun preferable.

28   1 Corinthians 15:24.

29   Joshua 10:12–13.

30   Daniel 11:15.

31   Gabaoth the Great is a translation of the Syriac *Gaba'ôt Ramtâ* ("Gaba'ôt the High"), and probably also refers to the location of the Arab victory over the Byzantines at the Battle of Yarmuk (636), which was fought near the town of Gabithas or Gabiia. Gaba'ôt Ramtâ was the place where, according to the Peshitta, the Syriac Bible, Gideon defeated the Midianites (Judges 7:1). It is consistent with Pseudo-Methodius's quest for historical correspondences that the second Ishmaelite invasion should be victorious where the first one was defeated; see Alexander (1985, 32).

32   See Ezekiel 39:17–18 (cf. Apocalypse 19:17–18).

33   See Genesis 16:12. In the Greek and Latin texts (as in the English), Ishmael is a "wild man," but in the Syriac Peshitta he is a "wild ass," a designation which was taken to refer to the desert habitation and the destructive and predaceous tendencies of his descendants; see Reinink, "Ismael, der Wildesel."

34   See 11.17 below.

35   See Deuteronomy 9:4–6.

36   Romans 1:26.

37   Romans 1:26–27.

38   Or "by men who are defiled."

39   Probably the Syrian frontier zone between Byzantine and Persian territory.

40   Judges 6:5, 7:12.

41   See Judges 16.

42 Literally, "at their entrances."

43 This is presumably a complaint about a poll tax being levied according to a census which included persons deceased, as well as those still living who would bear their tax burden.

44 The translator seems to have imperfectly understood this sentence, and it is not completely translated. The Syriac original reads something like "And their wisdom and education will be only from themselves. And the small will be regarded as greater and the despised as more venerable." The "they" referred to by "their" is the Ishmaelites, and the sentence suggests that they have their own nonsensical wisdom which makes what is small greater and what is despicable venerable. It is not clear who is referred to by the translator's "their." The inhabitants of the earth in the preceding sentence would seem to be the natural antecedent, but the Ishmaelite conquerors seem to possess the irrefutable words of the following clause. See Reinink, *Die syrische Apokalypse* (541), 49–50.

45 2 Thessalonians 2:3.

46 Romans 9:6.

47 Romans 11:4.

48 Luke 18:8.

49 1 Timothy 4:1–2.

50 2 Timothy 3:1–5.

51 See 2 Timothy 3:2, 1 Corinthians 5:10–11, Romans 1:31, 2 Timothy 3:3–4, 1 Corinthians 6:9–10, 1 Timothy 1:10, 2 Timothy 3:5.

52 The Greek word, χρεία, could be taken in the sense of "service," but considering the Syriac word being translated ("brasses" or "bronze objects") and the other concrete objects which make up the list, "equipment" or "necessities" seems intended.

53 Matthew 5:11–12, Matthew 10:22 = Matthew 24:13 = Mark 13:13.

54 Sections 13.7–13.10 do not appear in either the Syriac or Latin versions, nor in all Greek texts of the *Apocalypse*. They seem to represent an interpolation of the ninth century.

55 From this clause on, the number of the verbs in this paragraph switches from the plural to the singular, but the unnamed subject seems to remain the same. The phrase "this horde" is not found in the Greek text but is intended to reflect the grammar.

56   In the phrase "will overwhelm," the future tense, in which the prophetic passages of the Greek *Apocalypse* are otherwise conveyed,
is actually rejected in favor of the third-person imperative form,
which might be translated as the command "let it overwhelm"
and could be read as an endorsement or encouragement of the
Arab attack.

57   The meaning of the verb χειμάσει, here translated "turn the land
to winter barrenness," according to the lexicographer Hesychius
should be "to shudder with cold," which is clearly not the sense
here. This verb is also related to words which would suggest it
might mean "to winter (in a place)," which also seems inappro-
priate in this context. Aerts and Kortekaas (1998) II 49 think
the verb is intended to mean "to devastate." I agree, but have
tried to indicate the implications of the odd choice of words in
my translation.

58   Malagina was a district of Bithynia, which first enters the historical record in 786, when the empress Irene dispatched an army
there to fight the Arabs. The Arabs attacked Malagina in 798,
860, and around 875. Mention of Malagina is one of the indications that this interpolation is later than the rest of the text.

59   A rare word, which only appears in the *Lausiac History* of Palladius
otherwise, is used here. The winter of the Arab siege of Constantinople in 717–18 was exceptionally cold, and the weather
actually decimated the ranks of the Arab army.

60   "The cow": the *forum Bovis,* the cattle market of Constantinople.

61   Probably Xerolophos, one of the "seven hills" of Constantinople.

62   Deuteronomy 32:20.

63   See Psalm 78:65.

64   Cf. Apocalypse 13:10.

65   The Greek translator did not recognize "Hebron" in the Syriac
original. The Latin translation has "Aurania."

66   See Matthew 24:21.

67   See Ezekiel 28:26.

68   1 Thessalonians 5:3.

69   See Matthew 24:37–39.

70   See Matthew 24:38, Ezekiel 28:26.

71   See Psalm 79:3.

72   Psalm 79:3.

73   Matthew 11:21–23, Luke 10:13–15.

74   Here and in the next chapter the crown of the Roman emperor is called a *stemma*, "a wreath or chaplet," rather than a *stephanos*, the more common word for a crown and the one used throughout the Greek Testament. The Latin translation has *corona*, the simple word for a crown. The word choice is hard to explain. Perhaps the translator intended to distinguish the impermanent crown (*stemma*) of the ruler of an earthly kingdom from the incorruptible and unfading crown (*stephanos*) promised to the faithful in the New Testament (1 Corinthians 9:25, 1 Peter 5:4).

75   See 1 Corinthians 15:24.

76   Psalm 68:32.

77   See 1 Corinthians 15:24.

78   Genesis 49:17–18, according to the LXX.

79   See Matthew 11:5, 24:24; Acts 2:19–20; Apocalypse 6:12.

80   Or "a visage."

81   Genesis 49:18.

82   Matthew 24:24.

83   See 2 Thessalonians 2:3–4.

84   See Matthew 24:29.

85   Matthew 24:30, 2 Thessalonians 2:8.

86   Matthew 13:43, Philippians 2.15–16.

87   See Titus 3:4.

THE *APOCALYPSE* ATTRIBUTED TO SAINT METHODIUS (LATIN)

1   Leviticus 19:18, Matthew 22:39–40.

2   1 Corinthians 10:11.

3   It is unclear how *laboravi* was intended.

4   The Latin translator has rendered both κατεσχῆψησαν, the word found in the Greek text, with *conlapse,* and κατεχώψησαν, the word he apparently thought might have been intended, with *defusae.*

5   The Latin of this last phrase is ungrammatical, but the sense is clear.

6   The Latin rendering has literally translated the Greek genitive of comparison.

7   See Genesis 6:4.

8   See the note on the translation of the Greek text.

9   The translator seems not to have recognized ἑῴα as the Greek word for "the East" or "the dawn," and so a new and obscure country entered the geography of the Middle Ages.

10   Cf. Genesis 11:9.

11   While the noun *consilium* is singular, *quibus,* the pronoun which refers to it, is plural. This appears to be a simple error.

12   Neither of the senses of *rebello* is appropriate to the context. "To revolt" can hardly be a mutual activity, and "to renew the war" makes no sense when the war in question is the first one. Assuming that the translator was unfamiliar with the word he chose, I have tried to convey what I take to be his intended meaning.

13   I.e., "the lands which may be enumerated in succession beginning from the furthest West," so "as far as the West."

14   *Adposuerunt* is a literal translation of προσέθηκαν, with its sense of "give up, set aside," rather than an idiomatically correct usage of the verb *appono.*

15   See Judges 6:5, 7:12.

16   Judges 7:25, 8:3, 5–11; Psalm 83:11.

17   "Israel" may be assumed to be the subject of this sentence, but as it stands it is open to misconstruction.

18   See the note on the translation of the Greek text.

19   See Genesis 4:16.

20   As it stands the Latin should be translated "the land of Babylon prevailed over the kingdoms of the giants," but reference to the Greek would suggest that the translator took *regna* to be singular and *obtenuit* to take the ablative, giving a sense like that found in the Greek.

21   The Latin translation does not so much offer a version of Sennacherib's name as fail to recognize it.

22   1 Kings 19:37, Isaiah 37:38.

23   See Daniel 5:31, 9:1, 11:1.

24 See Daniel 7:2.

25 Cf. the Greek text.

26 The translator seems to be imagining all manner of unformed and deformed live and still births.

27 The next two paragraphs survive in two distinct but more or less equally reliable recensions in the Greek. The Latin text follows more closely the second of these two.

28 See Ezekiel 38:14–16, 18; Apocalypse 20:8–9.

29 Psalm 68:31.

30 I.e., "the scriptures."

31 2 Thessalonians 2:1–4, 7–8.

32 1 Corinthians 15:24.

33 See Joshua 10:12–13.

34 The point of this perhaps rather confusing paragraph is that while the forces of history of invasion and conquest have brought other kingdoms to an end, they have not done so to the kingdom of the Romans, nor will they. The kingdom of the Romans has resisted barbarian invasions in the past and will not be overcome by that of the Ishmaelites.

35 See Daniel 11:15.

36 Ezekiel 39:17–18; cf. Apocalypse 19:17–18.

37 See Genesis 16:12.

38 See Deuteronomy 9:4–6.

39 Romans 1:26.

40 Romans 1:26–27.

41 See note on translation of the Greek text.

42 Cf. Judges 6:5, 7:12.

43 The Latin translator has mistaken ὄρη ("mountains") for ὄρους ("boundary markers").

44 *In introitum eorum* is a literal translation of ἐν ταῖς εἰσόδοις αὐτῶν, and while it should mean something like "at their entrance," it is probably intended to convey a thought more like the one in our translation.

45 See note on translation of the Greek text.

46 2 Thessalonians 2:3.

47 This would appear to be the sense of *supergredientum raviem, ravies*

being a word invented by the translator, in ignorance of an approriate one like *agrestis,* on the basis of *ravus* ("hoarse") and *ravis* ("hoarseness").

48 That is, because there are fewer people, not because there is less humane sensibility.

49 *Praesipia,* from *praesaepia.*

50 Romans 9:6.

51 Cf. Romans 11:4.

52 The Latin translator seems to have assumed that any acceptable translation of παιδέα would convey all of the senses of the Greek word, including that of "chastisement."

53 *Putas* is also in the Vulgate.

54 Luke 18:8.

55 1 Timothy 4:1–2.

56 2 Timothy 3:1–5, Romans 1:29–31.

57 See 2 Timothy 3:2, 1 Corinthians 5:10–11, Romans 1:31, 2 Timothy 3:3–4, 1 Corinthians 6:9–10, 1 Timothy 1:10, 2 Timothy 3:5.

58 The translator apparently took *stercore* as a nominative form.

59 Seven weeks of years, that is, forty-nine years, are granted to the dominion of the Ishmaelites according to the prophecy of Pseudo-Methodius.

60 The sense, but not the word, is new.

61 The translator was apparently unaware of the appropriate word for "tools" and invented one of his own.

62 *Sed* is used here as the equivalent of *nisi.*

63 Matthew 5:11–12, 10:22 = Matthew 24:13 = Mark 13:13. The Latin text inexplicably mixes plural and singular in this last quotation.

64 See 8.1 above.

65 Lines 13.7–10 constitute an interpolation found only in the Greek text.

66 Cf. Psalm 78:65.

67 *Ipse* for *ipsi.*

68 Cf. Apocalypse 13:10.

69 The future perfect of this same verb ("will have been burned up") would have been a more suitable translation of the Greek.

70 See Matthew 24:21.

71 See Ezekiel 28:26.

72   1 Thessalonians 5:3.

73   See Matthew 24:37–39.

74   *Sese potantes,* an odd neologism translating πόντεω.

75   See Matthew 24:38, Ezekiel 28:26.

76   See Psalm 79:3.

77   Psalm 79:3.

78   *Cedunt,* from *caedunt.*

79   Matthew 11:21–23, Luke 10:13–15.

80   See 1 Corinthians 15:24.

81   Psalm 68:32.

82   See 1 Corinthians 15:24.

83   Genesis 49:17–18.

84   See Matthew 11:5, 24:24; Acts 2:19–20; Apocalypse 6:12.

85   Or "as if in the person of the human race."

86   Genesis 49:18.

87   Matthew 24:24.

88   See 2 Thessalonians 2:3–4.

89   See Matthew 24:29.

90   Matthew 24:30, 2 Thessalonians 2:8.

91   Matthew 13:43, Philip 2:15–16.

92   See Titus 3:4.

An Alexandrian World Chronicle

1   Cf. Genesis 5. The history of humanity is traced not to Adam per se but to his creation by God, just as God is the ultimate father in Genesis 5 and Luke's genealogy of Jesus (Luke 3:38).

2   This is the Septuagint's date for the years from Adam to the Flood. It also appears in such Latin works as the chronicle of Sulpicius Severus, *Hist. Sacr.* 1.3. There is no attempt in the chronology to accommodate the numbers and dates found in the Vulgate.

3   *Viginti* is required in the place of the *quinquaginta* of the MS. The translator probably misread the Greek text: χνέ for χκέ. He was apparently not checking the calculation as he translated it, since the next sum *(DCC nonaginta quinque)* appears correctly transcribed, as if there had been no intervening error.

4   The Greek and Latin versions of biblical names are not uniformly

consistent with the traditional English transcriptions of the Hebrew. For the sake of recognizability and comparison I have rendered all names as they are found in the Authorized Version.

5   Cf. Genesis 5:31, Septuagint: 753 years, Vulgate: 777 years. Perhaps the translator offers only the agreement between Greek and Latin texts, or perhaps the subsequent figures have merely fallen out.

6   The next two paragraphs are very close to the Vulgate Genesis 5:31–6:4, 6:11–14, for the most part verbatim. The translation has therefore freely borrowed from the equivalent passages in the Authorized Version in order to indicate the derivative nature of these parts of the text.

7   "And later" results from a confused rendering of the *postquam* in the Vulgate, Genesis 6:5 (and possibly καὶ μετ᾽ ἐκεῖνο in the Septuagint), which introduces the next clause. Here, however, it seems to indicate that giants inhabited the earth not only in the time before the Flood but also later; see Numbers 13:33 (34), cf. Numbers 13:29; Deuteronomy 1:28, 3:11; Joshua 14:12; 1 Samuel 17:4; 2 Samuel 21:16–22; 1 Chronicles 20:4–8.

8   The Vulgate speaks of *filii* at this point, and the Septuagint of υἱοί, but the Alexandrian text has ἄγγελοι. The use of "angels" corresponds to one school of interpretation which held the "sons of God" to be fallen angels.

9   The translator seems to have confused the meaning of *nominati* with that of *noti* and, not surprisingly, used the former word to render the ὀνομαστοί of Genesis 6:4 in the Septuagint (the Vulgate has *famosi*). He is probably not trying to introduce a new sense to the phrase (i.e., "the giants were called men by the world").

10   Although Genesis 6:13 in the Authorized Version reads "filled with violence," "filled with iniquity" is closer to the Vulgate *(repleta est iniquitate)*, which is followed by the *Excerpta* translator.

11   Cf. Genesis 6:14. "With pitch" appears as ἀσφάλτῳ in the Septuagint and as *bitumini* in the Vulgate. A similar reduplication of transcription and translation occurs at 1.6.2: *polyolbum et multoditatum.*

12   The further instructions to Noah and the revelation of God's in-

tention are summed up in a terse *et cetera.* It is unclear whether the translator excluded some text closely parallel to the Bible which he deemed unnecessary to repeat, or whether he found a similarly economical abbreviation in the Greek original.

13 Cf. Genesis 7:6.

14 Cf. Genesis 7:12, 17.

15 Cf. Genesis 7:21–23.

16 Cf. Genesis 8:13, 18–19.

17 I have some doubts about the lacuna postulated by Frick. It seems just as likely that *post diluvium* is borrowed from Genesis 11:10, at the beginning of the genealogy of Shem, which follows immediately here in the *Excerpta. Sic* also indicates information to follow at 1.2.1 and 1.2.2.

18 Cf. Genesis 11:10–17.

19 Cainan appears as the son of Arphaxad and the father of Sala in the Septuagint (Genesis 10:24, 11:13), but not in the Vulgate. Cainan is, however, found in all the versions of Christ's genealogy in the gospel of Luke (3:36).

20 The "twelve" of the codex must be "seventy-two" for the calculation to work. The translator apparently misread βωιβ′ for βωοβ′.

21 *Phalec* in the Vulgate.

22 An error of uncertain origin. In the biblical genealogies (Genesis 11:18, Luke 3:35, cf. 1 Chronicles 1:25) and according to the *Excerpta* itself (1.4.1), Reu is the son, not the brother, of Peleg.

23 I.e., that of Peleg; see Genesis 10:25, below 1.4.1.

24 This paragraph follows rather less closely than the previous block of narrative the Latin of the Vulgate, Genesis 11:1–9.

25 Both the place-name and the description of the place are of uncertain origin. Genesis 11:2 refers simply to "a plain" (*campum* in the Vulgate, πεδίον in the Septuagint). Frick suggested that the translator misread πεδίον as πανείον.

26 There is a nice distinction between the imperfect (*aedificabant*) of the Vulgate, Genesis 11:5 (God came to see the work in which men were engaged), and the *Excerpta* translator's pluperfect (God came to see what men had accomplished up to the point of his arrival).

27 The *Excerpta* translator uses *longitudo* for distance from north to

south and *latitudo* for distance from east to west, as we use their derivatives.

28   Although it is variously identified as the Pelusiac, or easternmost, branch of the Nile or the Wadi el-Arish in the north Sinai Desert, Rhinocorura was understood to mark the boundary between Egypt and Palestine.

29   Here and below (1.2.4) *Aethiops* is used as an epithet of Cush, perhaps naturally enough, as he is the progenitor of the Ethiopians, but *Aethiops* is also used as an epithet of Nimrod (1.2.4). The word is therefore probably being used to describe the physical characteristics of both men rather than to indicate either one as the ancestor of the Ethiopian race. Cush and Nimrod are both taken to be "burned faces," or black-skinned.

30   This interjection seems intended to detach Nimrod from the list of nations. No peoples are listed as descended from him (cf. 1.2.4). Just so in the Bible he appears as a builder of cities, not a father of nations (Genesis 10:10). Perhaps as a giant Nimrod is considered somehow separate from the human race. The phrase "for their food" is not taken from the Bible, although Nimrod is there called a hunter.

31   The association of Chaldeans and Galatians is apparently due to the Χαλδαῖοι being mistaken for Κελταῖοι. The error must have appeared already in the Greek text. The Celtic origins of the Galatians were well known.

32   Chattaim does not appear in the biblical lists of the names of the sons of Japheth (Genesis 10:2, 1 Chronicles 1:5). Kittim, the son of Javan, was variously identified as the ancestor of the Macedonians and of the Romans. When Kittim was assigned to the Romans, as here, it was necessary for the chronicle tradition to invent a new Japhethite progenitor for the Macedonians; this is Chattaim.

33   The Bible (Genesis 10:3) gives the second son of Gomer as Riphath (Ῥιφὰθ). Corruption seems likely, but it is difficult to explain. The Rhodians are usually assigned to the fourth son of Javan. The Septuagint (Genesis 10:4) does not transliterate the Hebrew name but interprets its ethnographic significance by rendering the last son of Javan as Ῥόδιοι.

34   The manuscript is corrupt at this point, but by comparison with equivalent passages below it would seem that *Citteis* was the translator's rendering of the Greek transliteration of Kittim. It is possible that this was not Κιτιαίοι, as in the Septuagint, Numbers 24:24, Isaiah 23:1, 1 Maccabees 8:5, or Syncellus (92), but something that would indicate the singular. It has been translated here and below as the name of an individual, not the people descended from him.

35   There was an old, but by no means uncontroversial, tradition that Athens had been founded by colonists from Sais in Egypt; see Anaximenes (*FGrHist* 72, F 20); Plato, *Timaeus* 21E; Diodorus Siculus, 1.28.4–5; Charax (*FGrHist* 103, F 39). While Athenian patriots insisted it was the other way around and Athens founded Sais, it must have served the purposes of Christian apologists in their battle with Hellenism to indicate that one of the centers of Hellenic culture was a barbarian foundation; see F. Jacoby, "The First Athenian Prose Writer," *Mnemosyne* 3rd ser. 13 (1947): 59.

36   The intent of this passage is debatable. At some point Carthaginians (Καρχηδόνιοι) seem to have been mistaken for the Chalcedonians (Χαλκηδόνιοι), and the Phoenician origins of the latter were imputed to the former, although Chalcedon was usually supposed to be a colony of Megara. Chalcedon seems to be intended, since the opening and closing indicate that the passage will deal with Greece. Otherwise, the Carthaginians might have been offered as a historical analogy that verified the Sidonian settlement of Thebes.

37   Probably the *Veneti,* among their neighbors, in the Greek original; cf. *Lib. Gen.* 12.19: *Uieni,* Syncellus (92): Οὐεννοί. The Huns (Οὔννοι) probably loomed larger in the translator's imagination.

38   Or perhaps "and north from there."

39   We are apparently supposed to imagine a block of territory as a geometric figure; cf. Tacitus, *Agricola* 10.3.

40   Comparison with the parallel Greek text shows that this should read "from the River Tanais (i.e., Don) to Mastousia."

41   Or perhaps "Mastousia across from Troy."

42 In the Table of Nations India usually belongs to Shem (see below, 1.2.6–7). *Lib. Gen.* 14.13 has *Collis Indiae* (?), and Chron. Pasch. 48.14 Ἰνδική. Frick suggests *Sindica.*

43 Achaea appears below in its proper geographical vicinity. Why it is anticipated here or whether this is a corruption is unclear.

44 *Molchia* is noted on the *Tabula Peutingeriana* (segm. 11.4, ed. Miller; segm. 10.4, ed. Levi and Levi) as a station in Armenia on the route from Tigranocerta to Isumbo, but considering the regions among which it is listed here, it seems to be a corruption of "Molossia."

45 The translator has mistaken Λυχνῖτις for an adjective, when it is actually another name in the list. "Lychnitis" should appear after Illyria.

46 "Gaul" seems to be Gallia Cisalpina (cf. Stephanus of Byzantium, Γαλλία, ἐντὸς Ἄλπεων χώρα), "Celtica" Transalpine Gaul or Gaul proper, and "Spanogallia" the border region between Gaul and Spain, perhaps Septimania.

47 Cf. Genesis 10:6–20, 1 Chronicles 1:8–16

48 *Patriae* in the *Excerpta* should be taken as something of a transliteration of the Greek πατριαί, which means "lineage" or "people," rather than a translation by means of the Latin *patria,* which means "homeland."

49 This indicates a quotation of Genesis 10:13–14. What follows is actually an elaborated version of the biblical verses, including the contemporary peoples sprung from the biblical peoples or sons of Mizraim. The indebtedness of lengthier and more faithfully rendered quotations is notably not signaled in this manner.

50 Cf. Genesis 10:15–18.

51 Josephus, *AJ* 1.138, indicates that Arucaeus settled Acre in Lebanon.

52 The Perizzites do not appear in either biblical list of the descendants of Canaan (Genesis 10:15–18, 1 Chronicles 1:13–16), nor in Josephus (*AJ* 1.138–39), but they do regularly occur in biblical lists of the inhabitants of Canaan (Genesis 15:20, Exodus 33:2, 34:11, Joshua 9:1, 11:3, etc.). This addition to the genealogies was perhaps necessary to arrive at a figure of twelve Canaanite nations, opposed to the twelve tribes of Israel.

53   The translator seems to be unaware that *septentrionem* means
      "northern," but he does know that it refers to one of the four
      cardinal compass points. He knows, moreover, that *aquilo* means
      "north" (1.2.1, 2, 3). He apparently assumes, however, that Latin
      does not possess synonyms for "north," and so uses *septentrio* of
      the south. Likewise *septentrionalem oceanum* below.

54   The Greek Ἰχθυοφάγοι ("Fish-eaters") was usually transliterated
      in Latin as *Ichthyophagi,* but the *Excerpta* translates it as *Pi-
      scescomeduli (pisces + comedo,* lit. "Fish-devourers").

55   Perhaps to be identified with the Psylloi.

56   Probably not to be identified with the Macae, noted below as in-
      habitants of Syrtis; rather somehow associated with Crete, an
      island in Hamite territory, whose ancient name was Macaris.

57   *Lib. Gen.* 20.7–8 reads: *sunt autem fines Cham a Rinocoryris, quae di-
      uidit Syriam et Aegyptum, usque Garira in longum.* This probably
      reflects the original, since Rhinocorura, "the stream of Egypt,"
      was thought to separate Egypt from Syria (broadly conceived
      so as to include Palestine). This would explain *et* in our text. If
      the text as it stands represents the thought of the translator, he
      must have imagined Rhinocorura extending much further than
      the Wadi el-Arish actually does, perhaps equating it with the
      Red Sea. It is also possible that *extendit* is an error for *diuidit.*
      The preposition does not preclude the possibility, since the MS
      reads *asyria,* not *a Syria.* This reading would demand an explana-
      tion for why Ethiopia is used as a name for the whole African
      continent.

58   The translator has offered a translation rather than a translitera-
      tion of this place-name. It could be the Egyptian city of *Erythra
      Bolos* ("Red Earth"; see Hdt., 2.111.3), but more likely the coastal
      region of the Red or Erythraean Sea, which would "look to the
      east."

59   Another instance of a Greek proper noun usually transliterated
      being translated into Latin. The Greek word *astu* ("city") had
      been borrowed into Latin, but as in Attic literature it almost ex-
      clusively referred to the city of Athens.

60   Rather than translating Μεγίστη as an adjective *(magna)* de-
      scribing Nisyra, the translator should have added Megiste as

another item in this list of islands; cf. *Lib. Gen.* 20.3, *Chron. Pasch.* 53.6.

61   Cf. Genesis 2:13.

62   The translator's rendering of this sentence is confused. The form of the original is preserved in *Chron. Pasch.* 53.14–15; cf. Syncellus (90): ὁρίζει δὲ μεταξὺ τοῦ Χὰμ καὶ τοῦ Ἰάφεθ τὸ στόμα τῆς ἑσπερινῆς θαλάσσης.

63   Cf. Genesis 10:22–29; 1 Chronicles 1:17–27.

64   Futh, the son of Shem, is not biblical (see Genesis 10:22). Josephus, *Lib. Gen.*, and Syncellus agree that the Persians belong to the family of Shem, but none offers a specific ancestor for them. Josephus (*AJ* 1.143) says the Persians were descendants of the Elymaeans. *Chron. Pasch.* 54.5 makes them descendants of Lud. Frick takes this phrase as a gloss, but it is also possible that it preserves a branch of the chronicle tradition which tried to account for the Persians in the Table of Nations.

65   The Hyantes were an ancient people of Boeotia, but it is difficult to see their connection with the man usually taken as the ancestor of the Syrians.

66   Cf. Genesis 10:23: "And the children of Aram; Uz, and Hul, and Gether, and Mash."

67   2 Kings 17:24 explains that the Samaritans were originally deportees from Babylon and other regions of Mesopotamia brought by the Assyrians to live in the depopulated northern kingdom of Israel.

68   This strange form of Sala's name might be a combination of the name itself and the conjunction which follows it, as in the Septuagint (Genesis 10:24): Σαλὰ δὲ.

69   Ptolemy, *Geographia*, mentions Σάλαθος (4.6.1–2) as the southern part of the west coast of Libya and Σαλάθα (7.2.22) as a village in inner India. Perhaps the Salathians are to be associated with one of these localities, the latter being more likely.

70   Cf. Genesis 10:26–29; 1 Chronicles 1.20–23. Josephus (*AJ* 1.147) has all of the descendants of "Iouctas" inhabiting various regions of India and Seria.

71   "Hazarmaveth and Jerah" in the Hebrew text (Genesis 10:26; 1

Chronicles 1:20) become Ἀσαρμὼθ καὶ Ἰαρὰχ in the Septuagint and *Asarmoth et Iare* in the Vulgate. It seems that some conflation of these two produces *Aram* here.

72 Stephanus Byzantius (apud Κάρμηλος) gives Καρμήλιος as an inhabitant of Mt. Carmel.

73 The Cedrusians or Cedrossians were a people on the Red Sea coast.

74 The translator has misunderstood ὁριζούσης to mean "stretching" rather than "dividing," and renders the relative clause as referring to *habitatio.* Comparison with the parallel Greek texts suggests that the sentence should read "Rhinocura, which divides Syria and Egypt, and the Red Sea from the outlet of Arsinoe, which is in India."

75 *Peoni* seems to be corrupt.

76 Germans also appear in the *Liber Generationis, Chronicon Paschale,* and Syncellus, but this is probably a corruption of "Carmanians."

77 Cossaea was a part of Persia; see Strabo, 16.1.17–18.

78 The Phoenicians are included among the descendants of Ham (1.2.4), but Phoenicia is not included in the territory of Ham (1.2.5). Tradition held that Canaan and his progeny unlawfully settled in the land which had fallen by lot to Shem; *Jubilees* 10.27–34; Syncellus (168). This is why the *Excerpta* compiler has appended a note insisting on the possession of Phoenicia by the sons of Shem.

79 These seventy-two tribes correspond to the seventy-two languages above (1.2.1).

80 According to Stephanus Byzantinus, the Ταηνοί were a southern tribe of the Saracens; see 1.3.2 below.

81 Presumably the same as the *Alamosyni* below (1.3.2).

82 According to Josephus (*AJ* 1.127), Tharsus was the original name of Cilicia, as is proven by the name of Tarsus, the principal city of the region.

83 A people of Pontus.

84 A Thracian people who gave their name to the district of Bessica.

85 The inhabitants of Noricum.

86 Pliny, *NH* 6.35(179), mentions the town of Macua on the "Arabian side" of the Nile; perhaps the Macuaci are to be associated with this place.

87 A people of Mauritania Caesariensis.

88 The *Chronicon Paschale* (57.13–15) lists the Outer Garamantes and the Nobadae "who extend as far as Ethiopia." Perhaps our chronicle is distinguishing inner and outer Garamantes, and one of the *exteriores* in the text is a mistake for *interiores*. Although the first *exteriores* seems to be defended by the text of the *Chronicon Paschale,* we would imagine the "outer Garamantes" (i.e., those furthest from the *oikoumene*) to be those whose territory stretched to Ethiopia, which was supposed to lie at the edges of the earth.

89 What may seem like a personal note is really taken over from the chronicle's source; cf. *Lib. Gen.* 28.5–6: *necessarium autem putavi et inhabitationes Gentium et cognominationes declarari.*

90 It seems that the chronicler did not intend the following list to refer in its entirety to the "unknown peoples," even if that was the understanding of the translator. The first part of what follows (down to the Graecosarmatians) is a list of colonists sent out by various ancient peoples and accounts for commonly known peoples who did not find a place in the Table of Nations. The list of unknown peoples comes after this.

The whole of this paragraph seems to be a translation of one very similar to a passage in the *Chronicon Paschale* (57.18–58.2): ἀναγκαῖον καὶ τὰς ἀποικίας τῶν ἐθνῶν καὶ τὰς προσηγορίας αὐτῶν δηλῶσαι καὶ τὰ κλίματα ἀγνώστων ἐθνῶν πῶς οἰκοῦσι καὶ τίς πλεῖον [*for* πλησίον] τίνος. ἄρξομαι δὲ διαγράφειν ἀπὸ τῆς ἀνατολῆς καὶ μέχρι δύσεως, πῶς οἰκοῦσι κατὰ τάξιν (It is necessary to show the colonists of the peoples and their names and the districts of the unknown peoples, how are they situated and who next to whom. I will begin to list them from east to west, how they are situated in order.).

91 The following examples indicate how peoples who have made a more recent appearance on the historical stage originated from the colonies sent out by more ancient ones. This explanation

was especially common in antiquity, and has yet to lose its grip on the popular imagination.

92 Or perhaps "the peoples of Peace round about." *Pacis* is almost certainly a translation of the Greek Εἰρήνης, but it is impossible to identify this place. Perhaps Irenopolis in Cilicia.

93 "The middle of Syria": a translation, rather than the usual transliteration, of *Coele Syria.*

94 The "Lucky Arabs," the Greek *Arabes Eudaimones,* and their country, *Arabia Eudaimon,* are usually found in Latin as *Arabes Felices* and *Arabia Felix.* The translator has imposed his own somewhat inaccurate rendering upon *Eudaimon.*

95 The Cinedocolpitae, who appear as *Cynedocolpitae* in the *Lib. Gen.* 28.13 and Κηναιδοκολπεῖται in the *Chronicon Paschale* 58.8, seem to be a corruption of the Cynamolgi (Κυναμολγοί) or "Bitch-milkers" who were known as neighbors of the Troglodytes and Ichthyophagi inhabiting the shores of the Red Sea (Diod. Sic., 3.31.1–3; Strabo, 16.4.10).

96 There is an apparent inconsistency in the chronicle at this point. Although the Greeks themselves are recorded above as descendants of Japheth (1.2.2), most of the peoples listed as their colonists here are included among the descendants of Ham (1.2.4, 5). Perhaps the colonists are supposed to be the present inhabitants of lands allotted to Ham, or perhaps this disagreement belies two disparate sources.

97 The Myrtoan Sea was that part of the Aegean which lay between the coasts of the Argolid and Attica.

98 Unidentified.

99 *Neraea* is a corruption, which occurs elsewhere in the chronicle tradition, of the name of Rhenea, a small island near Delos.

100 Cyrnos was the Greek name for the island of Corsica. Its inclusion among the Cyclades is as puzzling as that of Marathon, the plain on the coast of Attica!

101 The Sporades are the group of islands in the Aegean which lie off Cape Artemisium. Only the literal sense of their name ("scattered" islands) could allow such far-flung islands as Sicily and Cyprus to be included in their number, but this is apparently

how the chronicler used it of the "outer isles" settled by the Greeks.

102 "Settled," rather than "dwelled on," because the *Chronicon Paschale* (58.20) preserves the original: ἐν αἷς ἀπῳκίσθησαν Ἕλληνες.

103 Pontus was a region of Asia Minor far to the east of Ionia, on the shores of the Black Sea. Its inclusion among the cities of Ionia is inexplicable.

104 Amissus or Amisus was, next to Sinope, the largest city of Pontus. Its inclusion in a list of Ionian cities is perhaps justified by the fact that it was founded by colonists from Miletus, an Ionian city not included in this list. Its epithet is due, no doubt, to the city having been granted its freedom by Julius Caesar and again by Augustus. See Strabo, 12.3.14.

105 Possibly the inhabitants of the Roman *regio* of Aemilia in central Italy. The preponderance of members of the Aemilian *gens* in the annals of Roman history may have made it seem like a separate people.

106 Some of the Sicanians, an ancient people on the Tiber, allegedly migrated to Sicily and gave their name to its people.

107 The peoples listed are native Africans, but the islands are those colonized by the Phoenicians and Carthaginians. Either the chronicler meant by "Africans" the Carthaginians and took the native Africans to be derived from them, or he assumed that the native Africans had preceded the Punic settlers to these islands, just as they had to the African mainland.

108 The *Nebdini* and *Cnethi* are unidentified.

109 No attested African people can be identified with this name. The Saïi were known to Strabo (10.2.17, 12.3.20) as a Thracian people who had inhabited Samos, and the Sacae were a nomadic people of northern Asia (Hdt., 3.93.3; Pliny, *NH* 6.19.50); it is difficult to see how either of them could be transposed to Africa. It is possible that this was intended to refer to the Saites, although the proper forms of their ethnic name are Σαΐτις and Σαϊτηνός (Stephanus Byzantius, apud Σάις), and it is not certain that the inhabitants of an Egyptian city would be called "Africans."

110   Modern Djerba, also known as Meninx in antiquity.

111   Perhaps a corruption of either *Masaesyli* or *Massyli,* two different peoples of Numidia.

112   The people of Tinge or Tingi, the capital of Mauritania, modern Tangiers.

113   "Sarinaeans" should be "Caesariaeans." The translator read καίσαριναίοι, the inhabitants of Mauritania Caesariensis, as καὶ σαριναίοι, and so *et Sarinei* ("and the Sarinei").

114   So called from Tarraco, modern Tarragona, the capital of the Roman province of Hispania Citerior.

115   The translator apparently read Τάλλων for Γάλλων.

116   Presumably this name, which appears as Βελικοί in the *Chronicon Paschale* (60.4), became corrupted before entering the chronicle tradition. Certainly Strabo (4.1.1, 4.4.1, 3) knew of the Βέλγαι, and Stephanus Byzantius of Βελγικοί (*apud* Βελγίκα).

117   The *Sicani* were among the native inhabitants encountered by the Greek settlers in Sicily; Thucydides, 6.2.2; Strabo, 6.2.4. Perhaps they have been confused with the *Sequani,* a Gallic people.

118   Perhaps the *Ednii,* or Ἔδνοί in the *Chronicon Paschale* (60.4), who may represent a corruption of the name of the *Aedui,* a nation of Gaul.

119   Pliny, *NH* 4.14.99, agrees that there are five "kinds" of Germans but offers an altogether different list of the main groups.

120   While it seems possible to restore the names of three of these German tribes with reasonable certainty, the *Bardunii* and the *Berdilii* remain problematic. Perhaps the name of the *Varini* or *Varinnae,* a German tribe (Pliny, *NH* 4.14.99; Tacitus, *Germ.* 40.1), has been confused with that of the *Varduli,* an Iberian tribe (Strabo, 3.4.12; Pliny, *NH* 3.3.27, 4.20.11). The *Berdilii* might also be a corruption of the *Vandalii* or *Vandilii.*

121   The ancient geographers knew of a nomadic nation of "Wagondwellers" on the steppe of eastern Europe. Strabo (2.5.26, 7.2.4, 3.7, 11.2.1) speaks of the Ἁμάξοικοι, and Pliny (*NH* 4.12.80) of the *Hamaxobii.*

122   *Grecosarmates* is apparently otherwise unattested. These are possibly the mixed population of the Bosporan Kingdom, who were the descendants of Greek settlers as well as Scythians and

Sarmatians; see. T. Sulimirski, *The Sarmatians* (New York: Praeger, 1970), 150.

123 The "unknown peoples" (ἔθνη ἄγνωστα) seem to be nations outside the borders of the Roman Empire, not unheard of, but not belonging to the "known world" of the *oikoumene* either.

124 I.e., from east to west.

125 The text describes "in what manner" the unknown peoples live only in the sense of *how* their geographical locations are related to one another. There is no treatment of their habits or customs. The use of *quomodo* here is another example of the limitations of the translator's vocabulary.

126 Since the *Liber Generationis* provides the only recognizable ethnic name, I have assumed that it preserves the original reading.

127 In the *Chronicon Paschale* (60.13, 15) the same people appear twice, and it seems more likely that this is the original reading and that the multiplication of our text is due to corruption.

128 The Midianites were defeated and decimated by the Israelites under Moses on their progress to Canaan (Numbers 31). It is perhaps on this account that they are called *fortiores* here, on the assumption that the greater the enemy, the greater the victory. They are certainly distinguished from those Midianites to whom Moses was related by marriage and from whom he received counsel. The Midianites being presented both as friends of God's people and as their enemies was just the sort of problem which exercised the ingenuity of the chroniclers.

129 The father-in-law of Moses is called Reuel at Exodus 2:18 and Jethro throughout Exodus 18.

130 On the right as one proceeds eastward from Cappadocia, that is, to the south. *In leva*, likewise, means to the north.

131 Pliny, *NH* 6.4.12, 14, 21.45.77, identifies the *Sanni*, also known as the *Sanicae* or *Sannigae*, as a people of Pontus; cf. Strabo, 12.3.18.

132 The River Absarrus and the fort of the same name in its gorge are mentioned by Pliny, *NH* 6.4.12. The translator apparently took παρεμβολή in the alternate sense of "a drawing up in battle order."

133 I presume that the *Chronicon Paschale* best preserves the original, but I cannot claim to have identified this Black Sea port.

134 Presumably "further to the north," not merely "to the north as well," in addition to the peoples listed already.

135 The final sentence of this paragraph does not appear in either the *Liber Generationis* or the *Chronicon Paschale*. The two peoples it mentions are unidentified.

136 Sinai, undoubtedly a very important mountain from the Christian point of view, seems to have been added by the chronicler (this phrase does not appear in the *Liber Generationis*) to his source, whose list of famous mountains might have originated in pagan literature (cf., e.g., Ampelius, *Liber memorialis* 6.6–7). The phrase *deo spiratum* is probably a translation of θεοπνεύστου [ὄρους], as restored by Ducange (see Frick, *Chronica Minora,* 219). Its literal sense, that "God breathed upon" the mountain (a more powerful image than my rendering might suggest) would secure Sinai's place among the truly important mountains.

137 Νυσαῖος is usually found as the adjective derived from Νῦσα, Mt. Nysa, the reputed—and variously located—birthplace of the god Dionysus.

138 *Lycabantus* is attested only in the *Excerpta*. Perhaps it is an error for Liguria.

139 Pelineon and Epos are the two mountain peaks on the island of Chios. Mimas is a mountain range on the Ionian mainland which terminates on the promontory of Argennum facing Chios.

140 There are actually forty-one rivers listed here. Perhaps the discrepancy is explained by the fact that the Danube and the Ister, the same river, are listed separately.

141 The Hebrew equivalents of the Indus and the Nile, as well as the inclusion of the Jordan, indicate the Christian composition or reworking of this list. Otherwise it represents a basic understanding of Mediterranean geography, centered on the Aegean.

142 The Pison (LXX: Φισών, Vulg.: *Phison*) is one of the rivers of Paradise at Genesis 2:11. Eusebius *(Onomasticon)* identifies this river with the Ganges.

143 The Gihon (LXX: Γεών, Vulg.: *Geon*), Hebrew for the Nile, is also one of the rivers of Paradise (Genesis 2:13).

144 The Tigris and the Euphrates are the third and fourth rivers of Paradise (Genesis 2:14).

145 Unidentified.

146 Presumably the river in southern Spain which gave its name to the province of Hispania Baetica, now the Guadalquivir.

147 Occurring very near the three-thousand-year midpoint of the six-thousand-year cosmic cycle, the dispersion of the nations in the time of Peleg is an important event, and this goes some way to explaining the attention lavished on it in the chronicle tradition.

148 The translator probably misread μετὰ Ἴναχον as μετὰ Ἰνάχου, and this should read "after Inachus" rather than "with Inachus."

149 It was Ehud who slew Eglon (Judges 3:15–30). *Naoth* in the text is perhaps a misreading of [τὸ]ν Ἀώδ, or from Anath (Ἀνὰθ) the father of Shemgar (Judges 3:31).

150 The translator has misunderstood Argos's epithet of *Panoptes* ("All-seeing"), from the legend that his body was covered in eyes (Apollod., *Bibl.* 2.1.2), to mean *providens* ("foreseeing," or just possibly "far-seeing").

151 According to Apollodorus (*Bibl.*, 1.7.1), Prometheus molded men out of water and earth (ἐξ ὕδατος καὶ γῆς ἀνθρώπους πλάσας); cf. Lucian, *Dial. D.* 5(1).1; Pausanias, 10.4.4. We have evidence, particularly from Egypt, that witches in the imperial period employed humanoid figurines made of various materials in performing binding spells, especially those with an erotic intent; see F. Graf, *Magic in the Ancient World* (Cambridge, Mass.: Harvard University Press, 1997), 136–47. Our text rejects both the literal sense of the assertion that Prometheus molded men as well as an explanation which would have made Prometheus a sorcerer, in favor of an entirely metaphorical interpretation which preserves both mundane plausibility and Prometheus's good reputation.

152 The Latin *phitonissa*, from *Pythonissa* and ultimately *Pytho(n)*, was used throughout the Middle Ages and survived in the Italian *fi-*

tonissa and *fitonéssa*. The term was generally used with reference to the mantic or clairvoyant powers of the witch.

153   Literally "lovable" rather than "admirable;" perhaps ἄριστος was read as ἀρεστός.

154   Apuleius, *Met.* 1.8, speaks of a witch in Thessaly who was able to "bring down the sky" *(caelum deponere)*. This seems to be related to some reputed power over celestial objects, since Lucan, 6.499–500, said that it was by the Thessalian witches that "the stars were first brought down from the sky headlong" *(illis et sidera primum/praecipiti deducta polo)*. There were precedents for such ideas in the Greek world. Aristophanes, *Clouds* 749–52, has one of his characters consider hiring a Thessalian witch "to pull down the moon" (καθέλοιμι . . . τὴν σελήνην) and lock it in a case.

155   Possibly a reference to the several mentions of Atlas in Euripides, *Ion* 1, *Hippolytus* 747, *Hercules Furens* 405, but not clearly reflecting any one of them.

156   Jabin was king of the Canaanites according to Judges 4:2.

157   Cecrops received his epithet of *Diphyes* ("Double-form"), which has been transliterated—incorrectly, as *Dipsyis*—but not translated, because he was supposed to have had the upper body of a man and the lower body of a serpent or dragon (Apollod., *Bibl.* 3.14.1). Diodorus (1.28.7) rationalizes this fabulous form by suggesting that the epithet *Diphyes* referred to Cecrops's double Greek and barbarian citizenship.

158   Zeeb, who appears along with Oreb in the next paragraph, has apparently fallen out of the text here, because *Madianitis* should be plural.

159   Cf. Judges 7:25, 8:10.

160   Our sources are agreed that Zeus was the father of Zethus and Amphion by Antiope; we should expect, then, the translator to be rendering Διός. *Zini* indicates there might have been some effort to suggest a "Zenus" as the father of Zethus and Amphion and that Zeus crept into the story by way of a corruption of names.

161   Although he did rule Thebes, Amphion was not a descendant of

Cadmus; rather he belonged to a usurping dynasty which interrupted the line of Cadmus at Thebes. See Apollod., *Bibl.* 3.5.4–5.

162 This is a confused rendering of Judges 10:1–2, which tells us that Tola was "the son of Puah, the son of Dodo, a man of Issachar; and he dwelt in Shamir in Mount Ephraim." What *iterum* can mean here is hard to tell, as Tola seems to have been a judge only once.

163 The translator has confused Ἴλιος, the name of the city of Ilium or Troy, and ἥλιος, the Greek word for the sun, which, without the breathing marks, would have had the same pronunciation. The confusion is consistent throughout the *Excerpta,* and the various contexts in which *solis* occurs make it clear that the translator knew he was writing about a city and that this city had the same name as the sun (see 1.3.2, 2.7.1). This has been conveyed in rendering the *Excerpta* translator's *solis* as "Sun City."

164 See Homer, *Iliad* 20.213–41, for the traditional genealogy of the Trojan kings.

165 Corrected from *Siamus* by Scaliger.

166 The Greek word σχολαστικός, though not its Latin derivative *scholasticus,* might mean "leisurely" as well as "scholarly."

167 "Their work" should have been translated "the Argonauts." The translator has apparently mistaken Ἀργοναυτῶν for ἔργον αὐτῶν, hence *opus illorum.*

168 A reference to the third-century BCE poet Apollonius of Rhodes, who wrote the *Argonautica.*

169 *Pronepos* means "great-grandson," but we should not suppose that the translator was attempting to impute some relation to Cronus and Zeus (Picus) other than the canonical one of father and son. It seems, rather, that he was misled by the use of the word προπάτωρ ("ancestor, forefather") for Cronus, which appears in Malalas (1.9) and was probably also found in the Greek original of the *Excerpta,* into thinking that *propater* below was a variant of *pater,* and *pronepus* likewise a variant for *filius.*

170 The division of the earth is not mentioned in the parallel version of the Picus-Zeus narrative in Malalas. This seems to be an ef-

fort on the part of the compiler of the Greek *Excerpta* to adapt the account to his own purposes, downplaying the potentially irrelevant Assyrian origins of the gods and emphasizing the role of the god-kings in the west. This is an aborted effort, since Picus's earlier career in Assyria is mentioned shortly. He may also be trying to implicate a division of the earth among the gods (*Oracula Sibyllina* 3.110–16; cf. *Iliad* 15.187–92) in the division of the earth among the sons of Noah, an important topic in the chronicle.

171 The translator uses *patria* as if it meant *terra propria* or *terra eius*. But Picus's *patria* ("fatherland") is, after all, Assyria. A usage which appears to be similar, however, occurs several times in the *Leges Visigothorum* (ed. K. Zeumer [Hanover: Hahn, 1902] *MGH, Leges* 1.1) to refer to Spain as the *patria* of the Visigoths (2.1.8 [Zeumer 53.10, 54.16, 19], 3.5.7 [165.7], 5.7.19 [243.19], 6.1.4 [252.1], 6.1.6 [255.18], 6.1.7 [256.14], 9.2.8 [370.25, 371.8, 22], 9.2.9 [374.6]), even though the Visigoths were quite aware of their identity as fairly recent immigrants to Spain; see W. Liebeschuetz, *The Decine and Fall of the Roman City* (Oxford: Oxford University Press, 2001), 354–68. Perhaps in the Latin of the Germanic kingdoms *patria* had come to mean the land one ruled or possessed quite as much as one's original homeland.

172 As Frick (p. 236) suggests, *avortivos faciebat* (lit. "he was making them turned aside *or* estranged") is probably an unsuccessful attempt to translate the Greek διέφθειρε ("he ruined *or* corrupted"). This could refer to Picus' skill at causing abortions.

173 Or perhaps "as it pleased them."

174 Frick suspected that *strenuus valde* ("very busy *or* brisk") was intended to translate πανοῦργος ("crafty, villainous").

175 The translator may have intended *suspitiones* as the derivative of the verb *suspicio,* "to look upward" (i.e., for the purposes of augury), or he may have meant it to be taken closely with *divinationes,* so as to suggest that Faunus's prophecies were nothing more than guesses or suppositions (Cicero, *De natura deorum* 1.23.62, 3.25.64, uses *suspicio* in this sense of "a notion or idea").

176 The translator offers a transliteration of the Greek πολυόλβιον

and then translates the same word with *multoditatum*, apparently a word of his own invention. Such a combination of transliteration and translation is found above at 1.1.3.

177   The dating of Picus-Zeus from Adam should probably be *"quattuor milia CC"* rather than *"quattuor milia C,"* the second hundred having never been included in the translation, or having fallen out of the text. When the regnal years in the *Excerpta* for Picus (80), Faunus (35), Heracles (38), and Latinus (18) are added together, there are 171 years; if we subtract a year for Aeneas to travel from Troy to Latium, and remember that the *Excerpta* assumes Latinus to have been killed in the conflict precipitated by Aeneas's arrival in Italy (1.6.3), we arrive at a figure of 170 years between the fall of Troy and the beginning of the reign of Picus. Troy is supposed to have fallen during the priesthood of Heli (Eli), which lasted from the year of Adam 4355 to 4375 (1.5.5, 7.1). This leaves a difference of 255–275 years to be made up between the fall of Troy and the beginning of the reign of Picus in the year of Adam 4100 (1.6.2). If, however, we propose that the *ab Adam* date originally assigned to the beginning of the reign of Picus was 4200, the difference would be a neat 155–175 years, and the 170 years from Picus to Troy derived from the regnal years of the Italian kings would fall within it.

Although numbers are particularly susceptible to corruption (especially a single figure, in a concatenation of similar figures, like our *C*), it is possible that the change from 4200 to 4100 was not a transcriptional error but a deliberate adjustment. Elsewhere in the *Excerpta* we find that Deborah and Barach were judges from the year of Adam 4,071 to 4,111 (1.5.3), in their time it is noted (1.5.3): *omnes de Dena scribuntur esse* (all those things written about De[na] [?] took place). Frick assumes this to be a translation of πάντες οἱ ἐκ Διὸς γράφονται εἶναι (Frick, 23); the original could have referred to the children of Zeus, but neither this meaning nor the identification of *Dena* as Zeus (assuming a variant form of the accusative and a *dz* pronunciation of ζ) is clear from the translation in the *Excerpta*. In the *Canons* of Eusebius, certain acts of Zeus were said to have happened during the reign of Ce-

crops (see *ann. Abr.* CCCCLXX, CCCCLXXXVI), who is also mentioned as contemporaneous in the *Excerpta*'s note on *Dena* (1.5.3); it is perhaps noteworthy that Cecrops is supposed to have ruled Athens for fifty years in both the *Canons* and the *Excerpta.* One of the main premises of the introduction to the *Canons* is also that neither Zeus nor any of the other gods is older than Cecrops. The *Dena* of the *Excerpta* is probably, therefore, Zeus. In that case, it is possible that an editor changed the *ab Adam* 4,200 date of Picus-Zeus to 4,100 to agree with the apparent synchronism of Zeus with Deborah and Barach. This would be particularly easy if he were working with the Latin text, in which no change but simply the excision of a single letter would have been necessary. The likelihood that the change was made after translation is greater, moreover, since in certain prominent Christian Latin works Picus is synchronized with Deborah: Augustine, *De civ. dei,* 18.15; Isidore Iun., *Chronica* 76 (MGH, AA, 11.436). But this is obviously not the original intent of the *Excerpta* compiler; if Picus-Zeus began his reign only eleven years before the judgeship of Deborah and Barach ended and his reign lasted eighty years, it would be ludicrous to say that the events of his reign were contemporary with them.

The Zeus of the chronography from which the synchronism with Deborah and Barach was taken was probably never identified with Picus. We should assume that the date for Picus (4,200 years from Adam) was discreetly derived from the regnal years of the Italian kings, the occurrence of the fall of Troy in the time of Heli, and the *ab Adam* dates for the priesthood of Heli by the *Excerpta* compiler.

178   The original Greek phrase mistranslated as *Latothibis* is preserved in Malalas, 6.16: ἐν Λατῷ τῆς Θηβαΐδος. The sentence should read "Heracles was born in Latus of the Thebaid."

179   *Alminius* is obviously a misreading of Ἀλκμήνης.

180   *Cum omnia sua* need mean nothing more than "with his all," but something seems to have been lost.

181   The text is badly garbled at this point. Frick assumes that *ex ipsa*

neocorum Aleu filia was intended to translate ἐξ Αὔγης τῆς τοῦ νεωκόρου Ἀλέου θυγατρός. It is not clear why Aleus, the king of Arcadia, should be called a νεώκορος ("temple servant"), unless it is a reference to his building of the sanctuary of Athena Alea at Tegea (Pausanias, 8.4.8).

182   In *Telefonum* the translator has added the Latin accusative ending (*-um*) to his transliteration of the Greek accusative (Τήλεφον).

183   Traditionally Aeneas was supposed to have founded Lavinium and named it after his wife, Lavinia, the daughter of Latinus.

184   The translator seems to have read ἔτη for ἔτει, so this would have been "in the nineteenth year after the destruction of Troy" in the Greek original.

185   Our text asserts that Aeneas succeeded Latinus upon the latter's death in the war against the Rutulians, and that this war, which is supposed to have commenced upon Aeneas's arrival in Italy, took place nineteen years after the fall of Troy. The figure of nineteen years is confirmed below, at 2.4.1. This makes the wanderings of Aeneas last for a surprisingly long time. Eusebius's *Chronicle* (*ann. Abr.* DCCCXL) has Aeneas come to rule the Latins three or eight years after the fall of Troy, and Syncellus (323) nine years afterward. I would suggest that the death of Latinus fighting the Rutulians (not part of Virgil's canonical version) and the interval between the fall of Troy and Aeneas's ascension are taken from two different sources and combined with no thought to their implications.

186   The colony founded by Ascanius was generally remembered as Alba Longa.

187   This foundation is not commonly recognized.

188   The authoritative list of the kings of Rome (Cic., *Rep.* 2.10–24; Livy, 1) ran as follows: Romulus, Numa Pompilius, Tullus Hostilius, Ancus Martius, Lucius Tarquinius Priscus, Servius Tullius, Lucius Tarquinius Superbus. The *Excerpta*'s list is inconsistent in many points but does maintain the traditional number at seven.

189   Cf. Epiphanius, *De pond. et mens.* fragmenta; Isid., *Etym.* 16.18.10; John of Nikiu, 57.3.

190   The *nomen* of this fictitious king may have been invented on the basis of the clan of Sergius, which was prominent in later periods of early Roman history.

191   *Aedificationes* should mean "houses" in the sense of "buildings," rather than that of "noble houses," but it would be an acceptable translation for the Greek οἶκοι, which could mean either.

192   See 1.5.5 above.

193   That is, the beginning of monarchy among the Israelites.

194   1 Samuel 4:11.

195   1 Samuel 7:1–2.

196   The translator's choice of words is odd. Singular like the μόσχος of the Septuagint, rather than the plural *boves* of the Vulgate (2 Samuel 6:6), but the young of the species, which is not implied by either biblical version.

197   2 Samuel 6:2–11. In the lacuna in our text there must have been some mention of Uzzah's attempt to steady the ark shaken by the faltering calf and a change of subject to the Lord, who punished Uzzah's sacrilegious temerity.

198   1 Chronicles 2:16.

199   2 Samuel 24, 1 Chronicles 21.

200   See 2 Chronicles 9:29.

201   *Dammulae* is found in the Vulgate (Isaiah 13:14) and actually means "little deer" (diminutive of *damma*), but must have been used here because of its resemblance to the Greek δαμάλεις ("heifers"), which is used in the Septuagint of the idols set up by Jeroboam in one instance (1 Kings 12:28; cf. 2 Chronicles 13:8), whereas the Vulgate refers to *vituli,* "calves."

202   Shemaiah, the prophet who addressed Rehoboam, is not given a patronymic in the Bible (1 Kings 12:22; 2 Chronicles 11:2, 12:5, 15), and it is by no means obvious where the chronicler found a name for his father.

203   2 Chronicles 16:12.

204   A "Jehu the son of Hanani" (LXX: Ἰοὺ υἱοῦ Ἀνανὶ) was active as a prophet in the time of Jehoshaphat (1 Kings 16:1, 7; 2 Chronicles 19:2, 20:34), but the Greek chronicler seems to have confused him with a contemporary, Obadiah (LXX: Ἀβδιοὺ), Ahab's righ-

teous officer who showed great reverence for Elijah (1 Kings 18:3–4, 7) and shared a name with one of the minor prophets.

205   In the original, "Zedekiah the son of Chenaanah"; see 2 Chronicles 18:23.

206   The chronicler has conflated two different biblical stories here: the drought in Israel at the behest of Elijah (1 Kings 17, 18) and the famine in the besieged city of Samaria in the time of Elisha (2 Kings 6:24–25).

207   Presumably the *Abdoneus* of the text is to be identified with the Jehonadab who was called upon to witness the zeal of Jehu, who killed Ahaziah (2 Kings 10:15–28).

208   The plural here, "of her sons," is an error.

209   This passage has become confused through, I assume, the carelessness rather than the intention of the translator. *Uxor* must be used of *Godolia,* and so should be *mater,* but the slip was probably made because of the appearance of *uxor* closely before and after this sentence. That *Ochozias* was his mother's son hardly needs to be indicated, so *filii* should probably be *regis.*

210   "After these things" is the correct translation of *post haec,* but considering the chronicler's habit of introducing a new ruler with reference to the last one and the translator's lax grammar, it is possible that *post haec* refers to Athaliah and should be rendered "after her."

211   2 Chronicles 24:20–22, Matthew 23:35, Luke 11:51.

212   This phrase has been taken to mean that Jotham in his capacity as judge did not permit his leprous father to occupy the throne, but it could also mean that while Uzziah allowed his son to serve as regent, he did not allow him to actually assume the kingship. See 2 Kings 15:5, 2 Chronicles 26:21.

213   Jonah's hometown is not named in the Bible. Perhaps the chronicler added this note because the Ninevites, to whom Jonah preached, and the people of Sodom and Gomorrah are both mentioned in Christ's various predictions concerning the Day of Judgment (Matthew 10:15, 12:41).

214   The Latin text of the *Excerpta* consistently designates the high priest in Jerusalem the *princeps sacerdotum,* undoubtedly a translation of the Greek ἀρχιερεύς. The Vulgate offers various words

and phrases for the chief priest of the Jews: *sacerdos magnus* (see, e.g., Numbers 35:26), *pontifex* (Numbers 35:28; John 11:49, 51; Hebrews 4:14), *sacerdos primus* (2 Kings 25:18), *summus sacerdos* (Mark 14.47), but *primus sacerdotum* is favored by what might be considered the most historically and chronologically helpful of the gospels, Matthew (26:3) and Luke (3:2), and the Acts (4:6); the translator's choice was probably not altogether accidental. The phrase "high priest," customary in English, has been preferred to the more literal "chief of the priests."

215 In writing *illa prima olympiada venit ad Grecis*, the translator apparently misread ἦλθε for ἤχθη. The sentence would more correctly read "the first Olympiad took place among the Greeks."

216 Perhaps it is the two tribes of Judah and Benjamin who are destined to rule, rather than David.

217 2 Kings 23:14,16; 2 Chronicles 34:4–5.

218 The reference to the "keeper of the wardrobe" identifies *Elibasillim* as the prophetess Huldah the wife of Shallum (LXX: Ὄλδαν τὴν προφῆτιν γυναῖκα Σελλήμ), the keeper of the wardrobe in the time of Josiah (2 Kings 22:14; 2 Chronicles 34:22). It seems that the name of wife and husband have been compounded in *Elibasillim*, and then someone has taken the initiative to include Huldah again in this passage.

219 Unfamiliar with the Greek term λορδός, "bent backward," the translator has taken the word as a surname, *Lurdus*, for *Ananias*.

220 I.e., Necho.

221 Presumably this figure is to be identified with the father of Ezekiel; Ezekiel 1:3.

222 This sentence is copied wholesale from the earlier mention of Shalmaneser deporting the people of Israel to "Media and Babylon." The Bible speaks of Shalmaneser deporting the Israelites to Assyria and "the cities of the Medes" (2 Kings 17:6, 18:11) but does not mention Babylon, and of Nebuchadnezzar deporting the Jews to Babylon (2 Kings 24:14–16, 25:11; 2 Chronicles 36:20; Ezra 2:1). Both the repetition of phrasing in regard to Assyrian and Babylonian acts and the mingling of destinations are consistent with the confusion of eastern empires characteristic of the *Excerpta*.

223 The translator seems to have taken *ligamen* ("a tie or bandage") as a synonym for *vinculum*.

224 The translator apparently mistook ἐπρήσθη ("was burned down") for ἐπράθη ("was sold").

225 An extrabiblical tradition maintained that on Nebuchadnezzar's entry into Jerusalem, Habakkuk fled to the undistinguished town of Ostracina on the Mediterranean coast of eastern Egypt; *Vitae Prophetarum* 12.3.

226 This must refer to the vision of Daniel 9:20–27, which speaks of the restoration of Jerusalem and counts time in "weeks," but Daniel was supposed to have seen this vision in the first, not the fifth, year of Darius (Daniel 9:1).

227 Eusebius in the *Praeparatio Evangelica* (10.10.3–6) quotes Africanus to establish a synchronism of the fifty-fifth Olympiad, the accession of Cyrus, and the return of the Jews from exile; see M. Wallraff et al., eds., *Iulius Africanus, Chronographiae: The Extant Fragments* (Berlin: Walter de Gruyter, 2007), 72–74 (F 34). But the rebuilding of the temple is not mentioned in this passage. The source for the note in our chronicle seems to be Eusebius, *Chronicle, ann. Abr.* MCCCCLVII, which includes some mention of the temple along with the synchronism: *qui constructo altari templi fundamenta iecerunt.*

228 According to Herodotus's famous story (1.86–88), Croesus was condemned to death by Cyrus but saved by the miraculous intervention of Apollo. Ancient accounts of the fate of Croesus differed, however, and this passage may preserve a version in which Cyrus slew the Lydian king; see J. A. S. Evans, "What Happened to Croesus?" *Classical Journal* 74 (1978): 34–40.

229 The translator has mistaken νόθος ("bastard") for νωθής or νωθρός ("stupid"). *Nothos* was a nickname usually applied to Darius II Ochus, but at some point it has been decided that Darius Nothos and Darius Ochus were two different people, and the nickname of *Nothos* applied to Darius I, the son of Hystaspes, who was unrelated to Cyrus.

230 Syncellus (301.13–20) relates Xerxes's adventures in Greece in the following terms: τὰς Ἀθήνας ἐνέπρησε . . . δεινῶς πράξας μόλις

ἐπάνεισιν εἰς τὰ οἰκεῖα (he burned Athens . . . he did poorly and barely returned home). The original must have employed a similar phrase, and the translator seems to have misread μόλις ἐπάνεισιν ("barely returned") as μόλις ἔπνευσαν ("breathed with difficulty"). Perhaps the translator assumed that *suspiriosus* ("breathing with difficulty") might have the connotation of "frustrated."

231 Perhaps based on Daniel 9:25, but the derivation is not clear.

232 The seven and seventy weeks are taken from the prophecy of Daniel 9:24–27. Africanus interpreted the "weeks" as seven-year periods and the seventy "weeks" as 490 years, beginning from the rebuilding of the temple in Jerusalem under Nehemiah and ending with the Crucifixion and Resurrection of Christ; Wallraff, *Iulius Africanus,* 236–39 (F 78).

233 Sogdianus (Sekyndianos) was one of the bastard sons of Artaxerxes I who briefly held the throne in the bloody turmoil following Artaxerxes's death in 424; Ctesias (ed. Lenfant), *Pers.* F 15 §§ 47–50 (= Photius, *Bibl.* 72, pp. 41b–42b); Manetho, ed. Waddell FF 70–71, *FGrH* 609 FF 2, 3a, 3b; Diod. Sic., 12.71.1.

234 The epithet *Mnemon* is usually applied not to Darius II but to his son Artaxerxes II; see below.

235 I.e., Diagoras.

236 The Greek epithet of Artaxerxes II, Mnemon, is transliterated as a rule, but the translator has rendered it into Latin along with the rest of the text.

237 "Architect" (οἰκοδόμος) is an error for "comedian" (κωμῳδός).

238 The notion of Macedonian rule in Asia at this date is proleptic.

239 There were two high priests in Jerusalem between Eliashib and Jaddua, namely Jehoiada (Judas) and John (Joseph., *AJ* 11.297–301), as in the list of high priests below. The second Jehoiada here seems to be a mistake for John, but it may also be influenced by a source which did not recognize John's priesthood because of his sacrilegious fratricide.

240 On Alexandrian references to Alexander as "the Founder" (ὁ κτίστης), not uncommon in the imperial period, see P. M. Fraser, *Ptolemaic Alexandria* (Oxford: Clarendon, 1972), II: 360 n. 182.

241 On the tradition of Alexander's visit to Jerusalem, see S. Cohen, "Alexander the Great and Jaddus the High Priest According to Josephus," *AJS Review* 7 (1982): 41–68, esp. 59.

242 What follows is a version of part of the *Liber de Morte Testamentoque Alexandri Magni,* which appears to have originally been written in 317 BCE as a propaganda pamphlet for the party of Polyperchon in the disputes among Alexander's successors and was incorporated into the body of legendary material on the Macedonian conqueror, and particularly the *Alexander Romance;* see W. Heckel, *The Last Days and Testament of Alexander the Great: A Prosopographic Study* (Stuttgart: Franz Steiner, 1988).

243 Frick, 271, is surely correct in suggesting that *scriba memoratum* is intended to render ὑπομνηματογράφον, the term used of Eumenes in the version of Alexander's will in the *Alexander Romance* (3.33.14). Readers of the original Greek might have drawn a connection between Eumenes as ὑπομνηματογράφος and the important Alexandrian civic office holder who bore the same title; see Strabo, 17.1.12; P. Fraser, *Ptolemaic Alexandria* (Oxford: Clarendon, 1972), II: 182 n. 54, 189 n. 82; D. Delia, *Alexandrian Citizenship during the Roman Principate* (Atlanta: Scholars Press, 1991) 104–5.

244 In the other versions of the *Testament,* territory in India is granted to Porus, the defeated Indian king, but the Pytho of our text seems to be Peithon, the son of Agenor, who was in charge of territories on the borders of India; see Heckel, *Last Days and Testament of Alexander,* 65.

245 In the *Alexander Romance* (3.33.22), Oxydraces is identified with the father of Rhoxane, the wife of Alexander, more commonly known as Oxyartes.

246 Carmania is the portion of Tlepolemus in the *Alexander Romance* (3.33.22). The translator seems eager to find some familiar country in the territories of Alexander's empire, and it would not have been unreasonable to assume that conquests which stretched to the Pillars of Hercules also included Germany.

247 As in the list of famous rivers above (1.3.3). The Halys is mentioned in the bequest to Antigonus in the *Alexander Romance* (3.33.15).

248 Unlike the appearance of Germany above, inclusion of Spain in Alexander's empire does not seem to be the result of a mistake on the part of the translator. The *Excerpta's* source on Alexander has already said that his empire stretched from the Caspian Gates to the Pillars of Hercules and so would naturally include Spain. Antipater has had to be added to the beneficiaries of Alexander's will in order to accommodate this fabulous extension to his empire. It is, however, impossible to say what river is intended by the "Halys," whose namesake flows in Asia Minor.

249 On this list of cities and its place in the legendary history of Alexander, see P. M. Fraser, *Cities of Alexander the Great* (Oxford: Clarendon, 1996), 1–46.

250 From this point on the high priests of the Jews are synchronized with the Ptolemaic kings of Egypt, but the synchronisms are generally inaccurate; see S. Cohen, "Sosates, the Jewish Homer," *Harvard Theological Review* 74 (1981): 392–95.

251 As above (1.8.3), this is Menander the comic playwright (κωμῳδός), not the house builder (οἰκοδόμος).

252 From his accession Ptolemy XII Auletes ("the Fluteplayer"), the father of Cleopatra VII, bore the title *Neos Dionysus.*

253 On this otherwise unknown Hellenistic Jewish poet, see Cohen, "Sosates, the Jewish Homer."

254 P. Fraser, *Ptolemaic Alexandria* (Oxford: Clarendon, 1972), I: 17–20, surmises that the Pharos was largely constructed under Ptolemy I Soter (305–282 BCE).

255 Perhaps literally "kingdom," but this would hardly be appropriate for a power ruled by patriarchs, judges, and prophets.

256 In our Latin text the construction of this clause switches abruptly from passive to active. I have not tried to reproduce the translator's indecision.

257 Asia was, as the earlier narrative (1.6.1) indicates, the point of departure for Picus, and it further suggests that in Asia his name

was Ninus and he was called Picus when he came to Italy. Asia here, instead of Italy, represents a simple error in the original text or the translation.

258 The chronicle insists upon Semiramis-Rhea's unpleasant character at 1.6.1, but even there does not identify any of her outrages.

259 As Scaliger noted, the translator read a phrase perfectly consistent with the traditional Assyrian king list, Ἴτα or εἴτα Σφαῖρος ("then Sphaerus"), as two names, Ἴτας Φαῖρος.

260 This king, *Bellepares* in Jerome's translation of Eusebius's *Chronicle* (*ann. Abr.* DCVIII), usually appears as "Balatores."

261 Eusebius's *Chronicle* (*ann. Abr.* DCCCCLIII) has Eupales in this position as the thirtieth king of the Assyrians, but Syncellus (301) has "Eupacmes" in this same position as the thirty-fifth king of the Assyrians.

262 Sardanapallus is usually remembered, often in rather lurid and dramatic terms, as the last of the Assyrian kings. The appearance here of a successor named Ninus may be due to the corruption of a computation of reigns or years of the Assyrian kingdom from the first king, Ninus, to the last, set after the notice of the reign of Sardanapallus as in Eusebius's *Chronicle* (*ann. Abr.* MCXCVII).

263 Frick suspected that this phrase was originally a caption in smaller letters, but it may just as well have been a "concluding title" at the foot of a section.

264 Colloquial and inconsistent with the intended tenor of the chronicle, no doubt, but "will do" is the most apt translation of *faciam*.

265 Sosinosirim must represent some corruption in the rendering of the Greek text or transmission of the Latin, but it is impossible to determine just what the original might have been.

266 I.e., "ruler of the city."

267 Greek: ἡμίθεοι.

268 The text has been rendered as a reader of the Latin translation might have made sense of it, but it must be conceded that there is little enough sense to be found here. Frick, 287, plausibly reconstructed the Greek text as follows:

α΄. Πρῶτα Ἄνουβισ ἐτ. πγ΄.

β΄. Μετὰ τοῦτον Ἀμουσίν ⟨φασί τινες βασιλεῦσαι, ὃν⟩ Ἀπίων ὁ γραμματικὸς ὁ καὶ τὰς Αἰγυπτίων γραφὰς συνθεὶς κατὰ Ἴναχον ἑρμηνεύει τὸν ἐπ᾽ Ἀργείων ἀρχῆς βασιλεύσαντα, ἐτ. ξζ΄.

(1. First Anubis, 83 years.

2. After him some say Amosis reigned, whom Apion the grammarian who compiled the Egyptian records explains as a contemporary of Inachus who ruled the Argives at the beginning, 67 years.)

269 The translator has misunderstood a reference to the *Nekyes,* "the Dead, or the Corpses," who were recognized as one of the dynasties which ruled Egypt in earliest times.

270 Frick assumed that there would have been some mention of the mortal kings of Egypt at this point and that the 2,100 years referred to them.

271 If the translator had read the original correctly, this phrase would read "Inachus was the first to reign in Argos."

272 Perhaps intended to translate "Lynceus the son of Aegyptus."

273 For the place of this chronological relation in the context of Porphyry's work, see A.-Ph. Segonds, "Les fragments de l'Histoire de la Philosophie" in Porphyre, *Vie de Pythagore, Lettre à Marcella,* ed. E. des Places (Paris: Belles Lettres, 1982), 179; Porphyrius, *Fragmenta,* ed. A. Smith (Stuttgart: Teubner, 1993), 224.

274 The preponderance of the tradition maintains that Agamemnon returned home immediately after the fall of Troy and was killed upon his arrival by Clytemnestra and Aegisthus. How and why the variant offered here arose is difficult to say.

275 See Wallraff, *Iulius Africanus,* 138–45 (F 51).

276 Literally "diminishment," but a discussion of reigns must call for something more definite.

277 Should be "979."

278 Or perhaps "of Carnium"(?).

279 As it stands, this sentence makes no sense. Working from Scaliger's suggestion that in *Osuch* the translator misunderstood the introduction of a relative clause (ὃς οὐχ) as a name, Frick recon-

structed the original Greek as follows: ὃς οὐχ ὑπομείνας τὴν δαπάνην ἔφυγεν ([Charidemus,] who, not enduring the expense, fled). Even so, the intent of the sentence is not clear. It is by no means obvious that the original of *cibaria* ("food, victuals, rations") was δαπάνη, and the phrase in the Greek chronicle might have been something like "[Charidemus,] who, not maintaining(?) the food, fled." It would seem that as governing priest Charidemus failed to make provision for a famine and evaded the consequences. It would further seem that Charidemus's failure and flight brought about the demise of the institution of ruling priests at Sicyon.

280   Cecrops is described above (1.5.3) as particularly tall in order to explain his epithet of *Diphyes* ("Double-form").

281   Cranaus should precede Amphictyon, with a reign of nine years.

282   In Greek στοιχεῖον could refer to a letter of the alphabet, undoubtedly the intention of the original chronicle, and στοῖχος could be a line of poetry, apparently the source of the translator's misunderstanding.

283   Two years is required; cf. Eusebius, *Chronicle* (*ann. Abr.* MCCLXIII).

284   Presumably *Helladices* (as above, 2.3.1) has been read as *Hellenes* ("Greeks").

285   See 1.6.3.

286   *Imperium* rather than *regnum* seems to be used proleptically of the dominion of the Romans, since at this point they are ruled by kings and do not hold power over any foreign territories. *Romanorum imperium* may also appear here on account of force of habit.

287   The proper meaning of *diffamabatur* is "maligned," but the translator seems to have been misled, perhaps by such verbs as *differre* and *diffundere,* into thinking that it had some such sense as we have given it, as demanded by the context.

288   The translator rendered ἀρχὴν erroneously in the sense of "beginning" (*initium*), rather than correctly in that of "kingdom, or rule" (*regnum*).

289 The MS begins the numbering with this introductory line and in order to correct this mistake does not number Labotes.

290 Scaliger's suggestion that *Cemenelaus* is a corruption of καὶ Μενέλαος has been accepted by many scholars, but R. Ball, "'Menelaos' in the Spartan Agiad King-List," *Classical Quarterly* n.s. 27 (1977): 312–16, has advanced the theory that *Cemenelaus* is an interpolated invention (like Francus Siluius in 1.6.4, 2.4.1) related to the city of Cemenelum in southern Gaul.

291 See G. Huxley, "Automedon in the Slavonic Malalas," *Rivista di Filologia e di Istruzione Classica* 113 (1985): 304–6.

292 Correctly, "21st."

293 Correctly, "16th."

294 Frick, *Chronica Minora*, 306, suggests that the translator mistook ἐν τῇ ἑκατοστῇ πεντηκοστῇ τρίτῃ for ἔτη ἕκαστος τῇ πεντηκοστῇ τρίτῃ. The phrase would therefore properly be rendered "it ceased in the 153rd Olympiad."

295 Correctly, "2."

296 Properly "Amyntas again."

297 Amyntas and his six-year reign seem to have been transposed from before Argaius, cf. Eusebius, *Chron.* ann. Abr. MDCXVIII.

298 Correctly, "12."

299 Correctly, "42."

300 Properly, "Miles."

301 Correctly, "53."

302 Cf. Eusebius, *Chron. ann. Abr.* MCCXXVI, which has a thirty-year reign for Sosarmus.

303 Eusebius, *Chron. ann. Abr.* MCCLVI has "Madydus."

304 Or perhaps "the Great."

305 For the epithets of Darius and Artaxerxes, see 1.8.2–3 above and notes.

306 Note that Darius, mentioned in the preface to this list, has not been mentioned in the list itself. This is probably due to the misnumbering (Sogdianus in ninth place, but marked as "10"); there are fourteen kings in the Persian king list, and when "14" was reached the copyist or translator stopped. When the

appropriate corrections have been made to the regnal years, a subtraction from the total noted leaves six years for the reign of Darius, which is the length of reign assigned to Darius above (1.8.4).

307   *Nicanor* for *Nicator* also appears in the Greek chronicles, e.g., Syncellus (520).

308   The chronicler has assumed that "Caesar" was a princely title, as it was in his own day, rather than Gaius Julius's proper cognomen. The ignominious dissolution of the Seleucid kingdom in 64 BCE was actually accomplished under Caesar's rival, Pompey.

309   Considering certain Hellenistic theories of apotheosis, such a term, rather than "death," could be significant.

310   The address to God as "Only Prince," an addition to Alexander's prayer as it is found previously in the *Excerpta* (1.8.4), seems to be intended to suggest Alexander's imperfect understanding of God or to reveal the Christian origin of this story. *Princeps* in the Vulgate (and what Frick considered its Greek original, ἄρχων, in the Septuagint) is not a word used of God. It is used of the angelic powers that belong to nations (Daniel 10:13–21) and, in the Septuagint, at least, of the gods of the Gentiles (Leviticus 20:5). In the New Testament it is used of Satan as the "prince of devils" (Matthew 9:34) and "prince of this world" (John 12:31, 14:30, 16:11). Alexander addressing God in such terms might imply that although he worshipped God and recognized him as *solus,* he still did not make a proper distinction between the God of the Jews and the pagan gods he had worshipped previously. While *princeps* and ἄρχων are not used of God the Father, these terms are used in Isaiah's prophecy of the Messiah (9:6) and of Jesus Christ as "prince of the kings of this earth" (Apocalypse 1:5). There are both Jewish and Christian accounts of the visit of Alexander to Jerusalem, but whereas it might not have occurred to a Jewish author to have the Godhead addressed as *princeps/* ἄρχων, the Christians had authoritative precedent for such an address, and perhaps particularly appropriate precedent in the Apocalypse.

311   The exactions of Antiochus were not, of course, limited to a de-

mand that the Jews speak Greek. Scaliger proposed that *Greca loquutione coegebat* represents the translator's attempt to render ἑλληνίζειν ἠνάγκαζεν.

312   This passage indicates an interpretation of Daniel 9:24–27 inconsistent with that of Africanus referred to above (1.8.2), perhaps an entirely Jewish one. The 483 years work out very neatly if they begin with the first year of Cyrus's reign (559 BCE) and end with the death of Alexander Jannaeus in 76 BCE. The significance of 69 BCE, the completion of seventy "weeks," is harder to discern.

313   The translator has taken Salina as a man's name (see *post hunc* beginning the next entry) and indicated that he reigned along with his wife, Alexandra. In fact Salina (Salome) Alexandra was the widow of Aristobulus who made Alexander Janneus king, married him, and ruled in her own right after the death of her second husband; see Josephus, *AJ* 13.12.1, 16.1 (320, 405–7). So this entry is probably intended to render an original which read "After them his wife Salina (Salome) or Alexandra reigned."

314   The translator has misread νωθής/νωθρός for Ὄθων.

315   The reign of Vespasian has been transposed from its proper place following this line to item 14 below.

316   The reign of Vespasian should precede item 6 (Titus) above.

317   The Latin text's *Calerianus* is presumably a corruption of "Gallienus."

318   The annual limitation of the consulship was not, of course, an innovation of Caesar's, but rather one of the oldest institutions of the Roman Republic; see Cic., *Rep.* 2.31–32 (55–56); Livy, 1.60.3, 2.1.7–9.

319   The list of consuls which follows is woefully corrupt. I have not attempted to indicate every error or to explain every deviation from the canonical consular lists. Where names are corrupt but recognizable, I have corrected them. Where the text offers erroneous but plausible misreadings, I have transcribed the name in the text but given the putative original in square brackets. I have not indicated where the text appears to offer altogether imaginary consuls, but simply included their names along with

the authentic ones. Where possible I have given the year of the Christian era (BCE or CE) which corresponds to the consular year in square brackets after the entry, indicating BCE/CE where necessary and in the notes where all dates may be assumed to be either BCE or CE. Where the names of consuls have been taken from two different consular years, I give both years in the order in which the names appear in the entry.

320 In late antiquity, both *clarissimus* and *illustris* were not merely respectful descriptors but official titles corresponding to specific dignities.

321 Unless otherwise noted, dates are BCE from this point on.

322 The names of the first consuls, who according to tradition served in 509 BCE, are inexplicably interjected here.

323 Two individuals have been made out of L. Munatius Plancus, consul with M. Aemelius Lepidus in 42 BCE.

324 Frick conjectured that the translator mistook Κοκίου (Cocceius) for υἱοῦ.

325 Lit. "Cartagena," but it seems obvious that the translator was rendering the name of Carthage, which was resettled in the reign of Augustus.

326 See Luke 1:11.

327 The story of an annunciation by an angel to Elizabeth does not occur in the Bible or in any identifiable apochryphal work. Note that the annunciation to Elizabeth is supposed to occur on the same day of the year, though not in the same year, as the Annunciation to Mary.

328 See Luke 1:26, 27.

329 A close paraphrase of parts of the Vulgate, Luke 1:39–44. Cf. *Protevangelium Jacobi* 12.3–5.

330 On this date for the Incarnation, see G. Ogg, "Hippolytus and the Introduction of the Christian Era," *Vigiliae Christianae* 16 (1962): 13.

331 This sentence seems hopelessly corrupt. Its provenance and significance are apparently impossible to reconstruct.

332 The dating of the Incarnation 5500 years after the Creation ultimately depends on Africanus; Wallraff, *Iulius Africanus*, 24–25

(F 15), 274–75 (T 92), 288–89 (T 93c). His millennarian scheme placed the birth of Christ in the middle of the last of the thousand-year "days" before the millennial sabbath.

333 Unless otherwise noted, dates are CE from this point on.

334 This is the earliest known instance of the names of the Magi or the Three Wise Men; Matthew 2:1–12.

335 See Matthew 2:3, 16.

336 Some, but not all, of the elaborations on biblical material which appear here are taken from the so-called *Protevangelium Jacobi* or "Infancy Gospel of James," in this case *Protevan. Jac.* 23.

337 Cf. *Protevan. Jac.* 22.5–8.

338 Cf. *Protevan. Jac.* 24.11–14.

339 A partial quotation of the Vulgate, Luke 2:26, 29–32.

340 Although Asiaticus and Silanus were consuls in 46, another Silanus served as consul with Nerva in 28. The note here was probably intended to refer to this earlier consulate.

341 This refers to the institution of the Eucharist following the Last Supper; see Matthew 26:26–29, Mark 14:22–25, Luke 22:19–20.

342 The text seems to be corrupt at this point, since Christ was supposed to have been betrayed on the same night as the Last Supper, that is, the day before his crucifixion. The emendation would require only a single stroke being added to the *viii* here to make it agree with the *viiii* above.

343 See Matthew 26:69–75, esp. v. 73; cf. John 18.

344 A source cannot be offered for a number of the details added here to the biblical narrative, particularly the names of otherwise anonymous characters.

345 Tiberius did not actually serve a sixth consulship.

346 The tamarisk is one of a number of trees that have gone under the name of the "Judas tree" and is often associated with Judas in folklore; see D. Watts, *Elsevier's Dictionary of Plant Lore* (Amsterdam: Elsevier, 2007), 215.

347 There seems to be some confusion here. The martyrdom of Stephen was commemorated on December 26 from the late fourth century, and Epiphany was likewise celebrated on January 6. Eleven days after December 26 would be January 6. Perhaps the

count of eleven days is supposed to include December 26, or *pridie Epiphaniae* ("on the day before Epiphany") is a corrupt form of *die Epiphaniae* ("on the day of Epiphany").

348 More correctly, "14 years." Perhaps the *x* has fallen out of *xiiii*.

349 As with Claudius's above, the length of Nero's reign should be "14 years," not "4 years." It is likely, once again, that *iiii* is a corruption of *xiiii*.

350 There is a fairly lengthy gap in the text at this point. What material, besides a consular list, was included under the almost two hundred years covered by the missing portion we cannot say, but it seems likely that it was little more than the brief notices on the deaths and accessions of emperors and on Church history which are found in the surviving portions.

351 The very similar names of various members of the Flavian dynasty seem to have confused the translator or a later scribe. In our translation, the erroneous name in the text is given in *italics* and followed by the—sometimes presumably—correct name in square brackets.

352 Cf. Eusebius, *HE* 7.32, 9.6; see T. Vivian, *St. Peter of Alexandria, Bishop and Martyr* (Philadelphia: Fortress, 1988).

353 This word seems inexplicable. The Latin adjective means "of the camp," but that does not elucidate what it means here. It may be intended to indicate that a garrison was imposed upon Alexandria once Diocletian retook the city from a rebel army after the siege of 297–98; see D. van Berchem, *L'Armée de Dioclétien et la réforme constantinienne* (Paris: Imprimerie Nationale/Librairie Orientaliste Paul Geuthner, 1952), 61–63. But the benevolent sense of *donatus est* and the coupling with Diocletian's building of a bath complex suggest a benefaction to the city. Perhaps this is a reference to the Alexandrian grain dole instituted by Diocletian (Procopius, *HA* 26.41; cf. Eutropius, 9.23) and *castrisius* is somehow related to the *castrensis modius,* a grain measure used in Egypt.

354 Unlike Diocletian, Constantius did not in fact retire; rather he died in office and on campaign in York on July 25, 306. It is possible that "he went away and settled in Byzantium" *(abiens sedit in Bizantio)* is a corruption of "he went off and died in Britain" *(abi-*

ens obiit in Britannia), or perhaps the circumstances of Constantius's life have simply been confused with those of his son, who did indeed end his days in the vicinity of the city he refounded. Alternatively, there is no corruption here at all, and we have evidence of a tradition which associated Constantius, quite as much as his son, with the establishment of Byzantium. There is further evidence of the circulation of such a tradition in Egypt. John of Nikiu (77.42) states that Constantius "built the city of Byzantium" before his death.

355   Maximian was not related by blood to Diocletian but was Caesar to his Augustus.

356   Constantine first promoted his sons to the office of Caesar in 317, some years after the suicide of Maximian in 310. The chronicle seems to stress the collegiality of the house of Constantine.

357   Licinius was actually the brother-in-law of Constantine, the husband of his half-sister Constantia. Constantine's "fifth" son, who has fallen out of this list, would have been Constans — his youngest son, in fact.

358   I.e., Valerius Licinianus Licinius, the son of Constantine's rival.

359   Most of the Egyptian calendar dates given in the *Excerpta* are unproblematic, but in this instance the 8th of the calends of December should be the 28th of Hathyr and the 17th of Thoth should be the 18th of the Kalends of October.

360   Until quite recently the English word "symbol" could intelligibly be used in a sense precisely the same as that of *symbolus* here, that is, "a creed, confession, or statement of faith."

361   Cf. *Chronicon Athanasianum,* preface.

362   See D. Woods, "The Date of the Translation of the Relics of SS. Luke and Andrew to Constantinople," *Vigiliae Christianae* 45 (1991): 286–92, esp. n. 2.

363   Constantine died on May 22, 337. By this time his "five sons," mentioned here and identified earlier, had been reduced to three. Constantine had ordered the executions of Licinius in 325 and of his own son Crispus in 326.

364   The "new Constantine" must be Gallus (Flavius Claudius Constantius Gallus), the brother of Julian, who during his tenure as Caesar (351–354) served three times as consul with Constantius

II. The chronicler or the translator seems to have confused him with Constantine II (or Constantinus), the son of Constantine who ruled as senior Augustus from 337 to 340.

365   It is not altogether clear what is being referred to here. The latest *ludi saeculares* were due to be celebrated in 314 but were neglected by Constantine. The reign of Romulus falls one thousand years before this date in the chronicle, so the reference may be to a recalculated foundation date for Rome. "From the 532nd year" of what, however, remains to be determined.

366   The date agrees with that of an earthquake and subsequent tidal wave in 365 referred to in the *Chronicon Athanasianum* 37. Ammianus Marcellinus (26.10.15–19) describes in great detail how an earthquake in the first consulate of Valentinian and Valens (365) was followed by the retreat of the waters and then their violent return, causing considerable damage and loss of life; he mentions Alexandria specfically. Socrates (*Hist. eccl.* 4.3) also speaks of an earthquake and subsequent tidal waves in the same consulate, and John of Nikiu (82.21–23) recounts that in the days of Valens the sea rose against Alexandria and the city was saved from an inundation only by the prayerful intercession of Saint Athanasius.

367   The twenty-seventh of Epeiph would correspond to the twelfth of the calends of August.

368   From about 380, the chief civil official of the province of Egypt, formerly the *praefectus Aegypti,* was styled the *praefectus Augustalis.* The Index to the Festal Letters of Athanasius (*Chronicon Athanasianium*), written not long after the bishop's death, also gives dates with reference to the prefects of Egypt; see P. Schaff and H. Wace, eds., *Nicene and Post-Nicene Fathers, Second Series* (Grand Rapids: Eerdmans, 1890) IV: 500–506.

369   Frick conjectured that here and below *praeses* was employed to render the Greek ἔπαρχος, which, when translating a Roman title, was regularly used for *praefectus.* And each of the men referred to as a *praeses* in the *Excerpta,* with the possible exception of Bassianus, is known to have been a prefect of Egypt. The *praesides* were in fact subordinate officials in charge of the dioceses within the province of Egypt.

370 That is, the time-servers of Alexandria joined the Arian party to please the incumbent prefect. During the reign of Valens (364–378) the Arians enjoyed imperial favor and ecclesiastical ascendancy, and the persecution of the Nicene faithful in Egypt was extensive; see Theodoret, *Hist. Eccl.* 4.19; John of Nikiu, 82.17–18. The martyrdom of Dorotheus is also mentioned by Theophanes (a.m. 5870), but that chronicler's most recent translators suggest this Dorotheus may be a doublet for the possibly fictional Dorotheus of Tyre supposedly martyred in the reign of Julian; *The Chronicle of Theophanes Confessor: Byzantine and Near Eastern History AD 284–813,* trans. C. Mango and R. Scott (Oxford: Clarendon, 1997), 101 n. 8.

371 Valentinian did die on campaign against the Quadi and Sarmatians who had invaded Pannonia (for which "Campania" is probably an error), but he died not in battle but of a stroke, while berating the emissaries of the enemy; see Ammianus Marcellinus, 30.6.1–6. According to Ammianus, he died on November 18, 375.

372 According to John of Nikiu (82.20), Tatian built two stone gates for "the passage of the great river" at an unidentified place called Abrâkjûn in the Ethiopic text.

373 In fact, in this year the senior emperor Valens was serving his fifth consulship, and his nephew, Valentinian II, the son of Valentinian, was his colleague.

374 This date agrees with *Chronicon Athanasianum* 45.

375 The preposition in the Latin text is *sub,* a translation of the Greek ὑπό, which we have generally translated "in the time of" or "under." In this case and once again below the sense of ὑπό, indicating means or agency, called for the Latin preposition *a,* but the translator made no distinction and rendered ὑπό with *sub.* The import of the putative Greek original is discovered if "under" is replaced with "by."

376 "Under" should be "by," as above.

377 Cf. Theophanes Confessor, a.m. 5879.

378 This phrase is perhaps intentionally vague and ambiguous. In Theophilus's episcopate the Serapeum was destroyed, but Theophilus was no less vigorous in his efforts against Christians he deemed heretical than against pagans.

Bibliography

APOCALYPSE OF PSEUDO-METHODIUS

The following list is intended to be a thorough, if not necessarily exhaustive, guide to the current scholarship on Pseudo-Methodius accessible to the English reader, as well as important studies in other languages and some older works that remain fundamental. Cited or not, all of these books and papers have made some contribution to the introduction.

Editions

Sackur (below) includes an edition of the Latin text, and Nau offers a few Syriac fragments.

Aerts, W., and G. Kortekaas. *Die Apokalypse des Pseudo Methodius. Die ältesten griechischen und lateinischen Übersetzungen.* (Corpus scriptorum Christianorum orientalium, vv. 569–70. Subsidia, tt. 97–98.) Louvain: Peeters, 1998.

Istrin, V. *Otkrovenie Mefodiia Patarskago I Apokrificheskiia Videniia Daniila v Vizantiiskoi i Slaviano-Russkoi Literaturakh.* (Chteniia v Imperatorskom Obschchestvie Istorii i Drevnostei Rossiiskikh pri Moskovskom Universitete, 181 and 183.) Moscow, 1897.

Lolos, A. *Die Apokalypse des Ps.-Methodios.* (Beiträge zur klassischen Philologie, Heft 83.) Meisenheim am Glan: Anton Hain, 1976.

———. *Die dritte und vierte Redaktion des Ps.-Methodios.* (Beiträge zur klassischen Philologie, Heft 94.) Meisenheim am Glan: Anton Hain, 1978.

Reinink, G. *Die syrische Apokalypse des Pseudo-Methodius.* (Corpus scripto-rum Christianorum orientalium, vv. 540–41. Scriptores Syri, tt. 220–21.) Louvain: Peeters, 1993.

Thomson, F. "The Slavonic Translations of Pseudo-Methodius of Olympu *Apocalypsis.*" In *Kulturno razvitie na bulgarskata durzhava: krajat na XII–XIV vek: chetvurti Mezhdunaroden simpozium Veliko Turnovo, 16–18 ok-tomvri 1985,* ed. A. Davidov et al., 143–73. Sofia: Bulgarskata Akademiia na Naukite, 1985.

Translations

Translations of the Syriac text can be found in Alexander, *The Byz-antine Apocalyptic Tradition,* and Martinez, *Eastern Christian Apoca-lyptic;* a German translation in Reinink, *Die syrische pokalypse;* and a partial translation in Brock, "Two Seventh-Century Syriac Apocalyptic Texts." McGinn, *Visions of the End,* contains trans-lations of brief passages from the Latin text. There are at pres-ent no other modern translations of the complete Greek or Latin text.

Studies

Aerts, W. "Alexander's Wondercoating." In *Media Latinitas: A Collection of Essays to Mark the Occasion of the Retirement of L. J. Engels (Instrumenta Patristica XXVIII),* ed. R. Nip et al., 159–67. Turnhout: Brepols, 1996.

———. "Gog, Magog, Dogheads and Other Monsters in the Byzantine World." In *Gog and Magog: The Clans of Chaos in World Literature,* ed. A. A. Seyed-Gohrab et al., 23–36. Amsterdam: Rozenberg, 2007.

Alexander, P. *The Byzantine Apocalyptic Tradition.* Berkeley: University of California Press, 1985.

———. "Byzantium and the Migration of Literary Works and Motifs: The Legend of the Last Roman Emperor." *Medievalia et Humanistica* n.s. 2 (1971): 47–68.

———. "The Diffusion of Byzantine Apocalypses in the Medieval West and the Beginnings of Joachimism." In *Prophecy and Millenarianism:*

Essays in Honour of Marjorie Reeves, ed. A. Williams. Burnt Hill: Longman, 1980.

———. "Medieval Apocalypses as Historical Sources." *American Historical Review* 73 (1968): 997–1018.

———. "The Medieval Legend of the Last Roman Emperor and Its Messianic Origin." *Journal of the Warburg and Courtauld Institutes* 41 (1978): 1–15.

Anderson, A. *Alexander's Gate, Gog and Magog, and the Inclosed Nations,* 44–51. Cambridge, Mass.: Medieval Academy of America, 1932.

Bauckham, R. "The Martyrdom of Enoch and Elijah: Jewish or Christian?" *Journal of Biblical Literature* 95 (1976): 447–58.

Brock, S. "Syriac Sources for Seventh-History." *Byzantine and Modern Greek Studies* 2 (1976): 17–36.

———. "Syriac Views of Emergent Islam." In *Studies on the First Century of Islamic Society,* ed. G. Juynboll, 9–21. Carbondale: Southern Illinois University Press, 1982.

———. "Two Seventh-Century Syriac Apocalyptic Texts." In A. Palmer, *The Seventh Century in the West-Syrian Chronicles,* 222–50. Liverpool: Liverpool University Press, 1993.

Budge, E. A. Wallis, trans. *The Book of the Cave of Treasures.* London: Religious Tract Society, 1927.

———. *The History of Alexander the Great, Being the Syriac Version of Pseudo-Callisthenes.* Cambridge: Cambridge University Press, 1889.

Buonaiuti, E. "The Ethics and Eschatology of Methodius of Olympus." *Harvard Theological Review* 14 (1921): 255–66.

Cross, S. "The Earliest Allusion in Slavic Literature to the Revelations of Pseudo-Methodius." *Speculum* 4 (1929): 329–39.

D'Evelyn, C. "The Middle-English Metrical Version of the Revelations of Methodius: With a Study of the Influence of Methodius in Middle-English Writings." *Publications of the Modern Language Association of America* 33 (1918): 135–203.

Doufikar-Aerts, F. "Dogfaces, Snake-tongues, and the Wall against Gog and Magog." In *Gog and Magog: The Clans of Chaos in World Literature,* ed. A. A. Seyed-Gohrab et al., 39–52. Amsterdam: Rozenberg, 2007.

Drijvers, J. "Heraclius and the Restitutio Crucis: Notes on Symbolism and

Ideology." In *The Reign of Heraclius (610–641): Crisis and Confrontation,* ed. G. Reinink and B. Stolte. Leuven: Peeters, 2002.

Flori, J. *L'Islam et la fin des temps.* Paris: Éditions du Seuil, 2007.

Gero, S. "The Legend of the Fourth Son of Noah." *Harvard Theological Review* 73 (1980): 321–30.

Hill, T. "The Myth of the Ark-Born Son of Noe and the West-Saxon Royal Genealogical Tables." *Harvard Theological Review* 80 (1987): 379–83.

Jackson, P. "Medieval Christendom's Encounter with the Alien." *Historical Research* 74 (2001): 347–69.

Kaegi, W. "Initial Byzantine Reactions to the Arab Conquest." *Church History* 38 (1969): 139–49.

Kmosko, M. "Das Rätsel des PseudoMethodius." *Byzantion* 6 (1931): 273–96.

Magdalino, P. "The History of the Future and Its Uses: Prophecy, Policy and Propaganda." In *The Making of Byzantine History: Studies Dedicated to Donald M. Nicol,* ed. R. Beaton and C. Roueché, 3–34. Aldershot: Variorum, 1993.

Martinez, F. "The Apocalyptic Genre in Syriac: The World of Pseudo-Methodius." In *IV Symposium Syriacum: Literary Genres in Syriac Literature,* ed. H. Drijvers et al., 337–52. Rome: Pont. Institutum Studiorum Orientalium, 1987.

———. "Eastern Christian Apocalyptic in the Early Muslim Period: Pseudo-Methodius and Pseudo-Athanasius." PhD dissertation. Catholic University of America, Washington, D.C., 1985.

McGinn, B. *Visions of the End: Apocalyptic Traditions in the Middle Ages.* New York: Columbia University Press, 1979.

Meyendorff, J. "Byzantine Views of Islam." *Dumbarton Oaks Papers* 18 (1964): 113–32.

Nau, F. "Méthodius-Clement-Andronicus: Textes édités, traduites et annotés." *Journal Asiatique* ser. 9, no. 9 (1917): 415–71.

Ogle, M. "Petrus Comestor, Methodius, and the Saracens." *Speculum* 21 (1946): 318–24.

Perry, A. *Dialogus inter Militem et Clericum, Richard FitzRalph's Sermon: "Defensio Curatorum," and Methodius: the Bygynnyng of the World and the Ende of Worldes, by John Trevisa.* Early English Texts Society, no. 167. London: Humphrey Milford, 1925.

Pollard, R. "One Other on Another: Petrus Monachus' *Revelationes* and Islam." In *Difference and Identity in Francia and Medieval France,* ed. M. Cohen and J. Firnhaber-Baker, 25–42. Farnham: Ashgate, 2010.

Reinink, G. "Alexander the Great in Seventh-Century Syriac 'Apocalyptic' Texts." *Byzantinorossika* 2 (2003): 150–78.

———. "The Beginnings of Syriac Apologetic Literature in Response to Islam." *Oriens Christianus* 77 (1993): 165–87.

———. "Der edessenische 'Pseudo-Methodius.'" *Byzantinische Zeitschrift* 83 (1990): 31–45.

———. "Ismael, der Wildesel in der Wüste. Zur Typologie der Apokalypse des Pseudo-Methodios." *Byzantinische Zeitschrift* 75 (1982): 336–44.

———. "Pseudo-Methodius: A Concept of History in Response to the Rise of Islam." In *The Byzantine and Early Islamic Near East,* I: *Problems in the Literary Source Material,* ed. A. Cameron and L. Conrad, 149–87. Princeton: Darwin, 1992.

———. "Pseudo-Methodius and the Pseudo-Ephremian 'Sermo de Fine Mundi.'" In *Media Latinitas: A Collection of Essays to Mark the Occasion of the Retirement of L. J. Engels (Instrumenta Patristica XXVIII),* ed. R. Nip et al., 317–21. Turnhout: Brepols, 1996.

———. "Pseudo-Methodius und die Legende vom Römischen Endkaiser." In *The Use and Abuse of Eschatology in the Middle Ages,* ed. W. Verbeke, D. Verhelst, and A. Welkenhuysen, 82–111. Leuven: Leuven University Press, 1988.

———. "Tyrannen und Muslime: Die Gestaltung einer symbolischen Metapher bei Pseudo-Methodios." In *Scripta Signa Vocis: Studies about Scripts, Scriptures, Scribes and Languages in the Near East Presented to J. H. Hospers,* ed. H. Vanstiphout et al., 163–75. Groningen: Egbert Forsten, 1986.

Sackur, E. *Sibyllinische Texte und Forschungen: PseudoMethodius, Adso und die Tiburtinische Sibylle.* Halle: Max Niemeyer, 1898.

Stocks, H. "PseudoMethodius und die Babylonische 'Sibylle.'" *Byzantinisch-neu-griechische Jahrbücher* 15 (1939): 29–57.

Verhelst, M. "Pseudo-Methodius, Revelationes: Textgeschichte und kritische Edition. Ein Leuven-Groninger Forschungsprojekt." In *The Use and Abuse of Eschatology in the Middle Ages,* ed. W. Verbeke, D. Verhelst, and A. Welkenhuysen, 112–36. Leuven: Leuven University Press, 1988.

BIBLIOGRAPHY

An Alexandrian World Chronicle

Editions

Frick, Carl (Carolus). *Chronica Minora.* Leipzig: Teubner, 1892. Vol. I, lxxxiii–ccx (preface), 183–371.

Schoene, Alfred Kurt Immanuel. *Eusebi Chronicorum libri duo.* Berlin: Weidmann, 1866–1875. Vol. I, Appendix IV: 177–239. See also the comments on the manuscript in

Lowe, E. A. *Codices Latini Antiquiores: A Palaeographical Guide to Latin Manuscripts Prior to the Ninth Century.* Oxford: Clarendon, 1950. Part V (France: Paris): 13.

Translations

There are no translations of the *Excerpta* into any modern language, but on the facing pages of his edition Frick included an attempted reconstruction of the original Greek text. Though Frick's efforts have misled unwary readers into assuming that the Greek version of the *Excerpta* survives, they are often an invaluable asset in discerning the sense of the Latin text.

Studies

Burgess, Richard. "The Date, Purpose, and Historical Context of the Original Greek and the Latin Translation of the So-Called *Excerpta Latina Barbari.*" *Traditio* 68 (2013): 27–82.

Frick, Carl. "Beiträge zur griechischen Chronologie und Litteraturgeschichte." *Beilage zum Programm des König Wilhelms-Gymnasium zu Höxter,* 3–14. Höxter: C. Hillebrecht, 1880.

——. "Joseph Justus Scaliger und die Excerpta Latina Barbari." *Rheinisches Museum für Philologie* 43 (1888): 123–27.

Garstad, Benjamin. "Barbarian Interest in the *Excerpta Latina Barbari.*" *Early Medieval Europe* 19 (2011): 3–42.

——. "The Excerpta Latina Barbari and the 'Picus-Zeus Narrative.'" *Jahrbuch für Internationale Germanistik* 34 (2002): 259–313.

Hoeveler, Johann Joseph. "Die Excerpta Latina Barbari. II Teil: Die Sprache des Barbarus." In *Programm des Königlichen Kaiser Wilhelm-Gymnasiums zu Köln,* 1–29. Cologne: J. P. Bachem, 1896.

Jacoby, Felix. "Excerpta Barbari." In Pauly-Wissowa, *Realencyclopädie der classischen Altertumswissenschaft* VI 1566–1577 (Jan. 4, 1906) = *Griechische Historiker,* 257–62. Stuttgart: Alfred Druckenmüller, 1956.

Jouanaud, Jean-Louis. "Barbarus, Malalas et le *bissextus.*" In *Recherches sur la Chronique de Jean Malalas,* vol. I, ed. J. Beaucamp et al., 165–80. Paris: Association des Amis du Centre d'Histoire et Civilization de Byzance, 2004.

Index to *Apocalypse* of Pseudo-Methodius

Index to *Alexandrian World Chronicle*